# SECRETS FROM THE
# AGATHA CHRISTIE
## ARCHIVES

**Also by Jared Cade**

*Agatha Christie and the Eleven Missing Days*
*The Elusive Dietrich*
*Murder on London Underground*
*Murder in Pelham Wood*

# SECRETS FROM THE AGATHA CHRISTIE =ARCHIVES=

## JARED CADE

**WHITE OWL**

AN IMPRINT OF PEN & SWORD BOOKS LTD
YORKSHIRE - PHILADELPHIA

First published in Great Britain in 2024 by
PEN AND SWORD WHITE OWL
An imprint of
Pen & Sword Books Ltd
Yorkshire – Philadelphia

Copyright © Jared Cade Ltd., 2024

ISBN 978 1 03610 773 4

The right of Jared Cade to be identified as Author of this work has been asserted by him in accordance with the Copyright, Designs and Patents Act 1988.

A CIP catalogue record for this book is available from the British Library.

All rights reserved. No part of this book may be reproduced or transmitted in any form or by any means, electronic or mechanical including photocopying, recording or by any information storage and retrieval system, without permission from the Publisher in writing.

Typeset in Times New Roman 9.5/11.5 by
SJmagic DESIGN SERVICES, India.
Printed and bound in the UK by CPI Group (UK) Ltd, Croydon, CR0 4YY.

Pen & Sword Books Limited incorporates the imprints of Atlas, Archaeology, Aviation, Discovery, Family History, Fiction, History, Maritime, Military, Military Classics, Politics, Select, Transport, True Crime, Air World, Frontline Publishing, Leo Cooper, Remember When, Seaforth Publishing, The Praetorian Press, Wharncliffe Local History, Wharncliffe Transport, Wharncliffe True Crime, White Owl and After the Battle.

For a complete list of Pen & Sword titles please contact

PEN & SWORD BOOKS LIMITED
George House, Units 12 & 13, Beevor Street, Off Pontefract Road,
Barnsley, South Yorkshire, S71 1HN, England
E-mail: enquiries@pen-and-sword.co.uk
Website: www.pen-and-sword.co.uk

or

PEN AND SWORD BOOKS
1950 Lawrence Rd, Havertown, PA 19083, USA
E-mail: uspen-and-sword@casematepublishers.com
Website: www.penandswordbooks.com

# Contents

Acknowledgements and Sources ........................................................... 7
Preface: A Talent for Murder .............................................................. 10

### PART ONE: THE CLASSIC FULL-LENGTH MASTERPIECES
1920s ................................................................................................. 18
1930s ................................................................................................. 34
1940s ................................................................................................. 54
1950s ................................................................................................. 69
1960s ................................................................................................. 81
1970s ................................................................................................. 89
Afterword .......................................................................................... 95

### PART TWO: MASTERPIECES IN MINIATURE
The A – Z of Crime ........................................................................... 98
The Official Short Story Collections .............................................. 179
Special Short-Lived Collections ..................................................... 219

### PART THREE: OTHER GILDED VOLUMES
The Detection Club Writings ......................................................... 230
Dodd Mead Omnibus Editions ....................................................... 233
The Penguin Millions ..................................................................... 235
Continuation Cases ........................................................................ 237
The World's Thickest Book ........................................................... 239
The Quotable Christie .................................................................... 240

## PART FOUR: ADDITIONAL JEWELS IN THE CROWN

Million-Selling Mary Westmacott ................................................................... 242
Autobiographical Writings ............................................................................... 247
The Queen of Crime's Poetry .......................................................................... 251
Unpublished Work ........................................................................................... 257
Published Stage and Radio Plays ..................................................................... 258
Unpublished Plays ........................................................................................... 261
Forgotten Gems and Articles by Agatha Christie ............................................ 262
Recipes à la Agatha Christie ............................................................................ 264
Parodies and Tributes by Other Writers .......................................................... 265
Novels Featuring Agatha Christie as a Character ........................................... 269
Select Non-Fiction Articles by Other Writers ................................................. 274
Her Gift is Pure Genius: Non-Fiction Books by Other Writers ...................... 278

Index of Titles .................................................................................................. 287
Index of Newspapers ....................................................................................... 293
Index of Periodicals ......................................................................................... 299

# Acknowledgements and Sources

I would like to express my gratitude to the network of public libraries and organisations throughout the world whose archives of newspapers, periodicals and other materials have proven invaluable. The individuals and institutions listed below went far beyond the call of duty to assist me in researching this celebration of Agatha Christie's unique story-telling genius.

For their brilliant and continued support, I would like to thank Abby Yochelson, Gary Johnson, Josie Walters-Johnson, Valerie Haeder, Arlene Balkansky, Amber Paranick, Malea Walker, Cara Young, Karen Walfall, Megan Halsband, Peter Armenti, Rosemary Hanes, Travis Westly, Heather Thomas, Erin Sidwell, Laura Gottesman, David Sager, Amanda Zimmerman, Joanna Colclough, Zoran Sinobad, Meg Metcalfe, and Mark F. Hall of the Library of Congress; John Calhoun and Versenia Castro of the New York Public Library; Stephanie Barrett of New York State Library; Jenny Pickardt of Dag Hammarskjold Library, New York; Eileen F. King of the Los Angeles Public Library; Hilary Swett of the Writers Guild Foundation in Los Angeles; Karen Paige of the State Library of California; staff of the Kern County Library, California; Joseph Berger of the Washington County Free Library; Suzanne Stocking of the Detroit Public Library; Rebecca Johnson, director of the Fairfield Public Library, Connecticut, and her volunteer assistant Richard K. Thompson; Kelly Rhode of Mead Public Library in Sheboygan, Wisconsin; Lori B. Bessler of the Wisconsin Historical Society; Kara Ripley of Wisconsin's online library Badgerlink; Jay Trask of the University of Northern Colorado, Denver; Elizabeth Renedo of University of South Carolina; Melody Jones Lee of the Kansas City Public Library; Sarah Tenfelde-Dubois of State Library of Kansas; Donna K. Adams of the Sullivan County Public Library, Indiana; Leigh Anne Johnson of the State Library of Indiana; Jordan Orwig, Director of the Sullivan County Public Library, Indiana; Zach Downey and David Fraser of the Indiana University Bloomington; Sarah Hagan of the Boston Public Library and Alexandra Bernson of the State Library of Massachusetts; Susan Halpert of the Houghton Library, Harvard University, Massachusetts; and Andrew Isidoro, Burns Library, Boston College, Massachusetts.

Others to whom I am indebted include Leland Stange, Matthew Rowe and Anne Marie Menta of the Beinecke Rare Book and Manuscript Library; Yale University, Connecticut; Charles Dunham of the Corvallis-Benton County Library, Oregon; Esther N. Camacho of the McAllen Public Library, Texas; Michael Barera of the James Gee Library in Commerce, Texas; Kaitlyn Keever of the Rosenberg Library in Galveston, Texas; Danny Puckett of W. Walworth Harrison Public Library, Greenville, Texas;

— Secrets from the Agatha Christie Archives —

Kendall Newton of the Dolph Briscoe Center for American History at the University of Texas at Austin; Marcie Beard of the Provo Public Library, Utah; Pam Hunter of the Sedalia Public Library, Missouri; Tom Leimkuehler of Missouri State Library; Zachary Vickery, Senior Reference Librarian of the Library of Virginia; Brittney Falter of the George Mason University Library in Fairfax, Virginia; Addie Gilkerson, Assistant Director of Raleigh County Public Library, West Virginia; Christy Venham of the West Virginia and Regional History Center; Julie Dell and Jack Widner of Edinboro University of Pennsylvania; Frances Garrison of North Hall Library, Manfield University, Pennsylvania; Karen Holquist of the Benson Memorial Library, Pennsylvania; Andrew Marshall of Penn State University Libraries, Pennsylvania; Weckea Dejura Lilly of the Historical Society of Pennsylvania; and staff of the Library of Philadelphia.

Others include Holly Henley and Jennifer Shaffer Merry of the Arizona State Library; Janice M. Murphy of the Library of Michigan; Staff of the Capital Area District Libraries in Lansing, Michigan; staff of the Columbus Metropolitan Library, Ohio; Andrew Mayer of the Ohio History Connection; Ron Davidson, Special Collections Librarian of Sandusky Library, Ohio; Barbara Leden of the Akron-Summit County Public Library, Ohio; Sarah Karbassi and Cari Coe of the Butte Public Library, Montana; Jane Shambra of the Biloxi Public Library, Mississippi; Geoff Conwill of the Harrison County Library System, Mississippi; staff of Carnegie Library of Pittsburgh; Mary Grothause of the *Delphos Daily Herald*; Cathy Cottrell of Boone Public Library, Iowa; Shari S. Stelling of the State Historical Library and Archives, Iowa; Jeffrey L. Dawson of the Iowa Historical Society; Pam Rees of the State Library of Iowa; Perida Mitchell of the Thomasville County Public Library, Georgia; Janine Duncan of the Athens Historical Society, Georgia; Lydia Bramila of the University of Georgia; Jessie Moolman of the Library of Canada; Dan Cornier and Jonathan Jarvie of the Lethbridge Library, Alberta, Canada; and staff of the Winnipeg Public Library, Canada.

This roll call of honour also extends to Michael Herlihy, Scotia Ashley, Helen Wade, Danelle Edmondson, Ralph Sanderson, Mew Leng Mouy, Daniel Wee, Jess, Sue Chan and Rachel Pryor of the National Library of Australia; Monash University Library in Melbourne; Griffith University Library in Queensland; staff of Hard to Find Books in New Zealand; and Matthew Steindl and Sasha Hartmann-Hughes of the Alexander Turnbull Library of the National Library of New Zealand; and Kristen Gardner of Ancestry.com.

This book could not have been researched and written without the help of Stuart Butterfield; Kathy Barilly and Brigitte Loret of the National Library of France; Matthias Nepfer and Andreas Berz of the Swiss National Library; Jarle Aadna of The Royal Library of Denmark; Henrik Tvermoes of the Royal Danish Library; Svante Printz of National Library of Sweden; Krystyna Klejn-Podchorowska, Michalska Maria and Malgorzata Wojciechowska Marta of the National Library of Poland; Karolina Kostalova of the National Library of the Czech Republic; Sala de Prensa y Revistas of the National Library of Spain; Dorothee Scholian of the Swiss National Library; Ritva Leppanen and Pasi Koste of the National Library of Finland; Paola Londono of the National Library of Columbia; Rima Mažeikienė of the National Library of Lithuania; Monika Faulstich of the National Library of Germany; Sybille Stahl of National Library of Germany; Lars G. Karlsson, Head of the Archives Division, Ministry of Foreign Affairs, Copenhagen; Nora Geurtsen and Richard Westenbrink, National Library of

──────────────── Acknowledgements and Sources ────────────────

the Netherlands; staff of the National Library of Hungary; and Veronique Wese of the Royal Library of Belgium.

Special thanks is also due to Christi Cassidy of *The Publishers' Weekly*; the staff of Samuel French Ltd.; Adam Douglas and Pablo Pico of Peter Harrington Books; Rory Lalwan of the City of Westminster Archives Centre; the Royal Horticultural Society; Samantha Blake, Louise North and Jeff Walden of the BBC Written Archives; Dr Anne Mouron of Bodleian Library, Oxford; Noemi Shewan, Archivist at the University of Warwick; Joseph Harvey of Torre Abbey, Torquay; Storm Dunlop of the Society of Authors; Paul Stead of Daisybeck Studios; Iwan ap Dafydd of the National Library of Wales; and Angus Wark of the National Library of Scotland.

I am also grateful to Chris Verner; Rex Oman; John Dancy, Tammy Ryan; Debra Miller; Kate O'Brien, Erin Meiman; Derek Webb; Rachel Brett; Eric Mayer; John McCormick; Graham Holroyd; Robert Erwin; staff of Watermill Books; Karen Gainey; John Newland; Jance Leasure; James Hallgate; Richard Sylvanus Williams; Rushton Potts; Dale Weber; Nelson Ball; Andrea Parigi; Dan Magnuson; Graham Holroyd; Albert Tilley; Sue Lloyd-Davies; John W. Knott; Robert Erwin; John McCormick; Dave Downes; Jim Murphy; Jim Stachow; Steven Strange; David Aronovitz; Scott Herbertson; Diane Black; David Alexander; Doug Sulipa; David Murrills; James Pickard; Robert Tromp; Dick Wilson; Michael Harvey; Bernard Merry; Pat Koerber; Robert Grothe; Tina Haylor; Brainerd Phillipson; staff of Goldstone Books; Chris Jones; Kellie Paullin; Lauren Preston; Klaus Joergensen; Laura Festinger; Anya Melvin; Diane Sullivan; Kevin Murnane; Robert E. Ruffolo; Lisa Evans and Wyn Jones; Sarah Punshon; Annie Pritchard-Gordon; Meghan Constantinou; Jennifer K. Sheehan and Sophia Dahab of the Grolier Club, New York; Carl Williams; George Rapier; John Resenhouse; Jake Sullivan; and Martin Janal and Eve Hochwald of Alexanderplatz Books, New York City.

## Preface

# A Talent for Murder

Dame Agatha Christie, the world's most popular novelist, began her writing career in 1920 with the publication of *The Mysterious Affair at Styles*. She published at least one book a year over the next fifty-six years until her death in 1976 robbed the world of one of the greatest literary legends of the twentieth century.

Creator of Hercule Poirot and Miss Jane Marple, two of crime fiction's most famous sleuths, in addition to over 2,000 fascinating characters, Agatha Christie wrote sixty-six full-length crime novels and around 160 short stories that have sold billions of copies around the world. Under the secret pseudonym of Mary Westmacott, she published six straight novels that by 1972 had sold in excess of 6 million copies.

In 2000, America's Bouchercon World Mystery Convention honoured her with two posthumous Anthony Awards: the Hercule Poirot novels scooped the Best Series of the Century while their creator won Best Writer of the Century. In 2013, the British Crime Writers' Association celebrated its 60th anniversary by crowning her Best Ever Author and named her masterpiece *The Murder of Roger Ackroyd* the Best Ever Novel. Her breathlessly exciting elimination thriller *And Then There Were None* remains the bestselling mystery novel of all time, with sales in excess of 100 million copies. In 2015, fans from over 100 countries marked the 125th anniversary of her birth by voting it the world's favourite Agatha Christie novel.

As one of the leading lights in the firmament of crime fiction, Agatha Christie shaped and defined the genre of the murder mystery, dazzling readers with the outrageousness of her plots, the vividness of her characters, the exotic locations of her crimes, and the sheer unrivalled ingenuity of her denouements. She never broke the bond of trust between herself and her readers. A detective novel by Agatha Christie always gives readers access to the same clues as her detective, but only the most astute of fans ever guess the outcome before the unmasking of the criminal.

On a psychological level, the crimes in Agatha Christie's books are like a series of misdemeanours committed during the day in the nursery. By night, the children are sleeping peacefully in the glow of a lamp and their devoted nanny has tidied away the mess, thus ensuring order and harmony are restored. Her books make the world seem a much safer place – even though this is not really the case at all – and offer a temporary respite from the strains of everyday life. The Bible teaches us that David defeated a formidable enemy in Goliath by shooting him in the eye with a stone fired from a sling. Whatever physical ailments afflict the reader, he or she knows that by employing their mental acumen and following a similar line of reasoning as the detective, the guilty can be identified and banished from the Garden of Eden. The reader frequently finishes one of Agatha Christie's books feeling much better equipped to cope with the nastiness of reality. This, together with their sheer readability, forms part of her great charm, but the crimes themselves are far from cosy. They are distinctly vicious, like bindweed with roots that go far down into the soil. Religious mania, insanity, thwarted love, rape, incest, revenge, greed and envy are just some of the tortured motives that have prompted every conceivable type of villain to resort to murder in the guise of poisoning, throat-slitting, stabbing, strangling, shooting, deadly blow-pipe darts, drownings, hit-and-run collisions, fatal pushes and the placing of sulphuric acid in a glass of water on the victim's bedside table.

The English classical detective story, as typified by the works of Agatha Christie, is the thinking person's version of foxes and hounds. But even a literary goddess like Agatha Christie is not immune to critics and one suspects that some of the criticisms levelled at her are rooted in the fact that some readers do not like to admit she has outwitted them, time and time again, by unmasking the least likely person as the killer. Critics who find fault with the fact she ties up all the loose ends by the last chapter, in a way that frequently never happens in real-life, forget she regarded the detective story as 'the old Everyman Morality Tale, the hunting down of Evil and the triumphing of Good' and was a Christian for most of her life.

From 1921–1925, she was published in England by John Lane of The Bodley Head, who underpaid her for her work, so she moved to William Collins & Sons in 1926 and stayed with them for the rest of her life; in 1990, Collins merged with the US publisher Harper and Row to form HarperCollins. In America, the John Lane Company published her first book in 1920 before selling its assets to Dodd, Mead and Company, who valued her work more highly and became her official US hardback publisher. Following her death in 1976, Dodd Mead sold the publishing rights in her work to the Putnam Berkley Group in 1988.

During her lifetime, Agatha Christie's novels were serialized in some of the most prestigious magazines and newspapers of the day. In order to avoid offending their female readerships, British magazine editors tended to avoid words like 'murder' and 'death' in the title of their serials, and instead came up with substitute titles such as *Honeymoon for Three, No Other Love,* and *Sword in the Heart.* The lucrative US serial market paid huge sums of money for her work – far more than the UK market – and Collins and Dodd Mead frequently altered their publishing schedules to enable magazines and newspapers to snap up first serial rights to her work. Occasionally, when a suitable offer was not forthcoming from the American serial market, her New York-based literary agents Harold Ober Associates would grant first serial rights to a Canadian publication that was also distributed throughout the US.

To understand the importance of the UK and US serial market on the Christie coffers, it is first necessary to look at what her publishers were paying her. In 1928, Agatha Christie entered into a six-book contract with Collins that provided her with an advance on each title of £750, a royalty of 20 per cent for the first 8,000 copies sold rising thereafter to 25 per cent. That same year she signed a three-book contract with Dodd Mead that earned her an advance on each title of $2,500 and a 15 per cent royalty on the first 25,000 copies sold rising thereafter to twenty per cent. By 1939, Dodd Mead was paying her advances of $5,000, but it was not until 1941 that her advances from Collins rose to £2,000.

The archives of the following publications provide an intriguing snapshot of the prices Agatha Christie's novels were fetching for first-time serial rights. In America, *Collier's* magazine paid $17,500 for *Sad Cypress* and *Dead Man's Folly*, $30,000 for

— Secrets from the Agatha Christie Archives —

*Evil Under the Sun*, $19,325 for *One, Two, Buckle My Shoe*, $25,000 apiece for *Towards Zero* and *The Hollow* and $15,000 for *Hickory Dickory Dock*. Its rival, *The Saturday Evening Post*, acquired *Cards on the Table* for $14,000, *Dumb Witness* for $16,000, *The Body in the Library* for $24,780, *Sparkling Cyanide* for $27,000 and *Endless Night* for $25,000. *The Chicago Tribune* newspaper bought *A Pocket Full of Rye*, *After the Funeral* and *Destination Unknown* for $7,000 apiece. *Good Housekeeping* parted with $7,500 for *The Rose and the Yew Tree*, while *Cosmopolitan* magazine matched this for *Crooked House* and *They Do it with Mirrors*, as well as the novella *Three Blind Mice*. *Redbook* magazine's one-shot publication of the wartime thriller *N or M?* earned the writer a modest $5,000. In England, the London *Evening News* paid £500 for *The Man in the Brown Suit*. *Woman's Pictorial* secured *Murder in Mesopotamia* for £600, *Dumb Witness* for £700 and, owing to the exigencies of the war, *The Moving Finger* for the much smaller sum of £300. *Sparkling Cyanide* and *A Murder is Announced* went to the *Daily Express* newspaper for £550 and £1,000 respectively. *John Bull* magazine forked out £500 for *Crooked House*, £1,000 for *They Do it with Mirrors*, £1,500 for *A Pocket Full of Rye*, £2,000 for *Ordeal by Innocence*, £3,000 for *Destination Unknown* and £3,500 for *Hickory Dickory Dock*.

By way of capitalising on the publicity that had been generated, the writer's US hardback publisher Dodd, Mead and Company often published her latest novel under the substitute title bestowed on it by the magazine or newspaper that had first serialized it. On one occasion, the UK collection *Murder in the Mews: 4 Poirot Tales* was retitled *Dead Man's Mirror and Other Stories* for its US release because Dodd Mead did not think American readers would know that a mews is a house that has been converted from a former horse stable; Dodd Mead was also convinced the majority of American readers would not know that Paddington was a major railway terminus in London, so *4.50 from Paddington* was retitled *What Mrs McGillicuddy Saw!* Sometimes Dodd Mead's reasons for publishing Agatha Christie's work under different titles were hard to fathom. *The Thirteen Problems* morphed into *The Tuesday Night Club Murders* and *Destination Unknown* was altered to *So Many Steps to Death*. The US publishing giants Dell and Avon, to whom Dodd Mead granted paperback rights, were equally guilty of altering the title of her books. In the UK, William Collins & Sons almost invariably respected Agatha Christie's wishes and published her work under her preferred titles – a notable exception being her 1926 masterpiece *The Murder of Roger Ackroyd*, which she originally called *The Man Who Grew Vegetable Marrows*.

Agatha Christie's short stories enjoyed as much popularity as her novels, although naturally, they did not attract anywhere near the same large sums of money. In the mid-1920s, the UK's Amalgamated Press paid 27 guineas for the first serial rights of 'Wireless' in the *Sunday Chronicle Annual* and in 1939 *The Strand Magazine* forfeited £1,200 in return for the twelve labours of Hercule Poirot, although in the end, it decided against publishing the final labour because one of the characters in it resembled Hitler. By 1945, *Good Housekeeping* was offering $15,000 for a 30,000–40,000-word novella. That same year, *Ellery Queen's Mystery Magazine* concluded a two-year contract for reprints at $150 a story, which is the same amount that *Collier's* paid for 'Four and Twenty Blackbirds'. A reprint of 'The Under Dog' went to the *Toronto Star* for $400. *Woman's Journal*, a monthly British magazine, acquired 'Sanctuary' for one hundred guineas in 1954, while in America the same story was sold to *This Week* magazine for $3,500. Frederic Dannay and Manfred Lee, the crime writing team known as Ellery

Queen, both ardent admirers of Agatha Christie's work, took a positive delight in retitling her short stories for their legendary monthly periodical, although in fairness to them both, each issue of *Ellery Queen's Mystery Magazine* stated in small print the original title of the work. The pair were no less culpable than other magazine editors who retitled her short stories according to personal whim or to appeal to their respective readership demographics.

Agatha Christie's literary agents and publishers had enormous difficulty in keeping track of all her copyrights owing to her prolific output. To add to the confusion, the publication of her novels and collections of stories was not synchronized in the UK and the US, and several of her collections also contained different stories. By the mid-1960s Collins had published twelve major collections of short stories, while Dodd Mead had published fifteen collections, as well as several omnibus editions containing her novels. In a bid to sort out this complicated tangle, her literary agents granted Gordon C. Ramsey, an American lecturer in English at the Worcester Academy in Massachusetts, permission to write a bibliography about the mystery writer.

*Agatha Christie: Mistress of Mystery* was published in America in 1967 and a year later in England. Gordon Ramsey's slim volume listed in alphabetical order all the novels, stories and plays she had written to date, plus their alternate titles in the UK and the US. Gordon Ramsey concluded that a total of twenty-nine short stories remained unpublished by her UK publishers, while a further seventeen short stories had yet to be published in volume form by her US publishers. The figure was incorrect because several short stories, forgotten for decades, have come to light since Agatha Christie's death due in no small part to my own detective work and that of others. This, then, was the full extent of Gordon Ramsey's bibliography. Agatha Christie went on to write several more books and in 1971 received a Damehood for her services to literature. Following her death in 1976, a final Miss Marple novel, *Sleeping Murder*, was published. So, too, was her autobiography and three more collections of short stories, as well as novelizations of three of her plays by Charles Osborne, along with a series of superb graphic novels based on her novels, and a number of forgotten plays. More recently, the character of Hercule Poirot has appeared in several continuation novels by Sophie Hannah, with the full consent of Agatha Christie Ltd.

Gordon Ramsey made no attempt to provide his readers with a comprehensive catalogue of Dame Agatha's serializations despite being given full access to her literary agents' and publishers' records. In fairness, it must be pointed out that some of these records were destroyed by enemy action during the Second World War. Collins' publishing house in London received a direct hit in December 1940 while the offices of her UK literary agents Hughes Massie were damaged by a bomb exploding nearby. Moreover, Agatha Christie lost a lot of private papers when a landmine fell on the opposite side of the road to her home at 58 Sheffield Terrace in London; the force of the blast ripping out the cellar and top floor of her home. By totally ignoring the subject of serializations, Gordon Ramsey passed up a golden opportunity. This bibliography takes over from where he left off.

Initially, it was my intention to produce a definitive list of where all of Agatha Christie's writings were first serialized in the UK and the US before being published by Collins and Dodd Mead. But the picture of second serial rights in these territories that emerged during my extensive research revealed fascinating insight into how she conquered the serial market. Over 1,000 serializations are listed within these pages.

She also made such an indelible mark on the serial market in Australia and New Zealand (ANZ) that I decided to widen the scope of this book. Moreover, I also came across an intriguing number of foreign-language serializations. Although this information does not fall into the category of UK, US and ANZ serializations, I have included it in this book rather than risk the possibility of it being lost forever to historians.

The twenties, thirties and forties were the hey-day for magazines and newspapers competing to serialize Agatha Christie's work along with other bestselling authors of the day. The arrival in the 1950s of mass-produced television sets led to a shift in audiences' tastes throughout the world. Radio, theatre and movies fought a losing battle to retain their former supremacy. Magazine and newspaper sales dropped, too; some publications ceased altogether, others had already been consigned to memory years earlier. The advent of television resulted in the market for serializations shrinking radically, although demand for Agatha Christie's work remained high. She has triumphed in all these mediums, outlived numerous publications that once competed to serialize her work, weathered changes in public taste, survived enormous social and political change and upheaval, and emerged as a true cultural phenomenon.

*Secrets from the Agatha Christie Archives* focuses on the publishing timeline of her writings. A comprehensive bibliography is long over-due and essential if future writers are to establish an accurate chronology between her life and writings. In the past, others have all too often relied on guess work or their own speculations to bridge the gap in their knowledge and this has led to false assumptions gaining currency. For instance, on 31 March 1992, Agatha Christie's daughter Rosalind Hicks was dismayed by the criticisms levelled at her mother in the half-hour television programme *Without Walls: J'Accuse Agatha Christie*. The show's presenter, Michael Dibdin, enlisted the help of his fellow crime writers Joan Smith and Ruth Rendell in a calculated attempt to assassinate Agatha Christie's reputation as a writer, claiming she grotesquely perverted the form of the British crime novel by imposing her own imprint on it with such force that its development in the hands of other writers was stunted for years to come. The evolution of the modern realistic crime novel has, in the fullness of time, proved this claim to be incorrect. One charge Michael Dibdin levelled repeatedly at Agatha Christie is that her writing suffered from a lack of social realism. In particular, he criticized her 1926 masterpiece *The Murder of Roger Ackroyd* for making no reference to the largest industrial dispute in Britain's history. The General Strike, as it became known, saw the lower classes rise up in revolt against the government for a period of nine days from 4–12 May 1926 in a protest over poor wages and working conditions. What Michael Dibdin failed to realize is that *The Murder of Roger Ackroyd* was published two weeks later, on 27 May, and it would have been impossible, given Collins' tight publishing schedule, for any reference to the ill-fated dispute to have been incorporated into the book before its release, which would, of course, have been alien to Agatha Christie's wishes because she was not a political writer. Moreover, *The Murder of Roger Ackroyd* had already been serialized a year earlier as *Who Killed Ackroyd?* in the *Evening News* from 16 July to 16 September 1925.

This book, most emphatically, is not a record of all the adaptations of Agatha Christie's work in the mediums of stage, radio, television and film. However much this announcement may disappoint, her Midas touch in the entertainment industry is phenomenal and worthy of a complete book in itself. Volume one of this bibliography *Secrets from the Agatha Christie Archives* is a mere 90,000 words, while volume two – entitled *Agatha Christie's Spotlight on Murder* – runs to 120,000 and will hopefully be published in the not too distant future. So let it be understood, quite clearly, that this book is a celebration of her genius on the page that began over 100 years ago.

Dame Agatha once summed up her genius by saying simply, 'I'm a low-brow who appeals to high-brows'. It was a highly perceptive, yet typically understated comment from an innately modest woman who had suffered her fair share of emotional torment throughout her life. In *Curtain: Poirot's Last Case*, she wrote, 'Everyone is a potential murderer. In everyone there arises from time to time the *wish* to kill – though not the *will* to kill.' She devoted her career to writing about people who crossed that line and surrendered themselves to evil. Perhaps that is why we are still fascinated by her all these years later and why the magic spell of her legacy will undoubtedly continue to delight millions of readers for decades to come.

Part One

# THE CLASSIC FULL-LENGTH MASTERPIECES

# 1920s

## 1921 (UK) – *The Mysterious Affair at Styles* / 1920 (US)

As the First World War rages in Europe, events take a sinister turn at Styles, a manor house in the English countryside. A wealthy matriarch dies in the middle of the night of strychnine poisoning. Fortunately, a colony of refugees is residing nearby in the village of Styles St. Mary – one of whom is a former shining light in the Belgian police force. With his obsession for law and order, Hercule Poirot needs very little persuasion to come out of retirement and solve his first case in England.

### Inspiration for the Title

Agatha Christie's German-born maternal great-grandfather was Friedrich Conrad Heinrich Boehmer (1786–1826), who left his hometown of Pirmasens and moved to Harwich in Essex, England, prior to joining the British Army on 29 June 1805. The army anglicized his name and he saw active service during the Napoleonic Wars. He was married to Adelaide Styles (1793–1850), whose surname inspired the name of the country house in *The Mysterious Affair at Styles*.

### Pre-Publication Serialization

- In the UK, *The Mysterious Affair at Styles* appeared in eighteen instalments of *The Times Weekly Edition* from 27 February to 25 June 1920.

**Publication:** *The Mysterious Affair at Styles* was published in hardback in the UK by The Bodley Head on 26 January 1921 and in the US by the John Lane Company on 15 October 1920.

**Length:** UK 296pp. / US 296pp.

**Price:** UK 7s.6d / US $2.00

**Word Count:** 57,000

**Trivia:** Agatha Christie signed a five-book contract with John Lane of The Bodley Head on Thursday, 1 January 1920. What she did not realize at the time is that she was obliged to offer him a further four novels. An unfair clause in the contract meant she did not receive any royalties on the first 2,000 copies sold; she was only permitted a 10 per cent royalty on English copies sold after this figure was reached.

## Max Reinhardt Correspondence

The date 21 January 1921 is generally cited by Agatha Christie Ltd. and others as the date on which *The Mysterious Affair at Styles* was first published in the UK. However, during the research for this book a series of letters between Max Reinhardt of The Bodley Head and Agatha Christie's son-in-law Anthony Hicks came to light in the manuscript department of the British Library confirming the correct date as 26 January 1921. On 11 April 1979, Max Reinhardt wrote to Anthony Hicks at Agatha Christie's former home, Greenway, in Devon: 'We first published *The Mysterious Affair at Styles* on 26 January at 7s.6d.' Michael Rhodes, former archivist of The Bodley Head Archives at the University of Reading, has also confirmed 26 January is the correct date and this date is further endorsed by the *Catalog of Copyright Entries* held by the Library of Congress.

## *Publishers' Weekly* and the *Catalog of Copyright Entries*

While the publication dates for Agatha Christie's books are known in England, until now there has been a void of information about the American publication dates. Under the laws of the United States, it is a legal requirement for every book to be copyrighted and its official publication date filed. To this end, I have consulted the Library of Congress' *Catalog of Copyright Entries* and, for good measure, cross-referenced these dates with Dodd Mead's publicity campaigns in *Publishers' Weekly*. Otherwise known as the American book trade journal, it features an exhaustive indexing system that records the publication dates of all the books released each year in the US. Rather than rely on secondary sources for the 1,000 plus serializations listed in this book, I have gone to the original source material – the magazines, periodicals, and newspapers – and confirmed the serialization appeared there and verified the start and end dates of each one.

## Post-Publication Serialization

- In Birmingham, England, *The Mysterious Affair at Styles* appeared in the *Sunday Mercury* from 29 May to 11 September 1921.
- In the US, *The Mysterious Affair at Styles* was syndicated as *The Mystery at Styles* by King Features to the following newspapers:
  - *The Philadelphia Inquirer* (Pennsylvania) 29 May to 14 August 1927
  - *The Decatur Evening Herald* (Illinois) 29 June to 16 August 1927
  - *The Marion Star* (Ohio) 28 June to 14 July 1928
  - *East Liverpool Review* (Ohio) 11 July to 31 August 1928
  - *The Mysterious Affair at Styles* also appeared under its original title as a one-shot publication, 'the Sunday Novel', in *The Philadelphia Inquirer* on 6 April 1941, illustrated by R.J. Cavaliere, some fourteen years after the magazine first serialized the story as *The Mystery at Styles*.
- In Canada, *The Mysterious Affair at Styles* appeared in five monthly instalments of the *National Home Monthly* magazine from November 1938 to March 1939.

## Omnibus Edition

On 13 February 1931, *An Agatha Christie Omnibus* featuring *The Mysterious Affair at Styles*, *The Murder on the Links* and the UK edition of *Poirot Investigates* was published by The Bodley Head. The 931-page volume was priced at 7s.6d.

## Deleted Courtroom Scene

Agatha Christie first met John Lane of The Bodley Head in January 1920. He stipulated he would only publish *The Mysterious Affair at Styles* if she agreed to change the ending. The original denouement scene in which Poirot reveals the killer's identity in a packed courtroom had a ring of improbability about it that was solely attributable to its lack of adherence to correct legal procedure. Prior to her novel being published, Agatha Christie relocated the denouement scene to the drawing-room of Styles Court and the result was nothing short of stunning. On 5 September 2016, the deleted courtroom scene was published for the first time in the UK by HarperCollins. It appeared as an Appendix in a hardback edition of *The Mysterious Affair at Styles*, which was released in a boxset called *Styles: Hercule Poirot's First and Last Cases,* and also featured *Curtain: Poirot's Last Case.*

# 1922 – *The Secret Adversary*

**Working Title:** *The Joyful Adventure* / *The Young Adventurers* (as cited in Agatha Christie's autobiography)

After being demobbed at the end of the First World War, Tommy Beresford and Tuppence Cowley are hired to find a missing woman called Jane Finn. If the document in her possession falls into enemy hands, England will be plunged into anarchy. With only their wits and ingenuity to guide them, the patriotic pair embark on a dangerous mission to save their country and unmask an evil master criminal known only to his employees and enemies as 'Mr Brown'.

## Pre-Publication Serialization

- In the UK, *The Secret Adversary* appeared in seventeen instalments of *The Times Weekly Edition* from 12 August to 2 December 1921.

**Publication:** *The Secret Adversary* was published in hardback in the UK by The Bodley Head on 21 January 1922 and in the US by Dodd, Mead and Company on 10 June 1922.

**Length:** UK 312pp. / US 330pp.

**Price:** UK 7s.6d / US $1.75

**Word Count:** 76,000

## Post-Publication Serialization

- In Dundee, Scotland, *The Secret Adversary* appeared in forty-eight instalments of *The Courier* from 20 February to 15 April 1922.

- In Birmingham, England, *The Secret Adversary* appeared in thirty-six instalments of the *Sunday Mercury* from 27 May 1923 to 13 January 1924.
- In New Zealand, *The Secret Adversary* was serialized in twenty-two instalments of *The Auckland Star* newspaper from 10 November to 5 December 1923.
- In the US, *The Secret Adversary* was syndicated to the following newspapers:
    - *The Shamokin Dispatch* (Pennsylvania) 23 April to 21 May 1923
    - *The Wentzville Union* (Missouri) 4 May to 14 September 1923
    - *The Hudson Herald* (Kansas) 10 May to 20 September 1923
    - *The Index* (Hermitage, Missouri) 10 May to 9 August 1923
    - *The Daily Silver Belt* (Miami, Arizona) 11 May to 17 July 1923
    - *Johnson City Pioneer and Journal-News* (Kansas) 11 May to 21 September 1923
    - *American Fork Citizen* (Utah) 12 May to 15 September 1923
    - *Princeton Daily Democrat* (Indiana) 12 May to 2 July 1923
    - *The Daily Clintonian* (Clinton, Indiana) 14 May to 1 June 1923
    - *The Blue Mound Sun* (Kansas) 17 May to 12 May 1923
    - *Sullivan Daily Times* (Indiana) 17 May to 9 July 1923
    - *The Bicknell Daily News* (Indiana) 19 May to 23 June 1923
    - *The Cedar Vale Messenger* (Kansas) 25 May to 5 October 1923
    - *The Commerce Journal* (Texas) 25 May to 3 August 1923
    - *The Marthasville Record* (Missouri) 25 May to 5 October 1923.
    - *The Sedalia Capitol* (Missouri) 26 May to 24 June 1923
    - *Conway Springs Star* (Kansas) 31 May to 11 October 1923
    - *The Scott Republican* (Kansas) 31 May to 11 October 1923
    - *Seymour Daily Tribune* (Indiana) 6 June to 11 July 1923
    - *The Meade Globe-News* (Kansas) 7 June to 18 October 1923
    - *Postville Herald* (Iowa) 7 June to 18 October 1923
    - *The Monroe Journal* (Carolina) 8 June to 14 August 1923
    - *The Brownsburg Record* (Indiana) 8 June to 19 October 1923
    - *Twin Falls News* (Idaho) 12 June to 19 July 1923
    - *The Ruthven Free Press* (Iowa) 13 June to 24 October 1923
    - *The Boyden Reporter* (Iowa) 14 June to 25 October 1923
    - *Otis Reporter* (Kansas) 14 June to 27 September 1923
    - *The Marion Daily Star* (Ohio) 15 June to 16 July 1923
    - *The Muldrow Sun* (Oklahoma) 15 June to 26 October 1923
    - *The Swayzee Press* (Indiana) 15 June to 26 October 1923
    - *The Waterville Telegraph* (Kansas) 15 June to 26 October 1923
    - *Daily St. Charles Cosmos-Monitor* (Missouri) 18 June to 18 July 1923
    - *The Satanta Chief* (Kansas) 21 June to 1 November 1923
    - *The Colyer Advance* (Kansas) 28 June to 8 November 1923
    - *The Oxford Leader* (Iowa) 28 June to 8 November 1923
    - *Turon Weekly Press* (Kansas) 28 June to 8 November 1923
    - *The Beaver County News* (Utah) 29 June to 2 November 1923
    - *The L'Anse Sentinel* (Michigan) 29 June to 9 November 1923
    - *The Belton Journal* (Texas) 3 July to 20 November 1923
    - *The Sylvia Sun* (Kansas) 5 July to 15 November 1923
    - *The Mulvane News* (Kansas) 12 July to 15 November 1923

— Secrets from the Agatha Christie Archives —

- *The Cynthiana Argus* (Indiana) 6 July to 16 November 1923
- *Douglas Tribune* (Kansas) 6 July to 16 November 1923
- *The St. Mary's Star* (St. Mary's, Kansas) 12 July to 18 October 1923
- *The McHenry Plaindealer* (Illinois) 12 July to 22 November 1923
- *The Pomeroy Herald* (Iowa) 19 July to 8 November 1923
- *The Lake Park News* (Lake Park, Iowa) 19 July to 6 December 1923
- *The Leoti Standard* (Kansas) 26 July to 6 December 1923
- *The Wellsboro Gazette* (Pennsylvania) 26 July to 25 October 1923
- *The Bode Bugle* (Iowa) 10 August to 21 December 1923
- *Iron County New* (Hurley, Wisconsin) 11 August to 29 December 1923
- *State Center Enterprise* (Iowa) 16 August to 27 December 1923
- *The Courier-News* (Bridgewater, New Jersey) 23 August to 1 October 1923
- *The Francesville Tribune* (Indiana) 23 August 1923 to 24 January 1924
- *Albany Evening Herald* (Oregon) 27 August to 3 October 1923
- *The Sun-Herald* (Lime Springs, Iowa) 6 September 1923 to 17 January 1924
- *The Osawatomie World* (Kansas) 27 September 1923 to 7 February 1924
- *The Dallas Oil News* (Texas) – an instalment featuring chapter two of the novel appeared in the 29 September 1923 edition of the newspaper; the issue appeared for sale on eBay in 2018 but owing to its extreme rarity, it has not been possible to trace further editions of the newspaper through the Library of Congress or other US archives to establish the start and end dates of the serialization.
- *The Sunday Herald / Daily Herald* (Provo, Utah) 14 October to 18 December 1923
- *The Blockton News* (Iowa) 18 October 1923 to 6 March 1924
- *The Montezuma Press* (Kansas) 25 October 1923 to 27 March 1924
- *The Times Recorder* (Zanesville, Ohio) 6 November to 14 December 1923

• In the US, *The Secret Adversary* also appeared as a complete novel in:

- *Brief Stories* magazine, volume thirteen, number five, as *The Mysterious Mr Brown* in April 1926, illustrated by Van
- *The Philadelphia Inquirer* (Pennsylvania) 5 December 1937
- *The Big Book of Female Detectives*, edited by Otto Penzler, Vintage Crime / Black Lizard, October 2018

## Agatha Christie vs. P.G. Wodehouse

On 13 September 1923, *The Cherokee Times* in Gaffney, South Carolina, in the United States, announced that its current newspaper serial *The Branding Iron* by Katharine Newlin Burt would soon be ending. Readers were given a shortlist of novels that had already been serialized in other newspapers and asked to vote for the one they would like to read next in *The Cherokee Times*. They were instructed to fill out a voting form and return it to the newspapers' head office by 16th of that month. The nine shortlisted novels were Agatha Christie's *The Secret Adversary*, P.G. Wodehouse's *Three Men and a Maid*, Sidney Gowing's *The Joy of Giving*, Janet A. Fairbank's *The Courtlands of Washington Square*, Charles Tenney Jackson's *Captain Sazarac*, J. Allan Dunn's *Rimrock Trial*, Zane Grey's *The Light of the Western Stars*, and H. De Vere Stacpoole's *Satan*. The winning serial that ran in *The Cherokee Times* from 20 September to 25 October 1923 was *Three Men and a Maid* by P.G. Wodehouse.

Agatha Christie and P.G. Wodehouse became life-long admirers of each other's works. On 25 October 1968, he personally inscribed a copy of his 1967 omnibus *The World of Jeeves*: 'To Agatha Christie from P.G. Wodehouse. With homage and admiration and hoping that one of these days I may succeed in spotting who dun it before the final chapter.' Agatha Christie, in turn, dedicated her 1969 novel *Hallowe'en Party* 'To P.G. Wodehouse, whose books and stories have brightened my life for many years. Also to show my pleasure in his having been kind enough to tell me that he enjoys *my* books.'

**Comic Strip Edition:** *The Secret Adversary* was published as a hardback graphic novel by Harper, an imprint of HarperCollins, on 20 May 2008. Adapted by François Rivière and illustrated by Frank Leclercq, it was translated from the French edition originally published by Emmanuel Proust Editions in 2003 under the title of *Mister Brown*.

## 1923 – *The Murder on the Links*

Hercule Poirot receives a letter from a frightened millionaire begging him for help. On arriving in France with his trusted friend Captain Hastings, the Belgian sleuth finds his client has been murdered. If Hercule Poirot is to solve the case and maintain his reputation as English society's most famous detective, he must first outwit his rival Monsieur Giraud of the Surete and a merciless killer who is prepared to strike again.

### Pre-Publication Serialization

- In the UK, *The Murder on the Links* appeared in:
  - *The Grand Magazine* from December 1922 to March 1923 as *The Girl with the Anxious Eyes*
  - *Birmingham Daily Gazette,* 12 February to 3 April 1923

**Publication:** *The Murder on the Links* was published in hardback in the UK by The Bodley Head on 18 May 1923 and in the US by Dodd, Mead and Company on 17 March 1923.

**Length:** UK 319pp. / US 298pp.

**Price:** UK 7s.6d / US $1.75

**Word Count:** 59,000

### Post-Publication Serialization

- In the UK, *The Murder on the Links* appeared in sixteen instalments of *Reynolds's Illustrated News* ('Missing Novelist's Finest Serial Begins Today') from 12 December 1926 to 27 March 1927.
  At the time of the serialization, Agatha Christie was missing from her home Styles, in Sunningdale, Berkshire, England. She had left there on the night of Friday, 3 December 1926. The following morning her four-seater Morris Cowley car was

found abandoned at Newlands Corner in Surrey, a local beauty spot a mere 6 miles away from where her husband Colonel Archie Christie was spending the weekend with his mistress Nancy Neele at Hurtmore Cottage, near Godalming. A nationwide search followed in which the police and press competed with thousands of volunteers to find the moderately well-known writer. Many feared she was dead.

Within the space of a fortnight the unprecedented publicity led to Agatha Christie becoming one of the most famous women in the country. Both the *Liverpool Weekly Post* and *The Yorkshire Telegraph and Star* ran serialisations of *The Murder of Roger Ackroyd*, while the December issue of *The Storyteller* magazine debuted the first in a new series of six short stories entitled *The Magic of Mr Quin* – bringing the total serializations by Agatha Christie appearing in the British press to four. Is it any wonder some journalists suspected her disappearance was deliberately staged in order to publicize her career?

On Tuesday, 14 December 1926 she was found alive at the Harrogate Hydro Hotel in North Yorkshire. She had booked into the hotel as Mrs Neele shortly after seven o'clock on the evening of Saturday, 4 December – almost twenty-four hours after she had first left home. There are ten different ways of spelling the surname Neele – either beginning with the letter N or K – and when Agatha Christie had signed the hotel register as Mrs Neele she used the same spelling as her husband's mistress Nancy Neele. This immediately alerted the authorities and the press to the fact that Agatha Christie was not suffering from a genuine case of amnesia as was later claimed by her family who closed ranks around her to protect her from the consequences of her actions. The episode, along with its tragic repercussions and extensive cover-up, are discussed fully in my book *Agatha Christie and the Eleven Missing Days*.

- In the US, *The Murder on the Links* appeared as *The Merlinville Mystery* in volume twelve, number four of *Brief Stories* magazine in September 1925, illustrated by H. J. Gallagher.
- In Canada, *The Murder on the Links* appeared in five instalments of the *National Home Monthly* magazine from November 1937 to March 1938.
- In Montreal, Canada, *The Murder on the Links* appeared as *Le Crime du Golf* in *Mon Magazine Policier et D'Aventures* on 15 December 1943.

**Comic Strip Edition:** *The Murder on the Links* was published as a hardback graphic novel by Harper, an imprint of HarperCollins, on 16 July 2007. Adapted by François Rivière and illustrated by March Piskic, it was translated from the French edition originally published by Emmanuel Proust Editions in 2003 under the title of *Le Crime du Golf.*

## 1924 – *The Man in the Brown Suit*

**Working Title:** Agatha began plotting the novel in Notebook 24 under the heading: 'Adventurous Anne, Episode 1'; other titles she considered, as cited in her autobiography, were *The Mystery of the Mill House, Mystery in the Mill House* and *Murder in the Mill House*.

At Hyde Park tube station in London, a terrified man falls off the platform and onto the electrified rails. His death is clearly an accident, but Anne Beddingfeld's suspicions are aroused when a bogus doctor in a brown suit examines the dead man's body and drops a scrap of paper as he flees from the scene. What connection does the dead man have to the stranger in the brown suit and a woman found strangled in a deserted house in Marlow? Determined to find out, Anne embarks on a perilous journey halfway around the world – unaware her enemies are determined to silence her forever.

### Pre-Publication Serialization

- In the UK, *The Man in the Brown Suit* appeared as *Anne the Adventurous* in fifty instalments of the London *Evening News* from 29 November 1923 to 28 January 1924.
- In the US, *The Man in the Brown Suit* appeared in three instalments of *The Blue Book Magazine* from September to November 1924.

**Publication:** *The Man in the Brown Suit* was published in hardback in the UK by The Bodley Head on 22 August 1924 and in the US by Dodd, Mead and Company on 25 October 1924.

**Length:** UK 310pp. / US 275pp.

**Price:** UK 7s.6d / US $2.00

**Word Count:** 76,000

### Post-Publication Serialization

- In Montreal, Canada, *The Man in the Brown Suit* appeared as *L'Homme au Complet Marron* in *Mon Magazine Policier* on 15 October 1947.

**Trivia:** After the Second World War, Agatha Christie received a letter from a fan who was incarcerated in a German labour camp and had exchanged a piece of candle for a Polish translation of *The Man in the Brown Suit*, which 'I read and reread so often that I almost knew it by heart...for seven months it was my only link with a normal world.' The fan was Irena Malouzynska, who had the privileged of meeting the writer after the war was over.

**Comic Strip Edition:** *The Man in the Brown Suit* was published as a hardback graphic novel by Harper, an imprint of HarperCollins, on 3 December 2007. Adapted by Hichot and illustrated by Bairi, it was translated from the French edition originally published by Emmanuel Proust Editions in 2005 under the title of *L'Homme au Complet Marron*.

## 1925 – *The Secret of Chimneys*

A self-confessed adventurer with a dislike of regular work, Anthony Cade returns to England after many years' absence to deliver a dead man's political memoirs to a London publisher. What Anthony does not count on is crossing paths with a sinister organization known as the Comrades of the Red Hand and almost being knifed to death in his hotel room. Unable to resist the lure of mystery, Anthony follows the trail of clues to one of Britain's most historic homes, Chimneys, where he becomes the prime suspect in the murder of one of the guests. The only thing preventing Anthony from being arrested are his wits and the help of a beautiful woman.

**Publication:** *The Secret of Chimneys* was published in hardback in the UK by The Bodley Head on 12 June 1925 and in the US by Dodd, Mead and Company on 29 August 1925.

**Length:** UK 306pp. / US 310pp.

**Price:** UK 7s.6d / US $2.00

**Word Count:** 76,000

**Trivia:** This was the last novel of Agatha Christie's to be published by The Bodley Head. There was no reversion of rights clause in the five-book contract she had signed with them, and she was unable to get the rights back to the five full-length novels during her lifetime.

### Post-Publication Serialization

- In Dundee, Scotland, *The Secret of Chimneys* appeared in thirty-seven instalments of *The Courier* newspaper from 12 October to 23 November 1925.
- In the US, *The Secret of Chimneys* appeared in:
  - *Cleveland Plain Dealer* (*Fiction Magazine Supplement*) (Ohio) on 7 March 1926
  - *The Philadelphia Sunday Record* (Pennsylvania) on 10 October 1937
  - *The Syracuse Herald* (New York State) on 10 October 1937
- In Montreal, Canada, *The Secret of Chimneys* appeared as *Le Secret de Chimneys* in *Mon Magazine Policier* on 15 November 1944.

**Comic Strip Edition:** *The Secret of Chimneys* was published as a hardback graphic novel by Harper, an imprint of HarperCollins, on 20 August 2007. Adapted by François Rivière and illustrated by Laurence Suhner, it was translated from the French edition originally published by Emmanuel Proust Editions in 2002 under the title of *Le Secret de Chimneys*.

## 1926 – *The Murder of Roger Ackroyd*

**Working title:** *The Man Who Grew Vegetable Marrows* (as cited in an interview Agatha Christie gave *The Star*, a London-based newspaper, for its 16 May 1928 edition)

The famous detective Hercule Poirot has retired from his life of crime to grow vegetable marrows in the quiet English village of Kings Abbott. But a series of sinister events soon forces him to come out of retirement. First, Mrs Ferrars commits suicide after writing a letter to the man she loves, then the letter arrives in the evening post at the home of Roger Ackroyd. But he never gets the chance to finish reading it because someone has stabbed him in the neck with a Tunisian dagger. By the time police arrive the letter has disappeared…

## Pre-Publication Serialization

- In the UK, *The Murder of Roger Ackroyd* appeared as *Who Killed Ackroyd?* in fifty-four instalments of the London *Evening News* from 16 July to 16 September 1925.
- In the US, *The Murder of Roger Ackroyd* appeared in four instalments of *Flynn's Detective Weekly* from 19 June (volume 16, number 2) to 10 July 1926 (volume 16, number 5).

**Publication:** *The Murder of Roger Ackroyd* – one of the greatest landmark novels in detective fiction – was published in hardback in the UK by William Collins & Sons on 27 May 1926 and in the US by Dodd, Mead and Company on 16 July 1926.

**Length:** UK 312pp. / US 306pp.

**Price:** UK 7s.6d / US $2.00

**Word Count:** 70,000

**Trivia:** *The Murder of Roger Ackroyd* was the first title Agatha Christie wrote for Collins after signing a three-book deal with them on 27 January 1924, even though at the time she was obliged to deliver one more novel to John Lane of The Bodley Head. The publication of *The Murder of Roger Ackroyd* marked the beginning of a rewarding association with Collins that has lasted to the present day.

## Post-Publication Serialization

- In the UK, *The Murder of Roger Ackroyd* appeared in:
  - Eighteen front-page instalments of the *Liverpool Weekly Post* from 4 December 1926 to 2 April 1927, illustrated by E. Rubinson; 4 December was also the day on which the British police instigated a nation-wide search for Agatha Christie after her car was found abandoned in sinister circumstances at Newlands Corner in Surrey.
  - *The Yorkshire Telegraph and Star* from 13 December 1926 to 2 February 1927.
- In the US, *The Murder of Roger Ackroyd* was syndicated to the following newspapers:
  - *The Muscatine Journal and News-Tribune* (Iowa) 9 January to 1 March 1927
  - *Evening Star* (Washington D.C.) 5 February to 13 March 1927
  - *The Des Moines Register* (Iowa) 21 February to 28 March 1927
  - *Cincinnati Enquirer* (Ohio) 27 March to 23 April 1927
  - *The Decatur Evening Herald* (Illinois) 15 August to 15 September 1927
  - *The Sunday Milwaukee Journal* (Wisconsin) 23 September to 28 October
  - *The Wilkes-Barre Record* (Pennsylvania) 19 October to 6 December 1928
- In Canada, *The Murder of Roger Ackroyd* was syndicated to the following newspapers:
  - *The Toronto Star* (Toronto) 15 January to 19 February 1927
  - *Manitoba Free Press* (Winnipeg) 11 February to 15 March 1927

- o *The Lethbridge Herald* (Alberta) 19 March to 9 July 1927
- In the US, *The Murder of Roger Ackroyd* appeared as a 'complete novel' in:
  - o *The Great American Novel Magazine*, volume 1, number 3, in the June 1929 edition
  - o *The Brooklyn Daily Eagle* (New York) on 25 July 1937
    A full-page advertisement in the previous day's issue of the newspaper featured the first two chapters as well as the beginning of chapter three.
  - o *More Stories to Remember*, a hardback volume edited by Thomas B. Costain and John Beecroft, Popular Library, 1965
- In Alma-Ata, Kazakhstan, a Russian translation by I. Girov and T. Ozerskaya of *The Murder of Roger Ackroyd* appeared as *Ubiystvo Rodzhera Ekroyda* in *Prostor* journal in 1970 in issues № 1, pp.108-127; № 2, pp.108-127, № 3, pp.107-127.

**Comic Strip Edition:** *The Murder of Roger Ackroyd* was published as a hardback graphic novel by Harper, an imprint of HarperCollins, on 20 August 2007. Adapted and illustrated by Bruno Lachard, it was translated from the French edition originally published by Emmanuel Proust Editions in 2004 under the title of *Le Meurtre de Roger Ackroyd*.

# 1927 – *The Big Four*

Four ruthless megalomaniacs, known as 'the big four', are intent on ruling the world. They are prepared to resort to abduction, torture and murder on a global scale. Only two people stand in their way: the indomitable Hercule Poirot and his loyal and trusted friend Captain Hastings. If the pair are to rid the world of the evil designs of 'the big four', they will have to be on their guard, because one false step from either of them will invite instant death…

## Pre-Publication Serialization

- In the UK, *The Big Four* was serialized as *The Man Who Was Number Four: Further Adventures of M. Poirot* in twelve weekly instalments of *The Sketch* magazine from January to March 1924.
  - o 'The Unexpected Guest' (Chapters 1 and 2 of the book, The Unexpected Guest / The Man from the Asylum) appeared in *The Sketch* on 2 January 1924.
  - o 'The Adventure of the Dartmoor Bungalow' (Chapters 3 and 4 of the book, We Hear More About Li Chang Yen / The Importance of a Leg of Mutton) appeared in *The Sketch* on 9 January 1924.
  - o 'The Lady on the Stairs' (Chapters 5 and 6 of the book, Disappearance of a Scientist / The Woman on the Stairs) appeared in *The Sketch* on 16 January 1924.
  - o 'The Radium Thieves' (Chapter 7 of the book) appeared in *The Sketch* on 23 January 1924.
  - o 'In the House of the Enemy' (Chapter 8 of the book) appeared in *The Sketch* on 30 January 1924.

- o 'The Yellow Jasmine Mystery' (Chapters 9 and 10 of the book, The Yellow Jasmine Mystery / We Investigate at Croftlands) appeared in *The Sketch* on 6 February 1924.
- o 'The Chess Problem' (Chapter 11 of the book, A Chess Problem) appeared in *The Sketch* on 13 February 1924.
- o 'The Baited Trap' (Chapters 12 and 13 of the book, The Baited Trap / The Mouse Walks In) appeared in *The Sketch* on 20 February 1924.
- o 'The Adventure of the Peroxide Blonde' (Chapter 14 of the book, The Peroxide Blonde) appeared in *The Sketch* on 27 February 1924.
- o 'The Terrible Catastrophe' (Chapter 15 of the book) appeared in *The Sketch* on 5 March 1924.
- o 'The Dying Chinaman' (Chapter 16 of the book) appeared in *The Sketch* on 12 March 1924.
- o 'The Crag in the Dolomites' (Chapters 17 and 18 of the book, Number Four Wins the Trick / In the Felsenlabyrinth) appeared in *The Sketch* on 19 March 1924.

- In the US, *The Big Four* appeared in eleven monthly instalments of *The Blue Book* magazine between March 1927 and January 1928. The first five instalments were illustrated by L.R. Gustavson and the remaining six instalments were illustrated by William Molt. The eleven-part serialization was based on the text of the novel, which was 2,000 words longer than the original twelve-part serial that appeared in *The Sketch* magazine. Dodd, Mead and Company published *The Big Four* in hardback while the novel was still being serialized in *The Blue Book Magazine*.
  - o 'The Unexpected Guest' (Chapters 1 and 2 of the book, The Unexpected Guest / The Man from the Asylum) appeared in *The Blue Book* magazine in March 1927.
  - o 'The Dartmoor Adventure' (Chapters 3 and 4 of the book, We Hear More About Li Chang Yen / The Importance of a Leg of Mutton) appeared in *The Blue Book* magazine in April 1927.
  - o 'The Lady on the Stairs' (Chapters 5 and 6 of the book, Disappearance of a Scientist / The Woman on the Stairs) appeared in *The Blue Book* magazine in May 1927.
  - o 'The Radium Thieves' (Chapter 7 of the book) appeared in *The Blue Book* magazine in June 1927.
  - o 'In the House of the Enemy' (Chapter 8 of the book) appeared in *The Blue Book* magazine in July 1927.
  - o 'The Yellow Jasmine Mystery' (Chapters 9 and 10 of the book, The Yellow Jasmine Mystery / We Investigate at Croftlands) appeared in *The Blue Book* magazine in August 1927.
  - o 'The Chess Problem' (Chapter 11 of the book, A Chess Problem) appeared in *The Blue Book* magazine in September 1927.
  - o 'The Baited Trap' (Chapters 12 and 13 of the book, The Baited Trap / The Mouse Walks In) appeared in *The Blue Book* magazine in October 1927.
  - o 'The Peroxide Blonde' (Chapter 14 of the book) appeared in *The Blue Book* magazine in November 1927.

- o 'The Enemy Strikes' (Chapters 15 and 16 of the book, The Terrible Catastrophe / The Dying Chinaman) appeared in *The Blue Book* magazine in December 1927.
- o 'The Crag in the Dolomites' (Chapters 17 and 18 of the book, Number Four Wins the Trick / In the Felsenlabyrinth) appeared in *The Blue Book* magazine in January 1928.

**Publication:** *The Big Four* was published in hardback in the UK by William Collins & Sons on 27 January 1927 and in the US by Dodd, Mead and Company on 15 July 1927.

**Length:** UK 251pp. / US 276pp.

**Price:** UK 7s.6d / US $2.00

**Word Count:** 56,000

## Post-Publication Serializations

- In the US, *The Big Four* was syndicated by King Features to the following newspapers:
    - o *The Cedar Rapids Gazette* (Iowa) 24 April to 28 May 1936
    - o *The Owen Leader* (Spencer, Indiana) 30 May to 10 October 1936
    - o *The Mount Pleasance News* (Iowa) 15 September to 27 October 1936
    - o *The Bristol Courier* (Pennsylvania) 16 September to 27 October 1936
    - o *Victoria Daily Advocate* (Texas) 16 September to 27 October 1936
    - o *The Evening Journal* (Washington, Iowa) 16 September to 30 October 1936
    - o *The Logansport Pharos-Tribune* (Indiana) 23 September to 5 November 1936
    - o *Beckley Post-Herald* (West Virginia) 25 September to 5 November 1936
    - o *The Bradford Era* (Pennsylvania) 10 October to 28 November 1936
    - o *Roseburg News-Review* (Oregon) 12 October to 21 November 1936
    - o *Nanticoke Daily Press* (Pennsylvania) 21 October to 2 December 1936
    - o *San Mateo Times* (California) 21 October to 2 December 1936
    - o *The Daily Independent* (Elizabeth City, North Carolina) 31 October to 11 December 1936
    - o *Greenville Evening Banner* (Texas) 18 November 1936 to 6 January 1937
    - o *The Daily Boston Globe* (Massachusetts) 15 January to 11 March 1937
    - o *Daytona Beach Morning Herald* (Florida) 1 October to 19 November 1937

- In Canada, *The Big Four* was syndicated by King Features to the following newspapers:
    - o *The Ottawa Journal* (Ontario) 23 October to 26 November 1937
    - o *Brandon Daily Sun* (Manitoba) 6 July to 17 August 1938

**See Short Story section:** for reprints of 'A Chess Problem' and 'The Importance of a Leg of Mutton'

**Comic Strip Edition:** *The Big Four* was published as a hardback graphic novel by Harper, an imprint of HarperCollins, on 3 December 2007. Adapted and illustrated by Alain Paillou, it was translated from the French edition originally published by Emmanuel Proust Editions in 2006 under the title of *Les Quatre*.

## *The Big Four* 90th Anniversary Edition

**Publication:** *The Sketch* magazine's twelve-part serialization of *The Man Who Was Number Four* was published for the first time in volume form as *The Big Four* by HarperCollins on 1 December 2016 under its recently revived imprint, The Detective Story Club. The special edition is 2,000 words shorter than the official version and features twelve chapters instead of eighteen. It also includes an introduction by Christie enthusiast Karl Pike.

**Length:** UK 173pp.

**Price:** UK £9.99

**Word Count:** 54,000

# 1928 – *The Mystery of the Blue Train*

As the Blue Train roars across France, Ruth Kettering's romantic rendezvous turns to terror when her rubies are stolen and she is brutally murdered. Also on board is the celebrated detective Hercule Poirot. After the train arrives in Nice, he questions his fellow passengers, including the dead woman's lover and estranged husband. Later still, he takes another journey on the fabled train in order to stage an eerie re-enactment of the crime – complete with the killer.

## Pre-Publication Serialization

- In the UK, *The Mystery of the Blue Train* appeared in thirty-eight instalments of *The Star* newspaper (London) from 1 February to 15 March 1928.

**Publication:** *The Mystery of the Blue Train* was published in hardback in the UK by William Collins & Sons on 29 March 1928 and in the US by Dodd, Mead and Company on 20 July 1928.

**Length:** UK 295pp. / US 314pp.

**Price:** UK 7s.6d / US $2.00

**Word Count:** 71,000

## Post-Publication Serialization

- In Dundee, Scotland, *The Mystery of the Blue Train* appeared in thirty-one instalments of the *Evening Telegraph and Post* from 10 April to 22 May 1928.
- In the US, *The Mystery of the Blue Train* was syndicated to the following newspapers:
  - *The Muscatine Journal and News-Tribune* (Iowa) 9 January to 1 March 1929
  - *San Francisco Examiner* (California) 7 April to 12 May 1929
  - *Decatur Evening Herald* (Illinois) 18 April to 24 May 1929
  - *The Daily Times* (Davenport, Iowa) 1 May to 12 June 1929

— Secrets from the Agatha Christie Archives —

- *The Sandusky Register,* (Ohio) 9 June to 17 July 1929
- *The Beckley Post-Herald* (West Virginia) 13 June to 24 July 1929
- *The Montgomery Advertiser* (Alabama) 22 July to 1 September 1929
- *Gaffney Ledger* (South Carolina) 9 November 1929 to 30 January 1930

**Comic Strip Edition:** *The Mystery of the Blue Train* was published as a hardback graphic novel by Harper, an imprint of HarperCollins, on 3 December 2007. Adapted and illustrated by Marc Piskic, it was translated from the French edition originally published by Emmanuel Proust Editions in 2005 under the title of *Le Train Bleu*.

## 1929 – *The Seven Dials Mystery*

**Working Title:** *The Secret Six* (as cited in Agatha Christie's notebooks)

Being invited to stay at Chimneys, one of England's grandest stately homes, where history has been made on countless occasions, is an undeniable privilege. But one guest, Gerry Wade, a Home Office official, is constantly late coming down to breakfast. His fellow guests decide to play a prank on him to ensure he rises early, but their plan backfires when he is found dead in his bed the next day. Only one person suspects he was murdered; the young and resourceful Lady Eileen Brent. Her decision to unravel the truth leads her to a sinister organization called the Seven Dials, which is prepared to do anything to outwit its enemies...

### Pre-Publication Serialization

- In the UK, *The Seven Dials Mystery* appeared in thirty-four instalments of the *Daily News and Westminster Gazette* newspaper from 3 September to 18 October 1928. (The two London-based newspapers amalgamated in February 1928.)

**Publication:** *The Seven Dials Mystery* was published in hardback in the UK by William Collins & Sons on 24 January 1929 and in the US by Dodd, Mead and Company on 8 March 1929.

**Length:** UK 251pp. / US 310pp.

**Price:** UK 7s.6d / US $2.00

**Word Count:** 66,000

### Post-Publication Serialization

- In the US, *The Seven Dials Mystery* was syndicated to the following newspapers:
  - *The Washington Post* (Washington, D.C.) 15 September to 15 October 1929
  - *The Mansfield News* (Ohio) 29 September to 1 November 1929
  - *Lafayette Journal and Courier* (Indiana) 26 November 1929 to 27 January 1930
  - *The Cleveland Sunday News* (Ohio) 29 June 1930 as a 'complete novel'

- In Canada, *The Seven Dials Mystery* was syndicated to the following newspapers:
    - *Ottawa Evening Journal* (Ontario) 30 November 1929 to 17 January 1930.
    - *Manitoba Free Press* (Winnipeg) 8 October to 11 November 1929

## Bridge Extracts

Sir Oswald's and Lady Cootes' exchange of dialogue over a game of bridge in Chapter Two of *The Seven Dials Mystery* was quoted by author Wynne Ferguson in an article he wrote called *How to Play Bridge Auction or Contract* that was syndicated to the following US newspapers:

- *Hope Star*, (Arkansas) 22 November 1930
- *The Tipton Daily Tribune*, (Indiana) 20 December 1930
- *Ames Daily Tribune*, (Iowa) 19 January 1931
- *The Daily Inter Lake*, (Kalispell, Montana) 27 January 1931
- *The Brook Report*, (Indiana) 10 February 1931
- *Stanberry Headlight*, (Missouri) 19 February 1931
- *The Daily Times*, (New Philadelphia, Ohio) 24 February 1931
- *Republican Tribune*, (Union, Missouri) 24 February 1931
- *Bernardsville News*, (New Jersey) 9 April 1931
- *Altoona Tribune*, (Pennsylvania) 25 June 1931

# 1930s

## 1930 – *The Murder at the Vicarage*

Colonel Protheroe is an overbearing churchwarden with a talent for antagonizing everyone. The defalcations in the church accounts and his daughter's interest in a philandering artist are just some of the problems sent to annoy him. No one is upset when the colonel is found shot dead in the vicar's study. In fact, Miss Marple, St. Mary Mead's resident spinster sleuth, is convinced there are no less than seven potential suspects, any one of whom may have committed the good deed. But she will need to keep her wits about her if she is to prevent a further death and rid the village of the evil serpent in its midst.

### Pre-Publication Serialization

- In Agatha Christie's autobiography she is unable to recall writing her first full-length novel featuring Miss Marple, so it is all the more surprising to discover that in the UK alone *The Murder at the Vicarage* appeared as *Who Killed Colonel Protheroe?* in the following newspapers:

  - *Evening News* (London) 7 August to 17 September 1930
  - *The Citizen* (Gloucestershire) 19 August to 29 September 1930
  - *Evening Sentinel* (Staffordshire) 20 August to 30 September 1930
  - *Lincolnshire Echo* (Lincoln) 21 August to 18 October 1930, illustrated by Pisano
  - *Daily Mail* (Kingston upon Hull, East Riding of Yorkshire) 17 September to 27 October 1930

- In the US, *The Murder at the Vicarage* was syndicated by King Features to the following newspapers:

  - *Chicago Daily Tribune* (Illinois) 9 August to 20 October 1930
  - *The Pittsburgh-Post Gazette* (Pennsylvania) 22 August to 17 October 1930
  - *Daily News* (New York, New York State) 25 August to 18 October 1930
  - *The Sun* (Baltimore, Maryland) 16 September to 17 November 1930
  - *Rochester Democrat and Chronicle* (New York State) 20 September to 22 November 1930, as *The Crime at the Vicarage*
  - *The Atlanta Constitution* (Georgia) 24 September to 22 November 1930
  - *Daily Press* (Newport, Virginia) 27 September to 29 November 1930
  - *The Burlington Free Press* (Vermont) 13 October to 15 December 1930.

Three days earlier, on 10 October 1930, *The Burlington Free Press* ran a full-page advertisement for the newspaper's forthcoming serialization that quoted the first chapter of *The Murder at the Vicarage* in its entirety and also featured a picture of a man slumped dead over a desk.

- o *The St. Louis Star* (Missouri) 15 October to 18 December 1930

## *The Monroe Morning Post*

On 16 August 1930, *The Monroe News-Star*, an American newspaper based in Monroe, Louisiana, ran a full-page advertisement for *The Murder at the Vicarage* two days ahead of its scheduled serialization in *The Monroe Morning Post*. It is not possible to confirm the start and end dates because copies of *The Monroe Morning Post* do not appear to have survived. It was a short-lived newspaper published between June 1929 and October 1930. The State Library of Louisiana, along with the Northwestern State University of Louisiana, have confirmed there are no known issues of *The Monroe Morning Post* in existence for August, September and October 1930, and this is also confirmed by the Library of Congress' records. The advertisement in *The Monroe News-Star* is currently the only known clue indicating a serialization ever took place in *The Monroe Morning Post*.

- In Canada, *The Murder at the Vicarage* was syndicated by King Features to the following newspaper:
  - o *Manitoba Free Press* (Winnipeg) 12 September to 22 October 1930

**Publication:** *The Murder at the Vicarage* was published in hardback in the UK by the Collins Crime Club on 13 October 1930 and in the US by Dodd, Mead and Company on 24 October 1930.

**Length:** UK 254pp. / US 319pp.

**Price:** UK 7s.6d / US $2.00

**Word Count:** 70,000

**Trivia:** Agatha Christie states in her autobiography that she was unable to remember writing *The Murder at the Vicarage*, which is somewhat surprising given it was so widely serialized. However, 1930 was a busy year for her. Having divorced her husband Archie two years earlier, she met and married her second husband, the archaeologist Max Mallowan.

## Post-Publication Serialization

- In Leicester, England, *The Murder at the Vicarage* appeared as *Who Killed Colonel Protheroe?* in the *Leicester Evening Mail* from 27 April to 6 June 1931.
- In Dundee, Scotland, *The Murder at the Vicarage* appeared as *The Crime at the Vicarage* in the *Evening Telegraph and Post* from 26 December 1930 to 4 February 1931.
- In the US, *The Murder at the Vicarage* appeared in *The Minneapolis Tribune* (Minnesota) from 27 March to 16 April 1931.

**UK Omnibus Edition:** In 1932, *The Murder at the Vicarage* featured along with A. Fielding's *The Wedding Chest Mystery*, Victor L. Whitechurch's *Murder at the Pageant*, and John Rhode's *Tragedy on the Line* in *The Second Crime Omnibus* published by Collins. The volume is 1,014 pages long and was priced at 7s.6d.

**Comic Strip Edition:** *The Murder at the Vicarage* was published as a hardback graphic novel by Harper, an imprint of HarperCollins, on 20 May 2008. Adapted and illustrated by Norma, it was translated from the French edition originally published by Emmanuel Proust Editions in 2005 under the title of *L'Affaire Protheroe*.

## 1931 – *The Sittaford Mystery*

During a séance the snowbound inhabitants of Sittaford House on Dartmoor are shocked when the Ouija board reveals Captain Trevelyan has been murdered. The spirit world or a member of their group is playing a hoax, surely? But despite the appalling weather, Major Burnaby is determined to set his mind at rest and insists on trudging 6 miles to his friend's house in Exhampton. Someone has bludgeoned Captain Trevelyan to death. The police duly arrest the murdered man's destitute nephew, but his resourceful fiancé Emily Trefusis is convinced of his innocence and sets out to expose the real killer with help from a journalist – and the spirit world.

### Pre-Publication Serialization

- In the US, *The Sittaford Mystery* appeared as *The Murder at Hazelmoor* in six instalments of *Good Housekeeping* magazine from March (volume 92, number 3) to August 1931 (volume 93, number 2), illustrated by W. Smithson Broadhead.

**Publication:** *The Sittaford Mystery* was published in hardback in the UK by the Collins Crime Club on 7 September 1931 and in the US as *The Murder at Hazelmoor* by Dodd, Mead and Company on 14 August 1931.

**Length:** UK 250pp. / US 308pp.

**Price:** UK 7s.6d / US $2.00

**Word count:** 64,000

**Trivia:** The real-life setting for the lane leading to Sittaford house is Shilstone Lane in the village of Throwleigh, on Dartmoor, where Agatha Christie's brother Monty resided in a granite bungalow called Crossways. Monty and his servant Shebani were forerunners for the characters of Captain Wyatt and Abdul.

### Post-Publication Serialization

- In the US, *The Sittaford Mystery* was syndicated as *The Murder at Hazelmoor* by King Features to the following newspapers:
    - *Great Falls Tribune* (Montana) 1 June to 30 June 1932
    - *Sunday Journal and Star* (Nebraska) 5 June to 24 July 1932

- o *Arizona Republic* (Phoenix) 1 to 30 September 1932
- o *The Nashville Tennessean* (Tennessee) 4 September to 27 November 1932
- In Canada, *The Sittaford Mystery* was syndicated as *The Murder at Hazelmoor* by King Features to the following newspapers:
  - o *The Toronto Star*, (Toronto) 3 October to 28 November 1931
  - o *The Winnipeg Evening Tribune* (Manitoba) 6 June to 12 July 1932

## 1932 – *Peril at End House*

Hercule Poirot and Captain Hastings are holidaying at the Majestic Hotel in Cornwall when they meet Miss Buckley, the charming owner of End House. Poirot is alarmed when he learns Miss Buckley has had three escapes from death and suspects her 'accidents' were really attempted murder. Even more puzzling is the apparent lack of motive for the attacks. Poirot warns Miss Buckley to be on her guard, but even he is unable to prevent her assassin from striking again – with fatal consequences.

### Pre-Publication Serialization

- In the UK, *Peril at End House* appeared as *The Peril at End House* in eleven instalments of *Woman's Pictorial* magazine from 10 October (volume 22, number 561) to 19 December 1931 (volume 22, number 571), illustrated by Fred W. Purvis.
- In US, *Peril at End House* appeared as *The Peril at End House* in eleven instalments of *Liberty* magazine from 13 June (volume 8, number 24) to 22 August 1931 (volume 8, number 34), superbly illustrated by W.D. Stevens – making it an ideal item for collectors to own.

**Publication:** *Peril at End House* was published in hardback in the UK by the Collins Crime Club on 7 February 1932 and in the US by Dodd, Mead and Company on 26 February 1932.

**Length:** UK 250pp. / US 270pp.

**Price:** UK 7s.6d / US $2.00

**Word Count:** 55,000

**Trivia:** In February 1934, *Peril at End House*, along with Phillip MacDonald's *The Crime Conductor*, Alice Campbell's *The Click of the Gate* and John Rhode's *Dead Men at the Folly*, were published in *The Fifth Crime Club Omnibus* by Collins. The volume is 1,104 pages long and was priced at 7s.6d.

### Post-Publication Serialization

- In the US, *Peril at End House* was syndicated to the following newspapers:
  - o *The Philadelphia Inquirer* (Pennsylvania) 4 September to 8 October 1933

- *The Indianapolis Star* (Indiana) 25 September to 31 October 1933
- *Daily Times* (Davenport, Iowa) 26 October to 25 November 1933
- *Moorhead Daily News* (Minnesota) 31 October to 8 December 1933
- *Mag-a-Book,* vol. 1 no. 29, SABCO Communications, Inc., 1982 (US)

**Comic Strip Edition:** *Peril at End House* was published as a hardback graphic novel by Harper, an imprint of HarperCollins, on 31 August 2008. Adapted by Didier Quella-Guyot and illustrated by Thierry Jollet, it was translated from the French edition originally released by Emmanuel Proust Editions in 2009 under the title *La Maison du Peril.*

# 1933 UK – *Lord Edgware Dies* / US *Thirteen at Dinner*

Lord Edgware is disliked by almost everyone who knows him. No one is the least saddened when he is found murdered in his library. His estranged wife is one of several suspects including a ne'er-do well nephew, a handsome movie star and a mysterious butler – all of whom have excellent motives for stabbing him to death. But it is not until two other murders are committed and Hercule Poirot overhears a casual remark from a stranger in the street that the solution to the mystery becomes clear to him.

### Pre-Publication Serialization

- In the US, *Lord Edgware Dies* appeared as *13 for Dinner* in six monthly instalments of *The American Magazine* from March (volume 115, number 3) to August (volume 115, number 8) 1933, illustrated by Weldon Trench.

**Publication:** *Lord Edgware Dies* was published in hardback in the UK by the Collins Crime Club on 4 September 1933 and in the US as *Thirteen at Dinner* by Dodd, Mead and Company on 22 September 1933.

**Length:** UK 252pp. / US 305pp.

**Price:** UK 7s.6d / US $2.00

**Word Count:** 65,000

**Trivia:** *The Publishers' Weekly's* 9 September 1933 edition featured an attractive promotional poster for *Thirteen at Dinner* that was distributed to US stores. This is the only time Dodd Mead took out a full-page advertisement for a Christie title on the front cover of the trade journal.

### Post-Publication serialization

- In the US, *Lord Edgware Dies* appeared as *13 for Dinner* in *The Cincinnati Enquirer* from 18 November to 15 December 1934.

## 1934 – *Murder on the Orient Express*

The Orient Express is thundering across Europe when it is halted by a snowdrift. By morning, one of the passengers has been stabbed to death in his compartment. The unbroken snow outside indicates the killer is still on board. If Hercule Poirot is to discover the solution to one of the most celebrated cases of his career, he must first find out what happened to a mysterious wagon-lit conductor and a lady in a scarlet kimono who performed a seemingly impossible feat by vanishing from the train in the dead of the night.

### Pre-Publication Serialization

- In the US, *Murder on the Orient Express* appeared as *Murder in the Calais Coach* in six instalments of *The Saturday Evening Post* from 30 September to 4 November 1933. The change of title was deemed necessary to avoid confusion with Graham Greene's 1932 novel *Stamboul Train*, which was published in the US as *Orient Express*.

**Publication:** *Murder on the Orient Express* was published in hardback in the UK by the Collins Crime Club on 1 January 1934 and in the US as *Murder in the Calais Coach* by Dodd, Mead and Company on 28 February 1934.

**Length:** UK 254pp. / US 302pp.

**Price:** UK 7s.6d / US $2.00

**Word Count:** 59,000

### Post-Publication Serialization

- In the UK, *Murder on the Orient Express* appeared, without illustrations, in three monthly instalments of *The Grand Magazine* from March to May 1934.

The serialization omitted the plan of the Simplon Orient Express coach designating the victim's and suspects' compartments; it also adopted *The Saturday Post's* decision to change Princess Dragomiroff's name to Princess Dragiloff.

- In the UK, *Murder on the Orient Express* appeared in six instalments of *Detective Weekly* magazine (issue numbers 124 – 129) from 6 July to 10 August 1935.

The first two issues featured superb cover illustrations along with the plan of the Simplon Orient Express coach. All six instalments contain illustrations throughout depicting the suspects and scenes from the novel. From a collector's point of view, the artwork alone in *Detective Weekly* makes this a far more desirable item to acquire than *The Grand Magazine*.

- In the US, *Murder on the Orient Express* appeared as *Murder in the Calais Coach* in volume one of *A Treasury of Great Mysteries*, edited by Howard Haycraft and John Beecroft, published by Nelson Doubleday Inc. on 1 January 1957.

─────── Secrets from the Agatha Christie Archives ───────

- In the US, a small extract from *Murder on the Orient Express* appeared as *Murder in the Calais Coach* in *The Saturday Evening Post* in the July/August 1977 double issue as part of the magazine's special 250th anniversary celebration. The extract – taken from Part One, Chapter Seven – appeared in an article entitled 'Whodunits' and begins 'Ratchet lay on his back…' and ends with the line '… Que pensez-vous de ca!' The article also featured extracts from works featuring four other famous fictional detectives: *Mr. Motto is so Sorry* by Pulitzer prize-winning author John P. Marquand, Father Brown from 'The Strange Justice' (aka 'The Honour of Israel Gow') by G.K. Chesterton, Charlie Chan from *Keeper of the Keys* by Earl Derr Biggers, and Nero Wolfe from *The Frightened Men* (aka *The League of Frightened Men*) by Rex Stout.
- In the UK, *Murder on the Orient Express* appeared in four instalments of the London *Evening News* from 19 to 22 November 1974; the serialization was authored by William Hall and based on the screenplay Paul Dehn wrote for the superb 1974 film of the same name starring Albert Finney as Hercule Poirot. The fourth instalment of the serial featured a picture of Agatha Christie meeting Her Majesty Queen Elizabeth II at the Royal premiere of the film.

## Comic Strip Editions

- *Murder on the Orient Express* was published as a hardback graphic novel by Harper, an imprint of HarperCollins, on 16 July 2007. Adapted by François Rivière and illustrated by Solidor, it was translated from the French edition originally published by Emmanuel Proust Editions in 2003 under the title of *Le Crime de L'Orient-Express*.
- A second hardback graphic novel of *Murder on the Orient Express*, this one adapted and illustrated by Bob Al-Greene, was published in the UK by HarperCollins on 10 October 2024 and in the US by William Morrow on 12 September 2023.

# 1934 (UK) – *Why Didn't They Ask Evans?* / 1935 (US) *The Boomerang Clue*

Bobby Jones' game of golf goes from bad to catastrophic when he slices a ball over the edge of a cliff. Scrambling down the rocks to investigate the sound of a stricken cry, he discovers the body of a dying man whose final words are *'Why didn't they ask Evans?'* The answer to the baffling mystery draws Bobby and his friend Lady Frances Derwent into a world of sinister intrigue and hairbreadth escapes from danger in which the dead man's enemies are prepared to do anything to prevent the truth from being exposed.

## Pre-Publication Serialization

- In the UK, *Why Didn't They Ask Evans?* appeared in the London *News-Chronicle* from 19 September to 1 November 1933.
- In the US, *Why Didn't They Ask Evans?* appeared as *The Boomerang Clue* in *Redbook* magazine in November 1933, illustrated by Joseph Franké.

## First Hardback Edition

In the US, an abridged edition of *The Boomerang Clue* was first published in hardcover in *Six Redbook Novels* by The McCall Company in December 1933. The other abridged books in the volume were *White Piracy* by James Warner Bellah, *Parade Ground* by James L. Clifford, *The Figure in the Fog* by Mignon G. Eberhart, *The Cross of Peace* by Philip Gibbs, and *The Thin Man* by Dashiell Hammett.

**Publication:** *Why Didn't They Ask Evans?* was published in hardback in the UK by the Collins' Crime Club on 3 September 1934 and in the US as *The Boomerang Clue* by Dodd, Mead and Company on 18 September 1935.

**Length:** UK 252pp. / US 290pp.

**Price:** UK 7s.6d / US $2.00

**Word Count:** 64,000

## Post-Publication Serialization

- In the US, *Why Didn't They Ask Evans?* was syndicated as *The Boomerang Clue* by King Features to the following newspapers:
  - *The Rushville Republican* (Indiana) 15 January to 7 April 1936
  - *The Index-Journal* (South Carolina) 16 January to 4 March 1936
  - *The St. Cloud Daily Times* (Minnesota) 16 January to 5 March 1936
  - *The Daily News* (Frederick, Maryland) 16 January to 6 March 1936
  - *East Liverpool Review* (Ohio) 16 January to 6 March 1936
  - *The Corsicana Daily Sun* (Texas) 16 January to 7 March 1936
  - *Daily Herald* (Biloxi, Mississippi) 16 January to 7 March 1936
  - *The Daily Mail* (Hagerstown, Maryland) 16 January to 7 March 1936
  - *The Denton Record-Chronicle* (Texas) 16 January to 7 March 1936
  - *The Emporia Daily Gazette* (Kansas) 16 January to 7 March 1936
  - *The Evening Tribune* (Alberta Lea, Minnesota) 16 January to 7 March 1936
  - *The Express* (Lock Haven, Pennsylvania) 16 January to 7 March 1936
  - *The Fitchburg Sentinel* (Massachusetts) 16 January to 7 March 1936
  - *The Gettysburg Times* (Pennsylvania) 16 January to 7 March 1936
  - *Hattiesburg American* (Mississippi) 16 January to 7 March 1936
  - *The Hutchinson News* (Kansas) 16 January to 7 March 1936
  - *The Kingston Daily Freeman* (New York) 16 January to 7 March 1936
  - *The Maryville Daily Forum* (Missouri) 16 January to 7 March 1936
  - *The Monitor-Index and Democrat* (Moberly, Missouri) 16 January to 7 March 1936
  - *The Newark Advocate* (Ohio) 16 January to 7 March 1936
  - *The Oshkosh Northwestern* (Wisconsin) 16 January to 7 March 1936
  - *The Portsmouth Times* (Ohio) 16 January to 7 March 1936
  - *The Record-Argus* (Greenville, Pennsylvania) 16 January to 7 March 1936
  - *Salamanca Republican-Press* (New York State) 16 January to 7 March 1936
  - *The Sunset News* (Bluefield, West Virginia) 16 January to 7 March 1936
  - *Thomasville Times-Enterprise* (Georgia) 16 January to 7 March 1936

Secrets from the Agatha Christie Archives

- *The Warren Times-Mirror* (Pennsylvania) 16 January to 7 March 1936
- *The Abeline Morning Reporter-News* (Texas) 16 January to 8 March 1936
- *The Green Bay Press-Gazette* (Wisconsin) 16 January to 21 March 1936
- *Clovis Evening News-Journal* (New Mexico) 17 January to 7 March 1936
- *The Marion Star* (Ohio) 17 January to 7 March 1936
- *The Daily Corvallis Gazette-Times* (Oregon) 17 January to 9 March 1936
- *The Morning News* (Wilmington, Delaware) 18 January to 9 March 1936
- *Steubenville Herald-Star* (Ohio) 18 January to 9 March 1936
- *The Altoona Tribune* (Pennsylvania) 18 January to 10 March 1936
- *Journal-Every Evening* (Wilmington, Delaware) 18 January to 10 March 1936
- *The Racine Journal-Times* (Wisconsin) 21 January to 22 February 1936
- *Asbury Park Press* (New Jersey) 21 January to 7 March 1936
- *The Galveston Daily News* (Texas) 22 January to 9 March 1936
- *The Post-Register* (Idaho Falls, Idaho) 27 January to 18 March 1936
- *Lawrence Daily Journal-World* (Kansas) 1 February to 24 March 1936
- *Medford Mail Tribune* (Oregon) 4 February to 26 March 1936
- *The Paris News* (Texas) 4 February to 31 March 1936
- *Oakland Tribune* (California) 9 February to 8 March 1936
- *Big Spring Texas Daily Herald* (Texas) 10 February to 1 April 1936
- *The Daily Inter Lake* (Kalispell, Montana) 5 March to 24 April 1936
- *The Daily Messenger* (Canandaigua, New York State) 7 March to 2 May 1936
- *Santa Cruz Sentinel* (California) 15 March to 29 April 1936
- *The Sandusky Register* (Ohio) 26 March to 16 May 1936
- *Honolulu Star-Bulletin* (Hawaii) 4 April to 26 May 1936
- *The State Journal* (Lansing, Michigan) 8 May to 29 June 1936
- *The Enquirer and Evening News* (Battle Creek, Michigan) 11 June to 30 July 1936

# 1935 (UK) – *Three Act Tragedy* / 1934 (US) – *Murder in Three Acts*

**Working title:** *The Manor House Mystery* (as cited in Agatha Christie's notebooks)

The Reverend Stephen Babbington is sipping a cocktail at a party when he collapses and dies. His startled host, the distinguished actor Sir Charles Cartwright, is unused to being upstaged by one of his guests. His instincts warn him that Stephen Babbington was murdered, but the idea is dismissed by the other guests because the dead man was such a harmless and inoffensive individual. It is not until a second person dies after drinking a cocktail laced with deadly nicotine that it dawns on the great Hercule Poirot that he is in the middle of a three-act tragedy with death ringing the changes...

## Pre-Publication Serialization

- In the UK, *Three Act Tragedy* appeared as *Tragedy in Three Acts* in seven instalments of *Home Journal* magazine from 6 October (volume 2, number 31) to

17 November 1934 (volume 2, number 37). The serialization changed Sir Charles Cartwright's first name to Hugo and altered Hermione Lytton-Gore's nickname from Egg to Flip.
- In the US, *Three Act Tragedy* appeared as *Murder in Three Acts* in six instalments of *The Saturday Evening Post* from 9 June (volume 206, number 50) to 14 July 1934 (volume 207, number 2), illustrated by John La Gatta.

**Publication:** *Three Act Tragedy* was published in hardback in the UK by the Collins Crime Club on 7 January 1935 and in the US as *Murder in Three Acts* by Dodd, Mead and Company on 27 September 1934.

**Length:** UK 252pp. / US 279pp.

**Price:** UK 7s.6d / US $2.00

**Word Count:** 57,000

## Conflicting UK and US Versions

SPOILER ALERT

The British version of *Three Act Tragedy* is woven around the clever idea that it is impossible for a couple in England to get divorced if one of them is incurably insane. The killer poisons his best friend – the one person in the world who knows he is married to a woman residing in a mental asylum – to clear the way for his bigamous marriage to the girl he loves. In order to confuse the issue, he poisons another two victims at random although they pose no threat to him whatsoever.

*The Saturday Evening Post* in America refused to serialize the book unless Agatha altered the ending because insanity had been the grounds for divorce for many years in at least twenty states. Her revised ending has Hercule Poirot revealing the killer poisoned his three victims to prevent anyone from discovering he was insane. It was a weak substitute motive and the novel's characterisation consequently suffered.

Following the writer's centenary in 1990, Agatha Christie Ltd. rectified the problem, so that the solution in the British edition now also appears in the American edition. The decision was an entirely sensible one on their part given the novel is set in England. The rebranding, however, has not come without complications. The original US first edition of *Murder in Three Acts* contained a scene that has been left out of the UK edition of *Three Act Tragedy* for over eighty years. The missing scene from the second last chapter features Hercule Poirot receiving a visit from Oliver Manders *before* the great detective is visited by Egg Lytton-Gore, who finds him building a house of cards. The chapter currently begins with Hercule Poirot receiving a visit by Egg Lytton-Gore and there is no intimation whatsoever that he has had a previous caller in Oliver Manders.

SPOILER ALERT ENDS

## 1935 (UK) – *Death in the Clouds* / (US) – *Death in the Air*

*The Prometheus* is on a flight from France to England. Among the first-class passengers on board are a cocaine-addled countess, a Harley Street doctor and a celebrated crime writer. By the time the world's most brilliant detective, Hercule Poirot, wakes from his nap, Madame Giselle is dead, apparently stung to death by a wasp that was buzzing around the cabin. But Poirot soon discovers someone has fired a poisoned dart into her neck from a blow-pipe gun – and then had the audacity to plant the murder weapon on him...

### Pre-Publication Serialization

- In the UK, *Death in the Clouds* appeared as *Mystery in the Air* in six instalments of *Woman's Pictorial* magazine from 16 February (volume 29, number 736) to 23 March 1935 (volume 29, number 741), illustrated by Clive Upton.
- In the US, *Death in the Clouds* appeared as *Death in the Air* in six weekly instalments of *The Saturday Evening Post* from 9 February (volume 207, number 32) to 16 March 1935 (volume 207, number 37), illustrated by Frederick Mizen.

**Publication:** *Death in the Clouds* was published in hardback in the UK by the Collins Crime Club on 1 July 1935 and in the US as *Death in the Air* by Dodd, Mead and Company on 25 March 1935.

**Length:** UK 252pp. / US 304pp.

**Price:** UK 7s.6d / US $2.00

**Word Count:** 61,000

### Post-Publication Serialization

- In the US, forty-three years after it was first serialized in *The Saturday Evening Post*, *Death in the Clouds* became the magazine's '250th anniversary serial' and appeared once again as *Death in the Air* in six instalments of the magazine from October 1977 (volume 249, number 7) to April 1978 (volume 250, number 3), illustrated by Frederic Mizen. Five of the instalments appeared in monthly issues of the magazine while the January/February 1978 edition was a double bumper issue.

## 1936 – *The ABC Murders*

The British tabloid press is in a feeding frenzy. A deranged serial killer is working his way through the alphabet and striking fear into the heart of the nation: A is for Mrs Asher from Andover, B is for Betty Barnard from Bexhill-on-Sea, C is for Sir Carmichael Clarke from Churston... The only clue to the lunatic's identity is an ABC railway guide left at the scene of each murder. The police are determined to prevent him from working his way through the entire alphabet, but they have no idea where or when he will strike next. The killer's big mistake is to challenge Hercule Poirot to unmask him...

## Pre-Publication Serialization

- In the UK, *The ABC Murders* appeared in sixteen instalments of the *Daily Express* from 28 November to 12 December 1935, illustrated by Steven Spurrier.
- In the US, *The ABC Murders* appeared in volume 99, number 5 of *Cosmopolitan* magazine in November 1935, illustrated by Frederic Mizen.

**Publication:** *The ABC Murders* was published in hardback in the UK by the Collins Crime Club on 6 January 1936 and in the US by Dodd, Mead and Company on 14 February 1936.

**Length:** UK 252pp. / US 306pp.

**Price:** UK 7s.6d / US $2.00

**Word Count:** 59,000

## Post-Publication Serialization

- In the US, *The ABC Murders* appeared in:
  - *The Detroit Times* (Michigan) 16 November to 28 December 1936
  - *The San Antonio Light* (Texas) 14 December 1936 to 30 January 1937
  - *The Philadelphia Inquirer* (Pennsylvania) 15 November 1937 to 3 January 1938
- In Canada, *The ABC Murders* appeared in:
  - *Brandon Daily Sun* (Manitoba) 21 July to 8 September 1939
- *The ABC Murders* appeared in eight instalments of *The Australian Women's Weekly* from 4 July to 29 August 1936, illustrated by WEP.

# 1936 – *Murder in Mesopotamia*

Nurse Leatheran is hired by Dr Leidner to look after his neurotic wife on an archaeological camp in the Middle East. It takes the discovery of Mrs Leidner's body to convince everyone that her fears of being killed were justified. Hercule Poirot is convinced the killer must be a trusted member of Dr Leidner's archaeological team at Tell Yarimjah – and, tragically, further events prove him right...

## Pre-Publication Serialization

- In the UK, *Murder in Mesopotamia* appeared as *No Other Love* in eight instalments of *Woman's Pictorial* magazine from 8 February (volume 31, number 787) to 28 March 1936 (volume 31, number 794), illustrated by Clive Uptton. The serialization changed Amy Leatheran's surname to Seymour and Dr and Mrs Leidner became Mr and Mrs Trevor.

## Secrets from the Agatha Christie Archives

- In the US, *Murder in Mesopotamia* first appeared in six instalments of *The Saturday Evening Post* from 9 November (volume 208, number 19) to 14 December 1935 (volume 208, number 24), illustrated by F.R. Gruger.

**Publication:** *Murder in Mesopotamia* was published in hardback in the UK by the Collins Crime Club on 6 July 1936 and in the US by Dodd, Mead and Company on 17 September 1936.

**Length:** UK 284pp. / US 306pp.

**Price:** UK 7s.6d / US $2.00

**Word Count:** 68,000

### Post-Publication Serialization

- In Montreal, Canada, *Murder in Mesopotamia* appeared as *Meurtre de Mesopotamie* in *Mon Magazine Policier et D'Aventures* on 15 April 1943

**Comic Strip Edition:** *Murder in Mesopotamia* was published as a hardback graphic novel by Harper, an imprint of HarperCollins, on 1 July 2008. Adapted by François Rivière and illustrated by Chandre, it was translated from the French edition originally published by Emmanuel Proust Editions in 2005 under the title of *Meurtre en Mesopotamie*.

## 1936 – (UK) *Cards on the Table* / 1937 (US)

Mr Shaitana is a flamboyant dilettante with a fascination for killers who have never been caught. He invites Hercule Poirot and the crime novelist Mrs Ariadne Oliver, along with two other representatives of the law, to dinner to view his private collection. The evening ends with the discovery that one of Mr Shaitana's exhibits has stabbed him to death during a game of bridge. But the cycle of death is far from over...

### Pre-Publication Serialization

- In the UK, *Cards on the Table* appeared in seven instalments of *Home Journal* magazine from 2 May (volume 5, number 113) to 13 June 1936 (volume 5, number 119), illustrated by Clive Upton.
- In the US, *Cards on the Table* appeared in six instalments of *The Saturday Evening Post* from 2 May (volume 208, number 44) to 6 June 1936 (volume 208, number 49), illustrated by Orison MacPherson.

**Publication:** *Cards on the Table* was published in hardback in the UK by the Collins Crime Club on 2 November 1936 and in the US by Dodd, Mead and Company on 9 February 1937.

**Length:** UK 286pp. / US 262pp.

**Price:** UK 7s.6d / US $2.00

**Word Count:** 55,000

## Post-Publication Serialization

- *Cards on the Table* appeared in eight instalments of *The Australian Women's Weekly* from 20 May to 8 July 1939, illustrated by Wynne W. Davies.

**Comic Strip Edition:** *Cards on the Table* was published as a hardback graphic novel by Harper, an imprint of HarperCollins, on 17 June 2010. Adapted and illustrated by Frank Leclercq, it was translated from the French edition originally published by Emmanuel Proust Editions in 2009 as *Cartes Sur Table*.

# 1937 (UK) – *Dumb Witness /* (US) – *Poirot Loses a Client*

**Working title:** *The Murder at Littlegreen House*

Emily Arundell is nearly killed when she falls down a flight of stairs in the middle of the night. Everyone blames her accident on her adored wire-haired terrier Bob, who is suspected of leaving his ball at the top of the stairs. But Emily Arundell is not convinced she tripped on it and writes to Hercule Poirot for help. By the time he receives her letter, the same person who placed the tripwire at the top of the stairs has poisoned her to death.

## Pre-Publication Serialization

- In the UK, *Dumb Witness* appeared as *Mystery of Littlegreen House* in seven instalments of *Woman's Pictorial* magazine from 20 February (volume 33, number 841) to 3 April 1937 (volume 33, number 847), illustrated by Henry Raleigh.
- In the US, *Dumb Witness* appeared as *Poirot Loses a Client* in seven instalments of *The Saturday Evening Post* from 7 November (volume 209, number 19) to 19 December 1936 (volume 209, number 25), illustrated by Henry Raleigh. The change of title was deemed necessary by the magazine because earlier in the year Michael Sarne (1883–1961), an American writer, had published a book called *The Dumb Witness,* under the nom-de-plume of Thomas Arthur Plummer, in which Inspector Andrew Frampton investigates the disappearance of a public benefactor, assisted by a dog; the dumb and only witness of the crime.

**Publication:** *Dumb Witness* was published in hardback in the UK by the Collins Crime Club on 5 July 1937 and in the US as *Poirot Loses a Client* by Dodd, Mead and Company on 7 September 1937.

**Length:** UK 316pp. / US 302pp.

**Price:** UK 7s.6d / US $2.00

**Word Count:** 75,000

**Inspiration for the Novel:** *Dumb Witness* is an expanded version of 'The Incident of the Dog's Ball', which is not believed to have been published during Agatha Christie's lifetime. 'The Incident of the Dog's Ball' was found by her daughter Rosalind Hicks in a crate of her mother's personal belongings in 2004. It was published in the UK by HarperCollins in *Agatha Christie's Secret Notebooks: Fifty Years of Mysteries* by John Curran on 3 September 2009; subsequent reprints include the US quarterly October – January 2009 edition of *The Strand Magazine* as well as the UK anthology *Bodies from the Library 3* in 2020.

**Comic Strip Edition:** *Dumb Witness* was published as a hardback graphic novel by Harper, an imprint of HarperCollins, on 27 May 2010. Adapted and illustrated by Marek, it was translated from the French edition originally published by Emmanuel Proust Editions in 2009 under the title *Temoin Muet*.

# 1937 (UK) – *Death on the Nile* / 1938 (US)

Linnet Doyle has everything a woman could ask for: beauty, wealth and an adoring husband. But she is also surrounded by enemies who are travelling down the Nile with her on the luxury paddle-steamer SS *Karnak*. When someone fires a bullet into her brain, no one admits to seeing the killer enter or leave her cabin. The letter 'J' scrawled in blood on the wall suggests she recognized her killer before she died, but Hercule Poirot is not so easily fooled.

## Pre-Publication Serialization

- In the UK, *Death on the Nile* appeared as *Honeymoon for Three* in nine instalments of *Home Journal* from 2 October (volume 8, number 187) to 27 November 1937 (volume 8, number 195).
- In the US, *Death on the Nile* first appeared in eight instalments of *The Saturday Evening Post* from 15 May (volume 209, number 46) to 3 July 1937 (volume 210, number 1), illustrated by Henry Raleigh.

**Publication:** *Death on the Nile* was published in hardback in the UK by the Collins Crime Club on 1 November 1937 and in the US by Dodd, Mead and Company on 7 February 1938.

**Length:** UK 284pp. / US 327pp.

**Price:** UK 7s.6d / US $2.00

**Word Count:** 78,000

**Trivia:** *The Saturday Evening Post's* third instalment of *Death on the Nile* on 29 May coincided with the beginning of a four-part serialization of *The Case of the Lame Canary* by Erle Stanley Gardner, creator of crime fiction's most famous lawyer Perry Mason.

**Comic Strip Edition:** *Death on the Nile* was published as a hardback graphic novel by Harper, an imprint of HarperCollins, on 16 July 2007. Adapted by François Rivière and

Solidor, it was translated from the French edition originally published by Emmanuel Proust Editions in 2003 under the title of *Mort sur le Nil.*

## 1938 – *Appointment with Death*

**Working Title:** *The Petra Murder / Rose Red Murder / Rose Red Death* (as cited in Agatha Christie's notebooks)

Hercule Poirot is holidaying in the Holy Land when he hears about the death of an American tourist. Mrs Boynton was killed by a lethal injection of digitalis in a cave at Petra, the rose-red city half as old as time itself. If the Belgian detective is to fulfill his promise, then he has only twenty-four hours in which to find the killer. The dead woman was a sadistic tyrant and each member of her family has secrets they wish to keep, but Poirot nevertheless arrives at the truth in one of the most brilliant displays of deductive reasoning in his entire career.

### Pre-Publication Serialization

- In the UK, *Appointment with Death* appeared as *A Date with Death* in twenty-eight instalments of the London *Daily Mail* from 19 January to 19 February 1938, illustrated by Joseph van Abbé.
- In the US, *Appointment with Death* appeared in nine instalments of *Collier's* magazine from 28 August (volume 100, number 9) to 23 October 1937 (volume 100, number 17), illustrated by Mario Cooper.

**Publication:** *Appointment with Death* was published in hardback in the UK by the Collins Crime Club on 2 May 1938 and in the US by Dodd, Mead and Company on 8 September 1938.

**Length:** UK 252pp. / US 301pp.

**Price:** UK 7s.6d / US $2.00

**Word Count:** 54,000

**Trivia:** On 15 January 1938, four days prior to the serialization of *A Date with Death*, the *Daily Mail* published a tongue-in-cheek article by Agatha Christie called 'Hercule Poirot Fiction's Greatest Detective' in which she described how she created her sleuth and her mixed feelings towards him.

### Post-Publication Serialization

- In Sydney, Australia, a condensed version of *Appointment with Death*, comprising 15,000 words, appeared as a 16-page special in *Man* magazine (volume 4, number 3) in August 1938, illustrated by John Mills.
- In Brisbane, Australia, *Appointment with Death* appeared in thirty-three instalments of *The Courier-Mail* from 13 August to 20 September 1938.

———————— Secrets from the Agatha Christie Archives ————————

# 1938 (UK) – *Hercule Poirot's Christmas* / 1939 (US) *Murder for Christmas*

**Working Title:** *Blood Feast / Who Would Have Thought?* (as cited in Agatha Christie's notebooks)

> *Yet who would have thought the old man to have had so much blood in him?*
>
> Lady Macbeth, Act 5, Scene 1, *Macbeth*,
> William Shakespeare

Hercule Poirot is spending Christmas with the Chief Constable of Middleshire when a telephone call summons them both to Gorston Hall. Tyrannical Simeon Lee lies dead in a pool of blood – his throat cut – surrounded by a circle of relatives who loathed him. Greed, jealousy and betrayal are just some of the qualities the murdered man inspired in others, but that still does not explain how he was found inside a room that was locked on the inside or how the killer escaped without being seen.

## Pre-Publication Serialization

- In the UK, *Hercule Poirot's Christmas* appeared as *Murder at Christmas* in twenty instalments of the London *Daily Express* from 14 November to 10 December 1938.
- In the US, *Hercule Poirot's Christmas* appeared as *Murder For Christmas* in ten instalments of *Collier's* magazine from 12 November 1938 (volume 102, number 20) to 14 January 1939 (volume 103, number 2), illustrated by Mario Cooper.

**Publication:** *Hercule Poirot's Christmas* was published in hardback in the UK by the Collins Crime Club on 19 December 1938. Collins' originally planned to publish the novel the following year, which is why the copyright page is dated 1939. In the US, *Hercule Poirot's Christmas* was published in hardback as *Murder for Christmas* by Dodd, Mead and Company on 7 February 1939. The US title was changed in 1947 to *A Holiday for Murder* by the paperback publisher Avon Books.

**Length:** UK 251pp. / US 272pp.

**Price:** UK 7s.6d / US $2.00

**Word Count:** 60,000

**Trivia:** Agatha Christie became the victim of seasonal skulduggery when Howard Spring launched a vitriolic attack on *Hercule Poirot's Christmas* in the *Evening Standard* on 22 December 1938. His review provoked a storm of controversy, not least because it named the killer, with one of his less vitriolic comments being: 'If some madness urged me to murder my father, I should make a neater, sweeter and somehow less farcical job of it than is made in *Hercule Poirot's Christmas*.' The *Evening Standard* was bombarded by letters of complaint by indignant members of the British public and outraged fellow authors, as well of letters of support for Howard Spring. A letter of protest from the Detection Club's secretary John Dickson Carr was published in the *Evening Standard's* 4 January 1939 edition.

## Post-Publication Serialization

- In New Zealand, *Hercule Poirot's Christmas* appeared in twenty-two instalments of *The New Zealand Herald* newspaper from 24 December 1938 to 18 February 1939.

# 1939 (UK) *Murder Is Easy* / (US) *Easy to Kill*

Retired police officer Luke Fitzwilliam is skeptical of the claims made by the old lady sharing his train carriage. Miss Pinkerton is adamant a serial killer is on the loose in her village of Wychwood-under-Ashe. Somehow, the old dear's allegations seem so utterly preposterous, but after Miss Pinkerton dies in a mysterious hit-and-run car accident on the way to report her suspicions to Scotland Yard Luke discovers black magic rituals and a rising body count are just some of the strange things going on at Wychwood-under-Ashe.

## Pre-Publication Serialization

- In the UK, *Murder is Easy* appeared as *Easy to Kill* in twenty-three instalments of the London *Daily Express* from 10 January to 3 February 1939, illustrated by Prescott.
- In the US, *Murder is Easy* first appeared as *Easy to Kill* in seven instalments of *The Saturday Evening Post* from 19 November (volume 211, number 21) to 31 December 1938 (volume 211, number 27), illustrated by Henry Raleigh. The serial's change of title was deemed necessary by *The Saturday Evening Post* because *Murder is Easy* had already been appropriated by Armstrong Livingston for his 1933 mystery novel; the editor's decision failed to take into account that *Easy to Kill* had been used as a title in 1931 by Hulbert Footner.

## Pinkerton's National Detective Agency

*The Saturday Evening Post* altered Miss Pinkerton's name to Miss Fullerton to avoid confusion with the real-life US detective agency, and Agatha Christie's publishers Dodd, Mead and Company followed suit. Pinkerton's National Detective Agency was first founded in 1850 by Allan Pinkerton. The unblinking eye in the original Pinkerton logo – 'We never sleep' – became a symbol of vigilance and led to the term 'private eye' becoming part of the American lexicon. Throughout its rich history, Pinkerton created the forerunner to the US Secret Service, hired America's first woman detective and is recognized nowadays as the industry leader in developing security and risk management solutions for national and international corporations.

———————— Secrets from the Agatha Christie Archives ————————

**Publication:** *Murder is Easy* was published in hardback in the UK by the Collins Crime Club on 5 June 1939 and in the US as *Easy to Kill* by Dodd, Mead and Company on 19 September 1939.

**Length:** UK 254pp. / US 248pp.

**Price:** UK 7s.6d / US $2.00

**Word Count:** 58,000

### Post-Publication Serialization

- In New Zealand, *Murder is Easy* appeared as *Easy to Kill* in eighteen instalments of *The New Zealand Herald* newspaper from 5 August to 25 August 1939.

## 1939 (UK) – *Ten Little Niggers* / 1940 (US) – *And Then There Were None*

THE WORD'S BESTSELLING MURDER MYSERY OF ALL TIME
WITH SALES IN EXCESS OF 100 MILLION COPIES

The glorious summer evening offers no portent of the blood-drenched nightmare that is about to engulf ten people who have been lured to an island off the coast of Devon. The first intimation that something is wrong comes when their host U.N. Owen fails to appear. After dinner a gramophone record is played, and the voice of their absent host accuses every single one of them of hiding a terrible secret. Trapped on the island, each member of the ill-assorted group is haunted by a past they would rather forget, and soon their sanity is tested to the limit. As guilt, fear and paranoia take hold, the ten terrified inhabitants begin dying – one by one – murdered in accordance with a childish nursery rhyme that hangs on the wall in their bedrooms.

### Inspiration for the Title

*Ten little niggers went out to dine;*
   *Once choked his little self and then there were nine.*
*Nine little niggers sat up very late;*
   *One overslept himself and then there were eight.*
*Eight little nigger boys travelling in Devon;*
   *One said he'd stay there and then there were seven.*
*Seven little niggers chopping up sticks;*
   *One chopped himself in halves and then there were six.*
*Six little niggers playing with a hive;*
   *A bumblebee stung one and then there were five.*
*Five little niggers going in for law;*
   *One got into Chancery and then there were four.*
*Four little nigger boys going out to sea;*
   *A red herring swallowed one and then there were three.*
*Three little nigger boys walking in the zoo;*
   *A big bear hugged one and then there were two.*

*Two little nigger boys sitting in the sun;*
  *One got frizzled up and then there was one.*
*One little nigger boy left all alone;*
  *He went and hanged himself and then there were none.*

Frank Green, 1869

## Pre-Publication Serialization

- In the UK, *Ten Little Niggers* first appeared in twenty-three instalments of the London *Daily Express* from 6 June to 1 July 1939, illustrated by Prescott. The first instalment featured an illustration of Burgh Island off the coast of Devon, England, the inspiration for the setting of the story.
- In the US, *Ten Little Niggers* appeared as *And Then There Were None* in seven instalments of *The Saturday Evening Post* from 20 May (volume 211, number 47) to 1 July 1939 (volume 212, number 1), illustrated by Henry Raleigh.

**Publication:** *Ten Little Niggers* was published in hardback in the UK by the Collins Crime Club on 6 November 1939 and in the US as *And Then There Were None* by Dodd, Mead and Company on 20 February 1940.

**Length:** UK 252pp. / US 264pp.

**Price:** UK 7s.6d / US $2.00

**Word Count:** 53,000

**Trivia:** *The Saturday Evening Post* and Dodd Mead altered the title of *Ten Little Niggers* to *And Then There Were None* because they believed most Americans would not want to read a novel about black people. After decades of slavery, racial segregation of black people began in America in the late 1800s following the implementation of the Jim Crow laws and continued through and beyond the 1960s. In 1965, the US paperback publisher Pocket Books amended the title to *Ten Little Indians* in a bid to appease the wrath of civil rights groups. Contrary to intention, this only incited further controversy. Nowadays both the UK and US editions are known as *And Then There Were None*. The text of the nursery rhyme has been changed to 'Ten Little Soldier Boys', and Nigger Island and Indian Island are now called Solider Island. Ironically, all ten visitors to the slaughterhouse on the island were Caucasian. In the UK, the change of title to *And Then There Were None* was finally instigated by Collins in a Fontana paperback edition in August 1984.

## Post-Publication Serialization

- *Ten Little Niggers* appeared in nine instalments of *The Australian Women's Weekly* from 27 January to 23 March 1940, illustrated by WEP.

**Comic Strip Edition:** *And Then There Were None* was published as a hardback graphic novel by Harper, an imprint of HarperCollins, on 30 April 2009. Adapted by François Rivière and illustrated by Frank Leclercq, it was translated from the French edition originally published by Emmanuel Proust Editions in 2002 under the title of *Dix Petits Negres*.

# 1940s

## 1940 – *Sad Cypress*

Elinor Carlisle used to play with Mary Gerrard when they children, but those innocent, carefree days are long behind them now that the man Elinor loves beyond all reason covets Mary Gerrard. A black hatred enters Elinor's heart, then Mary Gerrard dies of morphine poisoning and Elinor is arrested for her murder. Only one man believes in Elinor's innocence and turns to Hercule Poirot for help in saving her from the gallows.

### Inspiration for the Title

> *Come away, come way, death,*
> *And in sad cypress let me be laid;*
> *Fly away, fly away breath!*
> *I am slain by a fair cruel maid.*
> *My shroud of white, stuck all with yew,*
> *O prepare it;*
> *My part of death no one so true,*
> *Did share it.*
>
> Act Two, Scene Four, *Twelfth Night*,
> William Shakespeare

In the fifteenth and sixteenth centuries coffins were made from cypress wood. The title of Agatha Christie's novel is a melancholic euphemism for a casket and no reference to the island in the Mediterranean Sea is intended.

### Pre-Publication Serialization

- In the US, *Sad Cypress* appeared in ten instalments of *Collier's* magazine from 25 November 1939 (volume 104, number 22) to 27 January 1940 (volume 105, number 4), illustrated by Mario Cooper.

**Publication:** *Sad Cypress* was published in hardback in the UK by the Collins Crime Club on 4 March 1940 and in the US by Dodd, Mead and Company on 10 September 1940.

**Length:** UK 252pp. / US 270pp.

**Price:** UK 8s.3d / US $2.00

**Word Count:** 56,000

## Post-Publication Serialization

- In the UK, *Sad Cypress* appeared in nineteen instalments of the London *Daily Express* from 23 March to 13 April 1940.
- In the US, *Sad Cypress* was syndicated by Kings Features to the following newspapers:

  - *The Nashville Tennessean* (Tennessee) 16 May to 26 June 1941
  - *The Beckley Post-Herald* (West Virginia) 24 June to 4 August 1942
  - *The Fairfield Daily Ledger* (Iowa) 2 July to 17 August 1942
  - *The Morning Herald* (Uniontown, Pennsylvania) 13 July to 22 August 1942
  - *The Lock Haven Express* (Pennsylvania) 15 July to 26 August 1942
  - *The Bristol Daily Courier* (Pennsylvania) 21 July to 29 August 1942
  - *The Odessa American* (Texas) 23 July to 31 August 1942
  - *The Bradford Era* (Pennsylvania) 30 July to 9 September 1942
  - *Valley Evening Monitor* (Harlingen, Texas) 31 July to 10 September 1942
  - *Elwood Call-Leader* (Indiana) 7 August to 29 September 1942
  - *The Staunton News Leader* (Virginia) 19 to 30 August 1942
  - *The Advocate-Messenger* (Kentucky) 27 August to 12 October 1942
  - *The Salem News* (Ohio) 3 September to 15 October 1942
  - *The Daily Clintonian* (Indiana) 4 September to 23 October 1942
  - *San Mateo Times* (California) 14 September to 24 October 1942
  - *The Times and Daily Leader* (San Mateo, California) 14 September to 24 October 1942

  **Following a three-year gap:**

  - *Monroe Evening Times* (Wisconsin) 1 June to 13 July 1945
  - *The Belvidere Daily Republican* (Illinois) 5 February to 23 March 1948

- In Canada, *Sad Cypress* was syndicated by Kings Features to the following newspapers:

  - *Brandon Daily Sun* (Manitoba) 14 October to 22 November 1941
  - *Toronto Daily Star* (Ontario) 8 July to 21 August 1941

- In Kingston, Jamaica, *Sad Cypress* appeared in *The Sunday Gleaner* from 12 May to 22 September 1940.
- In Switzerland, *Sad Cypress* appeared as *Morphium* in number 1 – 40 of *Basellandschaftliche Zeitung*, a daily newspaper published in the Swiss-German language in Liestal, from 20 May to 8 July 1976.

# 1940 (UK) – *One, Two, Buckle My Shoe* / 1941 (US)

As England enters the Second World War, Hercule Poirot's routine visit to his dentist is followed by the tragic news that Mr Morley has been found shot dead in his surgery. The police conclude Mr Morley killed himself after accidentally administering a fatal overdose to a patient who was a Greek spy. Poirot has his doubts, especially after a female patient, whose buckle fell off her shoe when she arrived at the surgery that morning, also disappears. But what motive could anyone have for killing a harmless dentist or any of his patients?

*One, two, Buckle my shoe,*
*Three, four, shut the door,*
*Five, six, pick up sticks,*
*Seven, eight, lay them straight,*
*Nine, ten, a big, fat hen,*
*Eleven, twelve, men must delve,*
*Thirteen, fourteen, maids are courting,*
*Fifteen, sixteen, maids in the kitchen,*
*Seventeen, eighteen, maids are waiting,*
*Nineteen, twenty, my plate's empty...*

## Pre-Publication Serialization

- In the US, *One, Two, Buckle My Shoe* appeared as *The Patriotic Murders* in nine instalments of *Collier's* magazine from 3 August (volume 106, number 5) to 28 September 1940 (volume 106, number 13), illustrated by Mario Cooper.

**Publication:** *One, Two, Buckle My Shoe* was published in hardback in the UK by the Collins Crime Club on 4 November 1940 and in the US as *The Patriotic Murders* by Dodd, Mead and Company on 25 February 1941. In the US, Dell paperbacks retitled the book *An Overdose of Death*.

**Length:** UK 252pp. / US 240pp.

**Price:** UK 7s.6d / US $2.00

**Word Count:** 53,000

**Trivia:** *Collier's* sixth instalment of *The Patriotic Murders* coincided with the beginning of a ten-part serialization of *Traitor's Purse* by Margery Allingham, creator of Albert Campion, whose crime novels were much admired by Agatha Christie. Ironically, Margery Allingham once wrote an obituary for Agatha Christie that was never used because she died before the Queen of Crime.

## Post-Publication Serialization

- *One, Two, Buckle My Shoe* appeared in ten instalments of *The Australian Women's Weekly* from 8 February to 12 April 1947, illustrated Wynne W. Davies.

## 1941 – *Evil Under the Sun*

The Jolly Rogers Hotel on Smugglers Island off the coast of Devon is the perfect place for a summer holiday. Hercule Poirot, detective extraordinaire, is taking a well-earned rest from his arduous professional activities. The arrival of beautiful *femme fatale*

Arlena Stuart soon ignites dangerous sexual passions. Someone hates Arlena enough to make a wax doll in her image and stick pins in it, then she is found strangled to death on the beach – the victim of an apparent *crime passionnel*. But as Hercule Poirot interrogates each of the suspects in turn, he suspects her murder was the culmination of something far more sinister.

## Inspiration for the Title

The title of Agatha Christie's novel is derived from Ecclesiastes 6:1–3: *'There is an evil that I have seen under the sun, and it lies heavy on mankind: God gives some people wealth, possessions and honour, so that they lack nothing their hearts desire, but God does not grant them the ability to enjoy them, and strangers enjoy them instead. This is meaningless, a grievous evil. A man may have a hundred children and live many years; yet no matter how long he lives, if he cannot enjoy his prosperity and does not receive proper burial, I say that a stillborn child is better off than he.'*

## Pre-Publication Serialization

- In the US, *Evil Under the Sun* appeared in eleven instalments of *Collier's* magazine from 14 December 1940 (volume 106, number 24) to 22 February 1941 (volume 107, number 8), illustrated by Mario Cooper.

**Publication:** *Evil Under the Sun* was published in hardback in the UK by the Collins Crime Club on 9 June 1941 and in the US by Dodd, Mead and Company on 7 October 1941.

**Length:** UK 252pp. / US 260pp.

**Price:** UK 7s.6d / US $2.00

**Word Count:** 58,000

**Triva:** Dodd Mead's advertisement in *The Publisher's Weekly* described *Evil Under the Sun* as 'Another breathless adventure in detection by the astute Hercule Poirot. You can sell Christie to any reader on the sparkle and entertainment of her writing.' The real-life setting for the island in the book is Burgh Island in Devon.

## Post-Publication Serialization

- *Evil Under the Sun* appeared in four instalments of *The Australian Women's Weekly* from 17 February to 10 March 1982; the serialisation was authored by David Badger and Greg Flynn and based on the screenplay Anthony Schaffer wrote for the 1982 film of the same name starring Peter Ustinov as Hercule Poirot.

**Comic Strip Novel:** *Evil Under the Sun* was published as a hardback graphic novel by Harper on 11 July 2013. Adapted by Didier Quella-Guyot and illustrated by Thierry Jollet, it was translated from the French edition originally published by Emmanuel Proust Editions in 2012 under the title *Les Vacances d'Hercule Poirot*.

## 1941 – *N or M?*

**Working Title:** *2nd Innings* (as cited in Agatha Christie's notebooks)

England is at war and its best agent Farquhar has just been killed by the driver of a hit-and-run lorry. Before Farquhar dies, he reveals that two of Germany's finest Nazi agents have infiltrated a seaside guesthouse called Sans Souci on the south coast of England. The British secret service is convinced Tommy Beresford is the right person to take over from Farquhar, but they do not reckon on the determination of his wife Tuppence to go uncover with him at Sans Souci to flush out the enemy agents. All the couple know for certain is that N is a man and M is a woman, and the two spies are prepared to stop at nothing to help Hitler invade England and win the war.

**Inspiration for the Title:** The title of the novel derives from a catechism in the Book of Common Prayer which poses the question 'What is your Christian name? Answer N or M.' In this instance, N or M stands for the Latin *nomen vel nomina*, meaning name or names.

### Pre-Publication Serialization

- In the UK, *N or M?* appeared as *Secret Adventure* in seven instalments of *Woman's Pictorial* from 26 April (volume 41, number 1059) to 7 June 1941 (volume 41, number 1065), illustrated by Clive Upton.
- In the US, an abridged version of *N or M?* appeared in volume 76, number 5 of *Redbook* magazine in March 1941, illustrated by Alan Haemer.

**Publication:** *N or M?* was published in hardback in the UK by the Collins Crime Club on 24 November 1941 and in the US by Dodd, Mead and Company on 17 June 1941.

**Length:** UK 192pp. / US 289pp.

**Price:** UK 7s.6d / US $2.00

**Word Count:** 56,000

**Trivia:** Following the publication of *N or M?*, Britain's security service MI5 feared the government's top-secret codebreaking centre at Bletchley Park in Buckinghamshire had an enemy mole within its organisation. Dilly Knox, one of the code-breakers, duly invited Agatha Christie to afternoon tea at his home, and asked her casually why she had named one of the characters in her book Major Bletchley. Her reply convinced MI5 that its fears were unfounded. 'Bletchley?' she replied. 'My dear, I was stuck there on my way by train from Oxford to London and took revenge by giving the name to one of my least lovable characters.'

### Post-Publication Serialization

- In Dundee, Scotland, *N or M?* appeared in twenty-nine instalments of the *Evening Telegraph and Post* from 5 August to 12 September 1941.

## 1942 – *The Body in the Library*

Mrs Bantry wakes from a pleasant dream to be told by her maid there is a dead body in the library at Gossington Hall. The identity of the strangled blonde lying on the hearth rug is as much a mystery to her as Colonel Bantry. Mrs Bantry realizes that if the crime goes unsolved, her husband will spend the rest of his life being ostracized by people who think he murdered the poor girl. Rather than let this happen, Mrs Bantry enlists the support of St. Mary Mead's resident spinster sleuth, Jane Marple.

### Pre-Publication Serialization

- In the US, *The Body in the Library* appeared in seven instalments of *The Saturday Evening Post* from 10 May (volume 213, number 45) to 21 June 1941 (volume 213, number 51), illustrated by Hy Rubin.

**Publication:** *The Body in the Library* was published in hardback in the UK by the Collins Crime Club on 11 May 1942 and in the US by Dodd, Mead and Company on 24 February 1942.

**Length:** UK 160pp. / US 245pp.

**Price:** UK 7s.6d / US $2.00

**Word Count:** 47,000

**Trivia:** By this time the appalling impact of the Second World War had led to paper shortages in England and Agatha Christie's literary agent Edmund Cork of Hughes Massie Ltd. was finding it harder to sell first serial rights to her novels in the UK.

## 1943 (UK) *Five Little Pigs* / 1942 (US) *Murder in Retrospect*

**Working Title:** *Post Mortem Justice* / *Retrospective Death* (as cited in Agatha Christie's notebooks)

When Carla Lemarchant comes of age, she learns her father was murdered by her mother. Refusing to accept the verdict, Carla turns to Hercule Poirot for help. His investigation into the events of sixteen years ago is complicated by the fact that Caroline Crayle has since died in prison, and everyone involved in the case is convinced she was guilty. In order to uncover the truth, Hercule Poirot must interview the five remaining suspects whose conduct reminds him curiously of a childhood nursery…

### Inspiration for the Title

> *This little pig went to market,*
> *This little pig stayed at home,*
> *This little pig had roast beef,*
> *This little pig had none,*
> *And this little pig cried wee wee wee all the way home.*
> 
> Traditional Nursery Rhyme, circa 1760

### Pre-Publication Serialization

- In the US, *Five Little Pigs* appeared as *Murder in Retrospect* in ten instalments of *Collier's* magazine from 20 September (volume 108, number 12) to 22 November 1941 (volume 108, number 21), illustrated by Mario Cooper.

**Publication:** *Five Little Pigs* was published in hardback in the UK by the Collins Crime Club on 11 January 1943 and in the US as *Murder in Retrospect* by Dodd, Mead and Company on 16 June 1942.

**Length:** UK 192pp. / US 234pp.

**Price:** UK 8s. / US $2.00

**Word Count:** 66,000

**Comic Strip Edition:** *Five Little Pigs* was published as a hardback graphic novel by Harper, an imprint of HarperCollins, on 22 July 2010. Adapted by Miceal O'Griafa and illustrated by David Charrier, it was translated from the French edition originally published by Emmanuel Proust Editions in 2009 under the title of *Cinq Petits Cochons*.

## 1943 (UK) – *The Moving Finger* / 1942 (US)

**Working Title:** *The Spider's Web / The Tangled Web* (as cited in Agatha Christie's notebooks)

Following a flying accident, Jerry Burton recuperates from his injuries in the village of Lymstock, where a spate of anonymous letters has shocked and outraged the residents. No one knows who is writing the obscene letters or who will be unfortunate enough to receive the next disgusting missive. What no one expects is that one of the vulgar letters will strike home and result in its recipient committing suicide, or that the mentally unbalanced writer will resort to murder to cover their tracks. In desperation, the vicar's wife calls in Miss Marple, an expert in human nature, to expose the evil poison-pen writer.

### Inspiration for the Title

> *The Moving Finger writes; and, having writ,*
> *Moves on; nor all they Piety nor Wit*
> *Shall lure it back to cancel half a Line,*
> *Nor all thy Tears wash out a Word of it.*
> Edward Fitzgerald's 1859 translation of the poem
> *The Rubaiyat of Omar Khayyam*.

### Pre-Publication Serialization

- In the UK, *The Moving Finger* appeared as *Moving Finger* in six instalments of *Woman's Pictorial* from 17 October (volume 44, number 1136) to 21 November 1942 (volume 44, number 1141), illustrated by Alfred Sindall.

- In the US, *The Moving Finger* appeared as *Moving Finger* in eight instalments of *Collier's* magazine from 28 March (volume 109, number 13) to 16 May 1942 (volume 109, number 20), illustrated by Mario Cooper.

**Publication:** *The Moving Finger* was published in hardback in the UK by the Collins Crime Club on 14 June 1943 and in the US by Dodd, Mead and Company on 6 October 1942. Avon Books, the US paperback publisher, altered the title to *The Case of the Moving Finger* throughout the 1940s and 1950s.

**Length:** UK 160pp. / US 229pp.

**Price:** UK 7s.6d. / US $2.00

**Word Count:** 57,000

## Post-Publication Serialization

- In Australia, *The Moving Finger* appeared in eighteen instalments of *The Sydney Morning Herald* from 20 April to 10 May 1946, illustrated by A. Ladd-Hudson.

**Conflicting UK and US Versions:** The Second World War created havoc with postal services and numerous letters and packages were lost at sea owing to enemy action. Agatha Christie's US publishers Dodd, Mead and Company were unable to locate a copy of her original manuscript of *The Moving Finger* in preparation for publishing, so they used the abridged version of the novel that appeared in *Collier's* magazine as the basis for their hardback edition. As a result, different versions of *The Moving Finger* were published in England and America for the duration of her life.

The UK version of *The Moving Finger* (which has fifteen chapters) begins: *'When at last I was taken out of the plaster, and the doctors had pulled me about to their hearts' content...'*

The US version (which is shorter and has eight chapters in line with *Collier's* serial) begins: *'I have often recalled the morning when the first of the anonymous letters came...'*

Scholars have frequently attributed the abridgement to an anonymous scribe on *Collier's* editorial staff, but Agatha Christie herself re-wrote the beginning of the novel and deleted several scenes to increase the story's pace, which Collier's thought was too slow for a serial. In fact, the magazine refused to serialize *The Moving Finger* unless she altered the text. Agatha Christie was compelled to make these changes because she was desperate for the money *Collier's* was paying her.

The writer often lived hand to mouth during this period because US legislation prevented her from receiving most of the large royalties she earned in America. Not only was she still obliged to pay taxes on these large sums in the UK, but she was also forced to pay double taxation in America despite spending all her time on British soil. Her battles with the Inland Revenue almost led to her declaring bankruptcy on three occasions. After the war it took many years for her advisors to sort out her bewildering labyrinthine tax problems.

Following Agatha Christie's centenary in 1990, the US edition of the novel was revised so the text is now the same as the UK edition. American fans should have no difficulty in obtaining a copy of the book as Agatha Christie originally wrote it with all fifteen chapters intact, although second-hand US editions of the novel with eight chapters remain readily available to those who wish to compare the two texts to see how she went about editing it for the American serial market.

# 1944 – *Towards Zero*

Mr Treves is a connoisseur of detective novels, although in his opinion they all make the mistake of beginning with the murder instead of ending with it. He believes the events culminating in a murder should start years before, with all the people and causes coming together from different parts of the world. When he accepts an invitation to dine at the seaside home of his old friend Lady Tressilian, he is unaware he is converging towards his own zero hero, or that he is about to become the victim of an insane killer.

## Pre-Publication Serialization

- In the US, *Towards Zero* appeared as *Come and Be Hanged* in three instalments of *Collier's* magazine from 6 May (volume 113, number 19) to 20 May 1944 (volume 113, number 21), illustrated by Charles La Salle.

**Publication:** *Towards Zero* was published in hardback in the UK by the Collins Crime Club on 3 July 1944 and in the US by Dodd, Mead and Company on 12 June 1944.

**Length:** UK 160pp. / US 242pp.

**Price:** UK 7s.6d. / US $2.00

**Word Count:** 57,000

## Post-Publication serialization

- In the US, *Towards Zero* was syndicated by King Features to the following newspapers:
    - *The Delphos Herald* (Ohio) 20 October to 3 December 1945
    - *The Evening Independent* (Massillon, Ohio) 20 October to 6 December 1945
    - *The Bradford Era* (Pennsylvania) 20 October to 7 December 1945
    - *The El Paso Times* (Texas) 21 October to 8 December 1945
    - *Kentucky Advocate* (Danville, Kentucky) 21 October to 13 December 1945
    - *The Record-Herald* (Washington, Ohio) 22 October to 7 December 1945
    - *The Daily News-Journal* (Wilmington, Ohio) 24 October to 9 December 1945
    - *The Daily Herald* (Circleville, Ohio) 24 October to 11 December 1945
    - *Macon Chronicle-Herald* (Missouri) 27 October to 15 December 1945
    - *The Journal-News* (Nyack, New York State) 30 October to 12 December 1945
    - *The Boone News-Republican* (Iowa) 30 October to 26 December 1945
    - *The Logan Daily News* (Ohio) 1 November to 19 December 1945
    - *The Gaffney Ledger* (South Carolina) 6 November 1945 to 9 February 1946
    - *Florence Morning News* (Eastern South Carolina) 9 November to 23 November 1945
    - *The Daily Courier* (Connellsville, Pennsylvania) 9 November to 28 December 1945

- *The Daily Clintonian* (Clinton, Indiana) 14 November 1945 to 11 January 1946
  - *The Montana Standard* (Butte, Montana) 17 November to 26 December 1945
  - *The Titusville Herald* (Pennsylvania) 22 November 1945 to 9 January 1946
  - *The Carbondale Free Press* (Illinois) 24 November 1945 to 11 January 1946
  - *The Daily Republican* (Monongahela, Pennsylvania) 5 December 1945 to 1 February 1946
  - *The Vidette-Messenger* (Valparaiso, Indiana) 7 December 1945 to 25 January 1946
  - *Monroe Evening Times* (Wisconsin) 26 December 1945 to 12 February 1946
  - *Waukesha Daily Freeman* (Wisconsin) 24 January to 13 March 1946
  - *Traverse City Record-Eagle* (Michigan) 8 April to 19 July 1946
  - *The Bonham Daily Favourite* (Texas) 31 May to 13 August 1946
  - *The Ludington Daily News* (Michigan) 2 May to 19 June 1947
- In Adelaide, Australia, *Towards Zero* appeared as *Come and Be Hanged* in five instalments of *The Mail* from 7 October to 4 November 1944.
- In Brisbane, Australia, *Towards Zero* appeared as *Come and Be Hanged* as a condensed one-shot publication in *The Sunday Mail* on 24 December 1944.

# 1945 (UK) – *Death Comes as the End* / 1944 (US)

Egypt 2000 BC. Following her husband's death, Renisenb turns to her father, a Ka Priest, for comfort. At first, she finds peace and respite in his household, but then her father's unexpected marriage to Nofret, a veritable hellcat, unleashes a maelstrom of hatred. When Nofret is found dead at the foot of a cliff, Renisenb is the only one to suspect Nofret's death might not have been an accident. As the killer's madness spirals out of control, the horrific body count that follows leaves everyone in Renisenb's family fearing for their lives.

**Publication:** *Death Comes as the End* was published in hardback in the UK by the Collins Crime Club on 29 March 1945 and in the US by Dodd, Mead and Company on 10 October 1944.

**Length:** UK 159pp. / US 233pp.

**Price:** UK 8s.6d. / US $2.00

**Word Count:** 63,000

## Post-Publication Serialization

- In Australia, *Death Comes as the End* appeared in twenty-one instalments of *The Sydney Morning Herald* from 16 November to 11 December 1945, illustrated by Charles Meere.
- In Perth, Australia, *Death Comes as the End* appeared in seventeen instalments of *Women's Magazine*, a supplement to the *Western Mail,* from 3 July to 23 October 1947, illustrated by Charles Meere.

— Secrets from the Agatha Christie Archives —

- In the Czech Republic, *Death Comes as the End* appeared as *Nakonec prijde smrt...* in nos. 1 – 29 of *Nase Rodino* from 2 January to 17 July 1974, translated by Eva Hruba.

# 1945 (UK) *Sparkling Cyanide* / (US) *Remembered Death*

**Working Title:** *In Memoriam* / *Remembered Death* (as cited in Agatha Christie's notebooks)

A year ago, Rosemary Barton sipped a glass of champagne laced with cyanide and died. The six people who were at her restaurant table are still unable to forget her purple convulsed face or the verdict of suicide. Since then, someone has been sending her husband George anonymous letters alleging she was murdered – and he's devised the perfect plan for flushing the killer out into the open…

## Pre-Publication Serialization

- In the UK, *Sparkling Cyanide* appeared in eighteen instalments of the London *Daily Express* from 9 July to 28 July 1945.
- In the US, *Sparkling Cyanide* appeared as *Remembered Death* in eight instalments of *The Saturday Evening Post* from 15 July (volume 216, number 3) to 2 September 1944 (volume 217, number 10), illustrated by Hy Rubin.

**Publication:** *Sparkling Cyanide* was published in hardback in the UK by the Collins Crime Club on 3 December 1945 and in the US as *Remembered Death* by Dodd, Mead and Company on 7 February 1945.

**Length:** UK 160pp. / US 209pp.

**Price:** UK 7s.6d. / US $2.00

**Word Count:** 63,000

## Post-Publication Serialization

- In Melbourne, Australia, *Sparkling Cyanide* appeared as *Remembered Death* in ten instalments of *The Argus* newspaper from 21 April to 23 June 1945, illustrated by Leslie H. Kelly and A. J. Shackel.
- *Sparkling Cyanide* appeared as *One Year Later* in ten instalments of *The Australian Women's Weekly* from 15 December 1945 to 16 February 1946, illustrated by Wynne W. Davies.

# 1946 – *The Hollow*

**Working Title:** *Echo* / *Tragic Weekend* / *Return Journey* (as cited in Agatha Christie's notebooks)

Dr John Christow is spending the weekend with relatives in the country. Surrounded by his unhappy wife and his calculating mistress, he is unprepared for an encounter with a former flame from long ago. Nor does he expect to be the main exhibit in a tableau of murder, in which he lies shot by the side of his hosts' swimming pool just before the legendary detective Hercule Poirot arrives for luncheon.

## Inspiration for the Title

> *I hate the dreadful hollow behind the little wood,*
> *Its lips in the field above are dabbled with blood-red heath,*
> *The red-ribb'd ledges drip with a silent horror of blood,*
> *And Echo there, whatever is ask'd her, answers 'Death.'*
>
> 'Maud: A Monodrama', Alfred, Lord Tennyson, 1855

## Pre-Publication Serialization

- In the UK, *The Hollow* appeared as *Sword in the Heart* in four monthly instalments of *Woman's Journal* from July to October 1946, illustrated by Albert Bailey.
- In the US, *The Hollow* appeared as *The Outraged Heart* in four abridged instalments of *Collier's* magazine between 4 May (volume 117, number 18) and 25 May 1946 (volume 117, number 21), illustrated by Mario Cooper. The abridgement was undertaken by Agatha Christie herself because, once again, she was in desperate need of money to alleviate her worsening tax position brought about by wartime legislation.

**Publication:** *The Hollow* was published in hardback in the UK by the Collins Crime Club on 25 November 1946 and in the US by Dodd, Mead and Company on 24 September 1946. In the US, a paperback edition released by Dell Books in February 1954 changed the title to *Murder After Hours*.

**Length:** UK 256pp. / US 279pp.

**Price:** UK 8s.6d. / US $2.50

**Word Count:** 73,000

## Post-Publication Serialization

- In the US, *The Hollow* was syndicated by King Features to the following newspapers:
    - *The Daily News* (Huntington, Philadelphia) 28 January to 19 March 1947
    - *The Linton Daily Citizen* (Indiana) 19 June to 15 September 1947
    - *The Evening Independent* (Massillon, Ohio) 25 June to 19 August 1947
    - *The Times Recorder* (Zanesville, Ohio) 25 June to 19 August 1947
    - *The Sheboygan Press* (Wisconsin) 26 June to 19 August 1947
    - *The Circleville Herald* (Ohio) 26 June to 21 August 1947
    - *The Courier-Express* (DuBois, Pennsylvania) 26 June to 21 August 1947
    - *The Montana Standard* (Butte, Montana) 29 June to 19 August 1947
    - *Wilmington News-Journal* (Ohio) 2 July to 27 August 1947

— Secrets from the Agatha Christie Archives —

- o *The Camden News* (Arkansas) 5 July to 29 August 1947
- o *The Norwalk Reflector-Herald* (Ohio) 7 July to 30 August 1947
- o *The Logan Daily News* (Ohio) 9 July to 3 September 1947
- o *The Journal-News* (Nyack, New York) 22 July to 16 September 1947
- o *The Morning Herald* (Hagerstown, Maryland) 25 July to 19 September 1947
- o *The Daily Courier* (Connellsville, Pennsylvania) 31 July to 27 September 1947
- o *The Gaffney Ledger* (South Carolina) 31 July to 22 November 1947
- o *Delphos Daily Herald* (Ohio) 4 August to 25 September 1947
- o *The Vidette-Messenger* (Valparaiso, Indiana) 23 August to 18 October 1947
- o *The Call-Leader* (Elwood, Indiana) 2 October 1947 to 13 February 1948
- o *The Daily Notes* (Canonsburg, Pennsylvania) 21 October 1947 to 21 January 1948

Following a three-year break:

- o *The Courier-Post* (Camden, New Jersey) 27 November 1950 to 27 January 1951

- In Canada, *The Hollow* was syndicated by King Features to the following newspaper:

- o *The Evening Citizen* (Ottawa) 20 February to 24 April 1947

## 1948 (UK) – *Taken at the Flood* / (US) *There is a Tide*

**Working Title:** *The Flowing Tide* / *The Incoming Tide* (as cited in Agatha Christie's notebooks)

When Gordon Cloade is killed in the Blitz, his entire fortune passes to his young bride Rosaleen. Five other members of Gordon Cloade's family have been promised a share in his fortune and their hatred for Rosaleen intensifies as their financial hardship worsens. Murder soon rears its ugly head and Hercule Poirot must discover which of the suspects resorted to violence to ensure a reversal of their fortunes.

### Inspiration for the Title

> 'There is a tide in the affairs of men,
> Which, taken at the flood, leads on to fortune;
> Omitted, all the voyage of their life
> Is bound in shallows and in miseries.
> On such a full sea are we now afloat,
> And we must take the current when it serves
> Or lose our ventures.'
>
> Brutus, Scene three, Act Four,
> *Julius Caesar*, William Shakespeare

**Cancellation of the Pre-Publication Serialization Deal:** Initially, Agatha Christie's US agents Harold Ober Associates were receptive to an offer to serialize *Taken at* *the Flood* as a one-shot publication in the *Star Weekly Complete Novel*, which was a Saturday supplement to *The Toronto Star*. The arrangement would also have enabled the Canadian newspaper to syndicate the novel to three smaller newspapers in America six weeks after its appearance in *The Toronto Star*. However, this could conceivably have thrown the work into the public domain in the US owing to possible ad interim copyright complications arising from the archaic laws of the time. The final fly in the ointment that led to Harold Ober Associates cancelling the deal arose when Agatha Christie's publishers Dodd, Mead and Company objected to the novel being serialized in three American newspapers so close to its own publication date.

**Publication:** *Taken at the Flood* was published in hardback in the UK by the Collins Crime Club on 12 November 1948 and in the US as *There is a Tide* by Dodd, Mead and Company on 15 March 1948.

**Length:** UK 192pp. / US 242pp.

**Price:** UK 8s.6d. / US $2.50

**Word Count:** 64,000

## Post-Publication Serialization

- In the US, *Taken at the Flood* was syndicated as *There is a Tide* by King Features to the following newspapers:
    - *Waukesha Daily Freeman* (Wisconsin) 17 July to 11 September 1948
    - *The Daily Republican* (Monongahela, Pennsylvania) 21 July to 24 September 1948
    - *The Daily Clintonian* (Clinton, Indiana) 22 July to 27 September 1948
    - *The Raleigh Register* (Beckley, West Virginia) 22 July to 28 September 1948
    - *The Sheboygan Press* (Wisconsin) 24 July to 16 September 1948
    - *The Circleville Herald* (Ohio) 26 July to 20 September 1948
    - *The Mason City Globe-Gazette* (Iowa) 28 July to 22 September 1948
    - *The Terre Haute Tribune* (Indiana) 30 July to 23 September 1948
    - *The Morning Herald* (Hagerstown, Maryland) 2 August to 28 September 1948
    - *The Camden News* (Arkansas) 10 August to 4 October 1948
    - *Tyrone Daily Herald* (Pennsylvania) 16 August to 11 October 1948
    - *Linton Daily Citizen* (Indiana) 1 September to 6 December 1948
    - *The Daily Notes* (Canonsburg, Pennsylvania) 30 November 1948 to 9 February 1949

- In Finland, *Taken at the Flood* appeared as *Vuoksi ja loude* (*Ebb and Flow of the Tide*) in volumes 9 – 22 of *Kotiliesi* from 2 May to 21 November 1973.

# *1949 – Crooked House*

Charles Hayward is in love with Sophia Leonides. They first met while she was working in the Foreign Office in Egypt during the Second World War. Charles is hoping to marry Sophia on his return to England, but his arrival is overshadowed by the discovery that her grandfather Aristides Leonides has been murdered. Unless Charles can find out who was responsible with help of his own father, who happens to be the police officer investigating the case, the lives of Sophia and her family will be ruined, forever tainted by the knowledge there is an unknown killer in their midst.

## Inspiration for the Title

*Crooked House* takes its title from the nursery rhyme, 'There Was a Crooked Man'. The novel's storyline deviates considerably from that of the popular childhood verse.

> *There was a crooked man and he walked a crooked mile. He found a crooked sixpence upon a crooked stile. He bought a crooked cat, which caught a crooked mouse. And they all lived together in a little crooked house.*
>
> *He met a crooked woman and he found a crooked preach. They had a crooked marriage on a crooked little beach. They had some crooked children and they lived a crooked life. The crooked man, the cat, the mouse, the children and the wife.*
>
> *They were happy for a number of crookedly long years. Lived a life of crooked happiness, no worries and no fears. Until one day the crooked wife upset the crooked man. He yelled a crooked yell and then he hit her and he ran.*
>
> *The crooked man came again at the stroke of twelve. That was when their crooked life became a living hell. There was a crooked man and he walked a crooked mile. And when he killed his wife and kids he smiled a crooked smile.*

## Pre-Publication Serialization

- In the UK, *Crooked House* appeared in seven instalments of *John Bull* magazine from 23 April (volume 85, number 2234) to 4 June 1949 (volume 85, number 2240), illustrated by Alfred Sindall.
- In the US, *Crooked House* appeared in volume 125, number 4 of *Cosmopolitan* magazine in October 1948, illustrated by Grushkin.

**Publication:** *Crooked House* was published in hardback in the UK by the Collins Crime Club on 23 May 1949 and in the US by Dodd, Mead and Company on 14 March 1949.

**Length:** UK 192pp. / US 211pp.

**Price:** UK 8s.6d. / US $2.50

**Word Count:** 56,000

## Post-Publication Serialization

- *Crooked House* appeared in ten instalments of *The Australian Women's Weekly* from 17 December 1949 to 18 February 1950

# 1950s

## 1950 – *A Murder is Announced*

**Working Title:** *A Murder Has Been Arranged* (as cited in Agatha Christie's notebooks)

*'A murder is announced and will take place on Friday October 29th, at Little Paddocks at 6.30 p.m...'* The advertisement in the local newspaper is clearly a joke, but several residents of Chipping Cleghorn cannot resist calling at Miss Blacklock's home Little Paddocks to find out who the practical joker is. At the appointed hour, the lights go out and the silence is shattered by the sound of revolver shots. When the lights come back on, a stranger is found lying dead in the hallway. But murder is no laughing matter as Miss Marple knows only too well and it takes all her perspicuity to unravel the mystery.

### Pre-Publication Serialization

- In the UK, *A Murder is Announced* appeared in eleven instalments of the London *Daily Express* from 28 February to 11 March 1950, illustrated by Andrew Robb.
- In the US, *A Murder is Announced* was syndicated to the following newspapers:
  - *Daily News* (New York) 28 February to 11 March 1950
  - *The Salt Lake Tribune* (Utah) 17 April to 10 June 1950
  - *The Chicago Daily Tribune* (Illinois) 17 April to 12 June 1950
  - *The Pittsburgh Sun-Telegraph* (Pennsylvania) 20 April to 13 June 1950
- In Ontario, Canada, *A Murder is Announced* appeared in *The Ottawa Journal* from 15 April to 10 June 1950.

**Publication:** *A Murder is Announced* was published in the UK by the Collins Crime Club on 5 June 1950 and in the US by Dodd, Mead and Company on 16 May 1950.

**Length:** UK 256pp. / US 248pp.

**Price:** UK 8s.6d. / US $2.50

**Word Count:** 71,000

## Post-Publication Serialization

- In the US, *A Murder is Announced* appeared in:
  - *Omnibook,* a magazine that specialized in abridgements of current bestsellers, November 1950
  - *Bakersfield Californian* (California) 15 July 1950 to 7 July 1951; the newspaper was published weekly on Sundays – hence the year-long serialization
  - *Fairbanks Daily-News Miner* (Alaska) 29 January to 16 April 1951
- In Australia, *A Murder is Announced* appeared in ten weekly instalments of *Woman's Day* magazine from 15 June to 21 August 1950, illustrated by Cecil Linaker.
- In Poland, *A Murder is Announced* appeared as *Inspektor i starsza pani* (*The Old Lady Inspector*) in *Trybuna Robotnicza*, a regional newspaper based in Katowice, from 27 September to 9 December 1973. The translator was Tadeusz Jan Dehnel.

# 1951 – *They Came to Baghdad*

**Working Title:** *The House in Baghdad* (as cited in Agatha Christie's notebooks)

After being fired from her boring London office job, Victoria Jones heads to Baghdad in pursuit of adventure and romance. The exotic old city is teeming with spies and counter-spies of all nations because of a forthcoming international summit between the world's two rival powers, America and Russia. Shortly after checking into her hotel room, Victoria finds herself saddled with the body of a murdered man. Surrounded by enemies and treachery at every turn, she is forced to choose between dying violently or playing the most dangerous role of her life.

## Pre-Publication Serialization

- In the UK, *They Came to Baghdad* appeared in eight instalments of *John Bull* magazine from 13 January (volume 89, number 2324) to 3 March 1951 (volume 89, number 2331), illustrated by Showell.
- In Canada, *They Came to Baghdad* appeared as a one-shot publication in *Star Weekly Complete Novel,* a Saturday supplement to *The Toronto Star* newspaper, on 1 September 1951.

**Publication:** *They Came to Baghdad* was published in the UK by the Collins Crime Club on 5 March 1951 and in the US by Dodd, Mead and Company on 26 March 1951.

**Length:** UK 256pp. / US 218pp.

**Price:** UK 8s.6d. / US $2.50.

**Word Count:** 70,000

## Post-Publication Serialization

- In Melbourne, Australia, *They Came to Baghdad* appeared in ten instalments of *Woman's Day* magazine from 16 April to 18 June 1951.

# 1952 – *Mrs McGinty's Dead*

When Mrs McGinty dies from a brutal blow to her head, her destitute lodger James Bentley is arrested and duly convicted of her murder. The only possible clues in support of his innocence are a bottle of ink and a faded newspaper article that were overlooked by the police. Hercule Poirot is convinced he is on the right track when one of Mrs McGinty's former employers is murdered, but if he is to save James Bentley from the gallows he must first survive an attack on his own life.

## Inspiration for the Title

*Mrs McGinty's Dead* is the name of a childhood game in which the participants form a row, going down on one knee and holding out their hand while chanting, in a question-and-answer format, the following rhyme before toppling over like ninepins:

> Mrs McGinty's dead! How did she die?
> *Down on one knee just like I.*
> Mrs McGinty's dead! How did she die?
> *Holding out her hand just like I.*
> Mrs McGinty's dead! How did she die?
> *Like this…*

## Pre-Publication Serialization

- In the UK, *Mrs McGinty's Dead* appeared in four instalments of *Woman's Journal* from December 1951 to March 1952, illustrated by Tanat Jones.
- In the US, *Mrs McGinty's Dead* appeared as *Blood Will Tell* in the following newspapers:
  - *The Chicago Daily Tribune* (Illinois) 7 October to 30 December 1951
  - *Sunday News* (New York) 7 October to 30 December 1951

**Publication:** *Mrs McGinty's Dead* was published in hardback in the UK by the Collins Crime Club on 3 March 1952 and in the US by Dodd, Mead and Company on 16 January 1952. The Detective Book Club in America released an edition of the novel in 1952 as *Blood Will Tell*.

**Length:** UK 187pp. / US 243pp.

**Price:** UK 9s.6d. / US $2.50

**Word Count:** 61,000

**Trivia:** The following novels by John Dickson Carr were also serialized by *Woman's Journal*: *Four False Weapons*, December 1937 to April 1938; *The Problem of the Green Capsule* as *Mystery in Limelight*, May to July 1939; *And So to Murder* as *Two Angry People*, June to September 1940; *Seeing is Believing* as *Invitation to a Mystery*, May to August 1941; *The Emperor's Snuff-Box*, February to May 1943; *He Wouldn't Kill Patience* as *Magicians Dine Out*, December 1943 to February 1944; *My Late Wives* as *Case of the Vanishing Brides*, April to June 1947; and *The Bride of Newgate*, June

——————— Secrets from the Agatha Christie Archives ———————

to September 1950. *Woman's Journal* also serialized Ngaio Marsh's *Opening Night*, March to May 1951; *Spinsters in Jeopardy*, October 1953 to January 1954; *Scales of Justice*, May to August 1955; *Singing in the Shrouds,* June to September 1958; *False Scent*, February to May 1960; *Hand in Glove*, April to July 1962; and *Death at the Dolphin*, July to November 1965. Both writers were admired by Agatha Christie, who knew them through the Detection Club.

### Post-Publication Serialization

- In the US, *Mrs McGinty's Dead* appeared as *Blood Will Tell* in the morning edition of *The Kansas City Times*, as well as the evening edition of *The Kansas City Star* (Missouri) from 25 April to 11 May 1955. There were two daily instalments, one in each newspaper, except for 1 May 1955 when both instalments appeared in the morning edition. The first instalment appeared in the Monday edition of *The Kansas City Times* (with the mistaken editorial note 'continued from *Sunday's Star*') while the final instalment appeared in *The Kansas City Star.*
- In Canada, *Mrs McGinty's Dead* appeared as *Blood Will Tell* in *Star Weekly Complete Novel*, a Saturday supplement to *The Toronto Star* newspaper, on 25 December 1954.

## 1952 (UK) *They Do it with Mirrors* / (US) *Murder with Mirrors*

Ruth van Rydock is worried about her sister Carrie Louise and asks Miss Marple to visit Carrie Louise at her vast Gothic mansion, which has been converted into a rehabilitation centre for juvenile delinquents. It seems to Miss Marple's shrewd eye that her elderly friend Carrie Louise is happy and quite unfazed by the cranks residing there, but when one of the guests is shot dead in puzzling circumstances Miss Marple suspects a far more cunning criminal intelligence is at work.

### Pre-Publication Serialization

- In the UK, *They Do it with Mirrors* appeared in six instalments of *John Bull* from 26 April (volume 91, number 2391) to 31 May 1952 (volume 91, number 2396), illustrated by George Ditton.
- In the US, *They Do it with Mirrors* appeared as a one-shot publication *Murder with Mirrors* in *Cosmopolitan* magazine (volume 132, number 4) in April 1952, illustrated by Joe Bowler.

**Publication:** *They Do it with Mirrors* was published in hardback in the UK by the Collins Crime Club on 17 November 1952 and in the US as *Murder with Mirrors* by Dodd, Mead and Company on 11 August 1952.

**Length:** UK 192pp. / US 182pp.

**Price:** UK 9s.6d. / US $2.50

**Word Count:** 52,000

## Post-Publication Serialization

- *They Do it with Mirrors* appeared in six instalments of *The Australian Women's Weekly* from 24 September to 22 October 1952, illustrated by Ron Laskie.

# 1953 (UK) – *After the Funeral* / (US) *Funerals are Fatal*

Richard Abernethie's funeral is an extremely dignified occasion. During the reading of the will his sister Cora remarks before the family, *'Still, it's been nicely hushed up, hasn't it..? But he wasn't murdered, wasn't he?'* The following day Cora receives a hatchet in the head by way of a reply and soon afterwards her companion is sent a piece of wedding cake steeped in arsenic. By then the family's solicitor has called in Hercule Poirot to unravel the mystery.

## Pre-Publication Serialization

- In the UK, *After the Funeral* appeared in seven instalments of *John Bull* magazine from 21 March (volume 93, number 2438) to 2 May 1953 (volume 93, number 2444) illustrated by William Little.
- In the US, *After the Funeral* appeared in the following newspapers:
    - *Daily News* (New York), 12 January to 7 March 1953
    - *The Chicago Daily Tribune* (Illinois) 20 January to 14 March 1953

**Publication:** *After the Funeral* was published in hardback in the UK by the Collins Crime Club on 18 May 1953 and in the US as *Funerals are Fatal* by Dodd, Mead and Company on 16 March 1953.

**Length:** UK 191pp. / US 244pp.

**Price:** UK 10s.6d. / US $2.50

**Word Count:** 72,000

**Trivia:** In the UK, *After the Funeral* was published as *Murder at the Gallop* by Fontana paperbacks, an imprint of William Collins & Sons, in 1963 to coincide with the release of the cinema film that was very loosely based on it. Much to Agatha Christie's disdain, Hercule Poirot was replaced in the picture by Miss Marple, who was played by Margaret Rutherford.

## Post-Publication Serialization

- In the US, *After the Funeral* appeared in fifty instalments of *The Daily Boston Globe* from 14 July to 29 September 1953.
- In Ontario, Canada, *After the Funeral* appeared in *The Ottawa Journal* from 9 May to 3 July 1953.
- In Sydney, Australia, *After the Funeral* appeared in seven instalments of *Woman's Day* magazine from 2 November to 14 December 1953.

Secrets from the Agatha Christie Archives

# 1953 (UK) – *A Pocket Full of Rye* / 1954 (US)

Rex Fortescue collapses while drinking tea in his office in London. Frightened staff wonder if he is suffering an epilepsy fit, but the autopsy shows the financial king was poisoned with taxine. Next, his wife Adele is poisoned in her parlour while eating bread and honey. Finally, Gladys the parlourmaid is strangled at the washing line – and a clothes peg is left clipped to her nose. The cruel, contemptuous gesture angers Miss Marple and brings her to Yewtree Lodge to ensure justice prevails for the poor girl. However, it takes all her ingenuity in this triple tragedy to fathom out the killer's bizarre motive for crime by rhyme.

## Inspiration for the Title

*Sing a song of sixpence*
*A pocket full of rye.*
*Four and twenty blackbirds*
*Baked in a pie.*
*When the pie was opened,*
*The birds began to sing;*
*Was not that a dainty dish,*
*To set before the King?*
*The King was in his counting house,*
*Counting out his money;*
*The Queen was in the parlour,*
*Eating bread and honey.*
*The maid was in the garden,*
*Hanging out the clothes,*
*When down came a blackbird*
*And nipped off her nose.*

Traditional Nursery Rhyme,
circa 1760

## Pre-Publication Serialization

- In the UK, *A Pocket Full of Rye* appeared in fourteen instalments of the London *Daily Express* from 28 September to 13 October 1953.
- In the US, *A Pocket Full of Rye* appeared in:
    - *The Chicago Daily Tribune* (Illinois) 11 January to 27 February 1954
    - *Daily News* (New York), 11 January to 27 February 1954
    - *The Paducah Sun-Democrat* (Kentucky) 17 January to 6 March 1954
    - *The Boston Daily Globe* (Connecticut) 31 May to 7 August 1954
- In Adelaide, Australia, *A Pocket Full of Rye* appeared in eight instalments of the *Sunday Advertiser* from (Saturday) 24 October to (Saturday) 12 December 1953, illustrated by Clem Seale. The *Sunday Advertiser* was always published on a Saturday because it was deemed inappropriate to work on the Sabbath.

- In Sydney, Australia, *A Pocket Full of Rye* appeared in six instalments of *The Sun-Herald* (the Sunday edition of the *Sydney Morning Herald* newspaper) from 25 October to 29 November 1953, illustrated by Clem Seale.

**Publication:** *A Pocket Full of Rye* was published in hardback in the UK by the Collins Crime Club on 9 November 1953 and in the US by Dodd, Mead and Company on 18 February 1954.

**Length:** UK 191pp. / US 211pp.

**Price:** UK 10s.6d. / US $2.75

**Word Count:** 59,000

### Post-Publication Serialization

- In the US, *A Pocket Full of Rye* was serialized in *The Evening Telegram* (Rocky Mount, North Carolina) from 11 January to 27 February 1954.
- In Perth, Australia, *A Pocket Full of Rye* appeared in seven instalments of *The Western Mail*, from 3 December 1953 to 14 January 1954, illustrated by Clem Seale.

## 1954 (UK) *Destination Unknown* / (US) *So Many Steps to Death*

Hilary Craven is on the brink of suicide when a member of the British government asks her to impersonate the wife of a missing scientist. Several scientists have recently disappeared, though whether they were abducted, brainwashed or murdered, no one knows. Unfazed by what might happen to her, Hilary accepts the commission, but by the time she realizes she wants to live again she is surrounded by danger at every turn.

### Pre-Publication Serialization

- In the UK, *Destination Unknown* appeared in five instalments of *John Bull* from 25 September (volume 96, number 2517) to 23 October 1954 (volume 96, number 2521), illustrated by William Little.
- In the US, *Destination Unknown* appeared as *Destination X* in the following newspapers:
    - *Daily News* (New York) 13 December 1954 to 5 February 1955
    - *The Chicago Daily Tribune* (Illinois) 12 April to 9 June 1955

**Publication:** *Destination Unknown* was published in hardback in the UK by the Collins Crime Club on 1 November 1954 and in the US as *So Many Steps to Death* by Dodd, Mead and Company on 8 February 1955.

**Length:** UK 191pp. / US 212pp.

**Price:** UK 10s.6d. / US $2.50

**Word Count:** 61,000

## Post-Publication Serialization

- In the US, *Destination Unknown* appeared as *Destination X* in the following newspaper:
  - *The Lake Charles American Press* (Louisiana) 17 January to 13 March 1955
- In Canada, *Destination Unknown* appeared as *Destination X* in the following newspaper:
  - *The Gazette* (Montreal) 24 January to 12 March 1955
- In Sydney, Australia, *Destination Unknown* appeared in eight instalments of *Woman* magazine from 18 October to 6 December 1954.

# 1955 (UK) *Hickory Dickory Dock* / (US) *Hickory Dickory Death*

Hercule Poirot's secretary Miss Lemon epitomizes efficiency, so when the great detective confronts her over three mistakes in the latest letter she has typed, she is forced to admit the cause of her current anxiety. Her sister, Mrs Hubbard, runs a students' hostel in Hickory Road where a series of thefts has caused a great deal of distress. Poirot is confident he can restore Miss Lemon's equilibrium by exposing the culprit, but no sooner does he fulfill his promise than the first of the murders occur...

## Inspiration for the Title

> *Hickory Dickory Dock*
> *The mouse ran up the clock*
> *The clock struck one,*
> *The mouse ran down,*
> *Hickory, dickory, dock.*
>
> Traditional Nursery Rhyme, circa 1744

## Pre-Publication Serialization

- In the UK, *Hickory Dickory Dock* appeared in six instalments of *John Bull* from 28 May (volume 97, number 2552) to 2 July 1955 (volume 98, number 2557) illustrated by Fancett.
- In the US, *Hickory Dickory Dock* appeared as *Hickory Dickory Death* in three instalments of *Collier's* magazine from 14 October to 11 November 1955, illustrated by Robert Fawcett.

**Publication:** *Hickory Dickory Dock* was published in hardback in the UK by the Collins Crime Club on 31 October 1955 and in the US as *Hickory Dickory Death* by Dodd, Mead and Company on 1 November 1955.

**Length:** UK 191pp. / US 241pp.

**Price:** UK 10s.6d. / US $3.00

**Word Count:** 57,000

## Post-Publication Serialization

- In Australia, *Hickory Dickory Dock* appeared in eight instalments of *Woman* magazine from 15 August to 3 October 1955, illustrated by Gerard Lants.

# 1956 – *Dead Man's Folly*

Sir George and Lady Stubbs are holding a garden fête at Nasse House in Devon. The distinguished crime novelist Mrs Ariadne Oliver has agreed to stage a 'Murder Hunt' on the day in question, but she soon suspects others of trying to manipulate her and turns to Hercule Poirot for help. Sure enough, Mrs Oliver's premonition of evil comes true on the day of the fête when a body is discovered in the boathouse. But what possible motive could anyone have for strangling a 14-year-old girl-guide?

## Pre-Publication Serialization

- In the UK, *Dead Man's Folly* appeared in six instalments of *John Bull* from 11 August (volume 100, number 2615) to 15 September 1956 (volume 100, number 2620), illustrated by Fancett.
- In the US, *Dead Man's Folly* appeared in three instalments of *Collier's* magazine from 20 July (volume 138, number 2) to 17 August 1956 (volume 138, number 4), illustrated by Robert Fawcett.

**Publication:** *Dead Man's Folly* was published in hardback in the UK by the Collins Crime Club on 5 November 1956 and in the US by Dodd, Mead and Company on 26 September 1956.

**Length:** UK 256pp. / US 216pp.

**Price:** UK 12s.6d. / US $2.95

**Word Count:** 57,000

**Trivia:** For the genesis of *Dead Man's Folly*, see 'Greenshore's Folly' in the short story section.

## Post-Publication Serialization

- *Dead Man's Folly* appeared in four instalments of *The Australian Women's Weekly* from 26 December 1956 to 16 January 1957, illustrated by John Mills. The first instalment also featured the short story 'Word in Season' by Margery Allingham.

——————— Secrets from the Agatha Christie Archives ———————

**Comic Strip Edition:** *Dead Man's Folly* was published as a hardback graphic novel by Harper, an imprint of HarperCollins, on 15 March 2012. Adapted and illustrated by Marek with colour by Christophe Bouchard, it was translated from the French edition originally published by Emmanuelle Proust Editions in 2011 under the title of *Poirot Joue le Jeu*. The English edition also features an introduction by Agatha Christie's grandson Mathew Prichard.

## 1957 (UK) – *4.50 from Paddington* / (US) *What Mrs McGillicuddy Saw!*

**Working Title:** *4.15 from Paddington / 4.30 from Paddington / 4.54 from Paddington* (as cited in Agatha Christie's notebooks)

Mrs McGillicuddy is relaxing in a first-class carriage after a day's busy Christmas shopping in London. After waking from a nap, she glances out of the train window. A few feet away, in the carriage of a train running parallel to hers, she sees a woman being strangled. Horrified, she watches as the end comes and the woman's body goes limp in the killer's hands, before the train then vanishes into the night. No one believes Mrs McGillicuddy's story of having witnessed a murder, no one, that is, apart from her old friend Miss Jane Marple.

### Pre-Publication Serialization

- In the UK, *4.50 from Paddington* appeared in five instalments of *John Bull* from 5 October (volume 102 number 2675) to 2 November 1957 (volume 102 number 2679), illustrated by K.J. Petts.
- In the US, *4.50 from Paddington* appeared in the following newspapers:
    - *Daily News* (New York) 20 October to 30 November 1957 as *Eyewitness to Death*
    - *The Chicago Daily Tribune* (Illinois) 27 October to 7 December 1957 as *Eyewitness to Death*

**Publication:** *4.50 from Paddington* was published in hardback in the UK by the Collins Crime Club on 4 November 1957 and in the US as *What Mrs McGillicuddy Saw!* by Dodd, Mead and Company on 11 November 1957.

**Length:** UK 256pp. / US 192pp.

**Price:** UK 12s.6d. / US $2.95

**Word Count:** 66,000

### Post-Publication Serialization

- In the US, *4.50 from Paddington* appeared as *Eyewitness to Murder* in *The Arizona Daily Star* (Texas) from 24 November 1957 to 4 January 1958.
- In Canada, *4.50 from Paddington* appeared as a one-shot publication entitled *Eye Witness to Death* in *Star Weekly Complete Novel,* a Saturday supplement to

*The Toronto Star* newspaper, on 28 December 1957, with a cover illustration by Maxine McCaffrey.
- *4.50 from Paddington* appeared in five instalments of *The Australian Women's Weekly* from 1 January to 29 January 1958, illustrated by Ron Laskie.

## 1958 (UK) – *Ordeal by Innocence* / 1959 (US)

**Working Title:** *The Innocent* (as cited in Agatha Christie's notebooks and on the front page of her manuscript)

*The Innocent* was a generic title that might have applied to any of Agatha Christie's detective novels, and one of Collins' readers suggested the following alternatives: *Viper's Point, A Serpent's Tooth, The Burden of Innocence* and *Cat Among the Pigeons*. Agatha Christie's decision to re-title her novel *Ordeal by Innocence* was based on her English literary agent Edmund Cork's suggestion.

Shortly before Rachel Argyle is killed by a blow to the head, she is overheard arguing with her destitute son. Jacko is convicted of her murder and sent to prison, where he dies for a crime he did not commit. Two years later, the peace of the Argyle household is shattered by a stranger who corroborates Jacko's alibi. Rachel Argyle's family are reluctant to accept that the real killer must still be living under the same roof as them – until a second murder confirms their worst fears.

### Pre-Publication Serialization

- In the UK, *Ordeal by Innocence* appeared in two instalments of *John Bull* magazine on 20 September (volume 104, number 2725) and 27 September 1958 (volume 104, number 2726) illustrated by Fancett.
- In the US, *Ordeal by Innocence* appeared as *The Innocent* in the following newspapers:
  - *Sunday News / Daily News* (New York) 4 January to 14 February 1959
  - *The Miami News* (Florida) 11 January to 21 February 1959
  - *The Chicago Daily Tribune* (Illinois) 1 February to 14 March 1959
- In Canada, *Ordeal by Innocence* appeared as a one-shot publication in *Star Weekly Complete Novel*, a Saturday supplement to *The Toronto Star* newspaper, on 21 February 1959, with a cover illustration by Russell Maebus; *The Toronto Star* was also distributed throughout the US.

**Publication:** *Ordeal by Innocence* was published in hardback in the UK by the Collins Crime Club on 3 November 1958 and in the US by Dodd, Mead and Company on 9 March 1959.

**Length:** UK 256pp. / US 247pp.

**Price:** UK 12s.6d. / US $2.95

**Word Count:** 69,000

## Post-Publication Serialization

- In Australia, *Ordeal by Innocence* appeared in three instalments of *Woman's Day* magazine on 5, 12 and 19 January 1959.

**Comic Strip Edition:** *Ordeal by Innocence* was published as a hardback graphic novel by Harper, an imprint of HarperCollins, on 1 July 2008. Adapted and illustrated by Chandre, it was translated from the French edition originally published by Emmanuel Proust Editions in 2006 under the title of *Temoin Indesirable*.

# 1959 (UK) – *Cat Among the Pigeons* / 1960 (US)

**Working Title:** *Death of a Games Mistress* (as cited in Agatha Christie's notebooks)

A revolution in the far-off country of Ramat sets in motion a series of frightening events at one of England's most distinguished schools for girls. Two teachers, investigating a mysterious light in the sports pavilion one night, stumble across the body of the games mistress. The police are baffled by the apparent lack of motive for the murder, until Hercule Poirot receives a visit from a schoolgirl who is determined to avoid becoming the killer's next victim.

## Pre-Publication Serialization

- In the UK, *Cat Among the Pigeons* appeared in six instalments of *John Bull* magazine from 26 September (volume 106, number 2771) to 31 October 1959 (volume 106, number 2776), illustrated by Fancett.
- In the US, *Cat Among the Pigeons* appeared in volume 76, number 11 of *Ladies' Home Journal* in November 1959, illustrated by Joe DeMers.

**Publication:** *Cat Among the Pigeons* was published in hardback in the UK by the Collins Crime Club on 2 November 1959 and in the US by Dodd, Mead and Company on 11 November 1960.

**Length:** UK 255pp. / US 224pp.

**Price:** UK 12s.6d. / US $2.95

**Word Count:** 68,000

# 1960s

## 1961 (UK) – *The Pale Horse* / 1962 (US)

**Working Title:** *The Thallium Mystery* (as cited in AC's notebooks)

Murder by black magic seems utterly absurd – or is it? A girl dies after having her hair pulled out and a priest is killed after hearing a death-bed confession. Historian Mark Easterbrook suspects their deaths are connected to a village pub which has been converted into a witches' coven specializing in murder by supernatural means. If Mark is to prevent the death toll from rising, he is going to need more than the moral support of the celebrated crime writer Ariadne Oliver to exorcise the evil spirits in their midst...

### Inspiration for the Title

> *And I looked, and behold a Pale Horse,*
> *And his name that sat on him was Death,*
> *And Hell followed with him.*
>
> Revelations 6:8

### Pre-publication serialization

- In the UK, *The Pale Horse* appeared in eight instalments of *Woman's Mirror* from 2 September to 21 October 1961, illustrated by Zelinksi.
- In the US, *The Pale Horse* appeared as a one-shot publication in *Ladies Home Journal* (volume 79, number 4) in April 1962, illustrated by Eugenie Louis.

**Publication:** *The Pale Horse* was published in hardback in the UK by the Collins Crime Club on 6 November 1961 and in the US by Dodd, Mead and Company on 24 September 1962.

**Length:** UK 256pp. / US 242pp.

**Price:** UK 15s. / US $3.75

**Word Count:** 64,000

### Post-Publication Serialization

- In Australia and New Zealand, *The Pale Horse* appeared in seven instalments of *The Australian Women's Weekly* from 13 December 1961 to 24 January 1962,

Secrets from the Agatha Christie Archives

illustrated by Laskie. (Prior to this, the magazine was only published in Australia, but over the next few years its growing popularity would result in it being distributed to other countries.)

## 1962 (UK) – *The Mirror Crack'd from Side to Side* / 1963 (US) *The Mirror Crack'd*

The residents of St. Mary Mead are thrilled when Gossington Hall is bought by the glamorous Hollywood movie star Marina Gregg. She endears herself to them by holding a fund-raising fete in the grounds, but the occasion is marred by the gate-crashing antics of rival actress Lola Brewster and producer Ardwyck Fenn, both of whom loathe Marina unconditionally. To make matters worse, the unexpected death of a local busy-body provides Miss Marple with a reason to put aside her knitting and investigate the first in a series of murders.

### Inspiration for the Title

*She left the web, she left the loom*
*She made three paces thro' the room*
*She saw the water-flower bloom,*
*She saw the helmet and the plume,*
  *She look'd down to Camelot.*
*Out flew the web and floated wide;*
*The mirror crack'd from side to side;*
*'The curse is come upon me,' cried*
  *The Lady of Shalott*

'The Lady of Shalott',
Alfred, Lord Tennyson, 1842

### Pre-publication serialization

- In the UK, *The Mirror Crack'd from Side to Side* appeared in eleven instalments of the London *Daily Express* from 29 October to 9 November 1962, illustrated by Robin Jacques.
- In Canada, *The Mirror Crack'd from Side to Side* appeared in two instalments of *Star Weekly Novel*, a Saturday supplement to *The Toronto Star* newspaper, on 9 and 16 March 1963, illustrated by Gerry Sevier.

**Publication:** *The Mirror Crack'd from Side to Side* was published in hardback in the UK by the Collins Crime Club on 12 November 1962 and in the US by Dodd, Mead and Company on 23 September 1963.

**Length:** UK 255pp. / US 246pp.

**Price:** UK 15s. / US $3.75

**Word Count:** 69,000

## Post-Publication Serialization

- *The Mirror Crack'd from Side to Side* appeared in six instalments of *The Australian Women's Weekly* from 6 February to 6 March 1963, illustrated by Boothroyd.

## 1963 (UK) – *The Clocks* / 1964 (US)

Sheila Webb is a typist employed by the Cavendish Secretarial Bureau. On arriving at 18 Wilbraham Crescent for her latest assignment, she finds the body of a murdered man in the living-room. The police are unable to identity the victim and the blind owner of the property has no idea how he got there. The most baffling aspect of the case for Hercule Poirot is why the killer left behind four clocks at the scene of the crime, each pointing to 4.13 p.m.

### Pre-Publication Serialization

- In the US, *The Clocks* appeared as a one-shot publication in *Cosmopolitan* magazine (volume 156, number 1) in January 1964, illustrated by Al Parker.

**Publication:** *The Clocks* was published in hardback in the UK by the Collins Crime Club on 11 November 1963 and in the US by Dodd, Mead and Company on 21 September 1964.

**Length:** UK 256pp. / US 276pp.

**Price:** UK 16s. / US $4.50

**Word Count:** 83,000

### Post–Publication Serialization

- In the UK, *The Clocks* appeared – two days after the publication of the book – in six instalments of *Woman's Own* from 9 November to 14 December 1963, illustrated by Herb Tauss.
- *The Clocks* appeared in five instalments of *The Australian Women's Weekly* from 11 December 1963 to 8 January 1964, illustrated by Wills.

## 1964 (UK) – *A Caribbean Mystery* / (US) 1965

**Working Title:** *Shadow in Sunlight* (as cited in Agatha Christie's notebooks)

Miss Marple is holidaying on the island of St. Honoré in the Caribbean. As she sits knitting in the sunshine, she listens patiently to old Major Palgrave's endless supply of stories, each one duller than the last. Most of the other guests avoid him and no one is interested in his claim to have a photograph of a murderer in his possession. Then one morning Major Palgrave is found dead, and the photograph is missing from his wallet. Not only does Miss Marple suspect he was murdered, but she has reason to believe the killer will strike again.

*Secrets from the Agatha Christie Archives*

### Pre-Publication Serialization

- In the UK, *A Caribbean Mystery* appeared in six instalments of *Woman's Own* magazine from 7 November to 12 December 1964, illustrated with photographic layouts by Abis Sida Stribley.
- In the US, *A Caribbean Mystery* was serialized in New York in the *Sunday News* and *Daily News* from 17 January to 20 February 1965
- In Canada, *A Caribbean Mystery* appeared in two instalments of *Star Weekly Novel,* a Saturday supplement to *The Toronto Star* newspaper, on 16 and 23 January 1965.

**Publication:** *A Caribbean Mystery* was published in hardback in the UK by the Collins Crime Club on 16 November 1964 and in the US by Dodd, Mead and Company on 7 September 1965.

**Length:** UK 256pp. / US 245pp.

**Price:** UK 16s. / US $4.50

**Word Count:** 53,000

## 1965 (UK) – *At Bertram's Hotel* / 1966 (US)

Miss Marple is enjoying a stay at Bertram's Hotel. Located in the heart of swinging London, Bertram's is a microcosm of Edwardian charm, patronized by the higher echelons of the clergy, dowager duchesses and teenagers returning abroad from finishing school. When a guest goes missing and the Irish mail train is robbed, Miss Marple suspects the two events are inextricably linked to Bertram's – and then a fatal shooting confirms her worst fears.

### Pre-Publication Serialization

- In the UK, *At Bertram's Hotel* appeared in five instalments of *Woman's Own* between 20 November and 18 December 1965, illustrated with photographic layouts by Abis Sida Stribley.
- In the US, *At Bertram's Hotel* appeared in two instalments of *Good Housekeeping* magazine in March and April 1966, illustrated by Sanford Kossin with a photograph by James Viles.

**Publication:** *At Bertram's Hotel* was published in hardback in the UK by the Collins Crime Club on 15 November 1965 and in the US by Dodd, Mead and Company on 26 September 1966.

**Length:** UK 255pp. / US 272pp.

**Price:** UK 16s. / US $4.50

**Word Count:** 62,000

## 1966 (UK) – *Third Girl* / 1967 (US)

Hercule Poirot's breakfast is interrupted by a dishevelled girl telling him she may have committed a murder. Before he can respond, she accuses him of being too old and vanishes. Poirot wonders whether the girl really *has* committed a murder or whether she is under the influence of a hallucinogenic drug. He has no idea who she is and where to find her. He concludes the business is probably best forgotten, until the crime novelist Mrs Ariadne Oliver puts him on the trail of the girl and decides to help him by playing detective herself with near fatal results.

### Pre-Publication Serialization

- In the US, *Third Girl* appeared as a one-shot publication in *Redbook* magazine (volume 128, number 6) in April 1967, with a photographic montage by Mike Cuesta.

**Publication:** *Third Girl* was published in hardback in the UK by the Collins Crime Club on 14 November 1966 and in the US by Dodd, Mead and Company on 5 September 1967.

**Length:** UK 256pp. / US 248pp.

**Price:** UK 18s. / US $4.50

**Word Count:** 72,000

### Post-Publication Serialization

- In the UK, *Third Girl* appeared in six instalments of *Woman's Own* from 19 November to 24 December 1966, illustrated by Richard Lewis with a series of photographs of models made-up to look like several of the characters in the story.

## 1967 (UK) – *Endless Night* / 1968 (US)

**Working Title:** *Gypsy's Acre* (as cited in Agatha Christie's notebooks)

*Endless Night* is a poignant, doom-laden murder mystery involving a young, romantic couple who meet and fall helplessly in love. They become obsessed with a beautiful piece of land known as Gipsy's Acre, where all sorts of nasty accidents and deaths have occurred over the years. Rather than heed the warnings of a local gypsy, they refuse to believe Gypsy's Acre is cursed and set about building their dream home on it, unaware that fate is about to come crashing down around them...

### Inspiration for the Title

*Man was made for Joy and Woe*
*And when this we rightly know*
*Thro' the World we safely go...*

*Every night and every morn*
*Some to misery are born,*
*Every morn and every night*
*Some are born to sweet delight.*
*Some are born to sweet delight,*
*Some are born to endless night.*

'Auguries of Innocence',
William Blake, c.1803

## Pre-Publication serialization

- In the US, *Endless Night* appeared in two instalments of *The Saturday Evening Post* on 24 February (volume 241, number 4) and 9 March 1968 (volume 241, number 5), illustrated by Tom Adams, famous the world over for his iconic cover illustrations of Agatha Christie's paperback series throughout the 1960s and 1970s.

**Publication:** *Endless Night* was published in hardback in the UK by the Collins Crime Club on 30 October 1967 and in the US by Dodd, Mead and Company on 18 March 1968.

**Length:** UK 224pp. / US 248pp.

**Price:** UK 18s. / US $4.95

**Word Count:** 62,000

## Post-Publication Serialization

- In Australia, *Endless Night* appeared in five instalments of *Woman's Day* magazine from 7 March to 4 April 1968.
- In India, *Endless Night* appeared in *Imprint,* a monthly magazine published in the English language by the Bombay Press, in September 1968.
- In Mexico, a Spanish translation of *Endless Night* appeared as *La Torre de la Gitana* (*The Tower of the Gypsy*) in *Kena* magazine in December 1971.
- In the US, *Endless Night* appeared in volume one of *A Treasury of Modern Mysteries*, Doubleday and Company 1973.

**Comic Strip Edition:** *Endless Night* was published as a hardback graphic novel by Harper, an imprint of HarperCollins, on 3 November 2008. Adapted by François Rivière and illustrated by Frank Leclercq, it was translated from the French edition originally published by Emmanuelle Proust Editions in 2003 under the title of *La Nuit Qui Ne Finit Pas.*

## *1968 – By the Pricking of My Thumbs*

**Working title:** *The House on the Canal*; other titles Agatha Christie considered were *The House by the Bridge* and *The House by the Canal* (as cited in her notebooks).

Tommy and Tuppence Beresford are visiting an eccentric aunt at Sunny Ridge Nursing Home where strange things happen. An elderly resident, Mrs Lancaster, tells Tuppence that the body of a dead child is buried behind a fireplace. However, before Tuppence can get to the bottom of the mystery bogus relatives spirit Mrs Lancaster away from the nursing home in the dead of night. The search for the endangered old lady leads Tuppence to the sinister village of Sutton Chancellor, where the sins of the past erupt into violence once more.

## Inspiration for the Title

> *By the pricking of my thumbs,*
> *Something wicked this way comes.*
> Second Witch, Act 4, Scene 1, *Macbeth*,
> William Shakespeare

## Pre-Publication serialization

- In Canada, *By the Pricking of My Thumbs* appeared in two instalments of *The Canadian Magazine Star Weekly Novel* on 1 and 8 February 1969, illustrated by Steve Mennie. (*Star Weekly* and *The Canadian Magazine* amalgamated on 7 October 1968 as *The Canadian Magazine Star Weekly Novel* until the last issue appeared 29 December 1973.)

**Publication:** *By The Pricking of My Thumbs* was published in hardback in the UK by the Collins Crime Club on 12 November 1968 and in the US by Dodd, Mead and Company on 2 December 1968.

**Length:** UK 255pp. / US 275pp.

**Price:** UK 21s. / US $4.95

**Word Count:** 71,000

**Trivia:** The novel was initially advertised by Dodd, Mead and Company in *The Publishers' Weekly* edition of 28 August 1968 as *The House on the Canal* before its title was changed to the far more evocative *By the Pricking of My Thumbs*. Agatha Christie also wrote the UK blurb for the book in which she stated it might well have been entitled *By the Chilling of Your Spine*. The personally inscribed copy she gave the creator of Jeeves and Wooster read: 'To P.G. Wodehouse with reverence, admiration and many long years of deeply enjoyed reading – no one like you! Agatha Christie.'

## Post-Publication serialization

- In Australia and New Zealand, *By the Pricking of My Thumbs* appeared in three instalments of *The Australian Women's Weekly* from 12 February to 26 February 1969; by this time the magazine was also being distributed in New Guinea and Malaysia.

# 1969 – *Hallowe'en Party*

**Working Title:** *Easeful Death* (as cited in Agatha Christie's notebooks)

During the preparations for a Hallowe'en party, 13-year-old Joyce Reynolds boasts she once saw a murder being committed. Everyone is convinced she is making the story up to impress the visiting crime novelist Mrs Ariadne Oliver. Later that night, after the party is over, Joyce is found dead after someone drowned her in a bucket of water while she was bobbing for apples. Mrs Oliver belatedly realizes that Joyce may have been telling the truth and asks her old friend Hercule Poirot to investigate. It soon transpires Joyce is not the only inhabitant of Woodleigh Common who has died in mysterious circumstances. Could the local witch really hold the key to the mystery?

## Pre-Publication serialization

- In the US, *Hallowe'en Party* appeared as a one-shot publication in *Cosmopolitan* magazine in December 1969, illustrated by Brian Sanders.

**Publication:** *Hallowe'en Party* was published in hardback in the UK by the Collins Crime Club on 10 November 1969 and in the US by Dodd, Mead and Company on 1 December 1969.

**Length:** UK 255pp. / US 248pp.

**Price:** UK 25s. / US $5.95

**Word Count:** 68,000

**Trivia:** Although the UK edition retailed at 25 shillings, it was also priced on the dustjacket at £1.25 in preparation for decimalisation on 15 February 1971. The book was officially dedicated to P.G. Wodehouse (see *1922 – The Secret Adversary: Agatha Christie vs P.G. Wodehouse*).

## Post-Publication serialization

- In the UK, *Hallowe'en Party* appeared in seven instalments of *Woman's Own* from 15 November to 27 December 1969.

**Comic Strip Edition:** *Hallowe'en Party* was published as a hardback graphic novel by Harper, an imprint of HarperCollins, on 3 December 2008. Adapted and illustrated by Chandre, it was translated from the French edition originally published by Emmanuel Proust Editions in 2007 under the title of *Le Crime d'Halloween*.

# 1970s

## 1970 – *Passenger to Frankfurt*

**Working Title:** *Passenger to Frankfort* (Agatha Christie's preferred spelling of the German city, as cited throughout her manuscript).

Sir Stafford Nye, a bored diplomat, agrees to help a frightened woman at Frankfurt Airport evade her enemies. On his return to London, he narrowly avoids being run over by a speeding car. Soon afterwards, he encounters the mystery woman again, masquerading as an aristocrat. By the time Sir Stafford realizes he is caught up in an international conspiracy with deadly, far-reaching consequences, it is too late for him to turn back.

**Publication:** *Passenger to Frankfurt* was published in hardback in the UK by the Collins Crime Club on 15 September 1970 and in the US by Dodd, Mead and Company on 16 November 1970.

**Length:** UK 256pp. / US 272pp.

**Price:** UK 25s. / £1.25 / US $5.95

**Word Count:** 69,000

### Post-Publication Appearance

*Passenger to Frankfurt* was a dystopian thriller and did not fare well in the serialization market because it was a far cry from the traditional whodunnits for which Agatha Christie was famous. Ironically, this did not prevent it from topping the bestseller lists in America owing to the author's immense fame.

- In the US, the introduction to *Passenger to Frankfurt* (in which Agatha Christie explained why she wrote the book and discussed how she got ideas for her work) appeared as 'Invention, Imagination and Reality' in *The Writer* magazine in June 1972.

## 1971 – *Nemesis*

Miss Marple receives a letter from a dead millionaire asking her to investigate a crime, without telling her who was involved or when it happened. Acting on instructions from 'beyond', she joins a coach tour of historic British homes and gardens. When

———————— Secrets from the Agatha Christie Archives ————————

disaster strikes a member of the coach party, it is apparent Miss Marple must rely on her flair for crime to expose the killer and ensure that 'justice rolls down like waters and righteousness like an everlasting stream'.

### Pre-Publication Serialization

- In the UK, *Nemesis* appeared in seven instalments of *Woman's Realm* from 25 September (volume 27, number 702) to 6 November 1971 (volume 27, number 708), illustrated by Len Thurston.
- In Canada, *Nemesis* appeared in two instalments of *The Canadian Magazine Star Weekly Novel* on 16 and 23 October 1971, illustrated by Laszlo Gal.

**Publication:** *Nemesis* was published in hardback in the UK by the Collins Crime Club on 18 October 1971 and in the US by Dodd, Mead and Company on 15 November 1971.

**Length:** UK 256pp. / US 271pp.

**Price:** UK £1.50 / US $6.95

**Word Count:** 78,000

**Trivia:** Following the publication of *Passenger to Frankfurt*, *Nemesis* marked a triumphant return to form. Is it any wonder the *Evening News* enthused: 'She is truly a phenomenon! At the age 81 she produces a whodunnit which for mystery and neat unravelling is up to the standard of her very best!'?

### Post-Publication Serialization

- In Australia, New Guinea, New Zealand and Malaysia, *Nemesis* appeared in four instalments of *The Australian Women's Weekly* from 15 December 1971 to 5 January 1972.

## 1972 – *Elephants Can Remember*

**Working Title:** *Elephants Can Forget* (as cited in Agatha Christie's notebooks)

Mrs Ariadne Oliver, the renowned crime writer, is attending a literary luncheon when she is accosted by a bossy stranger. The woman wants to know the solution to a long-forgotten tragedy. Who shot Sir Alistair and Lady Ravenscroft and why? Despite her dislike of the stranger, Mrs Oliver is aware old sins cast long shadows and turns to the only person capable of unravelling the conundrum – her old friend Hercule Poirot.

**Publication:** *Elephants Can Remember* was published in hardback in the UK by the Collins Crime Club on 6 November 1972 and in the US by Dodd, Mead and Company on 20 November 1972.

**Length:** UK 256pp. / US 243pp.

**Price:** UK £1.60 / US $6.95

**Word Count:** 44,000

## Post-Publication Serialization

- In Australia, New Guinea, New Zealand and Malaysia, *Elephants Can Remember* appeared in four instalments of *The Australian Women's Weekly* from 29 November to 20 December 1972.
- In Canada, *Elephants Can Remember* appeared in two instalments of *The Canadian Magazine Star Weekly Novel* on 10 February and 17 February 1973, with a cover illustration by Laszlo Gal.

## *1973 – Postern of Fate*

**Working Title:** *Doom's Caravan / Disaster's Caravan / Port of Fear / The Postern of Fate* (as cited in Agatha Christie's notebooks)

### Inspiration for the Title

*Four great gates has the city of Damascus…*
*Postern of Fate, the Desert Gate, Disaster's Cavern, Fort of Fear…*
*Pass not beneath, O Caravan, or pass not singing. Have you heard*
*That silence where the birds are dead yet something pipeth like a bird?*
          'The Gates of Damascus',
          James Elroy Flecker

Shortly after moving into their new home, Tommy and Tuppence Beresford come across an old book in an upstairs room that spells out a chilling message: *'Mary Jordan did not die naturally. It was one of us.'* The couple discover the schoolboy who wrote the message died soon afterwards in mysterious circumstances. The Beresfords have no reason to believe the shadows of the past will impact on the present, until someone murders their elderly gardener. After all these years, Mary Jordan's enemies are prepared to stop at nothing to ensure the secrets of the past remain buried forever.

**Publication:** *Postern of Fate* was published in hardback in the UK by the Collins Crime Club on 29 October 1973 and in the US by Dodd, Mead and Company on 26 November 1973.

**Length:** UK 253pp. / US 310pp.

**Price:** UK £2.00 / US $6.95

**Word Count:** 76,000

**Trivia:** As part of its promotional drive to enhance the Christie brand, Pocket Books in America commissioned Dorothy Anger to create an Agatha Christie Calendar for release in 1973. Each month was illustrated with a Christie paperback cover created for Pocket Books by the legendary artist Tom Adams. The Christie paperbacks were 95 cents each and for $95 dollars, US store owners could purchase a tall display stand capable of holding 100 of her titles. In Britain, fans had to wait until 1989 before Attica released an Agatha Christie Calendar featuring Tom Adams' cover illustrations.

## Post-Publication Serialization

- In Australia, New Guinea, New Zealand and Malaysia, *Postern of Fate* appeared in five instalments of *Woman's Day* magazine from 4 February to 4 March 1974.
- In Sweden, *Postern of Fate* appeared as *Mary Jordan dog inte naturlight (Mary Jordan Did Not Die Naturally)* in *Svenska Dagbladet*, a daily newspaper based in Stockholm, from 30 June to 14 September 1974.
- In Belgium, a Dutch translation of *Postern of Fate* appeared as *Moord in de Bibliotheek (Murder in the Library)* in *Gazet van Atwerpen*, a newspaper published in Antwerp and Flanders by Concentra, from 2 March to 1 July 1974. (Belgium has three official languages: French, German and Dutch.)

# 1975 – *Curtain: Poirot's Last Case*

**Working Title:** *Curtain* (as cited in Agatha Christie's notebooks and on the cover page of her manuscript)

An elderly Captain Hastings is summoned by Hercule Poirot to Styles Court – the scene decades earlier of their first murder investigation together. Styles is now a guest house run by a bickering couple called Colonel and Mrs Luttrell. Old and frail, Hercule Poirot is confined to a wheelchair and unable to leave his room without assistance, but his little grey cells are functioning as brilliantly as ever. He has sent for Captain Hastings one last time because he needs his faithful friend's help: one of the guests is a killer intent on playing a series of deadly games...

## Pre-Publication Serialization

- In the UK, *Curtain: Poirot's Last Case* appeared in seven instalments of *Woman's Own* magazine from 13 September to 25 October 1975, illustrated by Mike Ward.
- In the US, *Curtain: Poirot's Last Case* appeared in two instalments of *Ladies' Home Journal* in July (volume 92, number 7) and August 1975 (volume 92, number 8), illustrated by Mark English.

**Publication:** *Curtain: Poirot's Last Case* was published in hardback in the UK by the Collins Crime Club on 22 September 1975 and in the US by Dodd, Mead and Company on 15 October 1975.

**Length:** UK 221pp. / US 238pp.

**Price:** UK £2.95 / US $7.95

**Word Count:** 67,000

**Trivia:** On 6 March 1975, one of the biggest prepublication rights deals in publishing – and certainly the biggest in Dodd Mead's publishing history – occurred when nine major US publishers competed for the US paperback rights of *Curtain: Poirot's Last Case*. Jonathan Dodd, director of subsidiary rights at Dodd Mead, conducted the auction which had a floor of $100,000. By lunchtime the bidders had raised the price tag to over $500,000. Six publishers made it to the second and third round of bidding.

Pocket Books, Dell, New American Library, Bantam, Fawcett and Warner Paperbacks all bid over $700,000. Four of these dropped out when the figure rose to over $835,000 leaving Pocket Books and Dell to battle it out. By 7pm the bidding was finally over, with Pocket Books having secured its $935,000 prize.

## Post-Publication Serialization

- In the US, *Curtain: Poirot's Last Case* appeared in three instalments of the *Chicago Tribune* from 11 to 13 December 1977.
- In Australia, New Guinea, New Zealand and Malaysia, *Curtain: Poirot's Last Case* appeared in four instalments of *The Australian Women's Weekly* from 24 December 1975 to 14 January 1976, illustrated by D.E.
- In Mexico, a Spanish translation of *Curtain: Poirot Last Case* appeared as *Telon (Curtain)* in *Buenhogar* magazine in December 1975 and January 1976.

## 1976 – *Sleeping Murder: Miss Marple's Last Case*

**Working Title:** *Murder in Retrospect* (as cited in Agatha Christie's notebooks – other titles she considered were *The Late Mrs Dane* as well as *The Hand*)

Newly married Gwenda Reed is looking forward to decorating the charming old house she has bought for herself and her husband Giles. A visit to the theatre to see *The Duchess of Malfi* triggers a terrifying memory from Gwenda's childhood and she remembers witnessing a murder at Hillside. How could she have lived there as a child and have no recollection of the fact until now? Gwenda and Giles are determined to find out what happened with the help of that expert in human wickedness, Miss Jane Marple.

### Pre-Publication Serialization

- In the UK, *Sleeping Murder* appeared in six instalments of *Woman* magazine from 18 September to 23 October 1976, illustrated by Ian Beck. His illustration of Gwenda Reed bears a strong resemblance to the actress Joanna Lumley, later to feature in two television adaptations from the ITV Marple series.
- In the US, *Sleeping Murder* appeared in two instalments of *Ladies' Home Journal* from July (volume 93, number 7) to August 1976 (volume 93, number 8), illustrated by Fred Otnes.

**Publication:** *Sleeping Murder: Miss Marple's Last Case* was published in hardback in the UK by the Collins Crime Club on 11 October 1976 and in the US by Dodd, Mead and Company on 27 September 1976.

**Length:** UK 224pp. / US 242pp.

**Price:** UK £3.50 / US $7.95

**Word Count:** 59,000

**Trivia:** *Sleeping Murder* was published eight months after Agatha Christie's death triggered major headlines around the world. The Miss Marple novel was written over forty-five years earlier, during the hostilities of the Second World War, and was originally entitled *Murder in Retrospect* after chapter five in the novel. Her royalty statement for 15 March 1940 shows the secretarial agency that typed up copies of the Miss Marple manuscript charged her a total of £19 13s. 9. On 14 October 1940, Agatha Christie signed a deed of gift assigning copyright of the manuscript to her second husband Max Mallowan. Complications arose when the Hercule Poirot novel *Five Little Pigs* was serialized in America by *Collier's* magazine as *Murder in Retrospect* in 1941 and published under that title a year later by Dodd, Mead and Company. On 8 April 1964, the title of the last Miss Marple novel was belatedly changed to *Cover Her Face*. This was done before anyone realized that P.D. James' debut crime novel *Cover Her Face* had been published two years earlier. This meant the Miss Marple manuscript was once again in need of a new title. *She Died Young* is another title Agatha Christie considered. However, it was not until 1976 that the manuscript became known as *Sleeping Murder.* Although the novel was set during the 1930s, Collins added the sub-title *Miss Marple's Last Case* to maximise sales of the last ever full-length 'Christie for Christmas'.

On 13 May 1976, Dodd Mead set a record in the prepublication sale of paperback rights when it auctioned *Sleeping Murder*. The auction began at 9.30am and it says much for the power of the author's name that three of the six US publishers competing for the paperback rights had never had a single Christie title on their lists. The first round had a floor of $100,000. The second round started at $700,000 with five bidders still in the running while the third round narrowed the bidders down to two. By 8.30pm Bantam had fought off its competitors with a bid in excess of $1.1 million.

## Post-Publication Serialization

- In Australia, New Zealand, New Guinea and Malaysia, *Sleeping Murder* appeared in five instalments of *The Australian Women's Weekly* from 22 December 1976 to 19 January 1977.

# Afterword

On 29 January 1986, in his role of chairman of Agatha Christie Ltd., Matthew Prichard wrote to The Bodley Head, which still owned the publishing rights to the first six books his grandmother had written over sixty years earlier. He offered to buy the publishing rights to *The Mysterious Affair at Styles*, *The Secret Adversary*, *The Murder on the Links*, *The Man in the Brown Suit*, *Poirot Investigates*, and *The Secret of Chimneys* for £90,000. John Lane had long since died and The Bodley Head was now run by Max Reinhardt, who over the last three decades had rescued and revitalized the firm's ailing fortunes. He replied to Matthew Prichard's letter on 7 February stating he was prepared to sell the rights to him for £250,000. In July 1986, following extensive negotiations, Agatha Christie Ltd. acquired ownership of the publishing rights to the six titles for £155,000. The spirit of Agatha Christie – who had never forgiven John Lane for taking advantage of her as a first-time author – must surely have been pleased that her association with The Bodley Head was finally over.

# Part Two
# MASTERPIECES IN MINIATURE

# The A – Z of Crime

## 'Accident'
A retired police officer is determined to prevent a woman from killing her latest husband.

**Word Count:** 3, 200

**Pre-Publication Appearance**
UK – 22 September 1929, *Sunday Dispatch* as 'The Uncrossed Path'

**Official Collections**
*The Listerdale Mystery* 1934 (UK) / *The Witness for the Prosecution and Other* Stories 1948 (US)

**'Accident' was reprinted in**
- *My Best Thriller, An Anthology of Stories Chosen by Their Own Authors*, Faber and Faber, 1933 (UK)
- *The Thriller* magazine, 15 December 1934 (UK)
- *Ellery Queen's Mystery Magazine,* March 1943 (US)
- *The Star Weekly,* 6 November 1943 (CAN), as 'It Was an Accident'
- *Argosy,* May 1946 (UK)
- *Murder Without Tears: An Anthology of Crime,* edited by Will Cuppy, Sheridan House, 1946 (US)
- *Rogues' Gallery: The Great Criminals of Modern Fiction*, edited by Ellery Queen, Faber and Faber, 1947 (UK)
- *Short Story Magazine,* April 1947 (AUS)
- *Suspense Stories,* edited by Alfred Hitchcock, Dell, 1949 (US)
- *A Handbook for Poisoners,* edited by Raymond T. Bond, Rinehart and Company, New York and Toronto, 1951 (US)
- *Family Magazine,* November 1953 (US)
- *Creasey Mystery Magazine,* October 1957 (UK) as 'A Test for Murder'
- *Creasey Mystery Magazine,* February 1958 (AUS) as 'A Test for Murder'
- *Suspense,* March 1960 (UK)
- *A Butcher's Dozen of Wicked Women,* edited by Lee Wright, Pocket Books, 1960 (US)
- *Great Stories of Detection,* edited by R.C. Bull, Arthur Barker Ltd, 1960 (UK)
- *The Mystery Bedside Book,* edited by John Creasey, Hodder and Stoughton, 1960 (UK) as 'A Test for Murder'

- *Alfred Hitchcock Presents: A Baker's Dozen of Suspense Stories,* edited by Alfred Hitchcock, Dell, 1963 (US)
- *125th Anniversary Anthology, 1939-1964,* Dodd, Mead and Company, 1964 (US)
- *Read With Me,* selected and introduced by Thomas B. Constain, Doubleday, 1965 (US)
- *Ellery Queen's Mystery Magazine,* April 1974 (US)
- *65 Great Murder Mysteries,* edited by Mary Danby, Octopus Books, 1983 (UK)
- *The Mystery Hall of Fame: An Anthology of Classic Mystery and Suspense Stories,* William Morrow and Company, Inc., 1984 (US)
- *Great Murder Mysteries,* Octopus Books/Chartwell, 1998 (UK)
- *The Orion Book of Murder,* edited by Peter Haining, Orion, 1996 (UK)
- *Valentine's Day: Women Against Men: Stories of Revenge,* edited by Alice Thomas Ellis, Duckworth Publishing, 2001 (UK)

## 'The Actress'

A celebrated actress outwits a blackmailer when her past returns to haunt her.

**Word Count:** 2,600

### Pre-Publication Appearance
UK – May 1923, issue 218 of *The Novel Magazine* as 'A Trap for the Unwary', illustrated by Emile Verpilleux

### Official Collections
*While the Light Lasts and Other Stories* 1997 (UK) / *The Harlequin Tea Set and Other Stories* 1997 (US)

### 'The Actress' was reprinted in

- *20-Story Magazine,* Odhams, January 1931 (UK)
- *Agatha Christie Official Centenary Celebration 1890 – 1990* by Belgrave Publishing, 1990 (UK)

## 'The Adventure of Johnnie Waverly'

A distraught couple turn to Hercule Poirot for help after their son is kidnapped.

**Word Count:** 4,600

### Pre-Publication Appearance
UK – 10 October 1923, issue 1602 of *The Sketch* as 'The Kidnapping of Johnny Waverly'
US – June 1925, volume 41, number 2 of *The Blue Book Magazine*

### Official Collections
*Poirot's Early Cases* 1974 (UK) / *Three Blind Mice and Other Stories* 1950 (US)

### 'The Adventure of Johnnie Waverly' was reprinted in

- *The World's Best 100 Detective Stories*, edited by Eugene Thwing, Funk and Wagnalls, 1929 (US)
  [This marks the story's first publication in volume form.]
- *The Saint Detective Magazine*, July 1955 (US) as 'The Kidnapping of Johnny Waverley'
- *The Saint Detective Magazine*, November 1956 (AUS) as 'The Kidnapping of Johnny Waverley'
- *The Saint Detective Magazine*, January 1957 (UK) as 'The Kidnapping of Johnny Waverley'
- *Ellery Queen's Mystery Magazine*, July 1967 (US) as 'At the Stroke of Twelve'
- *Rogue's Gallery,* edited by Walter B. Gibson, Doubleday, 1969 (US) as 'At the Stroke of Twelve'
- *Mystery Stories,* chosen by Helen Reynolds, Kingfisher 1996 (US) as 'The Adventures of Johnnie Waverley'

## 'The Adventure of the Cheap Flat'

A couple's decision to rent a cheap flat in an expensive apartment block leads to a sinister chain of events for Hercule Poirot to unravel.

**Word Count:** 4,700

### Pre-Publication Appearance
UK – 9 May 1923, issue 1580 of *The Sketch*
US – May 1924, volume 39, number 1 of *The Blue Book Magazine*

### Official Collections
*Poirot Investigates* 1924 (UK) 1925 (US)

### 'The Adventure of the Cheap Flat' was reprinted in

- *Short Story Magazine*, February 1947 (AUS)
- *Ellery Queen's Mystery Magazine,* November 1965 (US) as 'Poirot Indulges a Whim'

## 'The Adventure of the Christmas Pudding' (shorter version)

Hercule Poirot is spending Christmas with a family when a body is found in the snow.

**Word Count:** 5,900

### Pre-Publication Appearance
UK – 12 December 1923, issue 1611 of *The Sketch* (there is a mistaken belief amongst some scholars that the story first appeared as 'Christmas Adventure'; however, I have viewed the magazine at the British Library and it definitely debuted as 'The Adventure of the Christmas Pudding').

**Official Collection**
*While the Light Lasts and Other Stories* 1997 (UK) as 'Christmas Adventure'

**Special Short-Lived Collection**
*Midwinter Murders* 2020 (UK) / *Midwinter Murders: Fireside Tales from the Queen of Mystery* 2020 (US) as 'Christmas Adventure' in both volumes

**'The Adventure of the Christmas Pudding' was reprinted in**

- *Guide and Ideas Christmas Number,* December 1935 (UK)
- *Problem at Pollensa Bay and Christmas Adventure,* Polybooks, 1943 (UK)
- *Poirot Knows the Murderer,* Polybooks, 1946 (UK / US)
- *Murder for Christmas,* edited by Thomas F. Godfrey, The Mysterious Press, 1982 (US)
- *The Strand Magazine,* issue 61, October 2020 – January 2021 (US) as 'Christmas Adventure'

## 'The Adventure of the Christmas Pudding' (expanded version)

Hercule Poirot's investigation into the theft of a royal ruby takes a sinister turn when he receives an anonymous note warning him not to eat any Christmas pudding.

**Word Count:** 15,500
[This novella is an expanded version of 'The Adventure of the Christmas Pudding', which first appeared in *The Sketch* on 12 December 1923.]

**Pre-Publication Appearance**
US – 25 September and 2 October 1960, *This Week*, as 'The Theft of the Royal Ruby', illustrated by William A. Smith. The magazine was distributed across America as a supplement to all the major Sunday newspapers, including *The Post-Standard Pictorial, The Salt Lake Tribune, The Des Moines Sunday Register, The Los Angeles Times, Democrat and Chronicle, The Daily Intelligencer* and *The Pittsburgh Press*, all of which advertised the story as a forthcoming attraction.

**Official Collections**
*The Adventure of the Christmas Pudding and a Selection of Entrees* 1960 (UK) / *Double Sin and Other Stories* 1961 (US) as 'The Theft of the Royal Ruby' with some alterations to the UK text.

**'The Adventure of the Christmas Pudding' was reprinted in**

- *Woman's Illustrated* magazine, 24 and 31 December 1960 and 7 January 1961 (UK) illustrated by Zelinksi (UK) as 'The Theft of the Royal Ruby'
- *Ellery Queen's Mystery's Magazine,* June 1968 (US) as 'The Theft of the Royal Ruby'
- *Murder for Christmas,* edited by Thomas Godfrey, Avenel Books, 1989 (US)
- *The Big Book of Christmas Mysteries,* edited by Otto Penzler, Vintage Crime / Black Lizard, October 2013 (US)
- *Christmas Crime Stories,* Folio Book Society, 2004 (UK)

## 'The Adventure of the Clapham Cook'

Hercule Poirot is hired to trace a missing cook who abandoned her post without giving notice.

**Word Count:** 4,800

**Pre-Publication Appearance**
UK – 14 November 1923, issue 1607 of *The Sketch*
US – September 1925, volume 41, number 5 of *The Blue Book Magazine* as 'The Clapham Cook'

**Official Collections**
*Poirot's Early Cases* 1974 (UK) / *The Under Dog and Other Stories* 1951 (US)

**'The Adventure of the Clapham Cook' was reprinted in**

- *Great Short Stories of Detection, Mystery and Horror*, second series, edited by Dorothy L. Sayers, Gollancz, 13 July 1931 (UK)
- *The Evening Standard*, 12 August 1933 (UK)
- *World's Great Mystery Stories*, edited by Will Cuppy, World Publishing Company, 1943 (US)
- *Ellery Queen's Mystery Magazine*, February 1956 (US) as 'Find the Cook'
- *Ellery Queen's Mystery Magazine*, January 1957 (AUS) as 'Find the Cook'
- *The Edge of the Chair*, edited by Joan Kahn, Harper and Row, 1967 (US)
- *The Graveyard Shift*, edited by Joan Kahn, Dell, 1970 (US)
- *The Television Detectives' Omnibus: Great Tales of Crime and Detection*, edited by Peter Haining, Artus, 1994 (UK)

## 'The Adventure of the Egyptian Tomb'

Poirot investigates the curse of the Men-her-Ra tomb after four archaeologists plunder its treasures and then die within a month of each other.

**Word Count:** 5,000

**Pre-Publication Appearance**
UK – 26 September 1923, issue 1600 of *The Sketch*
US – August 1924, volume 39, number 4 of *The Blue Book Magazine* as 'The Egyptian Adventure'

**Official Collections**
*Poirot Investigates* 1924 (UK) 1925 (US)

**'The Adventure of the Egyptian Tomb' was reprinted in**

- *The World's Greatest Detective Stories*, Syndicate Publishing Co., 1934 (US)
- *Suspense*, October 1959 (UK) as 'The Next Victim'
- *The Saint Mystery Magazine*, August 1963 (UK)

- *Ellery Queen's Mystery Magazine*, December 1967 (US)
- *Murder Intercontinental: Stories from Ellery Queen's Mystery Magazine and Alfred Hitchcock Mystery Magazine*, edited by Cynthia Manson and Kathleen Halligan, Caroll & Graff, 1996 (US)
- *Detective Stories*, chosen by Phillip Pullman, Kingfisher, 1998 (US)
- *In the Mummy's Tomb*, edited by Stephens Richard Stephens, Berkley Books, 2001 (US)
- *Detective Stories*, edited by Peter Washington, Alfred A. Knopf, 2009 (US)
- *The Oxford Book of Detective Stories*, edited by Patricia Craig, Oxford University Press, 2003 (UK)

## 'The Adventure of the Italian Nobleman'

A dying man phones Hercule Poirot after being attacked during a dinner party.

**Word Count:** 3,800

### Pre-Publication Appearance
UK – 24 October 1923, issue 1604 of *The Sketch*
US – December 1924, volume 40, number 2 of *The Blue Book Magazine* as 'The Italian Nobleman'

### Official Collections
*Poirot Investigates* 1924 (UK) 1925 (US)

### 'The Adventure of the Italian Nobleman' was reprinted in

- *Blue Book: Stories of Adventure for Men, by Men*, December 1941 (US) as 'The Italian Nobleman'
- *Ellery Queen's Mystery Magazine*, July 1963 (US) as 'The Regent's Court Murder'
- *Short Stories*, mid-August 1934 (UK)
- *Short Story Magazine*, number fifty-four, January 1949 (AUS)
- *Zabojstwo ksiecia*, February 1949 (Poland)
- *Ten Tales of Detection*, edited by Roger Lancelyn Green, Dent Dutton, 1967 (US)

## 'The Adventure of the Sinister Stranger'

A frightened doctor turns for help to Tommy and Tuppence Beresford of Blunts' Brilliant Detective Agency to prevent his house from being burgled.

**Word Count:** 5,200

### Pre-Publication Appearance
UK – 22 October 1924, in issue 1656 of *The Sketch* as 'The Case of the Sinister Stranger'

### Official Collections
*Partners in Crime* 1929 (UK / US)

**'The Adventure of the Sinister Stranger' was reprinted in**

- *Hutchinson's Adventure & Mystery Story Magazine*, June 1928 (UK)
- *The Daily Boston Globe,* 26 April 1931 (US)

## 'The Adventure of the Western Star'

Hercule Poirot finds himself on the trail of an evil Chinaman intent on stealing diamonds that form the eyes of a mysterious god.

**Word Count:** 7,300

### Pre-Publication Appearance
UK – 11 April 1923, issue 1576 of *The Sketch*
US – February 1924, volume 38, number 4 of *The Blue Book Magazine* as 'The Western Star'

### Official Collections
*Poirot Investigates* 1924 (UK) 1925 (US)

**'The Adventure of the Western Star' was reprinted in:**

- *Short Story Magazine*, number 27, October 1946 (AUS)
- *Ellery Queen's Mystery Magazine,* January 1964 (US) as 'Poirot Puts a Finger in the Pie'

## 'The Affair at the Bungalow'

Miss Marple's wisdom prevails when a playwright is lured to a bungalow and finds himself accused of a burglary.

**Word Count:** 5,100

### Pre-Publication Appearance
UK – May 1930, volume 46, number 277 of *The Story-Teller Magazine*

### Official Collections
*The Thirteen Problems* 1932 (UK) / *The Tuesday Club Murders* 1933 (US)

### 'The Affair at the Bungalow' was reprinted in

- *Ellery Queen's Mystery Magazine*, November 1959 (US)
- *Ellery Queen's Mystery Magazine*, January 1960 (UK)
- *Ellery Queen's Mystery Magazine*, January 1960 (AUS)

## 'The Affair at the Victory Ball'

Hercule Poirot demonstrates the brilliance of his little grey cells when an aristocrat and actress are murdered within hours of each other.

**Word Count:** 5,100

**Pre-Publication Appearance**
UK – 7 March 1923, issue 1571 of *The Sketch*
US – September 1923, volume 37, number 5 of *The Blue Book Magazine*

**Official Collections**
*Poirot's Early Cases* 1974 (UK) / *The Under Dog and Other Stories* 1951 (US)

**'The Affair at the Victory Ball' was reprinted in**

- *Ellery Queen's Mystery Magazine* October 1955 (US) as 'The Six China Figures'
- *Ellery Queen's Mystery Magazine* October 1955 (UK) as 'The Six China Figures'
- *Ellery Queen's Mystery Magazine* December 1955 (AUS) as 'The Six China Figures'

## 'The Affair of the Pink Pearl'

Blunt's Brilliant Detectives Tommy and Tuppence Beresford are hired to track down a thief who stole a pink pearl from a house party at Wimbledon.

**Word Count:** 5,200

**Pre-Publication Appearance**
UK – 1 October 1924, issue 1653 of *The Sketch*

**Official Collections**
*Partners in Crime* 1929 (UK / US)

**'The Affair of the Pink Pearl was reprinted in**

- *The Daily Boston Globe,* 19 April 1931 (US)
- *Ellery Queen's Mystery Magazine,* April 1960 (US) as 'Blunt's Brilliant Detectives'
- *Ellery Queen's Mystery Magazine,* June 1960 (AUS) as 'Blunt's Brilliant Detectives'
- *Ellery Queen's Mystery Magazine,* June 1960 (UK) as 'Blunt's Brilliant Detectives'

## 'The Ambassador's Boots'

Tommy and Tuppence Beresford are employed to find out why the American Ambassador's bag was switched with another passenger's following an ocean voyage.

**Word Count:** 3,300

**Pre-Publication Appearance**
UK – 12 November 1924, issue 1659 of *The Sketch* as 'The Matter of the Ambassador's Boots'

**Official Collections**
*Partners in Crime* 1929 (UK / US)

**'The Ambassador's Boots' was reprinted in**

- *Hutchinson's Adventure & Mystery Story Magazine*, April 1928 (UK)
- *The Daily Boston Globe,* 8 November 1931 (US)

## 'The Apples of Hesperides' – the eleventh labour

A millionaire asks Hercule Poirot to find a stolen goblet studded with green emeralds known as 'The Apples of Hesperides'.

**Word Count:** 4,800

**Pre-Publication Appearance**
UK – September 1940, volume 99, issue 597 of *The Strand Magazine,* illustrated by Ernest Ratcliff
US – 12 May 1940, *This Week* as 'The Poison Cup'; the magazine was distributed across America as a supplement to all the major Sunday newspapers, including the *Los Angeles Times* and *The Atlanta Constitution*, which advertised the story as a forthcoming attraction.

**Official Collections**
*The Labours of Hercules* 1947 (UK / US)

**'The Apples of Hesperides' was reprinted in**

- *The Australian Women's Weekly,* 23 May 1942 (AUS) as 'The Borgia Goblet'
- *Parade: The Middle East Weekly,* 17 January 1948 (Cairo, Egypt)
- *Bodies and Souls*, edited by Dan Herr and Joel Wells, Doubleday, 1961 (US)
- *The Saint Mystery Magazine*, May 1962 (UK)

## 'The Arcadian Deer' – the third labour

A distraught garage mechanic, who has fallen in love with a lady's maid, appeals to Poirot to find her after she disappears in disturbing circumstances.

**Word Count:** 5,500

**Pre-Publication Appearance**
UK – January 1940, volume 98, issue 589 of *The Strand Magazine,* illustrated by Ernest Ratcliff
US – 19 May 1940, *This Week* as 'Vanishing Lady'

**Official Collections**
*The Labours of Hercules* 1947 (UK / US)

**'The Arcadian Deer' was reprinted in**

- *The Australian Women's Weekly,* 6 October 1945 (AUS)
- *Parade: The Middle East Weekly,* 15 November 1947 (Cairo, Egypt)
- *Creasey Mystery Magazine*, August 1956 (UK)

## 'At the 'Bells and Motley'

A chance encounter at a village inn enables the 'love detectives' Mr Satterthwaite and Mr Quin to solve the mystery of Captain Harwell's disappearance.

**Word Count:** 5,100

**Pre-Publication Appearance**
UK – November 1925, *The Grand Magazine* as 'A Man of Magic'
US – 17 July 1926, volume 16, number 6 of *Flynn's Weekly* as 'A Man of Magic'

**Official Collections**
*The Mysterious Mr Quin* 1930 (UK / US)

**'At the Bells and Motley' was reprinted in**

- *Truth* magazine, 14 and 21 October 1951 (Sydney / AUS)
- *Ellery Queen's Mystery Magazine,* January 1954 (US)
- *Ellery Queen's Mystery Magazine,* May 1956 (UK)
- *Ellery Queen's Mystery Magazine,* June 1956 (AUS)

## 'The Augean Stables' – the fifth labour

Hercule Poirot averts a public scandal that threatens to engulf the British Prime Minister and his wife.

**Word Count:** 5,300

**Pre-Publication Appearance**
UK – March 1940, volume, issue 591 of *The Strand Magazine*, illustrated by Ernest Ratcliff

**Official Collections**
*The Labours of Hercules* 1947 (UK / US)

**'The Augean Stables' was reprinted in**

- *The Australian Women's Weekly,* 28 February 1942 (AUS) as 'Scandal in High Places'
- *Parade: The Middle East Weekly,* 29 November 1947 (Cairo, Egypt)
- *Creasey Mystery Magazine*, January 1957 (UK)

## 'The Big Four'

See 1927 in the Classic Full-Length Mysteries section

## 'The Bird with the Broken Wing'

Mr Satterthwaite and Mr Quin bring a woman's killer to justice after she is found hanging from her bedroom door with a wire around her throat.

**Word Count:** 6,200

**Official Collection**
*The Mysterious Mr. Quin* 1930 (UK / US)

**'The Bird with the Broken Wing' was reprinted in**

- *Modern Home,* January 1931 (UK)
- *Truth* magazine, 30 September and 7 October 1951 (Sydney/AUS)
- *MacKill's Mystery Magazine,* December 1953 (UK)
- *MacKill's Mystery Magazine,* February 1954 (US)
- *The Saint Detective Magazine,* December 1954 (US)
- *The Saint Detective Magazine,* June 1955 (AUS)
- *The Saint Detective Magazine,* August 1955 (UK)
- *Clubman,* October 1955 (UK)

## 'Blind Man's Buff'

Tommy and Tuppence Beresford are lunching in the Gold Room at the Blitz Hotel when a duke asks them to find his missing daughter.

**Word Count:** 3,600

**Pre-Publication Appearance**
UK – 26 November 1924, issue 1661 of *The Sketch*

**Official Collections**
*Partners in Crime* 1929 (UK / US)

**'Blind Man's Buff' was reprinted in**

- *Hutchinson's Adventure & Mystery Story Magazine,* August 1928 (UK)
- *The Daily Boston Globe,* 12 July 1931 (US)

## 'The Bloodstained Pavement'

An artist's holiday in Cornwall is blighted by some bloodstains and it falls to Miss Marple to unravel the mystery of how a woman was murdered miles away.

**Word Count:** 3,500

**Pre-Publication Appearance**
UK – March 1928, issue 353 of *The Royal Magazine*
US – 23 June 1928, volume 102, number 2 of *Detective Story Magazine* as 'Drip! Drip!'

**Official Collections**
*The Thirteen Problems* 1932 (UK) / *The Tuesday Club Murders* 1933 (US)

**'The Bloodstained Pavement' was reprinted in**

- *Hush,* December 1930 (UK)

- *Fifty Masterpieces of Mysteries*, Odhams Press, 1937 (UK)
- *Ellery Queen's Mystery Magazine*, November 1960, as 'Miss Marple and the Wicked World'
- *Ellery Queen's Mystery Magazine*, January 1961 (AUS) as 'Miss Marple and the Wicked World'
- *Ellery Queen's Mystery Magazine*, January 1961 (UK) as 'Miss Marple and the Wicked World'

## 'The Blue Geranium'

Miss Marple suspects a woman was murdered after the geranium on her bedroom wallpaper changes colour.

**Word Count:** 5,200

### Pre-Publication Appearance
UK – December 1929, volume 46, number 272 of *The Christmas Story-Teller Magazine*
US – February 1930, volume 31, number 5 of *Pictorial Review*, illustrated by De Alton Valentine

### Official Collections
*The Thirteen Problems* 1932 (UK) / *The Tuesday Club Murders* 1933 (US)

### 'The Blue Geranium' was reprinted in

- *The Mammoth Book of Thrillers, Ghosts and Mysteries*, edited by J.M. Parrish and John R. Crossland, Odhams Press, 1936 (UK)
- *The Mysterious Traveler* magazine, January 1952 (US)
- *Ellery Queen's Mystery Magazine*, March 1959 (US)
- *Ellery Queen's Mystery Magazine*, April 1959 (UK)
- *Ellery Queen's Mystery Magazine*, May 1959 (AUS)
- *Woman's Day*, 20 January 1964 (AUS)
- *Murderous Schemes: An Anthology of Classic Detective Stories*, Oxford University Press, 1996 (UK)
- *Senior Sleuths*, edited by Cynthia Manson and Constance Scarborough, Berkley Prime Crime, 1996 (US)
- *Crime Classics: The Mystery Story from Poe to the Present*, edited by Rex Burns and Mary Rose Sullivan, Viking, 1990 (US)
- *Classic Detective Stories*, MQ Publications, 1999 (US)
- *Classic Detective Stories from a Suitcase of Suspense*, Reader's Digest, 2002 (US)

## 'The Call of Wings'

A man hears strange pipe music after a road fatality that acts as a prelude to a far greater personal tragedy in his own life.

**Word Count:** 5,100

**Official Collections**
*The Hound of Death and Other Stories* 1933 (UK) / *The Golden Ball and Other Stories* 1971 (US)

**'The Call of Wings' was reprinted in**

- *The Magazine of Fantasy and Science Fiction,* June 1952 (US); the title is cited correctly on the contents page, but mistakenly referenced as 'The Sound of Wings' on the cover.
- *The Lucifer Society*, edited by Peter Haining, W.H. Allen, 1972 (UK); the paperback edition was retitled *Detours into the Macabre*, Pan, 1974 (UK)

## 'The Capture of Cerberus' (official version) – the twelfth labour

Hercule Poirot is invited to a nightclub operating on the wrong side of the law.

**Word Count:** 8,700
[There is another Hercule Poirot story featuring this title with an altogether different story-line – see 'The Capture of Cerberus', the original unpublished version known as 'The Thirteenth Labour'.]

**Pre-Publication Appearance**

- In the US, 'The Capture of Cerberus' appeared as 'Meet Me in Hell' in *This Week* on 16 March 1947; the magazine was distributed across America as a supplement to all the major Sunday newspapers, including the *Los Angeles Times, The Des Moines Register, The Indianapolis Star, The Cincinnati Enquirer,* and *Democrat and Chronicle*, all of which advertised the story as a forthcoming attraction.

**Official Collections**
*The Labours of Hercules* 1947 (UK / US)

**'The Capture of Cerberus' was reprinted in**

- *Parade: The Middle East Weekly,* 24 January 1948 (Cairo, Egypt)
- *Argosy*, December 1950 (UK) as 'Case of the Capture of Cerberus'
- *Ellery Queen's Mystery Magazine*, June 1961 (US) as 'Hercule Poirot in Hell'
- *Ellery Queen's Mystery Magazine*, August 1961 (AUS) as 'Hercule Poirot in Hell'
- *Ellery Queen's Mystery Magazine*, December 1961 (UK) as 'Hercule Poirot in Hell'

## 'The Capture of Cerberus' (the original unpublished version known as 'the thirteenth labour')

Poirot is asked by a man to prove his son did not assassinate a dictator despite the fact eyewitnesses caught him in the act.

**Pre-Publication Appearance**
UK – 28 August 2009, *Daily Mail*

**Word Count:** 4,900

**Official Collection**
The thirteenth labour appears as an Appendix in the 2014 paperback edition of *The Labours of Hercules* 1947 (UK). Prior to this, it was first published in volume form in the UK by HarperCollins in *Agatha Christie's Secret Notebooks* by John Curran on 3 September 2009 and in the US by Harper, an imprint of HarperCollins, on 22 February 2010.

## 'The Case of the Caretaker'

Miss Marple is given a manuscript and invited to solve the crime chronicled within its pages.

**Word Count:** 4,200

**Pre-Publication Appearance**
UK – January 1942, volume 102, issue 613 of *The Strand Magazine*
US – 5 July 1942, *Akron Beacon Journal, Chicago Sunday Tribune, Detroit Press* newspapers

**Official Collections**
*Miss Marple's Final Cases* 1979 (UK) / *Three Blind Mice and Other Stories* 1950 (US). This is a slightly shorter version of the 4,500-word story 'The Case of the Caretaker's Wife', which was first published in volume form in the UK by HarperCollins in *Agatha Christie's Murder in the Making* by John Curran on 1 September 2011 and in the US by Harper, an imprint of HarperCollins, as *Agatha Christie: Murder in the Making* on 22 November 2011.

**'The Case of the Caretaker' was reprinted in**

- *Winnipeg Free Press*, 25 July 1942 (CAN)
- *Ellery Queen's Mystery Magazine*, March 1969 (US)
- *Alle Kvinner*, a Norwegian magazine, 20 November 1973 as 'Den gamle kones forbannelse' ('The Old Lady's Curse')
- *Woman's Day* magazine, 17 September 1979 (AUS)

## 'The Case of the City Clerk'

A bored office worker travels to Geneva with a cryptogram and finds himself in far greater difficulty than he envisaged on the return journey home.

**Word Count:** 4,700

**Pre-Publication Appearance**
UK – November 1932, volume 84, issue 503 of *The Strand Magazine* as 'The £10 Adventure'

US – August 1932, issue 554 of *Cosmopolitan* magazine as 'The Clerk Who Wanted Excitement' under the series title of *Are You Happy? If Not, Consult Mr Parker Pyne*, illustrated by Marshall Frantz

**Official Collections**
*Parker Pyne Investigates* 1934 (UK) / *Mr. Parker Pyne, Detective* 1934 (US)

**'The Case of the City Clerk was reprinted in**
- *Woman's Pictorial*, 5 August 1933 (UK) as 'Romance – On Request'
- *The Thriller*, 29 September 1934 (UK) as 'The £10 Adventure', illustrated by Serge R. Drigin

## 'The Case of the Discontented Husband'

A man seeks professional help from Parker Pyne after his estranged wife challenges him to win her back.

**Word Count:** 4,100

**Pre-Publication Appearance**
UK – 29 October 1932, issue 616 of *Woman's Pictorial* as 'His Lady's Affair', illustrated by J.A. May
US – August 1932, issue 554 of *Cosmopolitan* magazine as 'The Husband Who Wanted to Keep His Wife' under the series title of *Are You Happy? If Not, Consult Mr Parker Pyne*, illustrated by Marshall Frantz

**Official Collections**
*Parker Pyne Investigates* 1934 (UK) / *Mr Parker Pyne, Detective* 1934 (US)

## 'The Case of the Discontented Soldier'

A retired soldier's life is lifted out of the doldrums when he meets an attractive woman targeted by confidence tricksters.

**Word Count:** 5,600

**Pre-Publication Appearance**
UK – 15 October 1932, issue 614 of *Woman's Pictorial* as 'Adventure – By Request', illustrated by J.A. May
US – August 1932, issue 554 of *Cosmopolitan* magazine as 'The Soldier Who Wanted Danger' under the series title of *Are You Happy? If Not, Consult Mr Parker Pyne*, illustrated by Marshall Frantz

**Official Collections**
*Parker Pyne Investigates* 1934 (UK) / *Mr Parker Pyne, Detective* 1934 (US)

**'The Case of the Discontented Soldier' was reprinted in**

- *MacKill's Mystery Magazine*, April 1953 (UK)
- *MacKill's Mystery Magazine*, May 1953 (US)
- *Malice Domestic 9,* Avon Twilight, 2000 (US)

## 'The Case of the Distressed Lady'

A young woman is faced with the dilemma of returning a stolen jewel to its rightful owner without being caught.

**Word Count:** 3,300

**Pre-Publication Appearance**
UK – 22 October 1932, issue 615 of *Woman's Pictorial* as 'Faked!', illustrated by J.A. May
US – August 1932, issue 554 of *Cosmopolitan,* as 'The Pretty Girl Who Wanted a Ring' under the series title of *Are You Happy? If Not, Consult Mr Parker Pyne*, illustrated by Marshall Frantz

**Official Collections**
*Parker Pyne Investigates* 1934 (UK) / *Mr Parker Pyne, Detective* 1934 (US)

**'The Case of the Distressed Lady' was reprinted in**

- *The Second Century of Detective Stories*, edited by E.C. Bentley, Hutchinson, 1938 (UK)
- *Ellery Queen's Mystery Magazine*, October 1957 (US)
- *Ellery Queen's Mystery Magazine*, October 1957 (UK)
- *Ellery Queen's Mystery Magazine*, December 1957 (AUS)

## 'The Case of the Middle-Aged Wife'

A married woman is worried her husband is paying too much attention to his secretary, so she consults Mr Parker Pyne.

**Word Count:** 4,100

**Pre-Publication Appearance**
UK – 8 October 1932, issue 613 of *Woman's Pictorial* as 'The Woman Concerned', illustrated by J.A. May

**Official Collections**
*Parker Pyne Investigates* 1934 (UK) / *Mr Parker Pyne, Detective* 1934 (US)

## 'The Case of the Missing Will'

A woman employs Poirot to find her uncle's missing will so she can inherit his estate.

**Word Count:** 3,300

**Pre-Publication Appearance**
UK – 31 October 1923, issue 1605 of *The Sketch*
US – January 1925, volume 40, number 3 of *The Blue Book Magazine* as 'The Missing Will'

**Official Collections**
*Poirot Investigates* 1924 (UK) 1925 (US)

**'The Case of the Missing Will' was reprinted in**

- *Suspense,* February 1959 (UK) as 'Where There's a Will'

[Not to be confused with the short story 'Wireless' – from the 1933 UK collection *The Hound of Death* – which has also been retitled 'Where There's a Will' by some publications.]

- *Short Story Magazine*, March 1947 (AUS)
- *The Australian Women's Weekly*, 20 January 1965 (AUS)
- *The Fourth Mystery Bedside Book,* edited by John Creasey, Hodder and Stoughton, 1963 (UK)
- *Argosy*, November 1965 (UK)
- *Literary Cavalcade,* April 1975 (US)

## 'The Case of the Perfect Maid'

Miss Marple investigates the disappearance of some jewellery after a servant goes missing from St. Mary Mead.

**Word Count:** 4,500

**Pre-Publication Appearance**
UK – April 1942, volume 103, issue 616 of *The Strand Magazine* as 'The Perfect Maid'
US – 13 September 1942, *Akron Beacon Journal, Chicago Sunday Tribune* and *Detroit Free Press* newspapers as 'The Case of the Perfect Maid'

**Official Collections**
*Miss Marple's Final Cases* 1979 (UK) / *Three Blind Mice and Other Stories* 1950 (US)

**'The Case of the Perfect Maid' was reprinted in**

- *20th Century Detective Stories,* edited by Ellery Queen, The Living Library, 1948 (US)
- *Ellery Queen's Mystery Magazine*, July 1957 (US) as 'The Servant Problem'
- *Ellery Queen's Mystery Magazine*, July 1957 (UK) as 'The Servant Problem'
- *Ellery Queen's Mystery Magazine*, September 1957 (AUS) as 'The Servant Problem'
- *Good Housekeeping's Best Book of Mystery Stories,* edited by Pauline Rush Evans, Prentice Hall, 1958 (US)
- *Favourite Sleuths,* edited by John Ernst, Doubleday and Company, 1965 (US)

- *Mystery Stories,* edited by James Higgins, Houghton Mifflin, 1973 (US)
- *Mystery,* Houghton Mifflin, 1989 (US)
- *Senior Sleuths: A Large Print Anthology of Mysteries and Puzzlers,* edited by Isaac Asimov, Martin H. Greenberg and Carol-Lynn Rossel Waugh, GK Hall, 1989 (US)
- *The Riverside Anthology of Short Fiction: Convention and Innovation,* Houghton Mifflin, 1998 (US)
- *Mystery,* Houghton Mifflin, 1989 (US)
- *The Television Detectives' Omnibus: Great Tales of Crime and Detection,* edited by Peter Haining, Artus, 1994 (UK)

## 'The Case of the Rich Woman'

A widow's search for happiness takes her to Parker Pyne with unexpected results.

**Word Count:** 4,800

### Pre-Publication Appearance
US – August 1932, issue 554 of *Cosmopolitan* as 'The Rich Woman Who Wanted Only To Be Happy' under the series title of *Are You Happy? If Not, Consult Mr Parker Pyne,* illustrated by Marshall Frantz

### Official Collections
*Parker Pyne Investigates* 1934 (UK) / *Mr Parker Pyne, Detective* 1934 (US)

## 'The Chess Problem'

A chess tournament is interrupted when one of the competitors dies of apparently natural causes and it falls to Poirot to reveal the ingenious method by which he was murdered.

**Word Count:** 4,600

### Pre-Publication Appearance
UK – 13 February 1924, issue 1620 of *The Sketch*
US – September 1927, volume 45, number 5 of *The Blue Book Magazine*
['The Chess Problem' was originally a self-contained episode from the serial *The Man Who Was Number Four* which ran in *The Sketch* magazine from 2 January to 19 March 1924.]

### Official Collections
*The Big Four* 1927 (UK / US)

**'A Chess Problem' (which forms chapter eleven of the 1927 novel *The Big Four*) was reprinted in**

- *101 Years' Entertainment: The Great Detective Stories 1841 – 1941,* edited by Ellery Queen, Little Brown, 1941 (US)

- *Sporting Detective Stories,* edited by Ellery Queen, Faber and Faber, 1946 (UK) aka *Sporting Blood: The Great Sports Detective Stories,* edited by Ellery Queen, Little, Brown and Company, 1942 (US)
- *The Great Detectives,* Hennel Locke, 1947 (UK)
- *Modern Short Story Classics of Suspense,* Readers Digest paperback, 1968 (US)
- *Ellery Queen's Mystery Magazine,* August 1972 (US)
- *Chess in Literature,* edited by Marcello Truzzi, Avon Books, 1975 (US)
- *Sinister Gambits,* edited by Richard Peyton, London: Souvenir Press, 1991 (UK)

## 'The Chocolate Box'

Poirot recalls for his friend Captain Hastings' benefit the time he overlooked a vital clue during the investigation of a Frenchman's murder.

**Word Count:** 5,100

### Pre-Publication Appearance
UK – 23 May 1923, issue 1582 of *The Sketch* as 'The Clue of the Chocolate Box'
US – February 1925, volume 40, number 4 of *The Blue Book Magazine*

### Official Collections
*Poirot's Early Cases* 1974 (UK) / *Poirot Investigates* 1925 (US edition only)

### 'The Chocolate Box' was reprinted in

- *Ellery Queen's Mystery Magazine,* November 1962 (US) as 'The Time Hercule Poirot Failed'
- *Bodies and Souls,* edited by Dan Herr and Joel Wells, Doubleday, 1961 (US)
- *Best Detective Stories 2,* edited by Edmund Crispin, Faber and Faber, 1962 (UK)
- *Ellery Queen's Mystery Magazine,* March 1963 (UK) as 'The Time Hercule Poirot Failed'
- *Ellery Queen's Mystery Magazine,* May 1963 (AUS) as 'The Time Hercule Poirot Failed'
- *The World of Mystery Fiction,* edited by Elliot L. Gilbert, University of California, San Diego, 1978 (US)

## 'A Christmas Tragedy'

Miss Marple is staying at a health hydro when she becomes convinced one of the guests is trying to murder his wife.

**Word Count:** 6,300

### Pre-Publication Appearance
UK – January 1930, volume 46, number 273 of *The Story-Teller Magazine* as 'The Hat and the Alibi'.

**Official Collections**
*The Thirteen Problems* 1932 (UK) / *The Tuesday Night Murders* 1933 (US)

**'A Christmas Tragedy' was reprinted in**

- *Best Crime Stories*, Faber and Faber, 1934
- *Ellery Queen's Mystery Magazine,* January 1961 (US) as 'Never Two Without Three'
- *Ellery Queen's Mystery Magazine,* March 1961 (AUS) as 'Never Two Without Three'
- *Ellery Queen's Mystery Magazine,* September 1961 (UK) as 'Never Two Without Three; or A Christmas Tragedy'
- *Centre View*, a quarterly magazine published by London Borough of Tower Hamlets' Health Department for the Prichard Road Day Centre, September and December 1968 (UK)
- *Crime for Christmas*, edited by Richard Dalby, O'Mara, 1991 (UK)
- *The Big Book of Christmas Mysteries*, edited by Otto Penzler, Vintage Crime / Black Lizard, October 2013 (US)

## 'The Clergyman's Daughter' and 'The Red House' (parts 1 and 2 of the same story)

A clergyman's daughter turns to Blunt's brilliant detectives for help when her home is plagued by poltergeists.

**Word Count:** 5,000

**Pre-Publication Appearance**
UK – December 1923, *The Grand Magazine* as 'The First Wish'

**Official Collections**
*Partners in Crime* 1929 (UK / US)

**'The Clergyman's Daughter' and 'The Red House' were reprinted in**

- *The Daily Boston Globe,* 25 October 1931 (US)
- *Ellery Queen's Mystery Magazine,* January 1960 (US) as 'Seek, and Ye Shall Find'
- *Ellery Queen's Mystery Magazine,* March 1960 (AUS) as 'Seek, and Ye Shall Find'
- *Ellery Queen's Mystery Magazine,* March 1960 (UK) as 'Seek, and Ye Shall Find'

## 'The Coming of Mr Quin'

Mr Satterthwaite meets a mysterious stranger called Mr Quin at a New Year's Eve house party and discovers why the former owner of Royston Hall shot himself.

**Word Count:** 5,800

### Pre-Publication Appearance
UK – March 1924, issue 229 *The Grand Magazine* as 'The Passing of Mr Quinn'
US – March 1925, volume 82, number 2 of *Munsey* magazine as 'Mr Quinn Passes By'

### Official Collections
*The Mysterious Mr Quin* 1930 (UK / US)

### 'The Coming of Mr. Quin' was reprinted in

- *Mystery and Detection,* July 1935 (UK)
- *Fifty Famous Detectives of Fiction,* Odhams Press, 1938 (UK)
- *The Saint Detective Magazine,* March 1954 (US)
- *The Saint Detective Magazine,* September 1954 (AUS)
- *The Saint Detective Magazine,* November 1954 (UK)
- *Clubman,* June 1955 (UK)

## 'The Companion'

Miss Marple unravels the riddle of a woman who drowns in suspicious circumstances while holidaying in the Canary Islands.

**Word Count:** 6,400

### Pre-Publication Appearance
UK – February 1930, volume 46, number 274 of *The Story-Teller Magazine* as 'The Resurrection of Amy Durrant'
US – March 1930, volume 31, number 6 of *Pictorial Review* as 'Companions', illustrated by De Alton Valentine

### Official Collections
*The Thirteen Problems* 1932 (UK) / *The Tuesday Club Murders* 1933 (US)

### 'The Companion' was reprinted in

- *Ellery Queen's Mystery Magazine,* December 1968 (US)

## 'The Cornish Mystery'

Hercule Poirot investigates the murder of a Cornish woman who was afraid her husband was planning to kill her.

**Word Count:** 4,800

### Pre-Publication Appearance
UK – 28 November 1923, in issue 1609 of *The Sketch*
US – October 1925, volume 41, number 6 of *The Blue Book Magazine*

### Official Collections
*Poirot's Early Cases* 1974 (UK) / *The Under Dog and Other Stories* 1951 (US)

**'The Cornish Mystery' was reprinted in**
*Ellery Queen's Mystery Magazine*, March 1973 (US)

## 'The Crackler'

Blunt's brilliant detectives Tommy and Tuppence Beresford track down a counterfeiter who has been flooding both sides of the English Channel with forged bank notes.

**Word Count:** 4,200

**Pre-Publication Appearance**
UK – 19 November 1924, issue 1660 of *The Sketch* as 'The Affair of the Forged Notes'

**Official Collections**
*Partners in Crime* 1929 (UK / US)

**'The Crackler' was reprinted in**

- *The Daily Boston Globe,* 16 August 1931 (US)
- *Ellery Queen's Mystery Magazine,* July 1968 (US)
- *Murder at the Races,* edited Peter Haining, Orion, 1995 (UK)

## 'The Cretan Bull' – the seventh labour

A woman enlists Poirot's help to determine if her boyfriend is going insane.

**Word Count:** 8,000

**Pre-Publication Appearance**
UK – May 1940, volume 99, issue 593 of *The Strand Magazine,* illustrated by Ernest Ratcliff
US – 24 September 1939, *This Week* as 'Midnight Madness'; the magazine was distributed as a supplement to all the major Sunday newspapers in America.

**Official Collections**
*The Labours of Hercules* 1947 (UK / US)

**'The Cretan Bull' was reprinted in**

- *The Star Weekly*, 19 July 1941 (CAN) as 'He Went Mad at Midnight'
- *Ellery Queen's Mystery Magazine*, April 1946 (US) as 'The Case of the Family Taint'
- *Ellery Queen's Mystery Magazine, Overseas Edition for the Armed Forces*, April 1946 (US) as 'The Case of the Family Taint'
- *Second Armchair Detective Reader,* edited by Ernest Dudley, Boardman, 1950 (UK)
- *Argosy*, October 1950 (UK) as 'Case of the Cretan Bull'

## 'The Dead Harlequin'

Mr Satterthwaite buys a painting by an artist that provides him and Mr Quin with a clue to a murder.

**Word Count:** 7,900

**Pre-Publication Appearance**
UK – March 1929, *The Grand Magazine*
US – 22 June 1929, volume 42, number 3 of *Detective Fiction Weekly*

**Official Collections**
*The Mysterious Mr. Quin* 1930 (UK / US)

**'The Dead Harlequin' was reprinted in**

- *Truth* magazine, 24 September and 1 October 1950 (Sydney / AUS)
- *Truth* magazine, 11 and 18 February 1951 (Brisbane / AUS)
- *Mackill's Mystery Magazine,* February 1953 (UK)
- *Mackill's Mystery Magazine,* February 1953 (US)
- *Clubman,* September 1955 (UK)
- *Edgar Wallace Mystery Magazine,* December 1966 (UK)
- *Ellery Queen's Mystery Magazine,* January 1955 (US) as 'The Man in the Empty Chair'
- *Ellery Queen's Mystery Magazine,* February 1956 (AUS) as 'The Man in the Empty Chair'

## 'Dead Man's Mirror'

Poirot finds himself on the trail of a killer after a man is shot dead in a locked room.

**Word Count:** 23,000

**Pre-Publication Appearance**
UK – the story is an expanded version of 'The Second Gong', which first appeared in volume 66, number 391 of *The Strand Magazine* in July 1923.
US – the story is an expanded version of 'The Second Gong', which appeared in volume 49, number 6 of *Ladies Home Journal* in June 1932, illustrated by R.J. Prohaska.

**Official Collections**
*Murder in the Mews: 4 Poirot Cases* 1937 (UK) / *Dead Man's Mirror* 1937 (US)
Following Agatha Christie's centenary in 1990, the title of the US collection was changed to *Murder in the Mews* for avoidance of confusion.

**'Dead Man's Mirror' was reprinted in**

- *MacKill's Mystery Magazine,* March 1954 (UK)
- *MacKill's Mystery Magazine,* May 1954 (US)

- *Murder Times Three*, edited by Howard Haycraft and John Beecroft, book club edition, three volumes in one, Doubleday and Company, 1964 (US)
- *Ellery Queen's Mystery Magazine*, February 1966 (US) as 'Hercule Poirot and the Broken Mirror'
- *The Folio Treasury of Shorter Crime Fiction, Volume 2: Superior Sleuths,* edited by Tim Heald and Sue Bradbury, Folio Society, 2007 (UK)

## 'Death by Drowning'

Miss Marple suspects murder when an unwed mother-to-be is found drowned in the river that runs through St. Mary Mead.

**Word Count:** 6,500

**Pre-Publication Appearance**
UK – November 1931, volume 88, number 462 of *Nash's Pall Mall Magazine*

**Official Collections**
*The Thirteen Problems* 1932 (UK) / *The Tuesday Club Murders* 1933 (US)

**'Death by Drowning' was reprinted in**

- *Detection Medley*, edited by John Rhode, Hutchinson, 1939 (UK)
- *The Avon Book of Modern Crime Stories*, edited by John Rhode, Avon Books, New York, 1942 (US)
- *The Mysterious Traveler*, June 1952 (US)
- *Ellery Queen's Mystery Magazine*, December 1957 (US)
- *Ellery Queen's Mystery Magazine*, December 1957 (UK)
- *Ellery Queen's Mystery Magazine*, February 1958 (AUS)

## 'Death on the Nile'

aka 'A Death on the Nile'

**Word Count:** 4,200
A woman is murdered on board a boat shortly after confiding to Parker Pyne that her husband is trying to kill her.

**Pre-Publication Appearance**
UK – July 1933, volume 91, issue 482 of *Nash's Pall Mall Magazine*, featuring Marshall Frantz's illustrations from *Cosmopolitan* magazine
US – April 1933, issue 562 of *Cosmopolitan* magazine under the series title of *Have You Got Everything You Want? If Not, Consult Mr Parker Pyne*, illustrated by Marshall Frantz

**Official Collections**
*Parker Pyne Investigates* 1934 (UK) / *Mr Parker Pyne, Detective* 1934 (US)

[This short story's title was altered to 'A Death on the Nile' when it was published on 2 April 2013 in the *Masterpieces in Miniature* e-book series. It is not to be confused with the 1937 Hercule Poirot novel *Death on the Nile*, which features a different plot and cast of characters.]

**'Death on the Nile' was reprinted in**

- *Ellery Queen's Mystery Magazine*, May 1969 (US)

## 'The Disappearance of Mr Davenheim'

After a banker goes missing Hercule Poirot wins a bet to solve the mystery without leaving his London flat.

**Word Count:** 5,000

### Pre-Publication Appearance
UK – 28 March 1923, issue 1574 of *The Sketch*
US – December 1923, volume 38, number 2 of *The Blue Book Magazine* as 'Mr Davenby Disappears'

### Official Collections
*Poirot Investigates* 1924 (UK) 1925 (US)

### 'The Disappearance of Mr Davenheim' was reprinted in

- *Sleuths: 23 Great Detectives of Fiction and Their Best Cases*, edited by Kenneth Macgowan, Harcourt, Brace and Company, 1931 (US)
- *Blue Book: Stories of Adventure for Men, by Men,* February 1942 (US) as 'Mr Davenby Disappears'
- *Short Story Magazine,* February 1948 (AUS)
- *Ellery Queen's Mystery Magazine,* November 1958 (US) as 'Hercule Poirot, Armchair Detective'
- *Ellery Queen's Mystery Magazine,* December 1958 (UK) as 'Hercule Poirot, Armchair Detective'
- *Ellery Queen's Mystery Magazine,* January 1959 (AUS) as 'Hercule Poirot, Armchair Detective'
- *Alfred Hitchcock's Daring Detectives*, Random House, 1969 (US)
- *Fiction 100: An Anthology of Short Stories*, Macmillan, 1978 (UK)
- *The Great British Detective,* edited by Ron Goulart, Mentor, 1982 (US)

## 'The Double Clue'

When some jewels are stolen during a party, Hercule Poirot narrows the field of suspects down to four individuals – one of whom must be guilty.

**Word Count:** 3,400

### Pre-Publication Appearance
UK – 5 December 1923, issue 1610 of *The Sketch*
US – August 1925, volume 41, number 4 of *The Blue Book Magazine*

**Official Collections**
*Poirot's Early Cases* 1974 (UK) / *Double Sin and Other Stories* 1961 (US)

**'The Double Clue' was reprinted in**

- *20th Century Detective Stories*, edited by Ellery Queen, The Living Library, 1948 (US)
- *Le Grandi Firme*, Torino 1935 (Italy) as *La Fidanzata Scomparsa*
- *Ellery Queen's Mystery Magazine*, July 1956 (US)
- *Ellery Queen's Mystery Magazine*, July 1956 (UK)
- *Ellery Queen's Mystery Magazine*, September 1956 (AUS)
- *Ellery Queen's Twentieth Century Detective Stories*, Popular Library, 1964 (US)
- *The Realm of Fiction,* edited James B. Hall and Elizabeth C. Hall, McGraw-Hill Book Company, 1977 (US)

## 'Double Sin'

Hercule Poirot and his sidekick Captain Hastings are travelling on a motor-coach to Charlock Bay when a passenger's valuable miniatures are stolen.

**Word Count:** 5,000

**Pre-Publication Appearance**
UK – 23 September 1928, *Sunday Dispatch* as 'By Road or Rail'
US – 30 March 1929, volume 108, number 6 of *Detective Story Magazine*

**Official Collections**
*Poirot's Early Cases* 1974 (UK) / *Double Sin and Other Stories* 1961 (US)

**'Double Sin' was reprinted in**

- *Ellery Queen's Mystery Magazine*, May 1971 (US)
- *Woman's Day* magazine, 25 December 1961 (AUS), illustrated by Frank McNamara
- *My Favourite Mystery Stories,* edited by Maureen Daly, Dodd Mead, 1966 (US)

## 'The Dream'

Hercule Poirot investigates the murder of a reclusive millionaire who was haunted by a re-occurring dream in which he killed himself.

**Word Count:** 7,800

**Pre-Publication Appearance**
UK – February 1937, volume 94, issue 566 of *The Strand Magazine*, illustrated by Jack M. Faulks
US – 23 October 1937, volume 210, number 17 of *The Saturday Evening Post*, illustrated by F.R. Gruger. [Reprinted 1977]

## Official Collections
*The Adventure of the Christmas Pudding and a Selection of Entrees* 1960 (UK) / *The Regatta Mystery and Other Stories* 1939 (US)

### 'The Dream' was reprinted in

- *Suspense,* September 1960 (UK)
- *Woman's Day,* 27 February 1961 (AUS)
- *The Saint Mystery Magazine,* June 1963 (UK)
- *Ellery Queen's Mystery Magazine,* December 1964 (US) as 'The Three Strange Points'
- *Danger: Great Stories of Mystery and Suspense from The Saturday Evening Post,* Gollancz, 1968 (UK) / Doubleday, 1967 (US)
- *Stories of Crime and Detection,* edited by Joan D. Berbrich, McGraw-Hill, 1974 (US)
- *Mystery and Suspense: Great Stories from the Saturday Evening Post,* edited by Julie Eisenhower, Curtis, 1976 (US)
- *The Saturday Evening Post,* January-February double issue (volume 249, number one) 1977 (US) [Reprint from 1937]
- *Murder Impossible: An Extravaganza of Miraculous Murders, Fantastic Felonies and Incredible Criminals,* edited by Jack Adrian and Robert Adey, Carrol and Graf, 1990 (US)
- *Detective Stories from The Strand,* edited by Jack Adrian with a foreword by Julian Symons, Oxford University Press, 1991 (UK / US)
- *The Black Lizard Big Book of Locked-Room Mysteries: The Most Complete Collection of Impossible-Crime Stories Ever Assembled,* Vintage Crime / Black Lizard, October 2014 (US)

## 'The Dressmaker's Doll'

Two dressmakers are menaced by a larger-than-life ragdoll that seems to follow them wherever they go.

**Word Count:** 6,300

### Pre-Publication Appearance
UK – December 1958, *Woman's Journal*
Canada – 25 October 1958, *Star Weekly Complete Novel*, a Saturday supplement to *The Toronto Star* newspaper; the magazine was also distributed across America as a supplement to all the major Saturday newspapers, including *The Times-Record* (Troy, New York State) *The Evening Independent* (Massillon, Ohio) *Democrat and Chronicle* (Rochester, New York State), all of which ran advertisements citing the story's forthcoming appearance.

### Official Collections
*Miss Marple's Final Cases* 1979 (UK) / *Double Sin and Other Stories* 1961 (US)

**'The Dressmaker's Doll' was reprinted in**

- *Ellery Queen's Mystery Magazine*, June 1959 (US)
- *Ellery Queen's Mystery Magazine*, August 1959 (UK)
- *Ellery Queen's 14th Mystery Annual*, Random House, 1959 (US)
- *The Australian Women's Weekly*, 18 November 1959 (AUS)
- *The Dark of the Soul*, edited by Don Ward, Tower, 1970 (US)
- *Argosy*, June 1972 (US)
- *Detective Fiction: Crime and Compromise*, edited by Dick Allen and David Chacko, Harcourt Brace Jovanovich, 1974 (US)
- *The Haunted Dolls*, edited by Seon Manly and Gogo Lewis, Doubleday, 1980 (US)
- *Handle with Care*, edited by Joan Kahn, Greenwillow Books, 1985 (US)

## 'The Edge'

A woman's jealousy is unleashed when she discovers the wife of a man she loves is being unfaithful.

**Word Count:** 5,600

**Pre-Publication Appearance**
UK – February 1927, volume 63, issue 374 of *Pearson's Magazine*

**Official Collections**
*While the Light Lasts and Other Stories* 1997 (UK) / *The Harlequin Tea Set and Other Stories* 1997 (US)

**'The Edge' was reprinted in**

- *Alfred Hitchcock's Mystery Magazine*, September 2010 (US)

## 'The Erymanthian Boar' – the fourth labour

Poirot travels to the Alps to capture a violent criminal.

**Word Count:** 6,700

**Pre-Publication Appearance**
UK – February 1940, volume 98, issue 590 of *The Strand Magazine*, illustrated by Ernest Ratcliff
US – 5 May 1940, *This Week* as 'Murder Mountain'; the magazine was distributed as a supplement to all the major Sunday newspapers in the country, including the *Los Angeles Times* and *The Atlanta Constitution*, which advertised the story as a forthcoming attraction.

**Official Collections**
*The Labours of Hercules* 1947 (UK / US)

## 'The Erymanthian Boar' was reprinted in

- *The Australian Women's Weekly,* 2 January 1943 (AUS) as 'Alpine Rendezvous'
- *Parade: The Middle East Weekly,* 22 November 1947 (Cairo, Egypt)
- *Argosy*, November 1950 (UK) as 'Case of the Erymanthian Boar'
- *Creasey Mystery Magazine*, December 1956 (UK)

## 'The Face of Helen'

Mr Satterthwaite's fascination with a lovely girl results in him preventing a particularly gruesome murder with the help of Mr Quin.

**Word Count:** 6,000

**Pre-Publication Appearance**
UK – April 1927, issue 240 of *The Story-Teller* magazine
US – 6 August 1927, *Flynn's Weekly Detective Fiction*

**Official Collections**
*The Mysterious Mr. Quin* 1930 (UK / US)

### 'The Face of Helen' was reprinted in

- *Truth* magazine, 4 and 11 February 1951 (Sydney / AUS)
- *Truth* magazine, 11 and 18 March 1951 (Brisbane / AUS)
- *Black Mask Detective Magazine,* July 1951 (US)
- *The Saint Detective Magazine,* Spring Issue 1953 (US)
- *The Saint Detective Magazine,* December 1954 (AUS)
- *The Saint Detective Magazine,* February 1955 (UK)
- *Clubman,* Summer / July 1955 (UK); this story is listed on the magazine's content's page, unlike 'The Man from the Sea', which also appears in the same issue.

## 'A Fairy in the Flat' and 'A Pot of Tea' (parts 1 and 2 of the same story)

An heir to an earldom hires Tommy and Tuppence Beresford to locate a missing girl.

**Word Count:** 5,100

**Pre-Publication Appearance**
UK – 24 September 1924, issue 1652 of *The Sketch* as 'Publicity'
US – 12 April 1931, *The Daily Boston Globe* as 'A Fairy in the Flat'

**Official Collections**
Chapters 1 and 2 of *Partners in Crime* 1929 (UK / US)

### 'A Fairy in the Flat' and 'A Pot of Tea' were reprinted in

- *Hutchinson's Adventure & Mystery Story Magazine,* February 1928 (UK)

- *20-Story Magazine*, Odhams Press, January 1930 (UK) as 'It Must Have Been a Fairy'
- *The Daily Boston Globe,* 12 April 1931 (US) as 'It Must Have Been a Fairy'

## 'Finessing the King'

Tommy and Tuppence Beresford investigate the murder of a woman stabbed to death at a ball.

**Word Count:** 4,600

### Pre-Publication Appearance
UK – 8 October 1924, issue 1654 of *The Sketch* as 'Finessing the King'

### Official Collections
*Partners in Crime* 1929 (UK / US)
[This story is divided into Chapters 7 and 8 of *Partners in Crime – Finessing the King / The Gentleman Dressed in Newspaper*]

### 'Finessing the King' was reprinted in

- *The Daily Boston Globe,* 31 May 1931 (US)
- *Ellery Queen's Mystery Magazine*, March 1971 (US)

## 'The Flock of Geryon' – the tenth labour

Poirot sets out to free a group of women brainwashed into joining a bogus religious cult that preys on its members for money.

**Word Count:** 6,200

### Pre-Publication Appearance
UK – August 1940, volume 99, issue 596 of *The Strand Magazine,* illustrated by Ernest Ratcliff
US – 26 May 1940, *This Week* as 'Weird Monster'

### Official Collections
*The Labours of Hercules* 1947 (UK / US)

### 'The Flock of Geryon' was reprinted in

- *The Australian Women's Weekly,* 8 August 1942 (AUS) as 'The Great Flock'
- *Parade: The Middle East Weekly,* 10 January 1948 (Cairo, Egypt)

## 'Four and Twenty Blackbirds'

The eating habits of a man who dies after being pushed down a flight of stairs provides Hercule Poirot with a vital clue to his killer's identity.

**Word Count:** 5,000

## Pre-Publication Appearance
UK – March 1941, volume 100, issue 603 of *The Strand Magazine* as 'Poirot and the Regular Customer'
US – 9 November 1940, volume 106, number 19 of *Collier's* magazine, illustrated by Mario Cooper

## Official Collections
*The Adventure of the Christmas Pudding and a Selection of Entrees* 1960 (UK) / *Three Blind Mice and Other Stories* 1950 (US)

## 'Four and Twenty Blackbirds' was reprinted in

- *Ellery Queen's Mystery Magazine*, June 1946 (US)
- *Ellery Queen's Mystery Magazine, Overseas Edition for the Armed Forces*, June 1946 (US)
- *A Cavalcade of Collier's*, edited by Kenneth McArdle, Barnes 1959 (US)
- *Argosy*, October 1960 (UK)
- *Honey* magazine, November 1966 (US)
- *The Gourmet Crook Book*, edited by Tony Wilmott, Everest Books 1976 (UK)
- *Murder on the Menu: A Gourmet Guide to Death*, edited by Peter Haining, Souvenir Press, 1991 (UK)

# 'The Four Suspects'

A former secret service spy is found dead at his home and it takes Miss Marple's perspicuity to work out which member of his household murdered him.

**Word Count:** 5,200

## Pre-Publication Appearance
UK – April 1930, issue 276 of *The Story-Teller Magazine*
US – January 1930, volume 31, number 4 of *Pictorial Review* as 'Four Suspects', illustrated by De Alton Valentine

## Official Collections
*The Thirteen Problems* 1932 (UK) / *The Tuesday Club Murders* 1933 (US)

## 'The Four Suspects' was reprinted in

- *Rex Stout Mystery Quarterly*, May 1945 (US)
- *Famous Stories of Code and Cipher*, edited by Raymond T. Bond, Rhinehart, 1947 (US)
- *Ellery Queen's Mystery Magazine*, March 1958 (US) as 'Some Day They Will Get Me'
- *Ellery Queen's Mystery Magazine*, April 1958 (UK) as 'Some Day They Will Get Me'
- *Ellery Queen's Mystery Magazine*, May 1958 (AUS) as 'Some Day They Will Get Me'
- *Famous Stories of Code and Cipher*, edited by Raymond T. Bond, Collier Books, 1965 (US)

*Publisher's Weekly* 9 September 1933 – Dodd Mead's advertisement for *13 at Dinner* aka *Lord Edgware Dies* featured the poster that was displayed throughout US stores to promote the book. (Copyright PWxyz LCC, Publishers' Weekly. Used by permission)

*The Grand Magazine*, May 1938, featured a superb cover illustration of Hercule Poirot meeting Katrina Reiger in 'How Does Your Garden Grown?' (Jared Cade Collection)

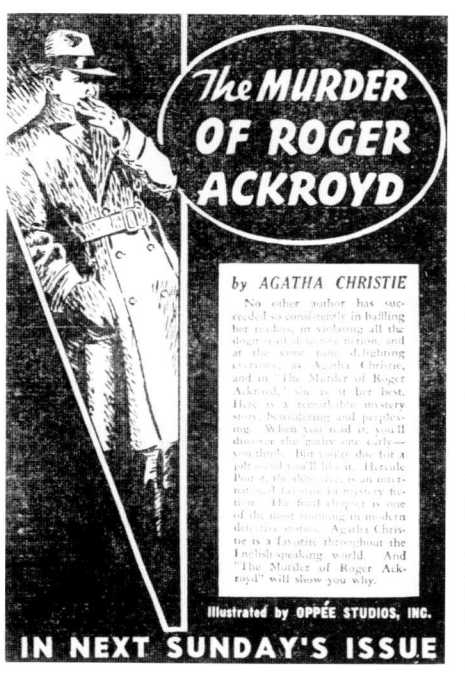

*Above left*: The Brooklyn Daily Eagle, New York, 18 July 1937, p. 60, advertisement for *The Murder of Roger Ackroyd*. (Newspapers.com)

*Above right*: Decatur Evening Herald, Illinois, 28 June 1927, p. 3, advertisement for *The Mystery at Styles*. (Newspapers.com)

*Above left*: Edinburg Daily Courier, Indiana, 7 February 1930, p. 3, advertisement for 'The Four Suspects' which was scheduled to appear in *Pictorial Review*. (Newspapers.com)

*Above right*: The Bristol Courier, Pennsylvania, 11 September 1936, p. 2, advertisement for *The Big Four*. (Newspapers.com)

# A Reviewer Grows Lyrical!

AGATHA CHRISTIE has done it again—
Hail to her Mystery of The Blue Train!
Roger Ackroyd she murdered most niftily,
Here is another crime done just as shiftily,
With Hercule Poirot to unravel the skein.

A millionaire father who dotes on his daughter,
Not guessing she loves where she really ought not-ter,
Blames his gay son-in-law for neglecting his Ruth,
Wants a divorce for her, finds out the truth
When Ruthie is strangled en route to her rotter.

Strangely enough, on the train at the time
Are Ruth's husband Derek—accused of the crime—
The dancer Mirelle, who wanted her dead,
Our heroine, Katherine, level of head,
And detective Poirot (who refuses to rhyme.)

Some Russian crown jewels he had bought for his child
Were missing, and father is awfully wild
To think they have brought death upon her. But zounds!
She omitted a will, and her two million pounds
Will go to her husband, who knew it—and smiled.

So here is the tangle—a love story in it,
And a sinister Marquis, right up to the minute;
Also Comte de la Roche and a noble Greek "fence."
How will Hercule Poirot know where to commence?
But he very soon does. You had better begin it.

### Selling Faster Than "THE MURDER OF ROGER ACKROYD"

### Agatha Christie's Mystery of The Blue Train

4th large printing ordered 10 days after publication.

$2.00

A mystery story built up with such care
For character, incident, writing, is rare.
Contributing issues will rivet attention,
There is much that these verses can't manage to mention;
But one thing they can say—the mystery's tension
Holds taut to the last. What joy to confess it:
Hercule TELLS the truth in the end. YOU CAN'T GUESS IT.
—*Louisville Courier Journal.*

**DODD, MEAD & CO., 449 Fourth Ave., New York, 215 Victoria St., Toronto**

*Publishers' Weekly*, 11 August 1928, Dodd Mead's advertisement for *The Mystery of the Blue Train* featured a poem that waxed lyrical about the book. (Copyright PWxyz LCC, Publishers' Weekly. Used by permission)

*Publishers' Weekly,* 23 February 1929, Dodd Mead's advertisement for *The Seven Dials Mystery* featured a picture of Agatha Christie and her beloved dog Peter. (Copyright PWxyz LCC, Publishers' Weekly. Used by permission)

The superbly illustrated British first edtions for *Murder in the Mews*, *Partners in Crime*, *Dumb Witness* and *Murder in Mesopotamia*. (Jared Cade Collection)

*Publishers' Weekly*, 13 February 1932, Dodd Mead's advertisement for *Peril at End House* demonstrated the growing demand for the author's work in America with many stores doubling their orders. (Copyright PWxyz LCC, Publishers' Weekly. Used by permission)

*Above left*: Publishers' Weekly, 19 April 1930, advertisement for *The Mysterious Mr Quin*. (Copyright PWxyz LCC, Publishers' Weekly. Used by permission)

*Above right*: Bradbord Evening Star and Bradford Daily Record, Pennsylvania, 17 October 1945, p. 4, advertisement for *Towards Zero*. (Newspapers.com)

*Above left*: Altoona Tribune, Pennsylvania, p. 4, advertisement for *The Boomerang Clue* aka *Why Didn't They Ask Evans?* (Newspapers.com)

*Above right*: Linton Daily Citizen, Indiana, 18 June 1947, p. 3, advertisement for *The Hollow*. (Newspapers.com)

*Above left*: *The Royal Magazine*, January 1928, featured Miss Marple in 'The Idol House of Astarte'. (Jared Cade Collection)

*Above right*: *The Strand Magazine*, February 1936, featured 'Poirot and the Crime in Cabin 66' aka 'Problem at Sea'. (Jared Cade Collection)

*Above left*: *Modern Home*, January 1931, featured the earliest known appearance of 'The Bird with the Broken Wing'. (Jared Cade Collection)

*Above right*: *The Strand Magazine*, November 1939, featured Poirot in 'The Nemean Lion'. (Jared Cade Collection)

*Detective Weekly*, 6 July 1935. *Murder on the Orient Express* is one of the major jewels in Agatha Christie's crown. The six-part reprint produced this splendidly atmospheric cover that sees Ratchett sleeping in his berth as the legendary train thunders across Europe to his appointment with death. (Jared Cade Collection)

*Detective Weekly*, 13 July 1935. The second instalment of *Murder on the Orient Express* depicts the terrifying moment Ratchett meets his death. The book's text, in fact, shows the train had run into a snowdrift and Ratchett was in a drugged sleep when he dies. Most readers will probably forgive this lack of fidelity to the plot owing to the cover's marvellously dramatic composition. (Jared Cade Collection)

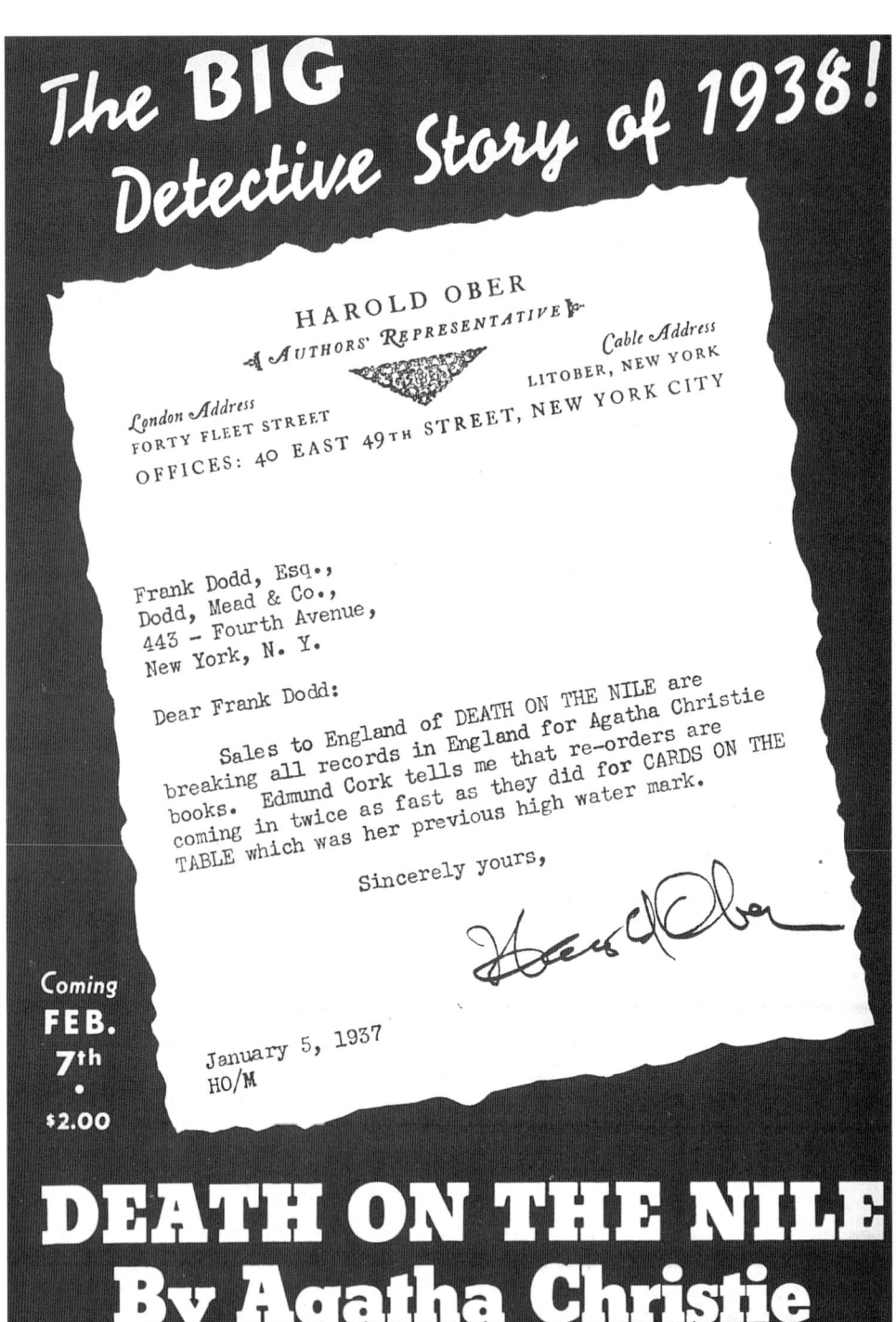

*Publishers' Weekly*, 5 February 1938, Dodd Mead's advertisement for *Death on the Nile* featured a letter from Agatha Christie's US literary agent Harold Ober describing the novel's runaway success in England. (Copyright PWxyz LCC, Publishers' Weekly. Used by permission)

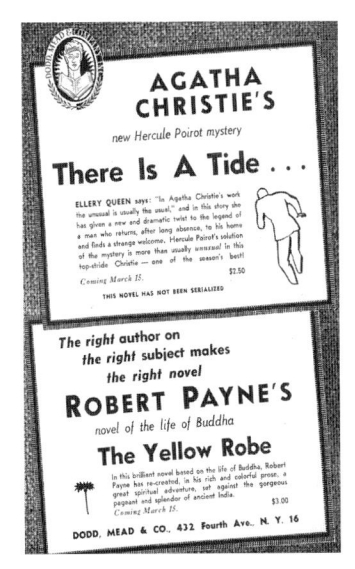

*Above left*: *Publishers' Weekly*, 4 July 1938, advertisement for *Murder for Christmas* aka *Hercule Poirot's Christmas*. (Copyright PWxyz LCC, Publishers' Weekly. Used by permission)

*Above right*: *Publishers' Weekly*, 28 February 1948, advertisement for *There is a Tide* aka *Taken at the Flood*. (Copyright PWxyz LCC, Publishers' Weekly. Used by permission)

*Above left*: *Publishers' Weekly*, 30 December 1939, advertisement for *And Then There Were None* aka *Ten Little Niggers*. (Copyright PWxyz LCC, Publishers' Weekly. Used by permission)

*Above right*: *Publishers' Weekly*, 18 March 1944, advertisement for *The Man with the Lumpy Nose* by Lawrence Lariar and the latest Christie – *Towards Zero*. (Copyright PWxyz LCC, Publishers' Weekly. Used by permission)

Publishers' Weekly, 3 February 1945, advertisement for *Remembered Death* aka *Sparkling Cyanide*. In the wake of the Second World War, Collins disliked Agatha Christie's preferred title of *Remembered Death*, believing it had too many grim associations for the public. She, in turn, disliked *Sparkling Cyanide*, which she considered sounded too frivolous and was suggested to her by Collins. (Copyright PWxyz LCC, Publishers' Weekly. Used by permission)

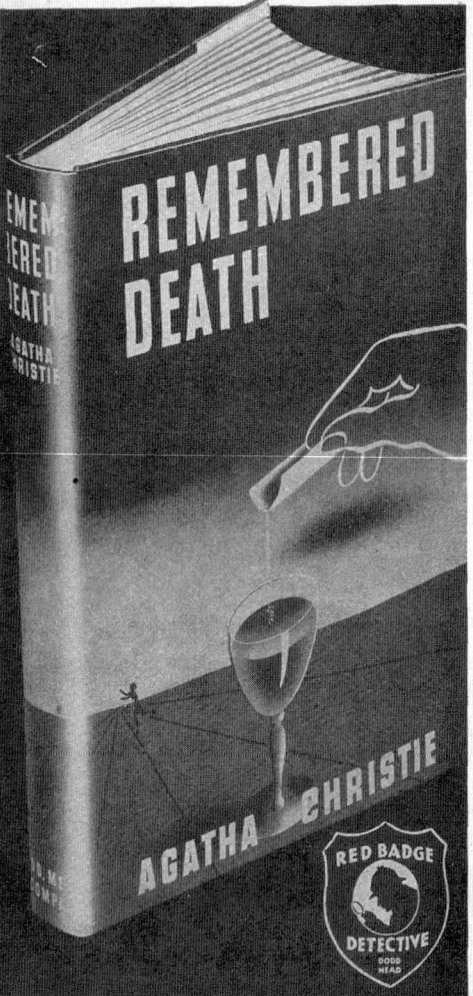

July 1946: the decision of *Woman's Journal* to reject *The Hollow* as a title in favour of *Sword in the Heart* conjures up a gruesome image – the victim John Christow is, in fact, shot. The title references Poirot's remark that Henrietta is one of those people who can live with pain and go on smiling. The woman on the cover is renowned concert pianist Eileen Joyce. (Jared Cade Collection)

# From DODD, MEAD

Coming December 1 • Brand new for Christmas!*

# AGATHA CHRISTIE
## HALLOWE'EN PARTY
### The new Hercule Poirot novel

*NOTICE: Last Christmas bookstore sales of the new Agatha Christie jumped twenty percent. "A Christie for Christmas" was so popular that many booksellers discovered—too late to reorder—they had sold out every copy and late shoppers were clamoring for more. Don't let this happen to you. This year order plenty now. DECEMBER 1. $5.95

**DODD, MEAD & COMPANY,** 79 Madison Avenue, New York 10016

Publishers' Weekly, 20 October 1969, advertisement for *Hallowe'en Party*. The plot was inspired by a hectic visit to America made by the author with her second husband Max Mallowan, whom she accompanied on a lecture tour to promote his book *Nimrud and Its Remains*. By now she was so famous that publishing her books was a licence to print money. (Copyright PWxyz LCC, Publishers' Weekly. Used by permission)

- *Mystery and Detection,* Great Neck and Roth Publishing, 1991 (US)
- *Murder British Style,* edited Martin H. Greenberg, Barnes and Noble, 1993 (US)
- *Lady on the Case: The World's Most Exciting Female Sleuths Portrayed by Twenty-Two Great Writers*, edited by Marcia Muller, Gramercy, 1994 (US)

## 'The Fourth Man'

During a train journey, three eminent men discuss the strange case of a woman with multiple personality disorder, unaware that the fourth man in their compartment holds the key to her life and death.

**Word Count:** 6,200

**Pre-Publication Appearance**
UK – December 1925, *Pearson's Magazine*
UK – October 1947, vol. 10 of *Ellery Queen's Mystery Magazine*

**Official Collections**
*The Hound of Death and Other Stories* 1933 (UK) / *The Witness for the Prosecution* 1948 (US)

**'The Fourth Man' was reprinted in**

- *The Grand Magazine*, February 1935 (UK)
- *Ellery Queen's Mystery Magazine,* October 1947 (US)
- *The Magazine of Fantasy and Science Fiction*, September 1955 (US)
- *Beware of the Trains!*, Ian Henry Publications, 1981 (UK)
- *The Agatha Christie Hour*, TV hard-back tie-in, Collins, 1982 (UK)

## 'A Fruitful Sunday'

A pair of lovers discover a priceless ruby and must decide whether to keep it for themselves or hand it over to the police.

**Word Count:** 2,800

**Pre-Publication Appearance**
UK – 11 August 1928, *Daily Mail*

**Official Collections**
*The Listerdale Mystery* 1934 (UK) / *The Golden Ball and Other Stories* 1971 (US)

**'A Fruitful Sunday' was reprinted in**

- *Sunday News*, 12 May 1929 (Sydney / AUS)
- *The Sunday Times*, 22 December 1929 (Perth / AUS)
- *The Second Mystery Bedside Book,* edited by John Creasey, Hodder and Stoughton, 1961 (UK)

## 'The Gate of Baghdad'

Parker Pyne is motoring with a group of passengers across the desert when a member of their coach party is murdered.

**Word Count:** 4,600

### Pre-Publication Appearance
UK – June 1933, volume 91, number 481 of *Nash's Pall Mall Magazine* as 'At the Gate of Baghdad', featuring Marshall Frantz's illustrations from *Cosmopolitan*

### Official Collections
*Parker Pyne Investigates* 1934 (UK) / *Mr Parker Pyne, Detective* 1934 (US)

### 'The Gate of Baghdad' was reprinted in
- *Ellery Queen's Mystery Magazine*, June 1966 (US) as 'The Gate of Death'

## 'The Gipsy'

A man with a phobia of gypsies, derived from a childhood nightmare, meets one who warns him of impending danger.

**Word Count:** 3,400

### Official Collections
*The Hound of Death and Other Stories* 1933 (UK) / *The Golden Ball and Other Stories* 1971 (US)

### 'The Gipsy' was reprinted in
- *Everywoman's* magazine, October 1935 (UK)
- *The Mail Magazine,* 13 April 1940 (Adelaide / AUS)
- *The Fontana Book of Great Horror Stories,* edited by Christine Bernard, Fontana, 1966 (UK)

## 'The Girdle of Hyppolita' – the ninth labour

Hercule Poirot's search for a painting called *The Girdle of Hyppolita* takes him to a finishing school in Paris.

**Word Count:** 4,700

### Pre-Publication Appearance
UK – July 1940, volume 99, issue 595 of *The Strand Magazine* as 'The Girdle of Hyppolyte', illustrated by Ernest Ratcliff

US – 10 September 1939, *This Week* as 'The Disappearance of Winnie King'; the magazine was distributed across the country as a supplement to all the major Sunday newspapers, including the *Los Angeles Times* and *The Spokesman-Review*, which advertised the story as a forthcoming attraction.

**Official Collections**
*The Labours of Hercules* 1947 (UK / US)

**'The Girdle of Hyppolita' was reprinted in**

- *The Australian Women's Weekly*, 17 January 1942 (AUS) as 'The Stolen Rubens'
- *Ellery Queen's Mystery Magazine*, January 1946 (US) as 'The Case of the Missing Schoolgirl'
- *Ellery Queen's Mystery Magazine*, Overseas Edition for the Armed Forces, January 1946 (US) as 'The Case of the Missing Schoolgirl'
- *Parade: The Middle East Weekly,* 3 January 1948 (Cairo, Egypt)

## 'The Girl in a Train'

A man's train journey is interrupted by a girl begging him to hide her from a sinister foreigner claiming to be her uncle.

**Word Count:** 6,500

**Pre-Publication Appearance**
UK – February 1924, *The Grand Magazine*

**Official Collections**
*The Listerdale Mystery* 1934 (UK) / *The Golden Ball and Other Stories* 1971 (US)

**'The Girl in a Train' was reprinted in**

- *The 20-Story Magazine*, Odhams Press, January 1929 (UK)
- *Mackill's Mystery Magazine*, November 1953 (UK)
- *Mackill's Mystery Magazine*, January 1954 (US)
- *Mysterious Railway Stories,* edited by William Pattrick, W.H. Allen, 1984 (UK)

## 'The Golden Ball'

A man and a society girl go on a pleasure drive into the country, only to find themselves terrorized at gunpoint by a sinister stranger and his accomplice.

**Word Count:** 3,400

**Pre-Publication Appearance**
UK – 5 August 1929, *Daily Mail* as 'Playing the Innocent', illustrated by Lowtham

**Official Collections**
*The Listerdale Mystery* 1934 (UK) / *The Golden Ball and Other Stories* 1971 (US)

**'The Golden Ball' was reprinted in**
*Tit-Bits Summer Special,* George Newnes Ltd., 1966 (UK)

―――――――― Secrets from the Agatha Christie Archives ――――――――

## 'Greenshaw's Folly'

Miss Marple investigates the murder of a woman after she is shot by an arrow fired from a bow.

**Word Count:** 5,100

**Working Title:** 'The Folly' / 'Sanderson's Folly' / 'Grandison's Folly' / 'Greenshore's Folly' (as cited in Agatha Christie's notebooks)

### Pre-Publication Appearance
UK – 3 to 7 December 1956, *Daily Mail*, illustrated by Caswell
Canada – *Star Weekly Complete Novel*, a Saturday supplement to *The Toronto Star* newspaper, 3 and 10 November 1956, illustrated by Russell Maebus

### Official Collections
*The Adventure of the Christmas Pudding and a Selection of Entrees* 1960 (UK) / *Double Sin and Other Stories* 1961 (US)

### 'Greenshaw's Folly' was reprinted in

- *Ellery Queen's Mystery Magazine*, March 1957 (US)
- *Woman's Day*, 22 April 1957 (AUS)
- *Sydney Morning Herald*, 13 May 1957 (AUS)
- *Ellery Queen's 13th Annual: 13 Famous Authors*, Random House, 1958 (US)
- *Woman's Journal*, August 1960 (UK)
- *Miss Marple's Final Cases*, 2002 paperback edition onwards (UK)

## 'The Harlequin Tea Set'

Mr Satterthwaite and Mr Quin prevent a tragedy from taking place at a family gathering.

**Word Count:** 10,900

### Pre-Publication Appearance
UK – November 1971, *Winter Crime's 3*, edited by George Hardinge, Macmillan
US – 11 November 1971, *Winter Crime's 3*, edited by George Hardinge, Macmillan

### Official Collections
*Problem at Pollensa Bay* and Other Stories 1991 (UK) / *The Harlequin Tea Set and Other Stories* 1997 (US)

### 'The Harlequin Tea Set' was reprinted in

- *The Australian Women's Weekly*, 24 May 1972 (AUS)
- *Ellery Queen's Mystery Magazine*, June 1973 (US)
- *Ellery Queen's Murdercade*, Random House, 1975 (US)
- *The Web She Weaves: An Anthology of Mystery and Suspense Stories by Women*, edited by Marcia Muller and Bill Pronzini, William Morrow and Company, 1983 (US)

- *The Mammoth Book of Modern Crime Stories,* edited by George Hardinge, Carrol and Graf, 1986 (US)
- *The Anthology of Crime Stories,* edited by George Hardinge, Tiger Books, 1994 (UK)

## 'Harlequin's Lane'

A harlequinade concert attended by Mr Satterthwaite provides the backdrop for a tragedy involving a ballerina and a house of dreams overlooking a quarry.

**Word Count:** 7,200

### Pre-Publication Appearance
UK – May 1927, issue 241 of *The Story-Teller* magazine under the series title of *The Magic of Mr Quin*
US – 27 August 1927, volume 26, number 4 of *Flynn's Weekly Detective Fiction*

### Official Collections
*The Mysterious Mr Quin* 1930 (UK / US)

### 'Harlequin's Lane' was reprinted in
- *MacKill's Mystery Magazine,* October 1953 (UK)
- *MacKill's Mystery Magazine,* December 1953 (US)

## 'Have You Got Everything You Want?'

Parker Pyne is travelling on the Simplon Express when a passenger's jewellery is stolen as the train crosses the bridge on the approach to Venice.

**Word Count:** 4,300

### Pre-Publication Appearance
UK – June 1933, volume 91, issue 481 of *Nash's Pall Mall Magazine* as 'On the Orient Express', with Marshall Frantz's illustrations from *Cosmopolitan* magazine
US – April 1933, issue 562 of *Cosmopolitan* magazine (unnamed) under the series title of *Have You Got Everything You Want? If Not, Consult Mr Parker Pyne,* illustrated by Marshall Frantz

### Official Collections
*Parker Pyne Investigates* 1934 (UK) / *Mr Parker Pyne, Detective* 1934 (US)

### 'Have You Got Everything You Want?' was reprinted in
- *The Grand Magazine,* September 1935 (UK) as 'Have You Got All You Want?'
- *The Golden Book of Stories,* John Leng and Co., 1937 (UK) as 'Parker Pyne Sees It Through'
- *Ellery Queen's Mystery Magazine,* June 1965 (US) as 'Express to Stamboul'

- *Murder on the Railways,* edited by Peter Haining, Orion, 1996 (UK) as 'Express to Stamboul'
- *Murder on the Railways,* edited by Peter Haining, Bounty Books, 2003 (UK) as 'Express to Stamboul'
- *Continental Crimes*, (British Library Classics), edited by Martin Edwards, British Library, 2017 (UK)

## 'The Herb of Death'

A house party ends in tragedy when the one of the guests dies after eating poisonous foxglove leaves mixed in with the sage.

**Word Count:** 4,800

**Pre-Publication Appearance**
UK – March 1930, issue 275 of *The Story-Teller Magazine*

**Official Collections**
*The Thirteen Problems* 1932 (UK) / *The Tuesday Club Murders* 1933 (US)

**'The Herb of Death' was reprinted in**

- *Ellery Queen's Mystery Magazine,* March 1962 (US) as 'Foxglove in the Sage'
- *Ellery Queen's Mystery Magazine,* July 1962 (UK) as 'Foxglove in the Sage'
- *Ellery Queen's Mystery Magazine,* September 1962 (AUS) as 'Foxglove in the Sage'

## 'Hercule Poirot and the Greenshore Folly' (novella)

The crime novelist Ariadne Oliver has a premonition that something is wrong during the planning of a murder hunt and soon afterwards a dead body is discovered in a boathouse.

**Word Count:** 20,000

**E-book Publication**
UK 31 October 2013 / US 12 November 2013

**Hardback Publication:** *Hercule Poirot and the Greenshore Folly* was published by HarperCollins in the UK on 31 July 2014. This novella was not published during Agatha Christie's lifetime because she expanded it into the 1956 novel *Dead Man's Folly* featuring Hercule Poirot.

**Length:** UK 160pp.

**Price:** UK £12.99

## 'The Horses of Diomedes' – the eighth labour

Hercule Poirot subdues a general's hell-raising daughters by capturing the person feeding them cocaine.

**Word Count:** 5,700

**Pre-Publication Appearance**
UK – June 1940, volume 99, issue 594 of *The Strand Magazine,* illustrated by Ernest Ratcliff
US – January 1945, volume 6, number 20 of *Ellery Queen's Mystery Magazine* as well as its *Overseas Edition for the Armed Forces,* as 'The Case of the Drug Peddler'
AUS – 21 March 1942, *The Australian Women's Weekly* as 'The Colonel's Daughters'

**Official Collections**
*The Labours of Hercules* 1947 (UK / US)

**'The Horses of Diomedes' was reprinted in**

- *Parade: The Middle East Weekly*, 27 December 1947 (Cairo, Egypt)

## 'The Hound of Death'

A nun with supernatural powers has disturbing visions of the hound of death prior to disaster striking a village in Cornwall.

**Word Count:** 5,800

**Official Collections**
*The Hound of Death and Other Stories* 1933 (UK) / *The Golden Ball and Other Stories* 1971 (US)

**'The Hound of Death' was reprinted in**

- *The Second Fontana Book of Great Horror Stories,* edited by Christine Bernard, Fontana, 1967 (UK)
- *Shapes of the Supernatural,* edited by Seon Manley and Gogo Lewis, Doubleday, 1969 (US)
- *The Hounds of Hell,* edited by Michel Parry, Gollancz, 1974 (UK)
- *Ellery Queen's Mystery Magazine,* August 1975 (US)
- *Stories of the Occult,* edited by Denys Val Baker, William Kimber, 1978 (UK)

## 'The House at Shiraz'

A pilot turns to Parker Pine to find out why the woman he loves will not see him following a fatality.

**Word Count:** 4,300
**Working Title:** 'The World's Forgetting' (as cited in Agatha Christie's notebooks)

**Pre-Publication Appearance**
UK – June 1933, volume 91, number 481 of *Nash's Pall Mall Magazine* as 'In the House at Shiraz', with Marshall Frantz's illustrations from *Cosmopolitan* magazine
US – April 1933, issue 562 of *Cosmopolitan* under the series title of *Have You Got Everything You Want? If Not, Consult Mr Parker Pyne*, illustrated by Marshall Frantz

**Official Collections**
*Parker Pyne Investigates* 1934 (UK) / *Mr Parker Pyne, Detective* 1934 (US)

**'The House at Shiraz' was reprinted in**

- *Ellery Queen's Mystery Magazine*, September 1966 (US) as 'The Dream House at Shiraz'

## 'The House of Dreams'

A man's reoccurring dream of a house of beauty is marred by the knowledge that something terrible lurks within it.

**Word Count:** 5,400

**Pre-Publication Appearance**
UK – January 1926, issue 74 of *The Sovereign Magazine*, illustrated by Stanley Lloyd

**Official Collections**
*While the Light Lasts and Other Stories* 1997 (UK) / *The Harlequin Tea Set and Other Stories* 1997 (US)

## 'The House of Lurking Death'

A woman hires Tommy and Tuppence Beresford to find out who sent her poisoned chocolates in the post.

**Word Count:** 5,700

**Pre-Publication Appearance**
UK – 5 November 1924, issue 1658 of *The Sketch*

**Official Collections**
*Partners in Crime* 1929 (UK / US)

**'The House of Lurking Death' was reprinted in**

- *The Daily Boston Globe,* 20 September 1931 (US)
- *Ellery Queen's Mystery Magazine*, December 1969 (US)

## 'How Does Your Garden Grow?'

The nursery rhyme 'Mistress Mary, Quite Contrary' provides Poirot with a clue to the identity of a killer.

**Word Count:** 5,700

**Pre-Publication Appearance**
UK – August 1935, volume 89, issue 536 of *The Strand Magazine*, illustrated by R.M. Chandler
US – June 1935, volume 52, number 6 of *Ladies' Home Journal*, illustrated by Mead Schaeffer

**Official Collections**
*Poirot's Early Cases* 1974 (UK) / *The Regatta Mystery and Other Stories* 1939 (US)

**'How Does Your Garden Grow?' was reprinted in**

- *Grand Magazine,* May 1938 (UK)
- *Ellery Queen's Mystery Magazine,* November 1954 (US)
- *Ellery Queen's Mystery Magazine,* September 1955 (UK)
- *Ellery Queen's Mystery Magazine,* November 1955 (AUS)
- *Ellery Queen's Anthology,* #3 1962 (US)
- *Ellery Queen's 12 Distinguished Tales of Detection*, Dell, 1964 (US)

## 'The Idol House of Astarte'

Miss Marple suspects murder when a man is struck dead by supernatural forces in an eerie grove on Dartmoor.

**Word Count:** 5,000

**Pre-Publication Appearance**
UK – January 1928, issue 351 of *The Royal Magazine*
US – 9 June 1928, volume 101, number 6 of *Detective Story Magazine* as 'The Solving Six and the Evil Hour'

**Official Collections**
*The Thirteen Problems* 1932 (UK) / *The Tuesday Club Murders* 1933 (US)

**'The Idol House of Astarte' was reprinted in**

- *Hush*, November 1930 (UK)
- *Great Detective*, October 1933 (US)
- *Fifty Famous Detectives of Fiction,* Odhams Press, 1938 (UK)
- *The Third Mystery Bedside Book,* edited by John Creasey, Hodder and Stoughton, 1962 (UK)
- *Woman's Day* magazine, 5 August 1963 (AUS)
- *Ellery Queen's Mystery Magazine*, September 1965 (US) as 'The Supernatural Murder'
- *High Adventure: A Treasury for Young Adults,* edited by Seon Manley and Gogo Lewis, Funk and Wagnalls, 1968 (US)
- *The Big Book of Detective Stories,* William Clowes, 1930 (UK)

## 'The Importance of a Leg of Mutton'

Hercule Poirot investigates the murder of an old man whose throat is slit in a bungalow on Dartmoor.

**Word Count:** 2,300
[This story was one of the episodes from the serial *The Man Who Was Number Four* that ran in *The Sketch* from 2 January to 19 March 1924.]

### Pre-Publication Appearance
UK – 9 January 1924, issue 1615 of *The Sketch* as 'The Adventure of the Dartmoor Bungalow'
US – April 1927, volume 44, number 6 of *The Blue Book Magazine* as 'The Dartmoor Adventure'

### Official Collections
*The Big Four* 1927 (UK / US)

### 'The Importance of a Leg of Mutton was reprinted in
- *Ellery Queen's Mystery Magazine*, May 1972 (US)

## 'In a Glass Darkly'

A guest at a house party has a psychic vision in which he sees a woman being strangled and later that night he meets her future killer.

**Word Count:** 2,500

### Pre-Publication Appearance
UK – December 1934, *Woman's Journal*
US – 28 July 1934, volume 94, number 4 of *Collier's* magazine, illustrated by Harry Morse Meyers

### Official Collections
*Miss Marple's Final Cases* 1979 (UK) / *The Regatta Mystery and Other Stories* 1939 (US)

### 'In a Glass Darkly' was reprinted in
- *Ellery Queen's Mystery Magazine*, March 1970 (US)
- *The Mammoth Book of 20th Century Ghost Stories*, edited by Peter Haining, Robinson, 1998 (UK)

## 'The Incident of the Dog's Ball'

Poirot receives a mysterious letter from a woman two and a half months after she was murdered.

**Word Count:** 6,800

## Post-Publication Appearance

- In the US, 'The Incident of the Dog's Ball' appeared in issue 29 of *The Strand Magazine* in its quarterly October 2009–January 2010 edition, illustrated by Pauline Hazelwood.

## Original Publication

'The Incident of the Dog's Ball' was expanded into the 1937 novel *Dumb Witness* and to date does not feature in any Agatha Christie short story collection. It was first published in volume form in the UK by HarperCollins in *Agatha Christie's Secret Notebooks* by John Curran on 3 September 2009 and in the US by Harper, an imprint of HarperCollins, on 22 February 2010.

## 'The Incident of the Dog's Ball' was reprinted in

- *Bodies from the Library 3*, edited by Tony Medawar, Collins Crime Club, 2020 (UK)

## 'The Incredible Theft'

A peer turns to Poirot for help when the plans of a secret bomber are stolen during a house party.

**Word Count:** 15,000
[This story is an expanded version of 'The Submarine Plans', which appeared in *The Sketch* on 7 November 1923.]

## Pre-Publication Appearance

UK – 6, 7, 8, 9, 10 and 12 April 1937, *Daily Express*, illustrated by Steven Spurrier.
US – no pre-publication serialization has been traced, although the story is an expanded version of 'The Submarine Plans' which appeared in volume 41, number 3 of *The Blue Book Magazine* in July 1925.
Canada – 29 May, 5, 12, 19, 26 June and 3 July 1937, *Toronto Star Weekly*, illustrated by Fred Wood, John Hanson, and D.M. Patterson.

## Official Collections

*Murder in the Mews: 4 Poirot Cases* 1937 (UK) / *Dead Man's Mirror* 1937 (US)
Following Agatha Christie's centenary in 1990, the title of the US collection was changed to *Murder in the Mews* for avoidance of confusion.

## 'The Incredible Theft' was reprinted in

- *The World's News*, 6 April to 11 May 1938 (Sydney / AUS)
- *The Daily News*, 5 – 12 October 1937 (Perth / AUS)
- *MacKill's Mystery Magazine,* August 1953 (UK)
- *MacKill's Mystery Magazine,* October 1953 (US)
- *Ellery Queen's Mystery Magazine,* March 1972 (US)

## 'Ingots of Gold'

Miss Marple's nephew is caught up in an illegal operation involving the salvaging of sunken treasure in Cornwall.

**Word Count:** 4,300

### Pre-Publication Appearance

UK – February 1928, issue 351 of *The Royal Magazine*; this issue features the first ever illustration of Miss Marple's nephew the novelist Raymond West, by Gilbert Wilkinson

US – 16 June 1928, volume 102, number 1 of *Detective Story Magazine* as 'The Solving Six and the Golden Grave'

### Official Collections

*The Thirteen Problems* 1932 (UK) / *The Tuesday Club Murders* 1933 (US)

### 'Ingots of Gold' was reprinted in

- *The Saturday Journal*, 24 March 1928 (Adelaide / AUS)
- *Hush,* January 1931 (UK)
- *Woman's Pictorial*, 23 July 1932 (UK) as *Bars of Gold*
- *Great Detective*, November 1933 (US)
- *The Big Book of Detective Stories,* William Clowes, 1930 (UK)

## 'Jane in Search of a Job'

Jane Cleveland finds herself in considerable danger when she agrees to act as a body double for a Grand Duchess whose enemies wish to get rid of her.

**Word Count:** 6,900

### Pre-Publication Appearance

UK – August 1924, *The Grand Magazine*

### Official Collections

*The Listerdale Mystery* 1934 (UK) / *The Golden Ball and Other Stories* 1971 (US)

### 'Jane in Search of a Job' was reprinted in

- *Home Journal,* 7 September 1935 (UK) as 'Here's to Adventure', illustrated by Moorsom
- *Gothic Stories,* May 1971 (US)
- *The Agatha Christie Hour*, TV hardback tie-in, Collins, 1982 (UK)

## 'The Jewel Robbery at the Grand Metropolitan'

Hercule Poirot is holidaying at a hotel in Brighton when a guest's pearls are stolen from her room.

**Word Count:** 5,000

### Pre-Publication Appearance
UK – 14 March 1923, issue 1572 of *The Sketch* as 'The Curious Disappearance of the Opalsen Pearls'
US – October 1923, volume 37, number 6 of *The Blue Book Magazine* as 'Mrs. Opalsen's Pearls'

### Official Collections
*Poirot Investigates* 1924 (UK) 1925 (US)

### 'The Jewel Robbery at the Grand Metropolitan' was reprinted in

- *Century of Thrillers*, volume 1, President Press, 1937 (US)
- *Fifty Famous Detectives of Fiction,* Odhams Press, 1938 (UK)
- *Blue Book: Stories of Adventure for Men, by Men,* August 1942 (US) as 'Mrs Opalsen's Pearls'
- *Avon Mystery Storyteller,* Avon, 1946 (US)
- *Short Story Magazine*, number 37, August 1947 (AUS)
- *Hit Parade of Mystery Stories,* edited Norma Reudi Ainsworth, Scholastic Book Services, 1963 (US)
- *Ellery Queen's Mystery Magazine,* November 1963 (US) as 'The Theft of the Opalsen Pearls'

## 'The Kidnapped Prime Minister'

Hercule Poirot has just over twenty-four hours to locate Britain's Prime Minister in order to avert an international catastrophe.

**Word Count:** 6,400

### Pre-Publication Appearance
UK – 25 April 1923, issue 1578 of *The Sketch*
US – July 1924, volume 39, number 3 of *The Blue Book Magazine* as 'The Kidnapped Premier' (the title of Prime Minister was used throughout the story)

### Official Collections
*Poirot Investigates* 1924 (UK) 1925 (US)

### 'The Kidnapped Prime Minister' was reprinted in

- *The Master Thriller Series: Tales of Mystery and Detection,* number 4, 1934, (UK)
- *The World's Greatest Detective Stories,* Syndicate Publications, 1934 (US)
- *Blue Book: Stories of Adventure for Men, by Men,* May 1942 (US) as 'The Kidnapped Premier'
- *Short Story Magazine*, August 1949 (AUS)
- *Ellery Queen's Mystery Magazine,* June 1960 (US)
- *Ellery Queen's Mystery Magazine,* August 1960 (AUS)
- *Ellery Queen's Mystery Magazine,* August 1960 (UK)

## 'The King of Clubs'

After his fiancé is suspected of murdering an unpleasant impresario, Prince Paul of Maurania calls in Poirot to get to the bottom of the mystery.

**Word Count:** 5,100

**Pre-Publication Appearance**
UK – 21 March 1923, issue 1573 of *The Sketch* as 'The Adventure of the King of Clubs'
US – November 1923, volume 38, number 1 of *The Blue Book Magazine*

**Official Collections**
*Poirot's Early Cases* 1974 (UK) *Poirot Investigates* 1925 (US edition only)

**'The King of Clubs' was reprinted in**

- *Ellery Queen's Mystery Magazine*, May 1955 (US) as 'Beware the King of Clubs'
- *Ellery Queen's Mystery Magazine*, May 1955 (UK) as 'Beware the King of Clubs'
- *Ellery Queen's Mystery Magazine*, July 1955 (AUS) as 'Beware the King of Clubs'
- *Win, Lose or Die: Stories from Ellery Queen's Mystery Magazine and Alfred Hitchcock Mystery Magazine,* edited by Cynthia Manson and Constance Scarborough, Carrol and Graf, June 1996 (UK) as 'Beware the King of Clubs'

## 'The Lamp'

Soon after a widow moves into a haunted house her child develops a special friendship with the ghost of a little boy.

**Word Count:** 2,700

**Inspiration for the title:** The story's title, along with the poem quoted in it, are taken from the *Rubaiyat of Omar Khayyam*, a selection of poems translated into English by Edward FitzGerald and attributed to the Persian astronomer, mathematician and poet Omar Khayyam (1048 – 1131).

> *'What Lamp has Destiny to guide*
> *Her little Children in the Dark?*
> *"A Blind Understanding," Heaven replied.'*

**Official Collections**
*The Hound of Death and Other Stories* 1933 (UK) / *The Golden Ball and Other Stories* 1971 (US)

**'The Lamp' was reprinted in**

- *A Gathering of Ghosts*, edited by Seon Manley and Gogo Lewis, Funk and Wagnalls, 1970 (US)
- *Nightfrights: An Anthology of Macabre Tales That Have Terrified Three Generations*, edited by Peter Haining, Gollancz, 1972 (UK)

- *Some Things Strange and Sinister*, edited by Joan Kahn, The Bodley Head (UK) / Harper and Row (US) 1973
- *Ghosts That Haunt You*, edited by Aidan Chambers, Kestrel, 1980 (UK)
- *The Seventeenth Fontana Book of Great Ghost Stories,* edited by R. Chetwynd-Hayes, Fontana, 1981 (UK)
- *Spooky Stories 5,* edited by Barbara Ireson, Carousel, 1983 (UK)
- *Spooky Tales,* Octopus Books, 1984 (UK)
- *Witches' Brew,* edited by Marcia Muller and Bill Pronzini, Macmillan, 1984 (US)
- *Favourite Ghost Stories,* edited by Aidan Chambers, Kingfisher, 2002 (US)

## 'The Last Séance'

A grieving mother's attempt to be united with her dead child leads to horrific consequences.

**Word Count:** 4,600

**Pre-Publication Appearance**
UK – March 1927, issue 87 of *The Sovereign Magazine* as 'The Stolen Ghost'
US – November 1926, volume 1, number 5 of *Ghost Stories* magazine as 'The Woman Who Stole a Ghost'

**Official Collections**
*The Hound of Death and Other Stories* 1933 (UK) / *Double Sin and Other Stories* 1961 (US)

**'The Last Séance' was reprinted in**

- *The Mystery Book*, edited by H. Douglas Thomson, Odhams Press, 1934 (UK)
- *The World's News,* 10 January 1942 (Sydney / AUS)
- *The Magazine of Fantasy and Science Fiction*, April 1951 (US)
- *Beyond the Barriers of Space and Time: 19 Astounding Stories of Science Fiction and Fantasy,* edited by Judith Merril, Sidgwick and Jackson (UK) / Random House, 1954 (US)
- *The Magazine of Fantasy and Science Fiction,* 1954 (AUS)
- *The Second Pan Book of Horror Stories,* edited by Herbert van Thal, Pan, 1960 (UK)
- *The Cold Embrace,* edited by Alex Hamilton, Transworld, 1966 (UK)
- *Dr. Caligari's Black Book,* edited by Peter Haining, W.H. Allen, 1968 (UK)
- *Ellery Queen's Mystery Magazine,* November 1971 (US)
- *Ladies of Horror,* edited by Seon Manley and Gogo Lewis, Lee and Shepard, 1971 (US)
- *The Eighth Fontana Book of Great Ghost Stories*, edited by Robert Aickman, Fontana, 1972 (UK)
- *The Venus Factor,* edited by Vic Ghidalia and Roger Elwood, Macfadden, 1972 (US)
- *Stories of the Macabre,* edited by Denys Val Baker, William Kimber, 1976 (UK)
- *Supernatural,* edited by James Gibson and Alan Ridout, John Murray, 1978 (UK)
- *65 Tales of Horror,* edited by Mary Danby, Octopus Books, 1981 (UK)

## 'The Lemesurier Inheritance'

A family curse states no first-born child shall ever inherit the Lemesurier estate and it falls to Poirot to exorcise the evil spirits once and for all.

**Word Count:** 4,000

### Pre-Publication Appearance
UK – December 1925, *The Christmas Magpie* as 'The Le Mesurier Inheritance'
US – November 1925, volume 42, number 1 of *The Blue Book Magazine* as 'The Le Mesurier Inheritance'

### Official Collections
*Poirot's Early Cases* 1974 (UK) / *The Underdog and Other Stories* 1951 (US)

## 'The Lernean Hydra' – the second labour

Hercule Poirot intervenes when a doctor is falsely accused of murder

**Word Count:** 7,200

### Pre-Publication Appearance
UK – December 1939, volume 98, issue 588 of *The Strand Magazine*, illustrated by Ernest Ratcliff
US – 3 September 1939, *This Week* as 'The Invisible Enemy'

### Official Collections
*The Labours of Hercules* 1947 (UK / US)

### 'The Lernean Hydra' was reprinted in

- *The Star Weekly*, 16 August 1941 (CAN) as 'Case of the Invisible Enemy'
- *The Australian Women's Weekly*, 11 July 1942 (AUS) as 'The Many-Headed Monster'
- *Ellery Queen's Mystery Magazine*, February 1946 (US) as 'The Case of the Gossipers'
- *Ellery Queen's Mystery Magazine*, Overseas Edition for the Armed Forces, February 1946 (US) as 'The Case of the Gossipers'
- *Parade: The Middle East Weekly*, 8 November 1947 (Cairo, Egypt)
- *Creasey Mystery Magazine*, September 1956 (UK)

## 'The Listerdale Mystery'

A woman becomes intrigued by the disappearance of a peer after renting his home.

**Word Count:** 6,000

### Pre-Publication Appearance
UK – December 1925, *The Grand Magazine* as 'The Benevolent Butler'

**Official Collections**
*The Listerdale Mystery* 1934 (UK) / *The Golden Ball and Other Stories* 1971 (US)

**'The Listerdale Mystery' was reprinted in**

- *MacKill's Mystery Magazine,* July 1953 (UK)
- *MacKill's Mystery Magazine,* September 1953 (US)

## 'The Lonely God'

At the British Museum, two lonely people are drawn to a heathen idol on display and over time, fall in love with each other.

**Word Count:** 4,700

**Pre-Publication Appearance**
UK – July 1926, issue 333 of *The Royal Magazine*, illustrated by H. Coller

**Official Collections**
*While the Light Lasts and Other Stories* 1997 (UK) / *The Harlequin Tea Set and Other Stories* 1997 (US)

**'The Lonely God' was reprinted in**

- *The Observer*, 11 September 1926 (Adelaide / AUS)

## 'The Lost Mine'

Hercule Poirot investigates the murder of a Chinese businessman robbed of secret papers revealing the whereabouts of a lost mine.

**Word Count:** 3,200

**Pre-Publication Appearance**
UK – 21 November 1923, issue 1608 of *The Sketch*
US – April 1925, volume 40, number 6 of *The Blue Book Magazine*

**Official Collections**
*Poirot's Early Cases* 1974 (UK) / *Poirot Investigates* 1925 (US edition only)

**'The Lost Mine' was reprinted in**

- *Ellery Queen's Mystery Magazine*, March 1965 (US)

## 'The Love Detectives'

Mr Satterthwaite is on his way to the scene of a murder when an encounter with the enigmatic Mr Quin has a profound effect on the outcome of the case.

**Word Count:** 6,600

### Pre-Publication Appearance
UK – December 1926, issue 236 of *The Story-Teller*
US – 30 October 1926, volume 19, number 3 of *Flynn's Weekly* as 'At the Cross Roads'

### Official Collections
*Problem at Pollensa Bay* 1991 (UK) / *Three Blind Mice and Other Stories* 1950 (US)

### 'The Love Detectives' was reprinted in

- *Ellery Queen's Mystery Magazine*, December 1946 (US)
- *Ellery Queen's Mystery Magazine*, April 1954 (UK)
- *Ellery Queen's Mystery Magazine*, June 1976 (US)
- *Argosy: Special Bicentennial Edition,* 1976 (US) as 'At the Crossroads'

## 'Magnolia Blossom'

A woman is running away with her lover when she sees a newspaper article that forces her to alter her plans.

**Word Count:** 5,600

### Pre-Publication Appearance
UK – March 1926, issue 329 of *The Royal Magazine*

### Official Collections
*Problem at Pollensa Bay and Other Stories* 1991 (UK) / *The Golden Ball and Other Stories* 1971 (US)

### 'Magnolia Blossom' was reprinted in

- *Me Naiset*, one of the largest women's magazines published in Helsinki, Finland, on 15 March 1974
- *The Agatha Christie Hour*, TV hardback tie-in, Collins, 1982 (UK)

## 'The Man from the Sea'

Mr Satterthwaite becomes fascinated by a woman living in a villa overlooking the sea where a man once drowned.

**Word Count:** 9,400

### Pre-Publication Appearance
UK – October 1929, volume 1, number 6 of *Britannia and Eve* magazine

### Official Collections
*The Mysterious Mr Quin* 1930 (UK / US)

**'The Man from the Sea' was reprinted in**

- *Truth* magazine, 17 and 24 December 1950 (Sydney / AUS)
- *Truth* magazine, 8 and 15 April 1951 (Brisbane / AUS)
- *Mackill's Mystery Magazine,* September 1953 (UK)
- *Mackill's Mystery Magazine,* November 1953 (US)
- *Clubman,* Summer / July 1955 (UK); this story is not listed on the magazine's content's page, unlike 'The Face of Helen', which also appears in the same issue.
- *'Holiday' Clubman,* Winter / December 1955-1956 (UK)

An editorial blooper in the winter edition of the *Holiday Clubman* cites 'The Man from the Sea' as the last in the series of adventures featuring Mr Satterthwaite and Mr Quin. Ironically, the story had already appeared months earlier in the Summer / July issue of the magazine, along with another story featuring the pair, 'The Face of Helen'.

## 'The Man in the Mist'

Tommy and Tuppence Beresford investigate the murder of an actress.

**Word Count:** 5,300

**Pre-Publication Appearance**
UK – 3 December 1924, issue 1662 of *The Sketch*

**Official Collections**
*Partners in Crime* 1929 (UK / US)

**'The Man in the Mist' was reprinted in**

- *The Daily Boston Globe,* 26 July 1931 (US)
- *Ellery Queen's Mystery Magazine,* September 1961 (US)
- *Ellery Queen's Mystery Magazine,* November 1961 (AUS)

## 'The Manhood of Edward Robinson'

After winning a cash prize in a newspaper competition, a man transforms his life by buying a magnificent car.

**Word Count:** 5,300

**Pre-Publication Appearance**
UK – December 1924, *The Grand Magazine* as 'The Day of His Dreams'
US – May 1925, volume one, number one of *Your Car: A Magazine of Romance, Fact and Fiction* as 'Romance and a Red Roundabout'

**Official Collections**
*The Listerdale Mystery* 1934 (UK) / *The Golden Ball and Other Stories* 1971 (US)

**'The Manhood of Edward Robinson' was reprinted in**

- *Gothic Stories*, May 1971 (US)
- *The Agatha Christie Hour*, a TV hardback tie-in, Collins, 1982 (UK)

## 'The Man Who Knew'

A man has a premonition of danger and shortly afterwards finds himself suspected of his uncle's murder.

**Word Count:** 1,800
[This story was expanded into 'The Red Signal'.]

**Original Publication:** 'The Man Who Knew' was first published in the UK by HarperCollins in *Agatha Christie's Murder in the Making* by John Curran on 1 September 2011 and in the US by Harper, an imprint of HarperCollins, as *Agatha Christie: Murder in the Making* on 22 November 2011.

**Official Collection**
This is one of the few Christie stories not to be included in a volume of her stories.

**'The Man Who Knew' was reprinted in**

- *Bodies from the Library 2*, selected and introduced by Tony Medawar, Collins Crime Club, 2019 (UK)

## 'The Man Who Was No. 16'

Tommy sets out to find Tuppence when she is abducted after lunching with a sinister man.

**Word Count:** 5,300
[This is the last story *The Sketch* published by Agatha Christie.]

**Pre-Publication Appearance**
UK – 10 December 1924, issue 1663 of *The Sketch*

**Official Collections**
*Partners in Crime* 1929 (UK / US)

**'The Man Who Was No. 16' was reprinted in**

- *Hutchinson's Adventure & Mystery Story Magazine*, July 1928 (UK)
- *The Daily Boston Globe,* 22 November 1931 (US)
- *My Best Secret Service Story,* edited by A.D. Divine, Faber and Faber, 1940 (UK)

## 'Manx Gold'

A letter from a dead man challenges his relatives to locate four chests of treasure on the Isle of Man. But the discovery of a body indicates someone is not prepared to play fair in a deadly case of winner takes all.

**Word Count:** 5,300

**Pre-Publication Appearance**
UK – 23 to 28 May 1930, *Daily Dispatch*

**Trivia:** In 1930, Alderman Arthur B. Crookall was the chairman of a committee of residents, known as the 'June Effort', who commissioned Agatha Christie to write 'Manx Gold' to boost tourism to the Isle of Man. The story provided the clues to a real-life treasure hunt in which four snuff-boxes, each containing a £100 voucher, were hidden around the island. A quarter of a million booklets entitled 'June in Douglas' featuring 'Manx Gold' were distributed to hotels and guesthouses around the island, making it Agatha Christie's biggest print run to date for a single title. Residents were banned from entering the competition.

**Official Collections**
*While the Light Lasts and Other Stories* 1997 (UK) / *The Harlequin Tea Set and Other Stories* 1997 (US)

## 'The Market Basing Mystery' (later expanded into the title story from the 1937 UK collection *Murder in the Mews: 4 Poirot Stories*)

Hercule Poirot and Captain Hastings are spending the weekend at Market Basing when word reaches them that a man has been shot in strange circumstances.

**Word Count:** 3,300

**Pre-Publication Appearance**
UK – 17 October 1923, issue 1603 of *The Sketch*
US – May 1925, volume 41, number 1 of *The Blue Book Magazine*

**Official Collections**
*Poirot's Early Cases* 1974 (UK) / *The Under Dog and Other Stories* 1951 (US)

**'The Market Basing Mystery' was reprinted in**

- *Thirteen for Luck!* 1966 (UK)
- *Ellery Queen's Mystery Magazine*, November 1973 (US)

## 'The Million Dollar Bond Robbery'

Hercule Poirot's little grey cells are challenged when Liberty Bonds are stolen from a locked briefcase inside a locked trunk on board the ocean liner *Olympia* en route to New York.

**Word Count:** 3,300

**Pre-Publication Appearance**
UK – 2 May 1923, issue 1597 of *The Sketch*
US – April 1924, volume 38, number 6 of *The Blue Book Magazine* as 'The Great Bond Robbery'

**Official Collections**
*Poirot Investigates* 1924 (UK) 1925 (US)

**'The Million Dollar Bond Robbery' was reprinted in**

- *The Boys' Second Book of Great Detective Stories*, edited by Howard Haycraft, Harper, 1940 (US)
- *Short Story Magazine,* October 1948 (AUS)
- *Ellery Queen's Mystery Magazine*, December 1962 (UK) as 'The $1,000,000 Bond Robbery'
- *The Boys' Second Book of Great Detective Stories,* edited by Howard Haycraft, Berkley, 1964 (US)

## 'The Case of the Missing Lady'

aka 'The Disappearance of Mrs Leigh Gordon
A man recently returned from an expedition to the North Pole hires Tommy and Tuppence Beresford to find his missing fiancé.

**Word Count:** 4,200

**Pre-Publication Appearance**
UK – 15 October 1924, issue 1655 of *The Sketch*

**Official Collections**
*Partners in Crime* 1929 (UK / US)

**'The Case of the Missing Lady' was reprinted in**

- *Hutchinson's Adventure & Mystery Story Magazine*, May 1928 (UK)
- *The Daily Boston Globe,* 28 June 1931 (US)
- *101 Years' Entertainment: The Great Detective Stories 1841 – 1941*, edited by Ellery Queen, Little Brown, 1941 (US) as 'The Disappearance of Mrs Leigh Gordon'
- *The Misadventures of Sherlock Holmes,* edited by Ellery Queen, Little Brown, 1944 (US) an anthology of thirty-three short stories written about Sherlock Holmes by writers other than his creator Sir Arthur Conan Doyle
- *Ellery Queen's Mystery Magazine*, September 1973 (US)

## 'Miss Marple Tells a Story'

Miss Marple recalls a murder she solved years ago when a Mr Rhodes stood falsely accused of killing his wife.

**Word Count:** 3,300

**Pre-Publication Appearance**
UK – 25 May 1935, volume 3, issue 64 of *Home Journal* as 'Behind Closed Doors', illustrated by Michael Bernard

**Official Collections**
*Miss Marple's Final Cases* 1979 (UK) / *The Regatta Mystery and Other Stories* 1939 (US)
Michael Bernard's excellent floorplan of the murdered woman's hotel suite – which adds clarity to the lay-out of the scene of the murder – does not appear in either volume.

**'Miss Marple Tells a Story' was reprinted in**

- *Ellery Queen's Mystery Magazine*, November 1969 (US)
- *Woman's Day* magazine, 24 September 1979 (AUS)
- *Murder Most Foul,* Treasure Press, 1982 (UK)

## 'Mr Eastwood's Adventure'

An author is suffering from writer's block when a series of strange events provide him with the plot of his next crime story.

**Word Count:** 5,600

**Pre-Publication Appearance**
UK – August 1924, issue 233 of *The Novel Magazine* as 'The Mystery of the Second Cucumber', illustrated by Wilmot Lunt
US – December 1924, volume 60, number 3 of *Macfadden Fiction-Lover's Magazine* as 'The Mystery of the Spanish Shawl'

**Official Collections**
*The Listerdale Mystery* 1934 (UK) / *The Witness for the Prosecution* 1948 (US) as 'The Mystery of the Spanish Shawl'.

**'Mr Eastwood's Adventure' was reprinted in**

- *The Grand Magazine*, December 1934 (UK) as 'The Mystery of the Second Cucumber'
- *Ellery Queen's Mystery Magazine,* April 1947 (US) as 'The Mystery of the Spanish Shawl' [Reprinted in 1976]
- *Ellery Queen's Mystery Magazine,* December 1976 (US) as 'Mr Eastwood's Adventure'

## 'Motive v Opportunity'

Miss Marple unravels the mystery of how Simon Clode's last will and testament disappeared in seemingly impossible circumstances.

**Word Count:** 4,700

**Pre-Publication Appearance**
UK – April 1928, issue 354 of *The Royal Magazine*
US – 30 June 1928, volume 102, number 3 of *Detective Story Magazine* as 'Where's the Catch?'

**Official Collections**
*The Thirteen Problems* 1932 (UK) / *The Tuesday Club Murders* 1933 (US)

**'Motive v Opportunity' was reprinted in**

- *Hush*, March 1931 (UK)
- *Ellery Queen's Mystery Magazine*, March 1966

## 'Murder in the Mews'

Chief Inspector Japp is not convinced a woman's death is suicide, so he calls in Hercule Poirot for a second opinion.

**Word Count:** 17,000
[This story is an expanded version of 'The Market Basing Mystery', which appeared in *The Sketch* on 17 March 1923.]

**Pre-Publication Appearance**
UK – December 1936, *Woman's Journal* as 'Mystery of the Dressing Case'; it is not until the last page of the story that Poirot refers to it as 'The Mystery of the Dressing Case'
US – September and October 1936, volume 67, numbers 5 and 6, of *Redbook* magazine, illustrated by John Fulton

**Official Collections**
*Murder in the Mews: 4 Poirot Stories* 1937 (UK) / *Dead Man's Mirror* 1937 (US)
Following Agatha Christie's centenary in 1990, the title of the US collection was changed to *Murder in the Mews* for avoidance of confusion.

**'Murder in the Mews' was reprinted in**

- *Aberdeen Evening News*, 22 May to 2 June 1939 (UK)
- *Daily Gazette for Middlesborough*, 22 May to 2 June 1939 (UK)
- *North-Eastern Gazette*, 22 May to 2 June 1939 (UK)
- *Newcastle Evening Chronicle*, 22 May to 5 June 1939 (UK)
- *Sheffield Evening Telegraph*, 22 June to 5 July 1939 (UK)
- *Mackill's Mystery Magazine*, May 1954 (UK)
- *Mackill's Mystery Magazine*, July 1954 (UK)
- *Ellery Queen's Mystery Magazine*, June 1964 (US) as 'Good Night for a Murder'

## 'The Mystery of the Baghdad Chest'

Hercule Poirot investigates the murder of a man whose body is found inside a trunk.

**Word Count:** 5,000

[This story was expanded into 'The Mystery of the Spanish Chest', which appeared in three instalments of *Woman's Illustrated* on 17 and 24 September and 1 October 1960.]

**Pre-Publication Appearance**
UK – January 1932, volume 83, issue 493 of *The Strand Magazine*
US – January 1932, volume 49, number 1 of *Ladies Home Journal*, illustrated by Robert E. Lee

**Official Collections**
*While the Light Lasts and Other Stories* 1997 (UK) / *The Regatta Mystery and Other Stories* 1939 (US)

**'The Mystery of the Baghdad Chest' was reprinted in**

- *Best Mystery Stories of the Year 1932*, Faber and Faber, 1933 (UK)
- *Poirot Knows the Murderer,* Polybooks, 1946 (UK).
- *Ellery Queen's Mystery Magazine*, August 1969 (US)
- *Murder Most British,* edited by Janet Hutchings, St. Martin's, 1996 (US)

## 'The Mystery of the Blue Jar'

A man's daily game of golf is interrupted by cries of 'murder' that have no physical manifestation, but then he meets an eminent specialist in paranormal mysteries who is able to shed light on the matter.

**Word Count:** 6,600

**Pre-Publication Appearance**
UK – July 1924, *The Grand Magazine*
US – March 1925, volume 60, number 6 of *Macfadden Fiction-Lovers Magazine*
From February 1895 through to September 1924, this periodical was known as *Metropolitan Magazine*; it was renamed *Macfadden Fiction-Lovers Magazine* in October 1924. Dwindling sales led to it ceasing publication after the release of the August 1925 issue.

**Official Collections**
*The Hound of Death and Other Stories* 1933 (UK) / *The Witness for the Prosecution and Other Stories* 1948 (US)

**'The Mystery of the Blue Jar' was reprinted in**

- *The Sunday Sun Magazine,* a supplement to the Sydney-based newspaper of the same name, 25 May 1941 (AUS)
- *Ellery Queen's Mystery Magazine,* May 1944 (US) [Reprinted in 1975]
- *Ellery Queen's Mystery Magazine 'Overseas Edition for the Armed Forces',* May 1944 (US)
- *MacKill's Mystery Magazine,* May 1953 (UK)
- *MacKill's Mystery Magazine,* June 1953 (US)
- *Ellery Queen's Anthology,* number 1, 1960 (US)
- *Ellery Queen's Mystery Magazine,* November 1975 (US) [Reprint from 1944]

## 'The Mystery of Hunter's Lodge'

A fatality at a hunting lodge in Derbyshire prompts the victim's grieving nephew and wife to ask Hercule Poirot for help in bringing the killer to justice.

**Word Count:** 4,500

### Pre-Publication Appearance
UK – 16 May 1923, issue 1581 of *The Sketch*
US – June 1924, volume 39, number 2 of *The Blue Book Magazine* as 'The Hunter's Lodge Case'

### Official Collections
*Poirot Investigates* 1924 (UK) 1925 (US)

### 'The Mystery of Hunter's Lodge' was reprinted in

- *Evening Standard*, number 6 of the 'Detective Cavalcade' series introduced by Dorothy L. Sayers, 4 August 1936 (UK)
- *The World's News,* number 5 of the 'Detective Cavalcade' series, 24 February 1937, (Sydney / AUS)
- *The Telegraph,* number 5 of the 'Detective Cavalcade' series, 9 and 10 March 1937 (Brisbane / AUS)
- *The Townsville Daily Bulletin,* number 5 of the Detective Cavalcade series, 16 November 1937 (Townsville / AUS)
- *Short Story Magazine*, March 1950 (AUS)
- *Giant Mystery Reader,* Avon, 1951 (US)
- *Ellery Queen's Mystery Magazine*, July 1958 (US) as 'Investigation by Telegram'
- *Ellery Queen's Mystery Magazine,* August 1958 (UK) as 'Investigation by Telegram'
- *Ellery Queen's Mystery Magazine,* September 1958 (AUS) as 'Investigation by Telegram'

## 'The Mystery of the Spanish Chest'

Hercule Poirot investigates the discovery of a murdered man's body inside a trunk.

[This story is an expanded version of 'The Mystery of the Baghdad Chest', which appeared in the UK in issue 493 of *The Strand Magazine* in January 1932.]

**Word Count:** 13,800

### Pre-Publication Appearance
UK – 17 and 24 September and 1 October 1960, three weekly instalments of *Woman's Illustrated* magazine

### Official Collections
*The Adventure of the Christmas Pudding and a Selection of Entrees* 1960 (UK) / *The Witness for the Prosecution and Other Stories* 1948 (US)

**'The Mystery of the Spanish Chest' was reprinted in**

- *Woman's Day* magazine, 26 December 1960 (AUS)

## 'The Nemean Lion' – the first labour

Sir Joseph and Lady Hoggin receive a ransom demand after her prized Pekingese dog is kidnapped during a walk in the park.

**Word Count:** 7,700

**Pre-Publication Appearance**
UK – November 1939, volume, 98 issue 587 of *The Strand Magazine* (the foreword to the book was not included), illustrated by Ernest Ratcliff
US – September 1944, volume 5, number 18 of *Ellery Queen's Mystery Magazine* as 'The Case of the Kidnapped Pekinese'

**Official Collections**
*The Labours of Hercules* 1947 (UK / US)

**'The Nemean Lion' was reprinted in**

- *The Australian Women's Weekly,* 2 October 1943 (AUS) as 'Pekingese Mystery'
- *Ellery Queen's Mystery Magazine,* September 1944 (US); cited as 'The Kidnapped Pekinese' on the cover and as 'The Case of the Kidnapped Pekinese' on the contents page
- *Ellery Queen's Mystery Magazine, Overseas Edition for the Armed Forces,* September 1944 (US); cited as 'The Kidnapped Pekinese' on the cover and as 'The Case of the Kidnapped Pekinese' on the contents page
- *To the Queen's Taste,* edited by Ellery Queen, Little, Brown and Company, August 1946 (US) as 'The Case of the Kidnapped Pekinese'
- *Parade: The Middle East Weekly,* 1 November 1947 (Cairo, Egypt)
- *Argosy,* September 1950 (UK) as 'Case of the Nemean Lion'
- *Creasey Mystery Magazine,* October 1956 (UK)
- *The Sixth Mystery Bedside Book,* edited by John Creasey, Hodder and Stoughton, 1965 (UK)

## 'Next to a Dog'

Joyce Lambert is desperate to find a job, but her love for her adorable wire-haired terrier is getting in the way of her prospects.

**Word Count:** 5,200

**Pre-Publication Appearance**
UK – September 1929, *The Grand Magazine*

**Official Collections**
*Problem at Pollensa Bay and Other Stories* 1991 (UK) / *The Golden Ball and Other Stories* 1971 (US)

## 'The Oracle at Delphi'

Mr Parker Pyne is holidaying in Greece when a distraught mother turns to him for help after her son is kidnapped.

**Word Count:** 4,000

### Pre-Publication Appearance
UK – July 1933, volume 91, issue 482 of *Nash's Pall Mall Magazine* under the series title of *More Arabian Nights of Parker Pyne*, illustrated by Marshall Frantz

US – April 1933, issue 562 of *Cosmopolitan* under the series title of *Have You Got Everything You Want? If Not, Consult Mr Parker Pyne*, illustrated by Marshall Frantz

### Official Collections
*Parker Pyne Investigates* 1934 (UK) / *Mr Parker Pyne, Detective* 1934 (US)

### 'The Oracle at Delphi' was reprinted in
- *Ellery Queen's Mystery Magazine*, March 1968 (US)
- *Reveille*, a weekly newspaper published every Thursday, issue number 1404, 23 February – 1 March 1967 (UK)

## 'The Pearl of Price'

Mr Parker Pyne exposes a thief who has stolen a tourist's valuable earrings on a trip to Petra.

**Word Count:** 3,900

### Pre-Publication Appearance
UK – July 1933, volume 91, issue 482 of *Nash's Pall Mall Magazine* as 'The Pearl' under the series title of *More Arabian Nights of Parker Pyne*, featuring Marshall Frantz's illustrations from *Cosmopolitan*

### Official Collections
*Parker Pyne Investigates* 1934 (UK) / *Mr Parker Pyne, Detective* 1934 (US)

### 'The Pearl of Price' was reprinted in
- *Woman's World*, March 1938 (AUS)
- *Ellery Queen's Mystery Magazine*, November 1957 (US) as 'Once a Thief'
- *Ellery Queen's Mystery Magazine*, November 1957 (UK) as 'Once a Thief'
- *Ellery Queen's Mystery Magazine*, January 1958 (AUS) as 'Once a Thief'

## 'Philomel Cottage'

A woman is unable to rid herself of a reoccurring nightmare in which her former lover murders her husband.

**Word Count:** 7,900

**Pre-Publication Appearance**
UK – November 1924, *The Grand Magazine*

**Official Collections**
*The Listerdale Mystery* 1934 (UK) / *The Witness for the Prosecution* 1948 (US)

**'Philomel Cottage' was reprinted in**

- *The World's Best 100 Detective Stories*, edited by Eugene Thwing, Funk and Wagnalls, 24 October 1929 (US)
- *My Best Detective Story*, Faber and Faber, London, 1931.
- *The Thriller*, 5 January 1935 (UK)
- *Tales of Detection,* edited by Dorothy L. Sayers, J.M. Dent & Sons, 1936 (UK)
- *Argosy of Complete Stories,* Allied Newspapers Ltd., 1940 (UK) as 'Love from a Stranger'
- *101 Years' Entertainment: The Great Detective Stories 1841 – 1941*, edited by Ellery Queen, Little Brown, 1941 (US)
- *Twelve Great Stories: A New Anthology No.31,* Avon, 1946 (US)
- *Hold Your Breath,* edited by Alfred Hitchcock, Dell, 1947 (US)
- *Ellery Queen's Mystery Magazine*, April 1951 (US)
- *Mackill's Mystery Magazine*, February 1954 (UK)
- *Mackill's Mystery Magazine*, April 1954 (US)
- *Best Legal Stories,* edited by John Welcome, Faber and Faber, 1962 (UK)
- *The Argosy Bedside Book,* edited by D. M. Sutherland, Odhams Press, 1965 (UK) as 'Love from a Stranger'

## 'The Plymouth Express' (later expanded into the 1928 novel *The Mystery of the Blue Train*)

A distraught magnate appeals to Poirot to find his daughter's killer after she is stabbed in a train.

**Word Count:** 4,700

**Pre-Publication Appearance**
UK – 4 April 1923, issue 1575 of *The Sketch* as 'The Mystery of the Plymouth Express'
US – January 1924, volume 38, number 3 of *The Blue Book Magazine* as 'The Plymouth Express Affair'

**Official Collections**
*Poirot's Early Cases* 1974 (UK) / *The Under Dog and Other Stories* 1951 (US)

**'The Plymouth Express' was reprinted in**

- *Blue Book: Stories of Adventure for Men, by Men,* October 1941 (US) as 'The Plymouth Express Affair'
- *Ellery Queen's Mystery Magazine*, March 1955 (US) as 'The Girl in Electric Blue'

- *Ellery Queen's Mystery Magazine*, March 1955 ((UK) as 'The Girl in Electric Blue'
- *Ellery Queen's Mystery Magazine*, May 1955 (AUS) as 'The Girl in Electric Blue'
- *Surprise! Surprise! A Collection of Mystery Stories with Unexpected Endings*, edited by Raymond T. Bond, Dodd, Mead and Company, 1965 (US)
- *The Crime-Solvers: 13 Classic Detective Stories,* edited by Stewart H. Benedict, Dell, 1966 (US)
- *Grande Dames of Detection: Two Centuries of Sleuthing Stories by the Gentle Sex*, edited by Seon Manley and Gogo Lewis, Lothrop, Lee & Shepard Co., 1973 (US)

**Comic Strip Edition:** 'The Plymouth Express' was published as a hardback graphic novel by Harper, an imprint of HarperCollins, on 3 December 2007. Adapted and illustrated by Marc Piskic, it was translated from the French edition originally published by Emmanuel Proust Editions in 2005 under the title of *Le Train Bleu*.

## 'Problem at Pollensa Bay'

Parker Pyne is holidaying in Mallorca when a guest at the same hotel approaches him to save her son from forming a mismatch with a girl from an artists' colony.

**Word Count:** 5,400

### Pre-Publication Appearance
UK – November 1935, volume 90, issue 539 of *The Strand Magazine*, illustrated by Stanley Davis

US – 5 September 1936, volume 13, number 36 of *Liberty* as 'Siren Business', illustrated by James Montgomery Flagg [Reprinted 1976]

### Official Collections
*Problem at Pollensa Bay and Other Stories* 1991 (UK) / *The Regatta Mystery and Other Stories* 1939 (US)

### 'Problem at Pollensa Bay' was reprinted in

- *Poirot Lends a Hand*, Polybooks,1946 (UK)
- *The Saint Detective Magazine*, October 1956 (US)
- *Liberty Magazine,* Fall 1975 (US) as 'Siren Business', illustrated by James Montgomery Flagg [Reprint from 1936]
- *The Complete Parker Pyne: Private Eye*, 2004 (UK)
- *Parker Pyne Investigates: A Parker Pyne Collection* (the complete stories) 2012 (US)

## 'Problem at Sea'

aka 'The Crime in Cabin 66'
A string of beads appears to be the only clue for Hercule Poirot when a woman is found murdered in her cabin.

**Word Count:** 5,100

**Pre-Publication Appearance**
UK – February 1936, volume 90, issue 542 of *The Strand Magazine* as 'Poirot and the Crime in Cabin 66', illustrated by Jack M. Faulks
US – 12 January 1936, *This Week*, illustrated by Stanley Parkhouse; the magazine was syndicated across the country to all the major Sunday newspapers, including *The Baltimore Sun, The Cincinnati Enquirer, The Indianapolis Star* and *The Pittsburgh Press*, all of which advertised the story as a forthcoming attraction.

**Official Collections**
*Poirot's Early Cases* 1974 (UK) / *The Regatta Mystery and Other Stories* 1939 (US)

**'Problem at Sea' was reprinted in**

- *The Mystery of the Crime in Cabin 66*, Bantam Books, 1943 (UK)
- *Poirot on Holiday,* Polybooks, 1943 (UK)
- *Crime in Cabin 66,* Vallancey Press, 1944 (UK)
- *Poirot Knows the Murderer,* Polybooks, 1946 (UK).
- *Ellery Queen's Mystery Magazine*, March 1964 (US) as 'The Quickness of the Hand'
- *Murder on Deck!: Shipboard and Shoreline Mystery Stories,* edited by Rosemary Herbert, Oxford University Press, 1998 (UK / US); in the UK this volume is published under the Clarendon Press imprint of the Oxford University Press.
- *Death Cruise: Crime Stories on the Open Seas,* edited by Lawrence Block, Cumberland House, 1999 (US)
- *Sleuths of the Century,* edited by Jon L. Breen and Ed Gorman, Carroll and Graf, 2000 (US)

## 'The Rajah's Emerald'

James Bond, a lowly paid clerk, is holidaying with his fiancée when a stolen emerald ends up in his possession.

**Word Count:** 6,000

**Pre-Publication Appearance**
UK – 30 July 1926, issue 420 of *Red Magazine*, illustrated by Jack M. Faulks

**Official Collections**
*The Listerdale Mystery* 1934 (UK) / *The Golden Ball and Other Stories* 1971 (US)

**'The Rajah's Emerald' was reprinted in**

- *The Grand Magazine,* October 1934 (UK)
- *Le Grandi Firme,* Torino 1935 (Italy) as *Lo Smeraldo del Rajah*

## 'The Red Signal'

A man has a premonition of approaching danger at a dinner party and soon afterwards becomes the chief suspect in the murder of his uncle.

**Word Count:** 6,800

['The Red Signal' is an expanded and superior version of 'The Man Who Knew', which to date has not appeared in any Agatha Christie collection. The shorter version was first published in volume form in the UK by HarperCollins in *Agatha Christie's Murder in the Making* by John Curran on 1 September 2011 and in the US by Harper, an imprint of HarperCollins, as *Agatha Christie: Murder in the Making* on 22 November 2011.]

**Pre-Publication Appearance**
UK – June 1924, *The Grand Magazine*
US – June 1947, vol. 9, no. 43 of *Ellery Queen Mystery Magazine*

**Official Collections**
*The Hound of Death and Other Stories* 1934 (UK) / *The Witness for the Prosecution and Other Stories* 1948 (US)

**'The Red Signal' was reprinted in**

- *Sydney Mail*, Christmas Number, 7 December 1938 (AUS)
- *Lancashire Daily Post,* Christmas Number 1938 (UK)
- *Portsmouth Evening News*, 12 December 1938 (UK)
- *Ellery Queen's Mystery Magazine,* June 1947 (US)
- *MacKill's Choice: A Book of Unfamiliar Mystery Stories Selected by the Editor of MacKill's Mystery Magazine,* Todd Publishing Group, 1952 (UK)
- *Ellery Queen's Anthology,* volume 2, 1961 (US)
- *Stories of the Night*, edited by Denys Val Baker, William Kimber, 1 October 1976 (UK)
- *Ellery Queen's Mystery Magazine,* October 1976 (US)
- *Mysterious Visions,* edited by Charles G. Waugh, Martin H. Greenberg and Joseph D. Olander, St. Martin's Press, 1979 (US)

## 'The Regatta Mystery'

A valuable diamond goes missing at the Royal George Hotel in Dartmouth and it falls to Hercule Poirot – or Parker Pyne – to solve the mystery depending on which version of the story you read.

**Word Count:** 5,200

**Pre-Publication Appearance**
UK – June 1936, volume 91, issue 546 of *The Strand Magazine* as 'Poirot and the Regatta Mystery'
US – 3 May 1936, syndicated as a Hercule Poirot story to the following newspapers: *Sunday News* (New York); *The Laredo Times* (Texas); *The Philadelphia Inquirer* (Pennsylvania); and *The Hartford Courant* (Connecticut) as 'Poirot and the Regatta Mystery'
Canada – 2 May 1936, *The Toronto Star Weekly* and 3 May 1936, *The Winnipeg Tribune* magazine (both with Hercule Poirot)

### Official Collections
*Problem at Pollensa Bay and Other Stories* 1991 (UK) / *The Regatta Mystery and Other Stories* 1939 (US) (both with Parker Pyne) and recent editions of *Parker Pyne Investigates*

### Other Collections
*The Complete Parker Pyne Private Eye*, featuring all fourteen stories, including 'Problem at Pollensa Bay' and 'The Regatta Mystery', was released in 2004 in the UK. The Poirot version of 'The Regatta Mystery' was incorporated into the 2008 UK omnibus ***Hercule Poirot: The Complete Short Stories***. 'Poirot and the Regatta Mystery' was also released as an e-book in the masterpieces in miniature series on 1 September 2011.

### 'The Regatta Mystery' (*featuring Hercule Poirot*) was reprinted in

- *Detroit Free Press* (Michigan) 22 November 1936 (*featuring Parker Pyne*):
- *13 for Luck! A Selection of Mystery Stories for Young Readers*, 1961 (US)
- *13 for Luck! A Selection of Mystery Stories for Young Readers*, 1966 (UK)
- *Ellery Queen's Mystery Magazine*, July 1971 (US)
- *The Complete Parker Pyne: Private Eye*, 2004 (UK)
- *Parker Pyne Investigates: A Parker Pyne Collection* (the complete stories) 2012 (US)

## 'Sanctuary'

A man seeking sanctuary is found dying in a church by the vicar's wife, who calls in Miss Marple to find out who killed him.

**Word Count:** 6,700
**Working Title:** 'Aftermath' (as cited in AC's notebooks)

### Pre-Publication Appearance
UK – October 1954, *Woman's Journal*
US – 12 and 19 September 1954, *This Week* as 'Murder at the Vicarage' (not to be confused with the 1930 novel of the same name), illustrated by Robert Fawcett; the magazine was syndicated across the country as a supplement to all the major Sunday newspapers, including *The Los Angeles Times, The De Moines Register, The Cincinnati Enquirer, Democrat and Chronicle* and *Arizona Republic*, all of which advertised the story as a forthcoming attraction.

### Official Collections
*Miss Marple's Final Cases* 1979 (UK) / *Double Sin and Other Stories* 1961 (US)

### 'Sanctuary' was reprinted in

- *This Week's Stories of Mystery and Suspense*, edited by Stewart Beach, Random House 1957 (US) as 'Murder at the Vicarage'
- *Argosy*, January 1959

- *This Week's Stories of Mystery and Suspense,* edited by Stewart Beach, Berkley, 1962 (US)
- *Ellery Queen's Mystery Magazine,* March 1963 (US) as 'Man on the Chancel Steps'
- *Ellery Queen's Mystery Magazine,* July 1963 (UK) as 'Man on the Chancel Steps'
- *Ellery Queen's Mystery Magazine,* September 1963 (AUS) as 'Man on the Chancel Steps'
- *Alfred Hitchcock's Mystery Magazine,* July 1983 (US)
- *More Murder Most Cozy: Mysteries in the Classic Tradition,* edited Cynthia Manson, Signet, 1993 (US)
- *Sins of the Fathers: An Anthology of Clerical Crime,* Victor Gollancz, 1996 (UK)

## 'The Second Gong'

Hercule Poirot investigates the murder of a man found shot dead in his study.

**Word Count:** 7,500

['The Second Gong' was expanded into the 1937 novella 'Dead Man's Mirror'.]

**Pre-Publication Appearance**
UK – July 1932, volume 84, issue 499 of *The Strand Magazine*
US – January 1932, volume 49, number 6 of *Ladies' Home Journal*

**Official Collections**
*Problem at Pollensa Bay and Other Stories* 1991 (UK) / *The Witness for the Prosecution and Other Stories* 1948 (US)

**'The Second Gong' was reprinted in**

- *Many Mysteries,* selected by E. Phillips Oppenheim, Rich and Cowan, 1933
- *Thrills, Crimes and Mysteries: A Specially Selected Collection of Sixty-Three Complete Stories by Well-Known Authors,* edited by John Gawsworth, Associated Newspapers, 1935
- *Tipperary* (Argentina) (Spanish language magazine) June 1938
- *Tales of Mystery and Suspense,* edited by Theodore W. Hipple, Allyn and Bacon, 1977 (US)

## 'The Shadow on the Glass'

A double shooting in the garden of Greenways House provides Mr Quin and Mr Satterthwaite with a mystery to solve.

**Word Count:** 7,100

**Pre-Publication Appearance**
UK – October 1924, *The Grand Magazine*

**Official Collections**
*The Mysterious Mr. Quin* 1930 (UK / US)

**'The Shadow on the Glass' was reprinted in**

- *Truth* magazine on 27 August 1950 (Sydney / AUS)
- *Truth* magazine, 25 February and 4 March 1951 (Brisbane / AUS)
- *MacKill's Mystery Magazine,* January 1954 (UK)
- *MacKill's Mystery Magazine,* March 1954 (US)
- *Clubman,* November 1955 (UK)
- *Ellery Queen's Mystery Magazine,* May 1959 (US) as 'Jealousy is the Devil'
- *Ellery Queen's Mystery Magazine,* July 1959 (UK) as 'Jealousy is the Devil'
- *Ellery Queen's Mystery Magazine,* July 1959 (AUS) as 'Jealousy is the Devil'
- *English Country House Murders: Classic Crime Fiction of Britain's Upper Crust,* edited by Thomas Godfrey, Readers Digest Association in conjunction with Mysterious Press, December 1988 (US)

## 'The Sign in the Sky'

Mr Satterthwaite realizes the wrong person is going to be hanged after discussing the outcome of a murder trial with his friend Mr Quin.

**Word Count:** 5,800

**Pre-Publication Appearance**
UK – July 1925, *The Grand Magazine* as 'A Sign in the Sky'
US – June 1925, *The Police Magazine*

**Official Collections**
*The Mysterious Mr Quin* 1930 (UK / US)

**'The Sign in the Sky' was reprinted in**

- *Weldon Ladies' Journal,* June 1932 (UK)
- *The Pocket Companion,* edited by Philip Van Doren Stern, May 1942 (US)
- *A Lady's Pleasure: A Modern Woman's Treasury of Good Reading,* introduction by Ilka Chase, William Penn Publishing Company, 1946 (US)
- *Story Digest,* October 1946 (US)
- *Murder Medley,* Hennel Locke, 1947 (UK)
- *Armchair Detective Reader,* edited by Ernest Dudley, Boardman, 1948 (UK)
- *Truth,* 4 September 1949 (Sydney / AUS)
- *MacKill's Mystery Magazine,* September 1952 (UK)
- *Ellery Queen's Mystery Magazine,* January 1959 (US)
- *Ellery Queen's Mystery Magazine,* February 1959 (UK)
- *Ellery Queen's Mystery Magazine,* March 1959 (AUS)
- *Alfred Hitchcock's Mystery Magazine,* December 2008 (US)

## 'Sing a Song of Sixpence'

The name of a restaurant provides a retired policeman with a clue to a woman's murder.

**Word Count:** 4,800

### Pre-Publication Appearance
UK – December 1929, *Holly Leaves*, the annual Christmas special of the *Illustrated Sporting and Dramatic News*, illustrated by C. Watson

### Official Collections
*The Listerdale Mystery* 1934 (UK) / *The Witness for the Prosecution and Other Stories* 1948 (US)

### 'Sing a Song of Sixpence' was reprinted in

- *A Century of Detective Stories*, Hutchinson 1935 (UK); SPOILER ALERT: G. K. Chesterton's introduction to 'Sing a Song of Sixpence' gives away the solution to *The Murder of Roger Ackroyd*
- *Ellery Queen's Mystery Magazine*, February 1947 (US) [Reprinted 1976]
- *Ellery Queen's Mystery Magazine*, August 1955 (UK)
- *Ellery Queen's Mystery Magazine*, October 1955 (AUS)
- *Ellery Queen's Mystery Magazine*, March 1976 (US) [Reprint from 1947]
- *The Mammoth Book of Great Detective Stories*, edited by Herbert Van Thal, Robinson 1995 (UK)

## 'S.O.S.'

After seeking refuge with a family during a storm, a man goes to his room and finds a distress signal scrawled in the dust on his nightstand. But who left it there and why?

**Word Count:** 5,800

### Pre-Publication Appearance
UK – February 1926, *The Grand Magazine*
US – December 1947, *Ellery Queen Mystery Magazine*

### Official Collections
*The Hound of Death and Other Stories* 1933 (UK) / *The Witness for the Prosecution and Other Stories* 1948 (US)

### 'S.O.S.' was reprinted in

- *Hutchinson's Adventure & Mystery Story Magazine*, May 1929 (UK)
- *Best English Detective Stories of 1929*, Horace Liveright, 1930 (US)
- *Christmas Pie*, 2 November 1939 (UK)
- *Evening Citizen*, a Glasgow-based newspaper, 20 – 21 June 1951 (UK)
- *Stories of Horror and Suspense*, edited by Denys Val Baker, William Kimble, 1977 (UK)
- *The Best Crime Stories*, Hamlyn, 1984 (UK)
- *The Best Crime Stories*, Mallard Press, 1990 (US)

## 'The Soul of the Croupier'

Mr Satterthwaite and Mr Quin are holidaying in Monte Carlo when they observe the strange culmination of a love affair between a proud croupier and a haughty countess.

**Word Count:** 5,700

**Pre-Publication Appearance**
UK – January 1927, issue 237 of *The Story-Teller* magazine
US – 13 November 1926, volume 19, number 5 of *Flynn's Weekly*

**Official Collections**
*The Mysterious Mr Quin* 1930 (UK / US)

**'The Soul of the Croupier' was reprinted in**

- *Truth* magazine, 19 and 26 November 1950 (Sydney / AUS)
- *Truth* magazine, 25 March and 1 April 1951 (Brisbane / AUS)
- *Clubman*, August 1955 (UK)

## 'The Strange Case of Sir Arthur Carmichael'

An eminent psychiatrist is summoned to a haunted house where a cat has been killed with prussic acid and an unbalanced man is now behaving like the dead feline.

**Word Count:** 6,900

**Official Collections**
*The Hound of Death and Other Stories* 1933 (UK) / *The Golden Ball and Other Stories* 1971 (US) as 'The Strange Case of Sir Andrew Carmichael'

**'The Strange Case of Sir Arthur Carmichael' was reprinted in**

- *MacKill's Mystery Magazine*, March 1953 (UK)
- *MacKill's Mystery Magazine*, April 1953 (US)
- *Realms of Darkness,* edited by Mary Danby, Octopus Books, 1985 (UK

## 'Strange Jest'

Miss Marple helps a young couple locate the missing fortune left to them by a dead relative.

**Word Count:** 3,900

**Pre-Publication Appearance**
UK – July 1944, volume 107, issue 643 of *The Strand Magazine* as 'A Case of Buried Treasure'
US – 2 November 1941, *This Week*; the magazine was distributed across country as a supplement to all the major Sunday newspapers, including *The Atlanta Constitution* and *Los Angeles Times*, which advertised the story as a forthcoming attraction.

**Official Collections**
*Miss Marple's Final Cases* 1979 (UK) / *Three Blind Mice and Other Stories* 1950 (US)

**'Strange Jest' was reprinted in**

- *The Star Weekly*, 13 June 1942 (CAN) as 'The Hidden Treasure Jest'
- *Ellery Queen's Mystery Magazine*, September 1946 (US)
- *Ellery Queen's Mystery Magazine*, December 1974 (US)
- *Woman's Day* magazine, 17 September 1979 (AUS)

## 'The Stymphalean Birds' – the sixth labour

A British politician finds himself being blackmailed while on holiday.

**Word Count:** 6,100

**Pre-Publication Appearance**
UK – April 1940, volume 98, issue 592 of *The Strand Magazine* as 'Birds of Ill-Omen', illustrated by Ernest Ratcliff
US – 17 September 1939, *This Week* as 'The Vulture Women'

**Official Collections**
*The Labours of Hercules* 1947 (UK / US)

**'The Stymphalean Birds' was reprinted in**

- *The Australian Women's Weekly*, 31 January 1942 (AUS) as 'Birds of Ill Omen'
- *Ellery Queen's Mystery Magazine*, September 1945 (US) cited as 'The Vulture Women' on the cover and 'The Case of the Vulture Women' on the contents page
- *Ellery Queen's Mystery Magazine, Overseas Edition for the Armed Forces*, September 1945 (US)
- *Parade: The Middle East Weekly*, 6 December 1947 (Cairo, Egypt)
- *Creasey Mystery Magazine*, February 1956 (UK)

## 'The Submarine Plans'

Hercule Poirot investigates the theft of the plans for a new submarine prototype.

**Word Count:** 4,800

[This story was later expanded into 'The Incredible Theft' from *Murder in the Mews: 4 Poirot Stories* 1937 (UK).]

**Pre-Publication Appearance**
UK – 7 November 1923, issue 1606 of *The Sketch*
US – July 1925, volume 41, number 3 of *The Blue Book Magazine*

**Official Collections**
*Poirot's Early Cases* 1974 (UK) / *The Under Dog and Other Stories* 1951 (US)

### 'The Submarine Plans' was reprinted in

- *Ellery Queen's Mystery Magazine*, August 1955 (US) as 'Shadow in the Night'
- *The Penguin Classic Crime Omnibus*, Penguin Books, 1984 (UK)
- *Masterpieces of Mystery and Suspense,* compiled by Martin H. Greenberg, Doubleday, 1988 (US)

## 'The Sunningdale Mystery'

Tommy and Tuppence Beresford investigate a fatal stabbing on a golf course.

**Word Count:** 4,700

**Pre-Publication Appearance**
UK – 29 October 1924, issue 1657 of *The Sketch*, as 'The Sunninghall Mystery'

**Official Collections**
*Partners in Crime* 1929 (UK / US)

## 'The Sunningdale Mystery' was reprinted in

- *Hutchinson's Adventure & Mystery Story Magazine*, March 1928 (UK) as 'Tommy and Tuppence: 2. The Sunninghall Mystery'
- December 1928, *Holly Leaves*, the annual Christmas special of the *Illustrated Sporting and Dramatic News*
- *The Daily Boston Globe,* 23 August 1931 (US)

## 'Swan Song'

A performance of *Tosca* turns to tragedy when the baritone playing Scarpia is stabbed to death during the last act.

**Word Count:** 4,800

**Pre-Publication Appearance**
UK – September 1926, *The Grand Magazine*

**Official Collections**
*The Listerdale Mystery* 1934 (UK) / *The Golden Ball and Other Stories* 1971 (US)

### 'Swan Song' was reprinted in

- *Home Journal,* 24 August 1935 (UK) as 'At Last – We Meet!'
- *Murder to Music: Musical Mysteries from Ellery Queen's Mystery Magazine and Alfred Hitchcock Mystery Magazine*, Carroll & Graf, July 1997 (US)
- *Murder at the Opera,* edited by Thomas Godfrey, Mysterious Press, 1989 (US)
- *The Methuen Book of Theatrical Short Stories,* edited by Sheridan Morley, Methuen, 1992 (UK)

- *Murder to Music,* edited by Cynthia Manson and Kathleen Halligan, Berkley Prime Crime, 1998 (US)

## 'The Tape-Measure Murder'

Miss Marple suspects the clue to the murder of Mrs Spenlow lies in a crime committed long ago.

**Word Count:** 4,700

**Pre-Publication Appearance**
UK – February 1942, volume 102, issue 614 of *The Strand Magazine* as 'The Case of the Retired Jeweller'
US – 16 November 1941, *This Week*, illustrated by Arthur Sarnoff

**Official Collections**
*Miss Marple's Final Cases* 1979 (UK) / *Three Blind Mice and Other Stories* 1950 (US)

**'The Tape-Measure Murder' was reprinted in**

- *The Female of the Species: The Great Women Detectives and Criminals,* edited by Ellery Queen, Little Brown, 1943 (US) as 'Village Murder'; the dust jacket of a Blue Ribbon edition of the book cites the title as *The Great Women Detectives and Criminals: The Female of the Species,* 1946 (US)
- *The Fifth Mystery Book,* Farrar and Rhinehart, 1944 (US)
- *Avon Detective Mysteries*, number 1, March 1947 (US)
- *Ellery Queen's Mystery Magazine*, January 1973 (US) as 'Village Murder'
- *Woman's Day* magazine, 24 September 1979 (AUS)
- *Crime Stories from the Strand,* edited by Geraldine Beare, Folio Society, 1991 (UK) as 'The Case of the Retired Jeweller'
- *Deadlier: 100 of the Best Crime Stories Written by Women,* selected and introduced by Sophie Hannah, Head of Zeus, 2017 (UK)

## 'The Third-Floor Flat'

Hercule Poirot is called upon to solve the murder of a woman residing in his apartment block.

**Word Count:** 6,000

**Pre-Publication Appearance**
UK – January 1929, volume 21, number 1 of *Hutchinson's Story Magazine*
US – 5 January 1929, volume 106, number 6 of *Detective Story Magazine* as 'In the Third Floor Flat'

**Official Collections**
*Poirot's Early Cases* 1974 (UK) / *Three Blind Mice and Other Stories* 1950 (US)

#### 'The Third Floor Flat' was reprinted in

- *Best English Detective Stories of 1929,* Horace Liveright, 1930 (US)
- *Ellery Queen's Mystery Magazine*, July 1942 (US)
- *Fourteen Great Detective Stories,* edited by Howard Haycraft, Modern Library, 1949 (US)
- *Suspense*, December 1958 (UK)
- *Alle Kvinner,* a Norwegian magazine, 20 December 1974 as 'Leiligheten i fjerde etasje' ('The Apartment on the Third Floor')
- *Ellery Queen's Mystery Magazine*, March 1975 (US)
- *Great Short Tales of Mystery and Terror,* Reader's Digest, 1982 (US)
- *Mystery,* Houghton Mifflin, 1989 (US)

## 'Three Blind Mice' (aka 'The Mousetrap')

The inhabitants of Monkswell Manor guest house are trapped by a blizzard and a raging psychopath.

**Word Count:** 21,000

#### Pre-Publication Appearance
UK – 31 December 1948 to 21 January 1949, four weekly instalments of *Woman's Own* magazine
US – May 1948, volume 124, number 5 of *Cosmopolitan* magazine

#### Official Collections

## *Three Blind Mice and Other Stories* 1950 (US only)

[Agatha Christie did not allow this story to be published in a UK collection during her lifetime because she did not want the public to be discouraged from seeing her West End play *The Mousetrap* and to this day her estate has respected her wishes.]

#### 'Three Blind Mice' was reprinted in

- *The Witness for the Prosecution and Three Blind Mice*, Detective Book Club, an imprint of Walter J. Black, December 1948 (US)
- *The Australian Women's Weekly*, 4 June to 25 June 1949 (AUS) illustrated by Des Gordon
- *Reader's Digest Condensed Books,* volume 59 Autumn, 1964 (US)

## 'The Thumb Mark of St. Peter'

Miss Marple sets out to clear her niece's name after she is suspected of murdering her husband.

**Word Count:** 4,700

**Pre-Publication Appearance**
UK – May 1928, issue 355 of *The Royal Magazine*
US – 7 July 1928, volume 102, number 4 of *Detective Story Magazine*

**Official Collections**
*The Thirteen Problems* 1932 (UK) / *The Tuesday Club Murders* 1933 (US)

**'The Thumb Mark of St Peter' was reprinted**

- *Hush*, February 1931 (UK)
- *The Big Book of Detective Stories,* William Clowes, 1930 (UK)
- *The Saint Mystery Magazine*, January 1964 (UK)
- *Ellery Queen Mystery Magazine*, June 1967 (US) as 'Ask and You Shall Receive'

[Not to be confused with 'The Clergyman's Daughter' and 'The Red House', parts 1 and 2 of the same story from the 1929 collection *Partners in Crime*, which appeared as 'Ask, and Ye Shall Receive' in *Ellery Queen's Mystery Magazine* in 1960.]

## 'The Tragedy at Marsdon Manor'

An insurance company hires Poirot to investigate the death of a man after he falls victim to a fatal cerebral haemorrhage.

**Word count:** 4,500

**Pre-Publication Appearance**
UK – 18 April 1923, issue 1577 of *The Sketch*
US – March 1924, volume 38, number 5 of *The Blue Book Magazine* as 'The Marsdon Manor Tragedy'

**Official Collections**
*Poirot Investigates* 1924 (UK) 1925 (US)

**'The Tragedy at Marsdon Manor' was reprinted in**

- *Modern Stories,* November 1934 (UK)
- *The World's Greatest Detective Stories,* Syndicate Pub. Co., 1934 (UK)
- *Short Story Magazine,* November 1946 (AUS)
- *Armchair Detective Reader,* editor Ernest Dudley, Boardman, 1948 (UK)
- *Ellery Queen's Mystery Magazine,* September 1964 (US) as 'Hercule Poirot, Insurance Investigator'
- *Suspense,* April 1959 (UK) as 'The Mystery at Marsdon Manor'

## 'Triangle at Rhodes'

Hercule Poirot is holidaying in Greece when he observes the formation of a romantic triangle that culminates in murder.

**Word Count:** 8,000

## Pre-Publication Appearance

UK – May 1936, volume 91, number 545 of *The Strand Magazine* as 'Poirot and the Triangle at Rhodes', illustrated by Jack M. Faulks

US – 2 February 1936, *This Week*, illustrated by Stanley Parkhouse; the magazine was syndicated across the country to all the major Sunday newspapers, including *The Baltimore Sun, The Cincinnati Enquirer, The Indianapolis Star* and *The Pittsburgh Press*, all of which advertised the story as a forthcoming attraction.

## Official Collections

*Murder in the Mews: 4 Poirot Cases* 1937 (UK) / *Dead Man's Mirror* 1937 (US)
Following Agatha Christie's centenary in 1990, the title of the US collection was changed to *Murder in the Mews* for avoidance of confusion.

## 'Triangle at Rhodes' was reprinted in

- *Glasgow Evening News*, 15 – 21 February 1940
- *MacKill's Mystery Magazine,* December 1952 (UK)
- *MacKill's Mystery Magazine,* December 1952 (US)
- *Ellery Queen's Mystery Magazine,* December 1956 (US) as 'Before It's Too Late'
- *Ellery Queen's Mystery Magazine,* December 1956 (UK) as 'Before It's Too Late'
- *Ellery Queen's Mystery Magazine,* February 1957 (AUS) as 'Before It's Too Late'
- *Suspense,* August 1958 (UK) as 'Double Alibi'
- *Berlingske Tidende*, a Danish-language daily newspaper based in Copenhagen, Denmark, 23 – 29 September 1973
- *Crime Stories from the Strand,* edited by Geraldine Beare, Folio Society, 1991 (UK) as *Poirot and the Triangle at Rhodes*

# 'The Tuesday Night Club'

Miss Marple solves the riddle of how a woman was poisoned to death after eating the same meal as her companions.

**Word Count:** 4,200

## Pre-Publication Appearance

UK – December 1927, issue 350 of *The Royal Magazine*; this issue features the first ever illustration of Miss Marple rendered by Gilbert Wilkinson

US – 2 June 1928, volume 101, number 5 of *Detective Story Magazine* as 'The Solving Six'

## Official Collections

*The Thirteen Problems* 1932 (UK) / *The Tuesday Club Murders* 1933 (US)

## 'The Tuesday Night Club' was reprinted in

- *The Best Detective Stories of the Year 1928*, edited by Ronald Knox and H. Harrington, Faber and Faber, 1929 (UK) aka *The Best English Detective Stories of 1928,* edited Horace Liveright, Faber and Faber, 1929 (US)

- *The Big Book of Detective Stories,* William Clowes, 1930 (UK)
- *Great Detective,* September 1933 (US) as 'The Tuesday Night Murders'
- *Creasey Mystery Magazine,* December 1957 (UK)
- *Creasey Mystery Magazine,* April 1958 (AUS)
- *Ellery Queen's Mystery Magazine,* June 1970 (US)
- *Alle Kvinner,* a Norwegian magazine, 19 March 1974 as *Tirsdagsklubben* ('The Tuesday Club')
- *Popular Fiction: An Anthology,* edited by Gary Hoppenstand, Addison-Wesley, January 1998 (US)

## 'The Unbreakable Alibi'

Tommy and Tuppence Beresford are hired to investigate reports that a woman was seen in two places at the same time.

**Word Count:** 5,600

**Pre-Publication Appearance**
UK – December 1928, *Holly Leaves,* the annual Christmas special of the *Illustrated Sporting and Dramatic News*

**Official Collections**
*Partners in Crime* 1929 (UK / US)

**'The Unbreakable Alibi' was reprinted in**

- *Tit-Bits,* 14 December 1929 (UK) as 'Alibi'
- *The Daily Boston Globe,* 1 November 1931 (US)
- *The 40 Story Book,* 1938 (UK)
- *Ellery Queen's Mystery Magazine,* January 1971 (US)

## 'The Under Dog'

Hercule Poirot rises to the challenge of identifying the killer of Sir Reuben Astwell after he is bludgeoned to death.

**Word Count:** 20,000

**Pre-Publication Appearance**
UK – October 1926, *The London Magazine*
US – 1 April 1926, volume 8, number 6 of *The Mystery Magazine*

**Official Collections**
*The Adventure of the Christmas Pudding and a Selection of Entrees* 1960 (UK) / *The Under Dog and Other Stories* 1951 (US)

## 'The Under Dog' was reprinted in

- *2 New Crime Stories*, also featuring 'Blackman's Wood' by E. Phillips Oppenheim, Readers' Library, an imprint of the London *Daily Express* newspaper, September 1929 (UK)
- *2 Thrillers*, also featuring 'Blackman's Wood' by E. Phillips Oppenheim, London *Daily Express* Fiction Library, 1936 (UK)
- *Ellery Queen's Mystery Magazine*, as a two-parter, May and June 1951 (US)
- *Star Weekly Complete Novel,* a Saturday magazine supplement to *The Toronto Star* newspaper, as a weekly five-parter, 10 November to 8 December 1951 (CAN)
- *MacKill's Mystery Magazine*, January 1953 (UK)
- *MacKill's Mystery Magazine*, January 1953 (US)
- *Woman's Mirror* magazine, 12, 19 and 26 November 1960 (UK)
- *Woman's Day* magazine, 5, 12 and 19 June 1961 (AUS)

## 'The Veiled Lady'

A distraught woman hires Poirot to rescue her from a blackmailer.

**Word Count:** 3,400

**Pre-Publication Appearance**
UK – 3 October 1923, issue 1601 *The Sketch* as 'The Case of the Veiled Lady'
US – March 1925, volume 40, number 5 of *The Blue Book Magazine*

**Official Collections**
*Poirot's Early Cases* 1974 (UK) / *Poirot Investigates* 1925 (US edition only)

### 'The Veiled Lady' was reprinted in

- *The Hospital Centenary Gift Book*, edited by Robert Ollenershaw, George G. Harrap and Company, 1935 (UK)
- *Evening Standard*, 2 December 1935 (UK)
- *The Star Weekly*, 25 September 1937 (CAN) issue omitted to print the first half of the story
- *The Evening Standard Second Book of Strange Stories*, Hutchinson, 1937 (UK)
- *The Veiled Lady*, Polybooks, 1944 (UK)
- *Poirot Lends a Hand*, Polybooks, 1946 (UK).
- *Nero Wolfe Magazine,* January 1954 (US)
- *12 Detective Stories,* edited by Grant Huffman, McCelland and Stewart, 1965 (CAN)
- *Spellbinders in Suspense,* edited Alfred Hitchcock, Random House, 1967 (US) as 'The Chinese Puzzle Box'
- *Spy and Mystery Stories,* edited by Kenneth Allen, Octopus Books, 1978 (UK)

## 'The Voice in the Dark'

Mr Satterthwaite and Mr Quin investigate the death of a woman who drowns in her bath after her daughter receives a mysterious message.

**Word Count:** 5,800

### Pre-Publication Appearance
UK – March 1927, issue 239 of *The Story-Teller* magazine
US – 4 December 1926, volume 20, number 1 of *Flynn's Weekly*

### Official Collections
*The Mysterious Mr Quin* 1930 (UK / US)

### 'The Voice in the Dark' was reprinted in

- *Truth* magazine, 2 October 1949 (Sydney / AUS)

## 'Wasps' Nest'

Hercule Poirot warns a man caught up in a love triangle that someone is planning to kill him.

**Word Count:** 3,800

### Pre-Publication Appearance
UK – 20 November 1928, *Daily Mail* as 'The Wasps' Nest'
US – 9 March 1929, volume 108, number 3 of *Detective Story Magazine* as 'Worst of All'

### Official Collections
*Poirot's Early Cases* 1974 (UK) / *Double Sin and Other Stories* 1961 (US)

### 'Wasps' Nest' was reprinted in

- *Evening News*, 3 – 5 July 1929 (Sydney / AUS) as 'The Wasps' Nest'
- *Mata Matters* (Malaysian Police Force magazine) 1937
- *Ellery Queen's Mystery Magazine*, March 1974 (US)
- *The Australian Women's Weekly*, 25 December 1974 (AUS)

## 'While the Light Lasts'

A widow is travelling through Rhodesia with her second husband when she is shocked to discover her first husband is still alive.

**Word Count:** 3,000

### Pre-Publication Appearance
UK – April 1924, issue 229 of *The Novel Magazine*, illustrated by Howard K. Elcock

**Official Collections**
*While the Light Lasts and Other Stories* 1997 (UK) / *The Harlequin Tea Set and Other Stories* 1997 (US)

## 'The Wife of the Kenite'

An officer fleeing from the Rand Rebellion discovers old sins cast long shadows.

**Word Count:** 2,400

**Pre-Publication Appearance**
AUS – *The Home: An Australian Quarterly*, volume 3, issue 3, 1 September 1922

**Official Collection**
This is one of the few Christie stories to date that is not included in a volume of her stories.

**Reprinted in**

- *Bodies from the Library,* selected and edited by Tony Medawar, Collins Crime Club, 2018 (UK)
- *The Last Séance: Tales of the Supernatural* by Agatha Christie HarperCollins 2019 (UK) William Morrow (US) [A one-off collection featured stories that have appeared in previous collections.]

## 'Wireless'

A widow hears the voice of her dead husband speaking to her over the wireless – with terrifying consequences.

**Word Count:** 4,900

**Pre-Publication Appearance**
UK – *Sunday Chronicle Annual* 1926
There is a mistaken belief amongst some commentators that 'Wireless' appeared in the *Sunday Chronicle Annual 1925*, but the actual year '1926' appears on the magazine's cover in bold type. The magazine has no official publisher's copyright date, but the back page bears the stamp of the British Library and the date '19 December 1925', which is when the magazine was recorded in their catalogue system. This would indicate the magazine was published in late 1925 by Allied Newspapers for distribution in early 1926.
US – 1 March 1926, volume 8, number 4 of *Mystery Magazine*

**Official Collections**
*The Hound of Death and Other Stories* 1933 (UK) / *The Witness for the Prosecution and Other Stories* as 'Where There's a Will' 1948 (US)

## 'Wireless' was reprinted in

- *The Grand Magazine*, June 1936 (UK)
- *The Australian Women's Weekly*, 5 December 1936 (AUS)
- *Detection Medley* (a series of short stories and articles by members of The Detection Club) Hutchinson, 1939 (UK)
- *The Central Queensland Herald*, 7 December 1939 (AUS)
- *Lancashire Daily Post,* Christmas Supplement 1939 (UK)
- *The Evesham Standard and West Midland Observer,* 23 December 1939 (UK)
- *Wireless Weekly,* 26 July 1941 (AUS)
- *The Avon Book of Modern Crime Stories*, edited by John Rhode, Avon Books, New York, 1942 (US)
- *Ellery Queen's Mystery Magazine,* August 1947 (US) as 'Where There's a Will' [Not to be confused with 'The Case of the Missing Will' from the 1924 UK collection *Poirot Investigates;* this story was also retitled 'Where There's a Will' when it was published in the UK by *Suspense* magazine in February 1959.]
- *Libelle*, a women's magazine published in Amsterdam, Netherlands, in the Dutch language, number 23, 7 June 1974 as 'De stem uit de radio' ('The Voice from the Radio')
- *Woman* magazine, 11 August 1973 (UK) as 'Where There's a Will' [The same issue also featured the first instalment of *The Burden* by Mary Westmacott.]
- *The Best Crime Stories,* Hamlyn, 1984 (UK)

## 'Within a Wall'

A painter is unaware he has a financial benefactor until a friend of the family dies.

**Word Count:** 5,800

**Pre-Publication Appearance**
UK – October 1925, issue 324 of *The Royal Magazine*, illustrated by Albert Bailey

**Official Collections**
*While the Light Lasts and Other Stories* 1997 (UK) / *The Harlequin Tea Set and Other Stories* 1997 (US)

## 'The Witness for the Prosecution'

A barrister finds defending a credulous young man in a murder trial the biggest challenge of his professional life.

**Word Count:** 7,500

**Pre-Publication Appearance**
US – 31 January 1925, volume IV, no 2 of *Flynn's Weekly* as 'Traitor Hands'

## Official Collections
*The Hound of Death and Other Stories* 1933 (UK) / *The Witness for the Prosecution and Other Stories* 1948 (US)

### 'The Witness for the Prosecution' was reprinted in

- *Morning Bulletin*, 24 December 1936 (Rockhampton / AUS)
- *Yorkshire Evening News,* Christmas 1936 (UK)
- *The Great Book of Thrillers*, edited Henry Douglas Thomson, Odhams Press, 1935 (UK)
- *Toronto Star Weekly*, 2 October 1937 (CAN)
- *Summer Pie*, 28 June 1939 (UK)
- *The Mail Magazine*, 23 November 1940 (Adelaide / AUS)
- *Ellery Queen's Mystery Magazine,* January 1944 (US)
- *Argosy*, June 1949, (UK) as 'Witness for the Prosecution'
- *MacKill's Mystery Magazine*, June 1953 (UK)
- *MacKill's Mystery Magazine*, July 1953 (US)
- An expanded version of 'Witness for the Prosecution', ghost-written by Peter Saunders (who produced Agatha Christie's record-breaking play *The Mousetrap*), was serialized in five instalments in the UK in the *Daily Express* from 6 – 10 February 1956, illustrated by Robb. The newspaper claimed each instalment was written 'by Agatha Christie' but the tell-tale words alluding to its real author 'SPECIAL (DAILY EXPRESS) ADAPTATION BY PETER SAUNDERS' appeared with each instalment. Peter Saunders' reason for writing an expanded version of the short story was to encourage Agatha Christie to adapt it into a play. His ploy worked and *Witness for the Prosecution* has since become one of the most famous courtroom dramas ever written for the stage.
- *Ten Great Mysteries: 2 Full-Length Novels: 3 Novelettes; 5 Short Stories*, edited by Howard Haycraft and John Beecroft, Doubleday, 1959 (US)
- *30 Stories to Remember,* edited by Thomas B. Costain and John Beecroft, Doubleday, 1962 (US)
- *The Fifth Mystery Bedside Book*, edited by John Creasey, Hodder and Stoughton, 1964 (UK)
- *Favorite Trial Stories,* edited by AK Adams, Dodd Mead, 1966 (US)
- *Short Story 17,* Aldine Modern English series, edited by Richard Lunn, J.M. Dent and Sons, 1966 (CAN)
- *Fiction 50: An Introduction to the Short Story*, edited by James H. Pickering, Prentice Hall, September 1992 (US)
- *Law and Order: Stories from Ellery Queen's Mystery Magazine and Alfred Hitchcock Mystery Magazine,* edited by Cynthia Manson, Berkley Prime Crime, 1997 (US)
- *Trial and Error: An Oxford Anthology of Legal Stories,* edited by Fred R. Shapiro and Jane Garry, Oxford University Press, Inc., 1998 (US)
- *Fiction 100: An Anthology of Short Stories, Vol. 8,* edited by James H. Pickering, Prentice Hall, 2001 (US)

## 'The World's End'

An encounter with an actress in Corsica enables Mr Satterthwaite and Mr Quin to resolve a terrible wrong.

**Word Count:** 6,400

### Pre-Publication Appearance
UK – February 1927, issue 238 of *The Story-Teller* magazine
US – 20 November 1926, volume 19, number 6 of *Flynn's Weekly*

### Official Collections
*The Mysterious Mr Quin* 1930 (UK / US)

### 'The World's End' was reprinted in

- *Truth* magazine, 16 and 23 September 1951 (Sydney / AUS)

## 'Yellow Iris'

An anonymous phone call summons Poirot to a restaurant where he finds a memorial dinner in progress for a woman who died a year ago.

**Word Count:** 4,200
[The story was expanded into the 1945 novel *Sparkling Cyanide* in which Hercule Poirot is replaced by Colonel Race.]

### Pre-Publication Appearance
UK – July 1937, volume 93, issue 559 of *The Strand Magazine*
US – 25 July 1937, *Chicago Tribune*
Canada – 24 July 1937, *Toronto Star Weekly*, as 'The Yellow Iris'

### Official Collections
*Problem at Pollensa Bay and Other Stories* 1991 (UK) / *The Regatta Mystery and Other Stories* 1939 (US)

### 'Yellow Iris' was reprinted in

- *The Winnipeg Evening Tribune*, 24 July 1937 (CAN)
- *The Hartford Courant* newspaper, 10 October 1937 (US) as *Poirot Wins Again!*
- *Ellery Queen's Mystery Magazine*, December 1966 (US) as 'Hercule Poirot and the Sixth Chair'
- *London After Midnight,* edited by Peter Haining, Barnes and Noble, 1996 (US)
- *London After Midnight: A Conducted Tour,* Royal National Institute of the Blind, 2002 (UK)

# The Official Short Story Collections

## 1924 (UK) – *Poirot Investigates* / 1925 (US)

**Working Title:** *The Grey Cells of M. Poirot* (as cited in Agatha Christie's contract with The Bodley Head and her autobiography)

Following his success in solving *The Mysterious Affair of Styles*, Hercule Poirot sets himself up in business as a private detective. By employing his famous little grey cells, he instils fear in the criminal fraternity and dazzles English society by solving a variety of crimes that establish him as the nation's favourite sleuth.

**Publication:** *Poirot Investigates* (featuring eleven stories) was published in hardback in the UK by The Bodley Head on 21 March 1924 and in the US (featuring fourteen stories) by Dodd, Mead and Company on 18 April 1925. Scholars frequently assume the US edition was published in 1924, but the year of publication, 1925, is stated unequivocally on the title page of the collection and the date is confirmed by the Library of Congress' *Catalog of Copyright Entries*.

**Length:** UK 319pp. / US 282pp.

**Price:** UK 7s.6d / US $2.00

**Word Count:** (UK) 49,000 (US) 65,000

**Trivia:** Various biographers and others, claiming exclusive access to archival material over the years, have stated that the contract Agatha Christie signed with John Lane of The Bodley Head on Thursday, 1 January 1920 was for a total of six books. This is factually incorrect; it was only for five full-length novels. Owing to the success of the Poirot stories in *The Sketch* magazine, Agatha Christie signed a one-off contract with The Bodley Head on 19 November 1923 for a collection of short stories to be published entitled *The Grey Cells of Monsieur Poirot*. Prior to publication, this was changed to Agatha Christie's preferred title of *Poirot Investigates*.

### Stories in the volume and pre-publication appearance

'The Adventure of the Western Star'
UK – 11 April 1923, issue 1576 of *The Sketch*
US – February 1924, volume 38, number 4 of *The Blue Book Magazine* as 'The Western Star'

'The Tragedy at Marsdon Manor'
UK – 18 April 1923, issue 1577 of *The Sketch*
US – March 1924, volume 38, number 5 of *The Blue Book Magazine* as 'The Marsden Manor Tragedy'

'The Adventure of the Cheap Flat'
UK – 9 May 1923, in issue 1580 of *The Sketch*
US – May 1924, volume 39, number 1 of *The Blue Book Magazine*

'The Mystery of Hunter's Lodge'
UK – 16 May 1923, issue 1581 of *The Sketch*
US – June 1924, volume 39, number 2 of *The Blue Book Magazine* as 'The Hunter's Lodge Case'

'The Million Dollar Bond Robbery'
UK – 2 May 1923, issue 1597 of *The Sketch*
US – April 1924, volume 38, number 6 of *The Blue Book Magazine* as 'The Great Bond Robbery'

'The Adventure of the Egyptian Tomb'
UK – 26 September 1923, issue 1600 of *The Sketch*
US – August 1924, volume 39, number 4 of *The Blue Book Magazine* as 'The Egyptian Adventure'

'The Jewel Robbery at the Grand Metropolitan'
UK – 14 March 1923, issue 1572 of *The Sketch* as 'The Curious Disappearance of the Opalsen Pearls'
US – October 1923, volume 37, number 6 of *The Blue Book Magazine* as 'Mrs Opalsen's Pearls'

'The Kidnapped Prime Minister'
UK – 25 April 1923, issue 1578 of *The Sketch*
US – July 1924, volume 39, number 3 of *The Blue Book Magazine* as 'The Kidnapped Premier' (the title of Prime Minister was used throughout the story)

'The Disappearance of Mr Davenheim'
UK – 28 March 1923, issue 1574 of *The Sketch*
US – December 1923, volume 38, number 2 of *The Blue Book Magazine* as 'Mr Davenby Disappears'

'The Adventure of the Italian Nobleman'
UK – 24 October 1923, issue 1604 of *The Sketch*
US – December 1924, volume 40, number 2 of *The Blue Book Magazine* as 'The Italian Nobleman'

'The Case of the Missing Will'
UK – 31 October 1923, issue 1605 of *The Sketch*
US – January 1925, volume 40, number 3 of *The Blue Book Magazine* as 'The Missing Will'

'The Veiled Lady' (not included in the UK version)
US – March 1925, volume 40, number 5 of *The Blue Book Magazine*

'The Lost Mine' (not included in the UK version)
US – April 1925, volume 40, number 6 of *The Blue Book Magazine*

'The Chocolate Box' (not included in the UK version)
US – February 1925, volume 40, number 4 of *The Blue Book Magazine*

# 1929 – *Partners in Crime*

Tommy and Tuppence Beresford are persuaded by British Intelligence to go under cover as Blunt's Brilliant Detectives to expose a dangerous criminal known only as Number Sixteen. The couple investigate baffling cases and pay homage to some of the most famous fictional detectives of the day before catching Number Sixteen in the ultimate *coup d'état*.

**Publication:** *Partners in Crime* was published in hardback in the UK by William Collins & Sons on 16 September 1929 and in the US by Dodd, Mead and Company on 16 August 1929.

## First true publication in volume form

The seven stories that comprise Chapters Eleven to Twenty-Two of *Partners in Crime* were published in paperback by Collins seven months earlier in February 1929 under the title *The Sunningdale Mystery* – see 'Short-Lived Collections'

**Length:** UK 251pp. / US 277pp.

**Price:** UK 7s.6d / US $2.00

**Word Count:** 69,000

## Stories in the volume and pre-publication appearance

Those stories appearing in *The Sketch* magazine were published under the umbrella title of ***Tommy and Tuppence: A Detective Series***

1 'A Fairy in the Flat'

and

2 'A Pot of Tea'
UK – 24 September 1924, issue 1652 of *The Sketch* as one story 'Publicity'

———————— Secrets from the Agatha Christie Archives ————————

3 'The Affair of the Pink Pearl'

4 'The Affair of the Pink Pearl' *(continued)*
UK – 1 October 1924, issue 1653 of *The Sketch*
Tommy uses a camera to emulate the technique of Dr Thorndyke, created by R. Austin Freeman (1862–1943).

5 'The Adventure of the Sinister Stranger'

6 'The Adventure of the Sinister Stranger' *(continued)*
UK – 22 October 1924, in issue 1656 of *The Sketch* as 'The Case of the Sinister Stranger'
The Beresfords adopt the methods of Francis and Desmond Okewood, created by Valentine Williams (1883–1946).

7 'Finessing the King'

and

8 'The Gentleman Dressed in Newspaper'
UK – 8 October 1924, issue 1654 of *The Sketch* as one story 'Finessing the King'
The couple spoof the detective duo of ex-policeman Tommy McCarty and fireman Denis Riordan, created by Isabel Ostrander (1885–1924).

9 'The Case of the Missing Lady'
UK – 15 October 1924, issue 1655 of *The Sketch*
Tommy and Tuppence reference Sherlock Holmes and Dr Watson with their investigation which features a direct parallel to the story 'The Disappearance of Lady Frances Carfax', created by Sir Arthur Conan Doyle (1859–1930).

10 'Blind Man's Buff'
UK – 26 November 1924, issue 1661 of *The Sketch*
Tommy pretends to be Thornley Colton, the blind problemist, created by Clinton Holland Stagg (1890–1916) who relies on his other senses to solve mysteries with the help of his secretary, who is played by Tuppence.

11 'The Man in the Mist'

12 'The Man in the Mist' *(continued)*
UK – 3 December 1924, issue 1662 of *The Sketch*
Tommy and Tuppence acknowledge Father Brown the Catholic priest, created by G.K. Chesterton (1874–1936).

13 'The Crackler'

14 'The Crackler' *(continued)*
UK – 19 November 1924, issue 1660 of *The Sketch* as 'The Affair of the Forged Notes'
Tommy and Tuppence draw inspiration from the Busies, created by Edgar Wallace (1875–1932).

15 'The Sunningdale Mystery'

16 'The Sunningdale Mystery' *(continued)*
UK – 29 October 1924, issue 1657 of *The Sketch* as 'The Sunninghall Mystery'
 The Beresfords pay their respects to the Old Man in the Corner and his newspaper reporter friend Polly Burton, created by Baroness Emma Orczy (1863–1947).

17 'The House of Lurking Death'

18 'The House of Lurking Death' *(continued)*
UK – 5 November 1924, issue 1658 of *The Sketch*
 Tommy and Tuppence refer to M. Hanard of the French Surete and his sidekick Mr Ricardo, created by A.E. Mason (1865–1948), with Tommy's final line at the end of the story – 'It is a great advantage to be intelligent and not look it' – being a quote from A.E. Mason's 1910 novel *At the Villa Rose.*

19 'The Unbreakable Alibi'
UK – December 1928, *Holly Leaves*, the annual Christmas special of the *Illustrated Sporting and Dramatic News*
 The Beresfords pay homage to Inspector French of Scotland Yard, created by Freeman Wills Croft (1879–1957), who was famous for inventing ingenious alibis based on railway timetables.

20 'The Clergyman's Daughter'

and

21 'The Red House'
UK – December 1923, *The Grand Magazine* as 'The First Wish'
 The Beresfords pattern themselves after Roger Sheringham, created by Anthony Berkeley (1893–1971).

22 'The Ambassador's Boots'
UK – 12 November 1924, issue 1659 of *The Sketch* as 'The Matter of the Ambassador's Boots'
The Beresfords' investigation parodies Dr Reggie Fortune, created by H.C. Bailey (1878–1961).

23 'The Man Who Was No. 16'
UK – 10 December 1924, issue 1663 of *The Sketch*
 Tommy and Tuppence bow to Hercule Poirot and come face to face with their mysterious enemy, Number Sixteen, whose name is a mathematical squaring of *The Big Four*, created by Agatha Christie (1890–1976).

## US Post-Publication Series

Throughout 1931 the stories from *Partners in Crime* appeared at sporadic intervals in **The Daily Boston Globe** newspaper:

- 'A Fairy in the Flat', 12 April 1931
- 'The Affair of the Pink Pearl', 19 April 1931

- 'The Adventure of the Sinister Stranger', 26 April 1931
- 'Finessing the King', 31 May 1931
- 'The Case of the Missing Lady', 28 June 1931
- 'Blind Man's Buff', 12 July 1931
- 'The Man in the Mist', 26 July 1931
- 'The Crackler', 16 August 1931
- 'The Sunningdale Mystery', 23 August 1931
- 'The House of Lurking Death', 20 September 1931
- 'The Clergyman's Daughter', 25 October 1931
- 'The Unbreakable Alibi', 1 November 1931
- 'The Matter of the Ambassador's Boots', 8 November 1931
- 'The Man Who Was No. 16', 22 November 1931

## 1930 – *The Mysterious Mr Quin*

Mr Harley Quin is an enigma who comes and goes like magic. An advocate for the living as well as the dead, he frequently appears when lovers are threatened. His presence acts as a catalyst for the elderly Mr Satterthwaite, who is tired of being an on-looker of life and yearns for romance and adventure. Mr Satterthwaite sees things he would otherwise have overlooked owing to the persuasive influence of Mr Quin. Together, the pair unravel human dilemmas and solve seemingly impenetrable mysteries in which those threatened by misfortune are unable to seek justice for themselves.

**Publication:** *The Mysterious Mr Quin* was published in hardback in the UK by William Collins & Sons on 14 April 1930 and in the US by Dodd, Mead and Company on 25 April 1930.

**Length:** UK 287pp. / US 290pp.

**Price:** UK 7s.6d / US $2.00.

**Word Count:** 79,000

**Trivia:** *Flynn's* (*Weekly*) (*Detective*) (*Fiction*) *Magazine*:
Launched by Frank A. Munsey in September 1924, this magazine was one of the longest running of all the US detective pulps. It notched up 929 issues over twenty-eight years under a variety of names, including *Flynn's, Detective Fiction Weekly, Flynn's Weekly, Flynn's Detective Fiction Magazine* and *Dime Detective Magazine*.

### Quin vs Quinn

The character of Mr Quin appeared with a double 'n' on the end of his surname in the first four stories published in *The Grand Magazine* in 1924; the second 'n' was dropped after this for his appearance in *The Story-Teller* magazine and other writings by Agatha Christie, although it was briefly revived for his appearance in the 1928 silent film *The Passing of Mr Quinn*.

'**At the Crossroads**': This story was the first in a sequence of six stories that appeared at monthly intervals in *The Story-Teller* magazine between December 1926 and May 1927 under the series title of ***The Magic of Mr Quin***. 'At the Crossroads' was not published in *The Mysterious Mr Quin* in 1930 because the central plot device was too similar to the one used in the first full-length Miss Marple book *The Murder at the Vicarage*, which also appeared that year. 'At the Crossroads' was retitled 'The Love Detectives' and eventually published in volume form in the US in *Three Blind Mice and Other Stories* (1950) and in the UK in *Problem at Pollensa Bay and Other Stories* (1991).

## Stories in the volume and pre-publication appearance

'The Coming of Mr. Quin'
UK – March 1924. *The Grand Magazine* as 'The Passing of Mr Quinn'
US – March 1925, volume 82, number 2 of *Munsey* magazine as 'Mr Quinn Passes By'

'The Shadow on the Glass'
UK – October 1924, *The Grand Magazine*

'At the Bells and Motley'
UK – November 1925, *The Grand Magazine* as 'A Man of Magic'
US – 17 July 1926, volume XVI, number 6 of *Flynn's Weekly* as 'A Man of Magic'

'The Sign in the Sky'
UK – July 1925, *The Grand Magazine* as 'A Sign in the Sky'
US – June 1925, *The Police Magazine*

'The Soul of the Croupier'
UK – January 1927, issue 237 of *The Story-Teller* magazine
US – 13 November 1926, volume 91, number 5 of *Flynn's Weekly*

'The Man from the Sea'
UK – October 1929, volume 1, number 6 of *Britannia and Eve* magazine

'The Voice in the Dark'
UK – March 1927, issue 239 of *The Story-Teller* magazine
US – 4 December 1926, volume 20, number 1 of *Flynn's Weekly*

'The Face of Helen'
UK – April 1927, issue 240 of *The Story-Teller* magazine
US – 6 August 1927, *Flynn's Weekly Detective Fiction*

'The Dead Harlequin'
UK – March 1929, *The Grand Magazine*
US – 22 June 1929, volume 42, number 3 of *Detective Fiction Weekly*

'The Bird with the Broken Wing'

'The World's End'
UK – February 1927, issue 238 of *The Story-Teller* magazine
US – 20 November 1926, volume 19, number 6 of *Flynn's Weekly*

'Harlequin's Lane'
UK – May 1927, issue 241 of *The Story-Teller* magazine
US – 27 August 1927, volume 26, number 4 of *Flynn's Weekly Detective Fiction*

## 1932 (UK) – *The Thirteen Problems* / 1933 (US) – *The Tuesday Club Murders*

The novelist Raymond West is fascinated by unsolved mysteries. So, too, is Sir Henry Clithering, former Commissioner of Scotland Yard, Dr Pender the elderly clergyman, Mr Petherick the solicitor and the artist Joyce Lempriere. The latter suggests they meet once a week and propound a series of unsolved mysteries for the other guests to elucidate. What no one anticipates is that Raymond West's elderly aunt Miss Jane Marple will be the only person to arrive at the correct solution to each crime.

**Publication:** *The Thirteen Problems* was published in hardback in the UK by the Collins Crime Club on 6 June 1932 and in the US as *The Tuesday Club Murders* by Dodd, Mead and Company on 24 February 1933. In 1940, Bantam Publications Inc., a Los Angeles-based paperback publisher, not to be confused with Bantam Books, retitled the collection *Mystery of the Blue Geranium and Other Tuesday Club Murders*.

**Length:** UK 250pp. / US 253pp.

**Price:** UK 7s.6d / US $2.00

**Word Count:** 66,000

### First Appearance in a Collection

In the UK, 'The Tuesday Night Club' debuted in the hardback collection *The Best Detective Stories of the Year 1928*, edited by Ronald Knox and H. Harrington (Faber and Faber, 1929); in the US the collection was renamed *The Best English Detective Stories of 1928*, edited by Horace Liveright (Faber and Faber, 1929).

### Stories in the volume and pre-publication appearance

'The Tuesday Night Club'
UK – December 1927, issue 350 of *The Royal Magazine*; this issue features the first ever illustration of Miss Marple rendered by Gilbert Wilkinson.
US – 2 June 1928, volume 101, number 5 of *Detective Story Magazine* as 'The Solving Six'

'The Idol House of Astarte'
UK – January 1928, issue 351 of *The Royal Magazine*
US – 9 June 1928, volume 101, number 6 of *Detective Story Magazine* as 'The Solving Six and the Evil Hour'

'Ingots of Gold'
UK – February 1928, issue 352 of *The Royal Magazine*; this issue features the first ever illustration of Miss Marple's nephew, the novelist Raymond West, by Gilbert Wilkinson.
US – 16 June 1928, volume 102, number 1 of *Detective Story Magazine* as 'The Solving Six and the Golden Grave'

'The Bloodstained Pavement'
UK – March 1928, issue 353 of *The Royal Magazine*
US – 23 June 1928, volume 102, number 2 of *Detective Story Magazine* as 'Drip! Drip!'

'Motive v Opportunity'
UK – April 1928, issue 354 of *The Royal Magazine*
US – 30 June 1928, volume 102, number 3 of *Detective Story Magazine* as 'Where's the Catch?'

'The Thumb Mark of St. Peter'
UK – May 1928, issue 355 of *The Royal Magazine*
US – 7 July 1928, volume 102, number 4 of *Detective Story Magazine*

'The Blue Geranium'
UK – December 1929, volume 46, number 272 of *The Christmas Story-Teller Magazine*
US – February 1930, volume 31, number 5 of *Pictorial Review*, illustrated by De Alton Valentine
   A year after the formation of the Tuesday Night Club, Miss Marple dines at the home of Colonel and Mrs Bantry, where a further series of six problems are propounded by the couple and their guests, including Sir Henry Clithering, elderly Dr Lloyd and the beautiful actress Jane Helier. Once again, the elderly spinster sleuth demonstrates her mental acumen over everyone else by arriving at the truth to each puzzle.

'The Companion'
UK – February 1930, volume 46, number 274 of *The Story-Teller Magazine* as 'The Resurrection of Amy Durrant'
US – March 1930, volume 31, number 6 of *Pictorial Review* as 'Companions', illustrated by De Alton Valentine

'The Four Suspects'
UK – April 1930, issue 276 of *The Story-Teller Magazine*
US – January 1930, volume 31, number 4 of *Pictorial Review* as 'Four Suspects', illustrated by De Alton Valentine

'A Christmas Tragedy'
UK – January 1930, volume 46, number 273 of *The Story-Teller Magazine* as 'The Hat and the Alibi'

'The Herb of Death'
UK – March 1930, issue 275 of *The Story-Teller Magazine*

'The Affair at the Bungalow'
UK – May 1930, volume 46, number 277 of *The Story-Teller Magazine*

'Death by Drowning'
UK – November 1931, volume 88, number 462 *Nash's Pall Mall Magazine*
Miss Marple's final problem takes place in the present against the backdrop of village life in St. Mary Mead.

# 1933 (UK only) – *The Hound of Death and Other Stories*

This chilling collection of twelve stand-alone mysteries is permeated by danger and horror at every turn, from a nun with physic visions…to the ghost of a child in an attic…to a man who assumes the personality of a cat that was poisoned to death with prussic acid…to a medium who pays the ultimatum price for summoning the spirit of the dead. The most famous story in the collection is 'The Witness for the Prosecution', which scored a huge success on the West End stage in 1953 and on Broadway in 1954.

**Publication:** *The Hound of Death* was published in hardback in the UK by Odhams Press on 23 October 1933. The reason it was not published by Collins is because Agatha Christie's literary agent Edmund Cork was negotiating a new contract with them on her behalf. *The Hound of Death* was released by Collins for the first time in February 1936, priced at £ 3s. 6d.

**Length:** 247pp.

**Price:** The Odhams Press' first edition of *The Hound of Death* was not available to buy in shops, but copies could be obtained by collecting coupons from *The Passing Show*, a weekly magazine published by Odhams Press. The coupons appeared in issues 81 to 83 of *The Passing Show*, published from 7– 21 October 1933, as part of the promotional re-launching of the magazine. In exchange for the coupons and 7s., customers could receive six books. The other five titles were *The Veil'd Delight* by Marjorie Bowen, *Jungle Girl* by Edgar Rice Burroughs, *The Sun Will Shine* by May Edginton, *Q33* by George Goodchild, and *The Venner Crime* by John Rhode.

**Word Count:** 66,000

## Stories in the volume and pre-publication appearance

Several of the stories' first true publication was in this collection.

─────────────── The Official Short Story Collections ───────────────

'The Hound of Death'

'The Red Signal'
UK – June 1924, *The Grand Magazine*

'The Fourth Man'
UK – December 1925, *Pearson's Magazine*

'The Gipsy'

'The Lamp'

'Wireless'
UK – *Sunday Chronicle Annual* 1926
There is a mistaken belief amongst some commentators that 'Wireless' appeared in the *Sunday Chronicle Annual 1925*, but the actual year '1926' appears on the magazine's cover in bold type.
US – 1 March 1926, volume 8, number 4 of *Mystery Magazine*

'The Witness for the Prosecution'
US – 31 January 1925, volume 4, no 2 of *Flynn's Weekly* as 'Traitor Hands'

'The Mystery of the Blue Jar'
UK – July 1924, *The Grand Magazine*
US – March 1925, volume 60, number 6 of *Macfadden Fiction-Lovers Magazine*

'The Strange Case of Sir Arthur Carmichael'

'The Call of Wings'

'The Last Séance'
UK – March 1927, issue 87 of *The Sovereign Magazine* as 'The Stolen Ghost'
US – November 1926, volume 1, number 5 of *Ghost Stories* magazine as 'The Woman Who Stole a Ghost'

'S.O.S.'
UK – February 1926, *The Grand Magazine*

## Alternate US Collections

*The Hound of Death and Other Stories* was not published in volume form in America, although the stories from it were later included in three collections.

- ***The Witness for the Prosecution and Other Stories*** (1948) features the title story as well as 'The Fourth Man', 'The Mystery of the Blue Jar', 'The Red Signal', 'S.O.S.', and 'Wireless' under the title of 'Where There's a Will'.
- ***Double Sin and Other Stories*** (1961) features 'The Last Séance'.
- ***The Golden Ball and Other Stories*** (1971) features 'The Hound of Death', 'The Gipsy', 'The Lamp', 'The Strange Case of Sir Arthur Carmichael' under the title of 'The Strange Case of Sir *Andrew* Carmichael' and 'The Call of Wings'.

Secrets from the Agatha Christie Archives

# 1934 (UK only) – *The Listerdale Mystery*

Romance, high spirits and adventure come together in plentiful supply in this collection of intriguing stories: a butler knows more about the disappearance of his employer than he admits; a young couple are faced with the dilemma of keeping stolen rubies or handing them over to the police; a man buys a magnificent car and becomes infatuated by a femme fatale engaged in nefarious activities; and a lowly paid clerk becomes embroiled in the disappearance of a rajah's emerald. On a far darker note, four of the tales feature betrayal and murder in various guises, none more so than 'Philomel Cottage', which became the inspiration for Frank Vosper's successful 1936 stage play 'Love from a Stranger' and a subsequent British movie starring Ann Harding and Basil Rathbone.

**Publication:** *The Listerdale Mystery* and Other Stories was published in hardback in the UK by William Collins & Sons under its Mystery Novel imprint on 11 June 1934.

## First true publication in volume form

'Philomel Cottage' was first published in volume form in *The World's Best 100 Detective Stories*, edited by Eugene Thwing, Funk and Wagnalls, on 24 October 1929.

**Length:** 251pp.

**Price:** 7s.6d

**Word Count:** 64,000

**Trivia:** Owing to the light-hearted nature of the stories, *The Listerdale Mystery* is only one of two Christie collections that appeared under the Collins Mystery Novel imprint. The other is *Parker Pyne Investigates*.

## Stories in the volume and pre-publication appearance

'The Listerdale Mystery'
UK – December 1925, *The Grand Magazine* as 'The Benevolent Butler'

'Philomel Cottage'
UK – November 1924, *The Grand Magazine*

'The Girl in a Train'
UK – February 1924, *The Grand Magazine*

'Sing a Song of Sixpence'
UK – December 1929, *Holly Leaves*, the annual Christmas special of the *Illustrated Sporting and Dramatic News,* illustrated by C. Watson.

'The Manhood of Edward Robinson'
UK – December 1924, *The Grand Magazine* as 'The Day of His Dreams'
US – May 1925, volume one, number one of *Your Car: A Magazine of Romance, Fact and Fiction* as 'Romance and a Red Roundabout'

———————— The Official Short Story Collections ————————

'Accident'
UK – 22 September 1929, *Sunday Dispatch* as 'The Uncrossed Path'

'Jane in Search of a Job'
UK – August 1924, *The Grand Magazine*

'A Fruitful Sunday'
UK – 11 August 1928, *Daily Mail*

'Mr. Eastwood's Adventure'
UK – August 1924, issue 233 of *The Novel Magazine* as 'The Mystery of the Second Cucumber', illustrated by Wilmot Lunt
US – December 1924, volume 60, number 3 of *Macfadden Fiction-Lover's Magazine* as 'The Mystery of the Spanish Shawl'

'The Golden Ball'
UK – 5 August 1929, *Daily Mail* as 'Playing the Innocent', illustrated by Lowtham

'The Rajah's Emerald'
UK – 30 July 1926, issue 420 of *Red Magazine*, illustrated by Jack M. Faulks

'Swan Song'
UK – September 1926, *The Grand Magazine*

## Alternate US Collections

*The Listerdale Mystery and Other Stories* was the second of Agatha Christie's UK collections not to be published in the US, although the stories from it were later included in two American collections:

- *The Witness for the Prosecution and Other Stories* (1948) features 'Philomel Cottage', 'Sing a Song of Sixpence', 'Accident', and 'Mr Eastwood's Adventure' under the title of 'The Mystery of the Spanish Shawl'.
- *The Golden Ball and Other Stories* (1971) features 'The Listerdale Mystery', 'The Girl in the Train', 'The Manhood of Edward Robinson', 'Jane in Search of a Job', 'A Fruitful Sunday', 'The Golden Ball', 'The Rajah's Emerald' and 'Swan Song'.

# 1934 (UK) – *Parker Pyne Investigates* / (US) *Mr Parker Pyne, Detective*

**Working Title:** *The Reminiscences of Parker Pyne* (as cited in Agatha Christie's notebooks)

'ARE YOU HAPPY? IF NOT, CONSULT MR PARKER PYNE, 17 RICHMOND STREET…' The advertisement in *The Times* newspaper intrigues several individuals who make their way to Mr Parker Pyne's consulting rooms in London in the hope of finding a solution to their problems. Whether Mr Parker Pyne is being assisted by his secretary Miss Lemon and the crime writer Mrs Ariadne Oliver, or travelling abroad on his own to such exotic locales as Damascus, Egypt, Teheran, Petra or Greece, he proves himself equally adept at solving mysteries as well as dilemmas of the human heart.

**Publication:** *Parker Pyne Investigates* was published in hardback in the UK by William Collins & Sons under its Mystery Novel imprint on 12 November 1934 and in the US as *Mr Parker Pyne, Detective* by Dodd, Mead and Company on 20 June 1934.

**Length:** UK 248pp. / US 244pp.

**Price:** UK 7s.6d / US $2.00

**Word Count:** 62,000

**Trivia:** This is the second Agatha Christie collection – *The Listerdale Mystery* from 1934 being the first – that appeared under the Collins Mystery Novel imprint because the majority of the stories in the volume feature personal dilemmas and mysteries of the human heart in contrast to the usual style of murder mystery published by the Collins Crime Club. The collection marks the fictional debut of Miss Lemon and Mrs Ariadne Oliver, who go on to have working relationships with Hercule Poirot.

## Stories in the volume and pre-publication appearance

'The Case of the Middle-Aged Wife'
UK – 8 October 1932, issue 613 of *Woman's Pictorial* as 'The Woman Concerned', illustrated by J.A. May

'The Case of the Discontented Soldier'
UK – 15 October 1932, issue 614 of *Woman's Pictorial* as 'Adventure – By Request', illustrated by J.A. May
US – August 1932, issue 554 of *Cosmopolitan* as 'The Soldier Who Wanted Danger' under the series title of *Are You Happy? If Not, Consult Mr Parker Pyne*, illustrated by Marshall Frantz

'The Case of the Distressed Lady'
UK – 22 October 1932, issue 615 of *Woman's Pictorial* as 'Faked!', illustrated by J.A. May
US – August 1932, issue 554 of *Cosmopolitan,* as 'The Pretty Girl Who Wanted a Ring' under the series title of *Are You Happy? If Not, Consult Mr Parker Pyne*, illustrated by Marshall Frantz

'The Case of the Discontented Husband'
UK – 29 October 1932, issue 616 of *Woman's Pictorial* as 'His Lady's Affair', illustrated by J.A. May
US – August 1932, issue 554 of *Cosmopolitan* as 'The Husband Who Wanted to Keep His Wife' under the series title of *Are You Happy? If Not, Consult Mr Parker Pyne*, illustrated by Marshall Frantz

———————— The Official Short Story Collections ————————

'The Case of the City Clerk'
UK – November 1932, volume 84, issue 503 of *The Strand Magazine* as 'The £10 Adventure'
US – August 1932, issue 554 of *Cosmopolitan* as 'The Clerk Who Wanted Excitement' under the series title of *Are You Happy? If Not, Consult Mr Parker Pyne*, illustrated by Marshall Frantz

'The Case of the Rich Woman'
US – August 1932, issue 554 of *Cosmopolitan* as 'The Rich Woman Who Wanted Only To Be Happy' under the series title of *Are You Happy? If Not, Consult Mr Parker Pyne*, illustrated by Marshall Frantz

'Have You Got Everything You Want?'
UK – June 1933, volume 91, issue 481 of *Nash's Pall Mall Magazine* as 'On the Orient Express' under the series title of *The Arabian Nights of Parker Pyne*, featuring Marshall Frantz's illustrations from *Cosmopolitan*
US – April 1933, issue 562 of *Cosmopolitan*; the story was unnamed and appeared under the series title of 'Have You Got Everything You Want? If Not, Consult Mr Parker Pyne', illustrated by Marshall Frantz

'The Gate of Baghdad'
UK – June 1933, volume 91, number 481 of *Nash's Pall Mall Magazine* as 'At the Gate of Baghdad'

'The House at Shiraz'
UK – June 1933, volume 91, number 481 of *Nash's Pall Mall Magazine* as 'In the House at Shiraz', with Marshall Frantz's illustrations from *Cosmopolitan* magazine
US – April 1933, issue number 562 of *Cosmopolitan* under the series title of *Have You Got Everything You Want? If Not, Consult Mr Parker Pyne*, illustrated by Marshall Frantz

'The Pearl of Price'
UK – July 1933, volume 91, issue 482 of *Nash's Pall Mall Magazine* as 'The Pearl' under the series title of *More Arabian Nights of Parker Pyne*

'Death on the Nile' aka 'A Death on the Nile' so as not to be confused with the 1937 novel of the same name
UK – July 1933, volume 91, issue 482 of *Nash's Pall Mall Magazine* under the series title of *More Arabian Nights of Parker Pyne*, featuring Marshall Frantz's illustrations from *Cosmopolitan*
US – April 1933, issue 562 of *Cosmopolitan* under the series title of *Have You Got Everything You Want? If Not, Consult Mr Parker Pyne*, illustrated by Marshall Frantz

'The Oracle at Delphi'
UK – July 1933, volume 91, issue 482 of *Nash's Pall Mall Magazine* under the series title of *More Arabian Nights of Parker Pyne*, featuring Marshall Frantz's illustrations from *Cosmopolitan*

*———— Secrets from the Agatha Christie Archives ————*

US – April 1933, issue 562 of *Cosmopolitan* under the series title of *Have You Got Everything You Want? If Not, Consult Mr Parker Pyne*, illustrated by Marshall Frantz

### Further Parker Pyne Exploits

In addition to the twelve stories in this collection, Parker Pyne features in two other stories that have collections named after them: *The Regatta Mystery and Other Stories* (1939 US) and *Problem at Pollensa Bay and Other Stories* (1991 UK). Ironically, 'The Regatta Mystery' was first published as a Poirot story in *The Strand* magazine in June 1936. Most recent paperback editions of *Parker Pyne Investigates* now also feature 'Problem at Pollensa Bay' and 'The Regatta Mystery', bringing the total of stories in the collection to fourteen.

## 1937 (UK) – *Murder in the Mews: 4 Poirot Stories* / (US) – *Dead Man's Mirror*

Hercule Poirot is at his best in these four-scintillating tales of intrigue and mystery. Whether he is assisting Chief Inspector Japp in 'Murder in the Mews' or gathering information from Mr Satterthwaite in 'Dead Man's Mirror' or taking a lone hand in 'The Incredible Theft' and 'Triangle at Rhodes', his little grey cells engage in a virtuoso display of deductive reasoning that enables him to unmask the guilty party in each case.

**Publication:** *Murder in the Mews: 4 Poirot Stories* was published in hardback in the UK by the Collins Crime Club on 15 March 1937 and in the US as *Dead Man's Mirror* by Dodd, Mead and Company on 22 June 1937.

**Disclaimer:** There is a prevalent belief among some Agatha Christie scholars that Dodd Mead's first edition of *Dead Man's Mirror* featured three stories instead of four, but this is factually incorrect. Dodd Mead's blurb asserts that the collection 'consists of two mystery novelettes and two short stories'. It was customary in the early years of paperback publishing for some publishers, not just Agatha Christie's, to drop one or more of an author's short stories from a collection in order to reduce publishing costs. This may well explain why 'The Incredible Theft' is absent from some early US paperback collections and why some scholars have assumed it was never included in the first edition issued by Dodd, Mead and Company. The current paperback by Harper features all four stories.

**Length:** UK 280pp. / US 290pp.

**Price:** UK 7s.6d / US $2.00

**Word Count:** 63,000

### Stories in the volume and pre-publication appearance

'Murder in the Mews'

UK – December 1936, *Woman's Journal*; this story is an expanded version of 'The Market Basing Mystery' which first appeared in issue 1603 of *The Sketch* on 17 October 1923.

US – September and October 1936, volume 67, numbers 5 and 6, *Redbook* magazine, illustrated by John Fulton.

'The Incredible Theft'
UK – 6, 7, 8, 9, 10 and 12 April 1937, *Daily Express*, illustrated by Steven Spurrier; this story is an expanded version based on 'The Submarine Plans', which first appeared in issue 1606 of *The Sketch* on 7 November 1923.
US – no pre-publication serialization has been traced; the story is an expanded version of 'The Submarine Plans', which appeared in volume 41, number 3 of *The Blue Book Magazine* in July 1925.

'Dead Man's Mirror'
UK – no pre-publication serialization has been traced; the story is an expanded version of 'The Second Gong', which first appeared in volume 66, number 391 of *The Strand Magazine* in July 1923.
US – once again no pre-publication serialization has been traced; the story is an expanded version of 'The Second Gong', which appeared in volume 49, number 6 of *Ladies Home Journal* in June 1932, illustrated by R.J. Prohaska.

'Triangle at Rhodes'
UK – May 1936, volume 91, number 545 of *The Strand Magazine* as 'Poirot and the Triangle at Rhodes', illustrated by Jack M. Faulks
US – 2 February 1936, *This Week*, illustrated by Stanley Parkhouse.

# 1939 (US only) – *The Regatta Mystery and Other Stories*

*The Regatta Mystery and Other Stories* provide ample proof that crime can strike anywhere and anytime. Not to mention in a variety of guises ranging from theft, stabbing, and poisoning. With there being so much wickedness in the world, both at home and abroad, it is just as well that three of Agatha Christie's most beloved detectives Hercule Poirot, Miss Jane Marple and Parker Pyne are around to protect the innocent and bring the perpetrators to account in this captivating collection of mysteries and crimes of the heart.

**Publication:** *The Regatta Mystery and Other Stories* was published in hardback in the US by Dodd, Mead and Company on 20 June 1939. These stories were not absorbed into collections in Britain until many years later and their appearance in this collection constitutes their first true publication in book form.

**Length:** 229pp.

**Price:** $2.00

**Word Count:** 45,000

### Stories in the volume and pre-publication appearance

'The Regatta Mystery' – Parker Pyne version
UK – June 1936, volume 91, issue 546 of *The Strand Magazine* as 'Poirot and the Regatta Mystery'.

US / Canada – 3 May 1936, syndicated as a Hercule Poirot story to the following newspapers: *Sunday News* (New York); *The Laredo Times* (Texas); *The Philadelphia Inquirer* (Pennsylvania); and *The Hartford Courant* (Connecticut – as 'Poirot and the Regatta Mystery') and *The Winnipeg Tribune* magazine (Canada)

'The Mystery of the Baghdad Chest' – Poirot
UK – January 1932, volume 83, issue 493 of *The Strand Magazine*
US – January 1932, volume 49, number 1 of *Ladies Home Journal*, illustrated by Robert E. Lee

'How Does Your Garden Grow?' – Poirot
UK – August 1935, volume 89, issue 536 of *The Strand Magazine*, illustrated by R. M. Chandler
US – June 1935, volume 52, number 6 of *Ladies' Home Journal*, illustrated by Mead Schaeffer

'Problem at Pollensa Bay' – Parker Pyne
UK – November 1935, volume 90, issue 539 of *The Strand Magazine*, illustrated by Stanley Davis
US – 5 September 1936, volume 13, number 36 of *Liberty* as 'Siren Business', illustrated by James Montgomery Flagg

'Yellow Iris' – Poirot
UK – July 1937, volume 93, issue 559 of *The Strand Magazine*; this story was later expanded into the 1945 novel *Sparkling Cyanide* in which Poirot was replaced by Colonel Race.
US – 25 July 1937, *Chicago Tribune*

'Miss Marple Tells a Story'
UK – 25 May 1935, volume 3, issue 64 of *Home Journal* as 'Behind Closed Doors', illustrated by Michael Bernard

'The Dream' – Poirot
UK – February 1937, volume 94, issue 566 of *The Strand Magazine*, illustrated by Jack M. Faulks
US – 23 October 1937, volume 210, number 17 of *The Saturday Evening Post*, illustrated by F.R. Gruger

'In a Glass Darkly' – stand-alone story
UK – December 1934, *Woman's Journal*
US – 28 July 1934, volume 94, number 4 of *Collier's*, illustrated by Harry Morse Meyers

'Problem at Sea' – Poirot
UK – February 1936, volume 90, issue 542 of *The Strand Magazine* as 'Poirot and the Crime in Cabin 66', illustrated by Jack M. Faulks
US – 12 January 1936, *This Week*, illustrated by Stanley Parkhouse

## Alternate UK Collections

*The Regatta Mystery and Other Stories* was not published in the UK, although the stories from it were later published in five British collections:

- *The Adventure of the Christmas Pudding and a Selection of Entrees* (1960) features 'The Dream' and an expanded version of 'The Mystery of the Baghdad Chest' entitled 'The Mystery of the Spanish Chest'.
- *Poirot's Early Cases* (1974) features 'Problem at Sea' and 'How Does Your Garden Grow?'
- *Miss Marple's Final Cases and Two Other Stories* (1979) features 'Miss Marple Tells a Story' and 'In a Glass Darkly'.
- *Problem at Pollensa Bay and Other Stories* (1991) plus 'Yellow Iris' and 'The Regatta Mystery'.
- *While the Light Lasts and Other Stories* (1997) features 'The Mystery of the Baghdad Chest'.

# 1947 – *The Labours of Hercules*

Vain and comical by turns, the world's greatest detective Hercule Poirot has decided to retire – once again. But before he does, he decides to exercise his little grey cells and solve twelve special cases that mirror the unique feats of his classical namesake from Greek mythology, the legendary Hercules.

**Publication:** *The Labours of Hercules* was published in hardback in the UK by the Collins Crime Club on 8 September 1947 and in the US by Dodd, Mead and Company on 23 June 1947.

**Length:** UK 256pp. / US 265pp.

**Price:** UK 8s.6d. / US $2.50

**Word Count:** 79,000

## Stories in the volume and pre-publication appearance

'The Nemean Lion' – the first labour
Hercules was instructed by King Eurystheus to kill the Nemean Lion, which was terrorizing the hills around Nemea and bring its skin back to him.
UK – November 1939, volume 98, issue 587 of *The Strand Magazine* (the foreword to the book was not included), illustrated by Ernest Ratcliff
US – September 1944, volume 5, number 18 of *Ellery Queen's Mystery Magazine* as 'The Case of the Kidnapped Pekinese'

'The Lernean Hydra' – the second labour
Hercules was tasked with destroying the Hydra, a nine-headed monster that was terrorizing the countryside, but each time one of its heads was chopped off another two would grow in its place.

UK – December 1939, volume 98, issue 588 of *The Strand Magazine,* illustrated by Ernest Ratcliff
US – 3 September 1939, *This Week* as 'Invisible Enemy'

'The Arcadian Deer' – the third labour
The Arcadian deer was incapable of being killed so Hercules followed it for a year before capturing it with an arrow between its forelegs and taking it back to King Eurystheus.
UK – January 1940, volume 98, issue 589 of *The Strand Magazine,* illustrated by Ernest Ratcliff
US – 19 May 1940, *This Week* as 'Vanishing Lady'

'The Erymanthian Boar' – the fourth labour
Hercules was instructed to capture the dangerous Erymanthian Boar, so he pursued it north until it became trapped in a snowdrift.
UK – February 1940, volume 98, issue 590 of *The Strand Magazine,* illustrated by Ernest Ratcliff
US – 5 May 1940, *This Week* as 'Murder Mountain'

'The Augean Stables' – the fifth labour
Faced with the challenge of cleaning the cattle manure out of King Augean's stables in a single day, Hercules diverted a river through it.
UK – March 1940, volume, issue 591 of *The Strand Magazine,* illustrated by Ernest Ratcliff

'The Stymphalean Birds' – the sixth labour
The man-eating Stymphalean Birds were destroying the crops and the townspeople of Lake Stymphalia, so Hercules shook a rattle and frightened the birds into the air, then shot them with his arrows.
UK – April 1940, volume 98, issue 592 of *The Strand Magazine* as 'Birds of Ill-Omen', illustrated by Ernest Ratcliff
US – 17 September 1939, *This Week* as 'The Vulture Women'

'The Cretan Bull' – the seventh labour
Hercules was instructed to capture the Cretan Bull, which was wreaking havoc on Crete, so he used his incredible strength to throttle it into unconscious and then shipped to back to Athens.
UK – May 1940, volume 99, issue 593 of *The Strand Magazine,* illustrated by Ernest Ratcliff
US – 24 September 1939, *This Week* as 'Midnight Madness'

'The Horses of Diomedes' – the eighth labour
Hercules was confronted with the challenge of capturing the mares of Diomedes, which became excitable each time they were fed human flesh, so he pursued them to a peninsula where he dug a ditch and filled it with water, thus cutting the horses off on an island.

UK – June 1940, volume 99, issue 594 of *The Strand Magazine,* illustrated by Ernest Ratcliff
US – January 1945, volume 6, number 20 of *Ellery Queen's Mystery Magazine,* as 'The Case of the Drug Peddler'

'The Girdle of Hyppolita' – the ninth labour
King Eurystheus' daughter Admete wanted the belt of Hippolyta for herself and so Hercules was sent to retrieve it from the Amazonian warrior queen Hyppolita.
UK – July 1940, volume 99, issue 595 of *The Strand Magazine* as 'The Girdle of Hyppolyte', illustrated by Ernest Ratcliff
US – 10 September 1939, *This Week* as 'The Disappearance of Winnie King'

'The Flock of Geryon' – the tenth labour
Confronted with the challenge of freeing some cattle held on the island of Erythea, Hercules killed a two-headed dog guarding the herd, followed by the herdsman and finally the owner of the herd of Geryon.
UK – August 1940, volume 99, issue 596 of *The Strand Magazine,* illustrated by Ernest Ratcliff
US – 26 May, *This Week* as 'Weird Monster'

'The Apples of Hesperides' – the eleventh labour
Securing the apples of Hesperides was no easy task so Hercules persuaded Atlas to steal them for him by relieving him of his burden of holding the world on his shoulders. On Atlas' return, he tricked him into handing over the apples and taking the world back onto his shoulders once again.
UK – September 1940, volume 99, issue 597 of *The Strand Magazine,* illustrated by Ernest Ratcliff
US – 12 May 1940, *This Week* as 'The Poison Cup'

'The Capture of Cerberus' – the twelfth labour
For his final labour Hercules was instructed to descend into the underworld and capture a three-headed dog called Cerberus who was guarding the entrance to Hades.
US – 16 March 1947, *This Week*

## The Thirteen Labour

The twelfth and last story in the series 'The Capture of Cerberus' was rejected by *The Strand Magazine* because it contained a character based on Adolf Hitler. The magazine's refusal to accept the story is not without irony because in the tenth labour, 'The Flock of Geryon', which appeared in the August 1940 issue of *The Strand*, Agatha Christie referred to Caesar, Napoleon and Hitler as 'poor, miserable, little fellows!' The author eventually wrote a second version of 'The Capture of Cerberus' that featured a totally different storyline involving a narcotic ring operating out of a London nightclub called Hell and it was this version that was published in the US by *This Week* on 16 March 1947.

The Hitleresque version of 'The Capture of Cerberus', known as the thirteenth labour for avoidance of confusion, was eventually published in the UK by the *Daily Mail* on

28 August 2009. It was first published in volume form in the UK by HarperCollins in *Agatha Christie's Secret Notebooks* by John Curran on 3 September 2009 and in the US by Harper, an imprint of HarperCollins, on 22 February 2010. In 2014, the Hitleresque version of 'The Capture of Cerberus' was added as an appendix to the UK paperback edition of *The Labours of Hercules*, so the collection now contains thirteen stories instead of the usual twelve labours.

## Post-Publication Series

Throughout 1947 and 1948 *The Labours of Hercules* appeared in **Parade: The Middle East Weekly**, an English-language magazine printed in Cairo, Egypt, and distributed to the Allies Forces:

- (Including foreword) 'The Nemean Lion', 1 November 1947
- 'The Lernean Hydra', 8 November 1947
- 'The Arcadian Deer', 15 November 1947
- 'The Erymanthian Boar', 22 November 1947
- 'The Augean Stables', 29 November 1947
- 'The Stymphalean Birds', 6 December 1947
- 'The Cretan Bull', 13 December 1947
- [No story from *The Labours of Hercules* was included in the 20 December Christmas issue, which instead featured a story by Roy Nash called 'The Upstairs Fairy'.]
- 'The Horses of Diomedes', 27 December 1947
- 'The Girdle of Hyppolita', 3 January 1948
- 'The Flock of Geryon', 10 January 1948
- 'The Apples of Hesperides', 17 January 1948
- 'The Capture of Cerberus', 24 January 1948

# 1948 (US only) – *The Witness for the Prosecution and Other Stories*

Agatha Christie's extraordinary ability to create suspense is on full display in this collection of sinister mysteries. A man ignores a premonition of danger and becomes the prime suspect in a murder... a radio is haunted by the voice of a dead man... a young girl dies after apparently strangling herself... and the shooting of an eccentric musician inside a locked room challenges Hercule Poirot's grey cells.... This dazzling miscellany highlighting the Queen of Crime's unrivalled skills in legerdemain has the additional interest of featuring the stories 'Accident', which was adapted by Margery Vosper into the excellent 1939 one-act play *Tea for Three*, and 'The Witness for the Prosecution', which Agatha Christie herself turned into one of the greatest stage courtroom dramas of all time.

**Publication:** *The Witness for the Prosecution and Other Stories* was published in hardback in the US by Dodd, Mead and Company on 7 September 1948.

**Length:** 272pp.

**Price:** $2.50

**Word Count:** 68,000

―――――――――― The Official Short Story Collections ――――――――――

## Stories in the volume and pre-publication appearance

'The Witness for the Prosecution'
US – 31 January 1925, volume 4, no 2 of *Flynn's Weekly* as 'Traitor Hands'

'The Red Signal'
UK – June 1924, *The Grand Magazine*

'The Fourth Man'
UK – December 1925, *Pearson's Magazine*

'S.O.S.'
UK – February 1926, *The Grand Magazine*

'Where There's a Will' (aka 'Wireless')
UK – *Sunday Chronicle Annual* 1926
US – 1 March 1926, volume 8, number 4 of *Mystery Magazine*

'The Mystery of the Blue Jar'
UK – July 1924, *The Grand Magazine*
US – March 1925, volume 60, number 6 of *Macfadden Fiction-Lovers Magazine*

'Sing a Song of Sixpence'
UK – December 1929, *Holly Leaves*, the annual Christmas special of the *Illustrated Sporting and Dramatic News*, illustrated by C. Watson.

'The Mystery of the Spanish Shawl' (aka 'Mr Eastwood's Adventure')
UK – August 1924, issue 233 of *The Novel Magazine* as 'The Mystery of the Second Cucumber'
US – December 1924, volume 60, number 3 of *Macfadden Fiction-Lover's Magazine* as 'The Mystery of the Spanish Shawl'

'Philomel Cottage'
UK – November 1924, *The Grand Magazine*

'Accident'
UK – 22 September 1929, *Sunday Dispatch* as 'The Uncrossed Path'

'The Second Gong'
UK – July 1932, volume 84, issue 499 of *The Strand Magazine*; this story was expanded into the novella *Dead Man's Mirror* from the 1937 collection *Murder in the Mews: 4 Poirot Cases* (UK) *Dead Man's Mirror* (US)
US – January 1932, volume 49, number 6 of *Ladies' Home Journal*

## Change of Titles

Following Agatha Christie's centenary in 1990, the titles of the two stories 'Where There's a Will' and 'The Mystery of the Spanish Shawl' were changed to 'Wireless' and 'Mr Eastwood's Adventure' in all US editions of this collection in order to coincide with the British listing of these stories for avoidance of confusion.

── Secrets from the Agatha Christie Archives ──

## Alternate UK Collections

*The Witness for the Prosecution and Other Stories* was not released in England because ten of the eleven stories had already appeared in two UK volumes. The eleventh story was published posthumously.

- ***The Hound of Death and Other Stories*** (1933) features 'The Red Signal', 'The Fourth Man', 'Where There's a Will' as 'Wireless', 'The Witness for the Prosecution', 'The Mystery of the Blue Jar', and 'S.O.S.'
- ***The Listerdale Mystery and Other Stories*** (1934) features 'Philomel Cottage', 'Sing a Song of Sixpence', 'Accident', and 'Mr Eastwood's Adventure' under the title 'The Mystery of the Spanish Shawl'.
- ***Problem at Pollensa Bay and Other Stories*** (1991) features 'The Second Gong'.

# 1950 (US only) – *Three Blind Mice and Other Stories*

This enthralling collection of short stories features four of the Queen of Crime's favourite detectives: the brilliant Hercule Poirot, the shrewd and kindly Miss Marple, and that elderly and wistful observer of life, Mr Satterthwaite and his enigmatic friend of magic Mr Harley Quin. The jewel in this collection is undoubtedly the title novella *Three Blind Mice*, which Agatha Christie adapted in 1952 into the world's longest running-play *The Mousetrap*, which continues to break records to this very day with every performance at St. Martin's Theatre in the West End of London.

**Publication:** *Three Blind Mice and Other Stories* was published in hardback in the US by Dodd, Mead and Company on 10 February 1950. In the US, Dell paperbacks retitled the collection *The Mousetrap and Other Stories*.

**Length:** 250pp.

**Price:** $2.50

**Word Count:** 62,000

## Stories in the volume and pre-publication appearance

'Three Blind Mice' – Stand Alone
UK – 31 December 1948 to 21 January 1949, four weekly instalments of *Woman's Own*
US – May 1948, volume 124, number 5 of *Cosmopolitan* magazine

'Strange Jest' – Miss Marple
UK – July 1944, volume 107, issue 643 of *The Strand Magazine* as 'A Case of Buried Treasure'
US – 2 November 1941, *This Week*

'The Tape-Measure Murder' – Miss Marple
UK – February 1942, volume 102, issue 614 of *The Strand Magazine* as 'The Case of the Retired Jeweller'
US – 16 November 1941, *This Week*, illustrated by Arthur Sarnoff

'The Case of the Perfect Maid' – Miss Marple
UK – April 1942, volume 103, issue 616 of *The Strand Magazine* as 'The Perfect Maid'
US – 13 September 1942, *Akron Beacon Journal, Chicago Sunday Tribune* and *Detroit Free Press* newspapers

'The Case of the Caretaker' (an abridged edition of 'The Case of the Caretaker's Wife') – Miss Marple
UK – January 1942, volume 102, issue 613 of *The Strand Magazine*
US – 5 July 1942, *Akron Beacon Journal, Chicago Sunday Tribune, Detroit Free Press* newspapers

'The Third Floor Flat' – Hercule Poirot
UK – January 1929, volume 21, number 1 of *Hutchinson's Story Magazine*
US – 5 January 1929, volume 106, number 6 of *Detective Story Magazine* as 'In the Third Floor Flat'

'The Adventure of Johnnie Waverly' – Hercule Poirot
UK – 10 October 1923, issue 1602 of *The Sketch* as 'The Kidnapping of Johnny Waverly'
US – June 1925, volume 41, number 2 of *The Blue Book Magazine*

'Four and Twenty Blackbirds' – Hercule Poirot
UK – March 1941, volume 100, issue 603 of *The Strand Magazine* as 'Poirot and the Regular Customer'
US – 9 November 1940, volume 106, number 19 of *Collier's* magazine, illustrated by Mario Cooper

'The Love Detectives' – Mr Satterthwaite and Mr Quin
UK – December 1926, issue 236 of *The Story-Teller* as 'The Magic of Mr Quin, No. 1: At the Crossroads'
US – 30 October 1926, volume 19, number 3 of *Flynn's Weekly* as 'At the Crossroads'

## Alternate UK Collections

*Three Blind Mice and Other Stories* was not published in England. All the stories, with the exception of 'Three Blind Mice', were later subsumed into the following collections.

**The Adventure of the Christmas Pudding and Other Stories** (1960) features 'Four and Twenty Blackbirds'.

**Poirot's Early Cases** (1974) features 'The Adventure of Johnnie Waverly' and 'The Third-Floor Flat'.

*Miss Marple's Final Cases and Two Other Stories* (1979) features 'Strange Jest', 'Tape-Measure Murder', 'The Case of the Caretaker', and 'The Case of the Perfect Maid'.

*Problem at Pollensa Bay and Other stories* (1991) features 'The Love Detectives'.

# 1951 (US only) – *The Under Dog and Other Stories*

Hercule Poirot takes centre-stage in this superb anthology based on his life in crime. Whether he is investigating a family curse, a killer who vanished from a speeding train or the disappearance of a domestic cook, his deductive skills are at their unmissable best. Each story is a marvellous feat of suspense, surprises and vivid characterization, which is the hallmark of Agatha Christie's style and has led to her being acclaimed the Queen of Crime the world over.

**Publication:** *The Under Dog and Other Stories* was published in hardback in the US by Dodd, Mead and Company on 7 September 1951.

**Length:** 248pp.

**Price:** $2.50

**Word Count:** 57,000

## Stories in the volume and pre-publication appearance

'The Under Dog'
UK – October 1926, *The London Magazine*
US – 1 April 1926, volume 8, number 6 of *The Mystery Magazine*

'The Plymouth Express' (later expanded into the 1928 novel *The Mystery of the Blue Train*)
UK – 4 April 1923, issue 1575 of *The Sketch* as 'The Mystery of the Plymouth Express'
US – January 1924, volume 38, number 3 of *The Blue Book Magazine* as 'The Plymouth Express Affair'

'The Affair at the Victory Ball'
UK – 7 March 1923, issue 1571 of *The Sketch*
US – September 1923, volume 37, number 5 of *The Blue Book Magazine*

'The Market Basing Mystery' (later expanded into the title story from the 1937 UK collection *Murder in the Mews: 4 Poirot Stories*)
UK – 17 October 1923, issue 1603 of *The Sketch*
US – May 1925, volume 41, number 1 of *The Blue Book Magazine*

'The Lemesurier Inheritance'
UK – December 1925, *The Christmas Magpie* as 'The Le Mesurier Inheritance'
US – November 1925, volume 42, number 1 of *The Blue Book Magazine*

'The Cornish Mystery'
UK – 28 November 1923, in issue 1609 of *The Sketch*
US – October 1925, volume 41, number 6 of *The Blue Book Magazine*

'The King of Clubs'
UK – 21 March 1923, issue 1573 of *The Sketch* as 'The Adventure of the King of Clubs'
US – November 1923, volume 38, number 1 of *The Blue Book Magazine*

'The Submarine Plans' (later expanded into 'The Incredible Theft' from the 1937 UK collection *Murder in the Mews: 4 Poirot Stories*).
UK – 7 November 1923, issue 1606 of *The Sketch*
US – July 1925, volume 41, number 3 of *The Blue Book Magazine*

'The Adventure of the Clapham Cook'
UK – 14 November 1923, issue 1607 of *The Sketch*
US – September 1925, volume 41, number 5 of *The Blue Book Magazine* as 'The Clapham Cook'

## Alternate UK Collections

The nine stories from *The Under Dog and Other Stories* were eventually incorporated into the following UK collections:

- ***The Adventure of the Christmas Pudding and a Selection of Entrees*** (1960) features 'The Under Dog'.
- ***Poirot's Early Cases*** (1974) features 'The Plymouth Express', 'The Affair at the Victory', 'The Market Basing Mystery', 'The Lemesurier Inheritance', 'The Cornish Mystery', 'The King of Clubs', 'The Submarine Plans', and 'The Adventure of the Clapham Cook'.

## 1960 (UK only) – *The Adventure of the Christmas Pudding and a Selection of Entrees*

**Working Title:** *The Mystery of the Spanish Chest and Other Stories* (as cited in Agatha Christie's notebooks)

Shakespeare once said of Cleopatra that age cannot wither nor custom stale her infinity variety, and fans would undoubtedly agree this is equally true of Agatha Christie. Her fertility of plot, colourful array of characters and nuanced understanding of human nature is amply displayed in these six striking tales – five of which are solved by the inimitable Hercule Poirot while the remaining one is elucidated by Miss Marple, the spinster sleuth of St. Mary Mead, who remains the most endearingly modest of all of Agatha Christie's literary creations. This impressive collection affirms what the Queen of Crime's admirers have long known: she stands *hors d'oeuvre* in a class of her own.

**Publication:** *The Adventure of the Christmas Pudding and a Selection of Entrées* was published in hardback in the UK by the Collins Crime Club on 24 October 1960.

**Length:** 256pp.

**Price:** 12s.6d.

**Word Count:** 71,000

## Stories in the volume and pre-publication appearance

*Foreword by the Author*

'The Adventure of the Christmas Pudding' – Hercule Poirot

UK – the title novella is an expanded version of 'The Adventure of the Christmas Pudding', which appeared in issue 1611 of *The Sketch* on 12 December 1923.

US – 25 September and 2 October 1960, *This Week*, illustrated by William A. Smith

'The Mystery of the Spanish Chest' – Hercule Poirot

UK – 17, 24 September and 1 October 1960, *Woman's Illustrated* magazine; the novella is an expanded version of 'The Mystery of the Baghdad Chest', which appeared in issue 493 of *The Strand Magazine* in January 1932.

'The Under Dog' – Hercule Poirot

UK – October 1926, *The London Magazine*

US – 1 April 1926, volume 8, number 6 of *The Mystery Magazine*

'Four and Twenty Blackbirds' – Hercule Poirot

UK – March 1941, volume 100, issue 603 of *The Strand Magazine* as 'Poirot and the Regular Customer'

US – 9 November 1940, volume 106, number 19 of *Collier's* magazine, illustrated by Mario Cooper

'The Dream' – Hercule Poirot

UK – February 1938, volume 94, issue 566 of *The Strand Magazine,* illustrated by Jack M. Faulks

US – 23 October 1937, volume 210, number 17 of *The Saturday Evening Post*, illustrated by F.R. Gruger

'Greenshaw's Folly' – Miss Marple

UK – 3 to 7 December 1956, *Daily Mail*, illustrated by Caswell

US – 12 and 19 September 1954, *This Week*

## Alternate US Collections

*The Adventure of the Christmas Pudding and a Selection of Entrées* was not published in the US because a number of the stories or earlier versions of them had already appeared in other collections.

─────────── The Official Short Story Collections ───────────

- *The Regatta Mystery and Other Stories* (1939) features the shorter version of 'The Mystery of the Spanish Chest' known as 'The Mystery of the Baghdad Chest' along with 'The Dream'.
- *The Under Dog and Other Stories* (1951)
- *Double Sin and Other Stories* (1961) features 'The Adventure of the Christmas Pudding' under the title of 'The Theft of the Royal Ruby'.

## 1961 (US only) – *Double Sin and Other Stories*

No one knows better than Agatha Christie how to weave a magical spell over her readers, and in this captivating collection she treats them to a veritable crimewave of skullduggery. Her two most famous sleuths, Hercule Poirot and Miss Marple, are on hand to test their legendary deductive skills in a variety of baffling cases ranging from theft to murder. Agatha Christie's adroit shuffling of clues and red herrings has never been better, and her solutions are guaranteed to take even the most hardened crime addicts by surprise. As a special bonus, she tantalizes her legion of devotees with two supernatural tales that are sure to remain in the mind long after they are finished.

**Publication:** *Double Sin and Other Stories* was published in hardback in the US by Dodd, Mead and Company on 5 July 1961.

**Price:** $3.50

**Length:** 247pp.

**Word Count:** 53,000

### Stories in the volume and pre-publication appearance

'Double Sin' – Hercule Poirot
UK – 23 September 1928, *Sunday Dispatch* as 'By Road or Rail'
US – 30 March 1929, volume 108, number 6 of *Detective Story Magazine*

'Wasps' Nest' – Hercule Poirot
UK – 20 November 1928, *Daily Mail* as 'The Wasps' Nest'
US – 9 March 1929, volume 108, number 3 of *Detective Story Magazine* as 'Worst of All'

'The Theft of the Royal Ruby' – Hercule Poirot
UK – 24, 31 December 1960 and 7 January 1961, *Woman's Illustrated* magazine as 'The Theft of the Royal Ruby', illustrated by Zelinksi
US – 25 September and 2 October 1960, *This Week* as 'The Theft of the Royal Ruby', illustrated by William A. Smith

This is one of the few stories in Agatha Christie's canon whose US title has not, as yet, reverted back to its original UK title 'The Adventure of the Christmas Pudding'.

'The Dressmaker's Doll' – Stand-Alone
UK – December 1958, *Woman's Journal*
Canada – 25 October 1958, *Star Weekly Complete Novel*, a Saturday supplement to *The Toronto Star* newspaper

'Greenshaw's Folly' – Miss Marple
UK – 3 to 7 December 1956, *Daily Mail*, illustrated by Caswell
US – 12 and 19 September 1954, *This Week*

'The Double Clue' – Hercule Poirot
UK – 5 December 1923, issue 1610 of *The Sketch*
US – August 1925, volume 41, number 4 of *The Blue Book Magazine*

'The Last Séance' – Stand-Alone
UK – March 1927, issue 87 of *The Sovereign Magazine* as 'The Stolen Ghost'
US – November 1926, *Ghost Stories* magazine as 'The Woman Who Stole a Ghost'

'Sanctuary' – Miss Marple
UK – October 1954, *Woman's Journal*
US – 12 and 19 September 1954, *This Week*, illustrated by Robert Fawcett

## Alternate UK Collections

*Double Sin and Other Stories* was not published in the UK, but the stories from it appeared in a number of collections.

- *The Hound of Death and Other Stories* (1933) features 'The Last Séance'.
- *The Adventure of the Christmas Pudding and a Selection of Entrees* (1960) features 'The Theft of the Royal Ruby' renamed as the title story and 'Greenshaw's Folly'.
- *Poirot's Early Cases* (1974) features 'Double Sin', 'Wasp's Nest' and 'The Double Clue'.
- *Miss Marple's Final Cases and Two Other Stories* (1979) features 'The Dressmaker's Doll' and 'Sanctuary'.

# 1971 (US only) – *The Golden Gall and Other Stories*

Agatha Christie's ability to surprise and delight her readers has seldom been in greater evidence than in the fifteen exquisitely crafted tales that comprise this anthology. Romance and sinister intrigue are never far from the surface in some of the stories such as 'The Girl in the Train', while others such as 'The Lamp' offer an eerie blend of the supernatural. The most poignant story of all, 'Next to a Dog', serves as a timely reminder that a dog is a man's best friend, while music, madness and murder take centre stage to brilliant effect in 'Swan Song'. Agatha Christie's storytelling genius has enthralled generations of readers and this stunning collection is sure to earn her even more admirers and tributes from around the world.

―――――――― The Official Short Story Collections ――――――――

**Publication:** *The Golden Ball and Other Stories* was published in hardback in the US by Dodd, Mead and Company on 21 July 1971.

**Length:** 280pp.

**Price:** $5.95

**Word Count:** 77,000

## Stories in the volume and pre-publication appearance

'The Listerdale Mystery'
UK – December 1925, *The Grand Magazine* as 'The Benevolent Butler'

'The Girl in a Train'
UK – February 1924, *The Grand Magazine*

'The Manhood of Edward Robinson'
UK – December 1924, *The Grand Magazine* as 'The Day of His Dreams'
US – May 1925, volume one, number one of *Your Car: A Magazine of Romance, Fact and Fiction* as 'Romance and a Red Roundabout'

'Jane in Search of a Job'
UK – August 1924, *The Grand Magazine*

'A Fruitful Sunday'
UK – 11 August 1928, *Daily Mail*

'The Golden Ball'
UK – 5 August 1929, *Daily Mail* as 'Playing the Innocent', illustrated by Lowtham

'The Rajah's Emerald'
UK – 30 July 1926, issue 420 of *Red Magazine*, illustrated by Jack M. Faulks

'Swan Song'
UK – September 1926, *The Grand Magazine*

'The Hound of Death'

'The Gipsy'

'The Lamp'

'The Strange Case of Sir Andrew Carmichael'

This is one of the few stories in Agatha Christie's canon whose US title has not, as yet, reverted back to its original UK title of 'The Strange Case of Sir *Arthur* Carmichael' for avoidance of confusion.

'The Call of Wings'
'Magnolia Blossom'
UK – March 1926, issue 329 of *The Royal Magazine*

'Next to a Dog'
UK – September 1929, *The Grand Magazine*

## Alternate UK Collections

This volume was not released in the UK because the stories had already appeared in two UK collections, with the exception of 'Magnolia Blossom' and 'Next to a Dog'.

- *The Hound of Death and Other Stories* (1933) features 'The Gipsy', 'The Lamp', 'The Strange Case of Sir Arthur Carmichael' and 'The Call of Wings'.
- *The Listerdale Mystery and Other Stories* (1934) features 'The Girl in the Train', 'The Manhood of Edward Robinson', 'Jane in Search of a Job', 'A Fruitful Sunday', 'The Golden Ball', 'The Rajah's Emerald' and 'Swan Song'.
- *Problem at Pollensa Bay and Other Stories* (1991) features 'Magnolia Blossom' and 'Next to a Dog'.

# 1974 (UK only) *Poirot's Early Cases*

Millions of fans, who were saddened when Hercule Poirot died last year in *Curtain: Poirot's Last Case*, have reason to rejoice again. The legendary detective is back – and he has seldom been on better form than in this brilliant series of stories that were written by Agatha Christie during the 1920s and 1930s. The stories are all vintage Christie and a superb reminder as to why the eccentric Belgian with his egg-shaped head and little grey cells has captured the hearts of so many admirers around the world. The tales also affirm why the Queen of Crime has brooked no near rival in years and has long resided within a realm of her own.

**Publication:** *Poirot's Early Cases* was published in hardback in the UK by the Collins Crime Club on 23 September 1974. The stories were also published in the US in the short-lived 1974 collection *Hercule Poirot's Early Cases*. *Thirteen for Luck* (1966) marks the first publication in an Agatha Christie collection of 'The Market Basing Mystery'.

**Length:** 253pp.

**Price:** £2.25

**Word Count:** 81,000

## Stories in the volume and pre-publication appearance

'The Affair at the Victory Ball'
UK – 7 March 1923, issue 1571 of *The Sketch*
US – September 1923, volume 37, number 5 of *The Blue Book Magazine*

'The Adventure of the Clapham Cook'
UK – 14 November 1923, issue 1607 of *The Sketch*
US – September 1925, volume 41, number 5 of *The Blue Book Magazine* as 'The Clapham Cook'

———————— The Official Short Story Collections ————————

'The Cornish Mystery'
UK – 28 November 1923, in issue 1609 of *The Sketch*
US – October 1925, volume 41, number 6 of *The Blue Book Magazine*

'The Adventure of Johnnie Waverly'
UK – 10 October 1923, issue 1602 of *The Sketch* as 'The Kidnapping of Johnny Waverly'
US – June 1925, volume 41, number 2 of *The Blue Book Magazine*

'The Double Clue'
UK – 5 December 1923, issue 1610 of *The Sketch*
US – August 1925, volume 41, number 4 of *The Blue Book Magazine*

'The King of Clubs'
UK – 21 March 1923, issue 1573 of *The Sketch* as 'The Adventure of the King of Clubs'
US – November 1923, volume 38, number 1 of *The Blue Book Magazine*

'The Lemesurier Inheritance'
UK – December 1925, *The Christmas Magpie* as 'The Le Mesurier Inheritance'
US – November 1925, volume 42, number 1 of *The Blue Book Magazine* as 'The Le Mesurier Inheritance'

'The Lost Mine'
UK – 21 November 1923, issue 1608 of *The Sketch*
US – April 1925, volume 40, number 6 of *The Blue Book Magazine*

'The Plymouth Express' (later expanded into the 1928 novel *The Mystery of the Blue Train*)
UK – 4 April 1923, issue 1575 of *The Sketch* as 'The Mystery of the Plymouth Express'
US – January 1924, volume 38, number 3 of *The Blue Book Magazine* as 'The Plymouth Express Affair'

'The Chocolate Box'
UK – 23 May 1923, issue 1582 of *The Sketch* as 'The Clue of the Chocolate Box'
US – February 1925, volume 40, number 4 of *The Blue Book Magazine*

'The Submarine Plans' (later expanded into 'The Incredible Theft' from the 1937 collection *Murder in the Mews: 4 Poirot Stories*)
UK – 7 November 1923, issue 1606 of *The Sketch*
US – July 1925, volume 41, number 3 of *The Blue Book Magazine*

'The Third-Floor Flat'
UK – January 1929, volume 21, number 1 of *Hutchinson's Story Magazine*
US – 5 January 1929, volume 106, number 6 of *Detective Story Magazine* as 'In the Third Floor Flat'

'Double Sin'
UK – 23 September 1928, *Sunday Dispatch* as 'By Road or Rail'
US – 30 March 1929, volume 108, number 6 of *Detective Story Magazine*

―――――― Secrets from the Agatha Christie Archives ――――――

'The Market Basing Mystery' (later expanded into the title story from the 1937 collection *Murder in the Mews: 4 Poirot Stories*)
UK – 17 October 1923, issue 1603 of *The Sketch*
US – May 1925, volume 41, number 1 of *The Blue Book Magazine*

'Wasps' Nest'
UK – 20 November 1928, *Daily Mail* as 'The Wasps' Nest'
US – 9 March 1929, volume 108, number 3 of *Detective Story Magazine* as 'Worst of All'

'The Veiled Lady'
UK – 3 October 1923, issue 1601 *The Sketch* as 'The Case of the Veiled Lady'
US – March 1925, volume 40, number 5 of *The Blue Book Magazine*

'Problem at Sea'
UK – February 1936, volume 90, issue 542 of *The Strand Magazine* as 'Poirot and the Crime in Cabin 66', illustrated by Jack M. Faulks
US – 12 January 1936, *This Week*, illustrated by Stanley Parkhouse

'How Does Your Garden Grow?'
UK – August 1935, volume 89, issue 536 of *The Strand Magazine*, illustrated by R.M. Chandler
US – June 1935, volume 52, number 6 of *Ladies' Home Journal*, illustrated by Mead Schaeffer

# 1979 (UK only) – *Miss Marple's Final Cases and Two Other Stories*

Aficionados of Agatha Christie's favourite detective will be delighted by Miss Marple's return to form in this collection of vintage stories written during the 1930s and 1940s. A man with a bullet wound is found dying in a church...a couple anxious to inherit a fortune ask Miss Marple to find where it is buried...and a series of thefts at Old Hall sets tongues wagging... The spinster sleuth of St. Mary Mead solves a total of six tantalizing cases with her usual customary modesty, and for added measure the collection is rounded off with two eerie stand-alone stories with supernatural overtones that are sure to send a chill down the reader's spine.

**Publication:** *Miss Marple's Final Cases and Two Other Stories* was published in hardback in the UK by the Collins Crime Club on 18 October 1979.

**Length:** 138pp.

**Price:** £4.50

**Word Count:** 36,000

### Stories in the volume and pre-publication appearance

'Sanctuary'
UK – October 1954, *Woman's Journal*
US – 12 and 19 September 1954, *This Week*, illustrated by Robert Fawcett.

— The Official Short Story Collections —

'Strange Jest'
UK – July 1944, volume 107, issue 643 of *The Strand Magazine* as 'A Case of Buried Treasure'
US – 2 November 1941, *This Week*

'Tape-Measure Murder'
UK – February 1942, volume 102, issue 614 of *The Strand Magazine* as 'The Case of the Retired Jeweller'
US – 16 November 1941, *This Week*

'The Case of the Caretaker'
UK – January 1942, volume 102, issue 613 of *The Strand Magazine*
US – 5 July 1942, *Akron Beacon Journal, Chicago Sunday Tribune, Detroit Free Press* newspapers

'The Case of the Perfect Maid'
UK – April 1942, volume 103, issue 616 of *The Strand Magazine* as 'The Perfect Maid'
US – 13 September 1942, *Akron Beacon Journal, Chicago Sunday Tribune* and *Detroit Free Press* newspapers

'Miss Marple Tells a Story'
UK – 25 May 1935, volume 3, issue 64 of *Home Journal* as 'Behind Closed Doors', illustrated by Michael Bernard

'The Dressmaker's Doll' – Stand-Alone
UK – December 1958, *Woman's Journal*
Canada – 25 October 1958, *Star Weekly Complete Novel*, a Saturday supplement to *The Toronto Star* newspaper

'In a Glass Darkly' – Stand-Alone
UK – December 1934, *Woman's Journal*
US – 28 July 1934, volume 94, number 4 of *Collier's* magazine, illustrated by Harry Morse Meyers

## Alternate US Collections

*Miss Marple's Final Cases and Two Other Stories* was not published in the US because the stories had already appeared in other collections:

- **The Regatta Mystery and Other Stories** (1939) features 'Miss Marple Tells a Story' and 'In a Glass Darkly'.
- **The Under Dog and Other Stories** (1951) features 'Strange Jest', 'Tape-Measure Murder', 'The Case of the Perfect Maid' and 'The Case of the Caretaker'.
- **Double Sin and Other Sins** (1961) features 'The Dressmaker's Doll' and 'Sanctuary'.

## Greenshaw's Folly

Since 2002, UK paperback editions of *Miss Marple's Final Cases* have also featured 'Greenshaw's Folly', which was first published in *The Adventure of the Christmas Pudding and a Selection of Entrees* in 1960 and remains a part of that collection, too. In the US, *Miss Marple's Final Cases* was released in 2010 as an audio book and e-book, also featuring 'Greenshaw's Folly'.

## 1991 (UK only) – *Problem at Pollensa Bay*

As devoted fans of Agatha Christie know only too well, there is nothing more satisfying than a Christie for Christmas. This timely posthumous collection of stories features three of her most beloved detectives. Whether Parker Pyne is solving a romantic dilemma in 'Problem at Pollensa Bay' or tackling a jewel robbery in 'The Regatta Mystery', he radiates his usual kindness and ingenuity. Hercule Poirot unravels a locked-room puzzle in 'The Second Gong' and responds to a damsel in distress in 'Yellow Iris' with his usual blend of brilliance and outrageous conceit. An elderly Mr Satterthwaite and his supernatural friend Mr Quin rescue a pair of tormented lovers from danger in 'The Love Detectives' and end their career in crime-solving by triumphing over evil in 'The Harlequin Tea-Set'. Each story is a masterpiece of skillful plotting, suspense and characterization and guaranteed to delight the Queen of Crime's multitude of fans.

**Publication:** *Problem at Pollensa Bay and Other Stories* was published in hardback in the UK by HarperCollins in November 1991. 'Magnolia Blossom' was first published in hardback in the 1982 UK collection *The Agatha Christie Hour* to promote the television series of the same name.

**Length:** 227pp.

**Price:** £13.99

**Word Count:** 51,000

### Stories in the volume and pre-publication appearance

'Problem at Pollensa Bay' – Parker Pyne
UK – November 1935, volume 90, issue 539 of *The Strand Magazine*, illustrated by Stanley Davis
US – 5 September 1936, volume 13, number 36 of *Liberty* as 'Siren Business', illustrated by James Montgomery Flagg

'The Second Gong' – Hercule Poirot
UK – July 1932, volume 84, issue 499 of *The Strand Magazine*; this story was expanded into the novella *Dead Man's Mirror* from the 1937 collection *Murder in the Mews: 4 Poirot Cases* (UK) *Dead Man's Mirror* (US).
US – January 1932, volume 49, number 6 of *Ladies' Home Journal*

'Yellow Iris' – Hercule Poirot
UK – July 1937, volume 93, issue 559 of *The Strand Magazine*; this story was later expanded into the 1945 novel *Sparkling Cyanide* in which Poirot was replaced by Colonel Race.
US – 25 July 1937, *Chicago Tribune*

'The Harlequin Tea Set' – Mr Satterthwaite and Mr Quin
UK – November 1971, *Winter Crime's 3*, edited by George Hardinge, Macmillan
US – 11 November 1971, *Winter Crime's 3*, edited by George Hardinge, Macmillan

'The Regatta Mystery' – Parker Pyne version
UK – June 1936, volume 91, issue 546 of *The Strand Magazine* as 'Poirot and the Regatta Mystery', illustrated by Jack M. Faulks; the Poirot version can be found in the 2008 paperback collection: *Hercule Poirot: The Complete Short Stories*.
US / Canada – 3 May 1936, syndicated as a Hercule Poirot story to the following newspapers: *Sunday News* (New York); *The Laredo Times* (Texas); *The Philadelphia Inquirer* (Pennsylvania); and *The Hartford Courant* (Connecticut – as 'Poirot and the Regatta Mystery') and *The Winnipeg Tribune* magazine (Canada)

'The Love Detectives' – Mr Satterthwaite and Mr Quin
UK – December 1926, issue 236 of *The Story-Teller* as 'The Magic of Mr Quin, No. 1: At the Crossroads'
US – 30 October 1926, volume 19, number 3 of *Flynn's Weekly* as 'At the Cross Roads'

'Next to a Dog' – Stand-Alone
UK – September 1929, *The Grand Magazine*

'Magnolia Blossom' – Stand-Alone
UK – March 1926, issue 329 of *The Royal Magazine*

## Alternate US Collections

*Problem at Pollensa Bay and Other Stories* was not published in America because the stories had already been included in other collections.

- ***The Regatta Mystery and Other Stories*** (1939) also features 'Yellow Iris'.
- ***The Witness for the Prosecution and Other Stories*** (1948) features 'The Second Gong'.
- ***Three Blind Mice and Other Stories*** (1950) features 'The Love Detectives'.
- ***The Golden Ball and Other Stories*** (1971) features 'Magnolia Blossom' and 'Next to a Dog'.
- ***The Harlequin Tea-Set and Other Stories*** (1997)

## 1997 (UK) *While the Light Lasts* / (US) *The Harlequin Tea Set*

This fascinating collection brings together for the first time in volume form several newly unearthed stories by Agatha Christie, plus magazine versions of two Poirot stories she later rewrote for mainstream publication. The stories are some of the earliest she ever penned, including 'The House of Dreams', which recounts the impact of a macabre dream on a man's life. The title character in 'The Actress' is forced to act fast to prevent her past from overtaking her, and in 'While the Light Lasts' a woman receives a visit from beyond the grave. The most unusual story in the collection is 'Manx's Gold', which formed the basis of a real-life treasure hunt that was enacted on the Isle of Man in the summer of 1930. Published twenty-one years after the legendary crime writer's death, this unique collection offers her fans a rare posthumous treat.

**Publication:** *While the Light Lasts and Other Stories* was published in hardback in the UK by HarperCollins on 4 August 1997 and in the US and Canada as *The Harlequin Tea Set and Other Stories* by G. P. Putnam's Sons on 14 April 1997.

**Length:** UK 181pp. / US 281pp.

**Price:** UK £14.95 / US & CAN $21.95 / $29.50

**Word Count:** UK 49,000 / US 58,000

**Trivia:** The UK edition features editorial notes for each story acknowledging the help of Jared Cade and Geoff Bradley, among others, in tracing the stories which were lost for several decades; the US edition only reproduces the editorial notes written for 'Manx Gold' explaining why the story came to be written.

**Differences in the UK and US Editions:** 'Christmas Adventure' is omitted from the US volume, along with 'The Mystery of the Baghdad Chest', which appears in its longer format 'The Mystery of the Spanish Chest'.

## Stories in the UK volume and pre-publication appearance

'The House of Dreams'
UK – January 1926, issue 74 of *The Sovereign Magazine*, illustrated by Stanley Lloyd

'The Actress'
UK – May 1923, issue 218 of *The Novel Magazine* as 'A Trap for the Unwary', illustrated by Emile Verpilleux

'The Edge'
UK – February 1927, volume 63, issue 374 of *Pearson's Magazine*

'Christmas Adventure' – Hercule Poirot
UK – 12 December 1923, issue 1611 of *The Sketch* as 'The Adventure of the Christmas Pudding'; this story was later expanded into the title novella from the 1960 UK collection *The Adventure of the Christmas Pudding and a Selection of Entrees*.

'The Lonely God'
UK – July 1926, issue 333 of *The Royal Magazine*, illustrated by H. Coller

'Manx Gold'
UK – 23 to 28 May 1930, five-parter, *Daily Dispatch*

'Within a Wall'
UK – October 1925, issue 324 of *The Royal Magazine*, illustrated by Albert Bailey

'The Mystery of the Baghdad Chest'
UK – January 1932, volume 83, issue 493 of *The Strand Magazine*; this story was later expanded into the novella 'The Mystery of the Spanish Chest' from the 1960 UK collection *The Adventure of the Christmas Pudding and a Selection of Entrees*.

'While the Light Lasts'
UK – April 1924, issue 229 of *The Novel Magazine*, illustrated by Howard K. Elcock

## Stories in the US volume and pre-publication appearance

'The Edge'

'The Actress'

'While the Light Lasts'

'The House of Dreams'

'The Lonely God'

'Manx Gold'

'Within a Wall'

'The Mystery of the Spanish Chest'
US – no pre-publication appearance has been traced although this novella is an expanded version of the short story 'The Mystery of the Baghdad Chest', which first appeared in volume 49, number 1 of *Ladies' Home Journal* in June 1932

'The Harlequin Tea Set'
US – June 1973, *Ellery Queen's Mystery Magazine*

―――― Secrets from the Agatha Christie Archives ――――

## 2014 (UK only) – *Hercule Poirot and the Greenshore Folly*

The celebrated crime writer Mrs Ariadne Oliver is hired by Sir George and Lady Stubbs to arrange a 'murder hunt' that will take place in the grounds of Nasse House during a fête. Mrs Oliver's premonition of evil comes true on the day in question when a dead body is discovered in the boathouse. The police are baffled as to the motive for the crime and overwhelmed by the plethora of suspects attending the fête. But luckily for everyone Mrs Oliver has already called in Hercule Poirot to solve the mystery.

**Publication:** 'Hercule Poirot and the Greenshore Folly' (a novella on which the 1956 novel *Dead Man's Folly* is based) was published in hardback in the UK by HarperCollins on 19 June 2014 featuring a specially commissioned cover design and introduction by Tom Adams, as well as a preface by Agatha Christie's grandson Mathew Prichard.

**Length:** 159pp.

**Price:** £12.95

**Word Count:** 20,000

### Pre-Publication Appearance

UK – 31 October 2013, HarperCollins Kindle e-book available from www.amazon.co.uk

US – 12 November 2013, HarperCollins Kindle e-book available from www.amazon.com

# Special Short-Lived Collections

## 1929 (UK only) – *The Sunningdale Mystery*

Newlywed Tommy and Tuppence Beresford get a new lease of life by running a detective agency and solving a host of extraordinary crimes.

### Stories in the volume

1. 'The Man in the Mist'
2. 'The Man in the Mist' – (*Continued*)
3. 'The Crackler'
4. 'The Crackler' – (*Continued*)
5. 'The Sunningdale' Mystery
6. 'The Sunningdale' Mystery – (*Continued*)
7. 'The House of Lurking Death'
8. 'The House of Lurking Death' – (*Continued*)
9. 'The Unbreakable Alibi'
10. 'The Clergyman's Daughter'
11. 'The Red House'
12. 'The Ambassador's Boots'

### Pre-Publication Appearance

See – 'Official Collections: 1929 – *Partners in Crime*'

**Publication:** *The Sunningdale Mystery* was published in paperback in the UK by Collins in February 1929.

**Length:** 128pp.

**Price:** 6d.

**Trivia:** Another three printings of *The Sunningdale Mystery* followed in 1929 in April, June and August. It was reprinted in February and September 1931, as well as in January 1932 and February 1933. The copy held by the British Library is the February 1933 version. The cover features a green background and depicts a pair of eyes staring over a hand holding a gun, below which lies the body of a man in evening tails. Despite its popularity, *The Sunningdale Mystery* was a relatively short-lived publication. The seven stories that appeared in it became Chapters Eleven to Twenty-Two of *Partners in Crime*. Collins' reason for publishing *The Sunningdale Mystery* was to capitalize on the notoriety of Agatha Christie's real-life disappearance. She became famous in December 1926 when she vanished for eleven days from her home Styles in Sunningdale, Berkshire. See *Agatha Christie and the Eleven Missing Days* by Jared Cade.

## 1929 (UK only) – *2 New Crime Stories* featuring 'The Under Dog' by Agatha Christie and 'Blackman's Wood' by E. Phillips Oppenheim

**Publication:** *2 New Crime Stories* was published in hardback in the UK by the Reader's Library, an imprint of the *Daily Express* newspaper, in September 1929.

**Length:** 188pp.

**Price:** no retail price on the dust jacket

### Reprint

- *2 New Crime Stories* was retitled *Two Thrillers* and reprinted by the *Daily Express* Fiction Library in 1936. *Two Thrillers* does not have a copyright page but bears a British Library date stamp of 2 December 1936, which is when it was processed through their cataloguing system and not the actual publication date. Further clues within *Two Thrillers* narrows the timeframe in which the volume was published. The editor's foreword refers to Agatha Christie's play 'Alibi' (based on *The Murder of Roger Ackroyd*) having been staged in London 'about eight years ago' (i.e. 1928), and there is also a mention of her 'excellent new novel *Murder in Mesopotamia*', which was published in the UK on 6 July 1936, thus indicating *2 New Crimes Stories* was published sometime between then and 2 December 1936.

### Official Collections

'The Under Dog' appears in *The Adventure of the Christmas Pudding and a Selection of Entrees* 1960 (UK) / *The Under Dog and Other Stories* 1951 (US)

## Agatha Christie Booklets (1943–1946)

During the Second World War and its aftermath, a series of booklets were published that are nowadays considered a great rarity among collectors:

**1943 – THE MYSTERY OF THE CRIME IN CABIN 66** (aka 'Problem at Sea') was published by Bantam Books, an imprint of Todd Publishing, in April 1943

———————— Special Short-Lived Collections ————————

(UK) 4d. / 16pp. It was processed through the British Library's cataloguing system on 23 June 1943.

**1943 – POIROT AND THE REGATTA MYSTERY** was published by Bantam Books, an imprint of Todd Publishing, in April 1943 (UK) 4d. / 16pp. It was processed through the British Library's cataloguing system on 16 August 1943.

**1943 – PROBLEM AT POLLENSA BAY** was published by Polybooks, an imprint of Todd Publishing, in 1943 (UK) 6d. / 16pp. There is no copyright page stating the year of publication. CONTENTS: 'Problem at Pollensa Bay' and 'Christmas Adventure' (aka the 1923 version of 'The Adventure of the Christmas Pudding'). It was processed through the British Library's cataloguing system on 16 August 1943.

**1943 – POIROT ON HOLIDAY**, was published by Polybooks, an imprint of Todd Publishing, in November 1943 (UK) 6d. / 16pp. CONTENTS: 'The Regatta Mystery' and 'The Crime in Cabin 66' (aka 'Problem at Sea'). It was processed through the British Library's cataloguing system on 16 November 1943.

**1944 – THE VEILED LADY** was published by Polybooks, an imprint of Todd Publishing, in April 1944 (UK) 6d. / 16pp. CONTENTS: 'The Veiled Lady' and 'The Mystery of the Baghdad Chest'. It was processed through the British Library's cataloguing system on 17 May 1944.

**1944 – CRIME IN CABIN 66** (aka 'Problem at Sea') was published by Vallancey Press in 1944 (UK) 4d. / 16pp. The booklet does not feature a copyright page citing the year of publication, but it was processed through the British Library's cataloguing system on 10 July 1944.

**1946 – POIROT KNOWS THE MURDERER** was published by Polybooks, an imprint of Todd Publishing, in March 1946 (UK) 6d. / 62pp. CONTENTS: 'The Mystery of the Baghdad Chest', 'The Crime in Cabin 66' (aka 'Problem at Sea') and 'Christmas Adventure' (aka the 1923 version of 'The Adventure of the Christmas Pudding'). The British Library processed the booklet through its cataloguing system on 28 June 1946.

**1946 – POIROT LENDS A HAND** was published by Polybooks, an imprint of Todd Publishing, in March 1946 (UK) 6 d. / 62 pp. CONTENTS: 'Problem at Pollensa Bay' (featuring Parker Pyne) 'Poirot and the Regatta Mystery' and 'The Veiled Lady'. The title of this booklet is misleading because Hercule Poirot only appears in the last two stories. The British Library processed the booklet through its cataloguing system on 6 April 1946.

**1965 (US only)** *Surprise! Surprise! A Collection of Mystery Stories with Unexpected Endings*

## Stories in the volume

'Double Sin'
– from *Poirot's Early Cases* (UK 1974) / *Double Sin and Other Stories* (US 1961)

'The Arcadian Deer'
– from *The Labours of Hercules* (UK / US 1947)

'The Adventure of Johnnie Waverly'
– from *Poirot's Early Cases* (UK 1974) / *Three Blind Mice and Other Stories* (US 1950)

'Where There's a Will'
– aka 'Wireless' from *The Listerdale Mystery and Other Stories* (UK 1934) / *The Witness for the Prosecution and Other Stories* (US 1948)

'Greenshaw's Folly'
– from *The Adventure of the Christmas Pudding and a Selection of Entrees* (UK 1960) and *Miss Marple's Final Cases and Two Other Stories* (included in the UK 2002 paperback editions onwards) / *Double Sin and Other Stories* (US 1961)

'The Case of the Perfect Maid'
– from *Miss Marple's Final Cases and Two Other Stories* (UK 1979) / *Three Blind Mice and Other Stories* (US 1950)

'At the Bells and Motley'
– from *The Mysterious Mr. Quin* (UK / US 1930)

'The Case of the Distressed Lady'
– from *Parker Pyne Investigates* (UK 1934) / *Mr. Parker Pyne, Detective* (US 1934)

'The Third Floor Flat'
– from *Poirot's Early Cases* (UK 1974) / *Three Blind Mice and Other Stories* (US 1950)

'The Plymouth Express'
– from *Poirot's Early Cases* (UK 1974) / *The Under Dog and Other Stories* (US 1951)

'The Mystery of the Spanish Shawl'
– aka 'Mr Eastwood's Adventure' from *The Listerdale Mystery and Other Stories* (UK 1934) / *The Witness for the Prosecution and Other Stories* (US 1948)

'The Cornish Mystery'
– from *Poirot's Early Cases* (UK 1974) / *The Under Dog and Other Stories* (US 1951)

'The Witness for the Prosecution'
– from *The Hound of Death and Other Stories* (UK 1933) *The Witness for the Prosecution and Other Stories* (US 1948)

**Publication:** *Surprise! Surprise! A Collection of Mystery Stories with Unexpected Endings*, edited by Raymond T. Bond, was published in hardback in the US by Dodd, Mead and Company on 15 August 1965. It was a short-lived collection designed to introduce the author's work to the teenage market and was not published in the UK.

**Length:** 246pp.

**Price:** $3.50

―――――― Special Short-Lived Collections ――――――

# 1966 (UK) – *13 for Luck! A Selection of Mystery Stories for Young Readers* / 1961 (US)

## Stories in the volume

'The Nemean Lion' – Hercule Poirot
   – from *The Labours of Hercules* (UK / US 1947)

'The Girdle of Hyppolita' – Hercule Poirot
   – from *The Labours of Hercules* (UK / US 1947)

'The Market Basing Mystery' – Hercule Poirot
   – from *Poirot's Early Cases* (UK 1974) / *The Under Dog and Other Stories* (US 1951)

'The Blue Geranium' – Miss Marple
   – from *The Thirteen Problems* (UK / US 1932)

'The Four Suspects' – Miss Marple
   – from *The Thirteen Problems* (UK / US 1932)

'Greenshaw's Folly' – Miss Marple
   – from *The Adventure of the Christmas Pudding* (UK 1960) / *Double Sin and Other Stories* (US 1961)

'The Face of Helen' – Mr. Satterthwaite and Mr. Quin
   – from *The Mysterious Mr. Quin* (UK / US 1930)

'The Bird with the Broken Wing' – Mr. Satterthwaite and Mr. Quin
   – from *The Mysterious Mr. Quin* (UK / US 1930)

'The Unbreakable Alibi' – Tommy and Tuppence Beresford
   – from *Partners in Crime* (UK / US 1929)

'Where There's a Will' – Stand-Alone
   – aka 'Wireless' from *The Hound of Death* (UK 1933) / *The Witness for the Prosecution and Other Stories* (US 1948)

'The Mystery of the Spanish Shawl' – Stand-Alone
   – aka 'Mr. Eastwood's Adventure' from *The Listerdale Mystery* (UK 1934) / *The Witness for the Prosecution* (US 1948)

'Accident' – Stand-Alone
   – from *The Listerdale Mystery* (1934) / *The Witness for the Prosecution* (US 1948)

**Publication:** *13 for Luck! A Selection of Mystery Stories for Young Readers* was a short-lived collection published in hardback by Collins in October 1966 and in the US five years earlier on 21 August 1961.

**Length:** UK 224 pp / US 248 pp

**Price:** UK 15s / US $3.50

## 1966 (US only) – *13 Clues for Miss Marple*

### Stories in the volume

'The Tape-Measure Murder' (aka 'The Case of the Retired Jeweller')
   – from *Miss Marple's Final Cases* (UK 1997) / *Three Blind Mice and Other Stories* (US 1950)

'Strange Jest'
   – from *Miss Marple's Final Cases* (UK 1997) / *Three Blind Mice and Other Stories* (US 1950)

'Sanctuary'
   – from *Miss Marple's Final Cases* (UK 1997) / *Three Blind Mice and Other Stories* (US 1950)

'Greenshaw's Folly'
   – from *The Adventure of the Christmas Pudding and a Selection of Entrees* (UK 1960) and *Miss Marple's Final Cases and Two Other Stories* (included in the UK 2002 paperback editions onwards) / *Double Sin and Other Stories* (US 1961)

'The Case of the Perfect Maid'
   – from *Miss Marple's Final Cases* (UK 1979) / *Three Blind Mice and Other Stories* (US 1950)

'The Case of the Caretaker' (an abridged edition of 'The Case of the Caretaker's Wife')
   – from *Miss Marple's Final Cases* (UK 1979) / *Three Blind Mice and Other Stories* (US 1950)

'The Blue Geranium'
   – from *The Thirteen Problems* (UK / US 1932)

'The Companion'
   – from *The Thirteen Problems* (UK / US 1932)

'The Four Suspects'
   – from *The Thirteen Problems* (UK / US 1932)

'Motive v Opportunity'
   – from *The Thirteen Problems* (UK / US 1932)

'The Thumb Mark of Saint Peter'
   – from *The Thirteen Problems* (UK / US 1932)

'The Bloodstained Pavement'
   – from *The Thirteen Problems* (UK / US 1932)

'The Herb of Death'
   – from *The Thirteen Problems* (UK / US 1932)

**Publication:** *13 Clues for Miss Marple* was published in hardback by Dodd, Mead and Company on 14 August 1966.

**Length:** 241pp.

**Price:** $3.50

―――― Special Short-Lived Collections ――――

# 1974 (US only) *Hercule Poirot's Early Cases*

## Stories in the volume

'The Affair at the Victory Ball'

'The Adventure of the Clapham Cook'

'The Cornish Mystery'

'The Adventure of Johnnie Waverly'

'The Double Clue'

'The King of Clubs'

'The Lemesurier Inheritance' aka 'The Le Mesurier Inheritance'

'The Lost Mine'

'The Plymouth Express' (later expanded into the 1928 novel *The Mystery of the Blue Train*)

'The Chocolate Box'

'The Submarine Plans' (later expanded into 'The Incredible Theft' from the UK 1937 collection *Murder in the Mews: 4 Poirot Stories / Dead Man's Mirror* US 1937).

'The Third-Floor Flat'

'Double Sin'

'The Market Basing Mystery' (later expanded into the title story from the 1937 UK collection *Murder in the Mews: 4 Poirot Stories /* US *Dead Man's Mirror*)

'Wasps' Nest'

'The Veiled Lady'

'Problem at Sea'

'How Does Your Garden Grow?'

**Publication:** *Hercule Poirot's Early Cases* was published in hardback by Dodd, Mead and Company on 16 September 1974.

**Length:** 250pp.

**Price:** $6.95

## Alternate US Collections

*Hercule Poirot's Early Cases* was a short-lived collection because all the stories from it had already appeared in the following official US collections:

- The US edition of ***Poirot Investigates*** (1924) features fourteen stories including 'The Chocolate Box', 'The Veiled Lady' and 'The Lost Mine' – all three of which were omitted from the UK edition.
- ***The Regatta Mystery and Other Stories*** (1939) features 'Problem at Pollensa Bay' and 'How Does Your Garden Grow?'

- ***Three Blind Mice and Other Stories*** (1950) features 'The Adventure of Johnny Waverly' and 'The Third Floor Flat'.
- ***The Under Dog and Other Stories*** (1951) features 'The Affair at the Victory Ball', 'The King of Clubs', 'The Plymouth Express', 'The Market Basing Mystery', 'The Submarine Plans', 'The Adventure of the Clapham Cook', 'The Cornish Mystery', and 'The Lemesurier Inheritance'.
- ***Double Sin and Other Stories*** (1961) features 'The Double Clue' and 'Wasps' Nest'.

## 1982 (UK only) – 'Magnolia Blossom' from *The Agatha Christie Hour*

'The Fourth Man' – Stand-Alone
– from *The Hound of Death* (1933) / *The Witness for the Prosecution* (US 1948)

'The Case of the Discontented Soldier' – Parker Pyne
– from *Parker Pyne Investigates* (1934) / *Mr. Parker Pyne, Detective* (US 1934)

'The Red Signal' – Stand-Alone
– from *The Hound of Death* (1933) / *The Witness for the Prosecution* (US 1948)

'The Girl in the Train' – Stand-Alone
– from *The Hound of Death* (1933) / *The Golden Ball and Other Stories* (US 1971)

**'Magnolia Blossom'** – Stand-Alone
– first published in the UK by Collins in this volume / official collection *Problem at Pollensa Bay and Other Stories* (UK 1991) / *The Golden Ball and Other Stories* (US 1971)

'Jane in Search of a Job' – Stand-Alone
– from *The Listerdale Mystery* (1934) / *The Golden Ball and Other Stories* (US 1971)

'In a Glass Darkly' – Stand-Alone
– *Miss Marple's Final Cases and Two Other Stories* (1979) / *The Regatta Mystery and Other Stories* (US 1939)

'The Case of the Middle-Aged Wife' – Parker Pyne
– from *Parker Pyne Investigates* (1934) / *Mr. Parker Pyne, Detective* (US 1934)

'The Manhood of Edward Robinson' – Stand-Alone
– from *The Listerdale Mystery* (1934) / / *The Golden Ball and Other Stories* (US 1971)

**Publication:** 'Magnolia Blossom' was published in hardback in the UK by Collins in a short-lived collection of stand-alone stories called *The Agatha Christie Hour* in September 1982 as a tie-in with the ten-part Thames Television series of the same name.

**Length:** 190pp.

**Price:** £6.50

──────── Special Short-Lived Collections ────────

**2018 – 'The Wife of the Kenite'** from *Bodies from the Library*
See short story section The A – Z of Crime

**2019 – 'The Man Who Knew'** from *Bodies in the Library 2*
See short story section The A – Z of Crime

**2020 – 'The Incident of the Dog's Ball'** from *Bodies in the Library 3*
See short story section The A – Z of Crime

**2022 – *Personal Call*** from *Ghosts from the Library*
See the Published Stage and Radio Plays section

Part Three

# OTHER GILDED VOLUMES

# The Detection Club Writings

The Detection Club was founded by a group of British crime writers in 1930. Its founding members included Agatha Christie, G.K. Chesterton, Dorothy L. Sayers, Ronald Knox, E.C. Bentley, Anthony Berkeley, Freeman Wills Croft, and Baroness Orczy. From time to time, certain members wrote a series of round-robin novels, novellas and short stories to raise funds for the club. Agatha Christie contributed to two novellas *Behind the Screen* and *The Scoop* as well as the full-length novel *The Floating Admiral*.

## 1983 (UK) / 1984 (US) – *The Scoop* and *Behind the Screen*

*Behind the Screen* was originally broadcast in six instalments on BBC radio in 1930, while *The Scoop* was broadcast in twelve instalments the following year. After each instalment was read out loud by its contributor, it was serialized in the latest edition of *The Listener* magazine which was published four days later. The order of the novellas in the volume contradicts their listing in the title:

- ***Behind the Screen*** – The Ellis family is relaxing in the drawing-room after dinner when Mrs Ellis notices some blood trickling out from behind the Chinese screen. The family's odious lodger Paul Dudden is found lying murdered behind it. The police investigation that follows reveals a tangled web of secrets.
- ***The Scoop*** – Johnson, the *Morning Star* newspaper reporter, is hot on the heels of the Jumbles murderer when he is stabbed to death in a phone box at Victoria Station. For his shell-shocked colleagues at the *Morning Star*, it becomes a matter of pride to upstage their newspaper rivals by hunting down his killer and scoring the ultimate front-page scoop of the capture and arrest.

### Pre-Publication Serialization

- ***Behind the Screen***
  In the UK, *Behind the Screen* was serialized in six instalments of *The Listener* magazine:

    1. 'Behind the Screen I' by **Hugh Walpole** – 18 June 1930
    2. 'Behind the Screen II' by **Agatha Christie** – 25 June 1930
    3. 'Behind the Screen III' by **Dorothy L. Sayers** – 2 July 1930

4. 'Behind the Screen IV: In the Aspidistra' by **Anthony Berkeley** – 9 July 1930
 5. 'Behind the Screen V' by **E.C. Bentley** – 16 July 1930
 6. 'Behind the Screen VI: Mr. Parsons on the Case' by **Ronald Knox** – 23 July 1930

- *The Scoop*
  In the UK, *The Scoop* was serialized in twelve instalments of *The Listener* magazine:

  1. 'Over the Wire' by **Dorothy L. Sayers** – 14 January 1931
  2. 'At the Inquest' by **Agatha Christie** – 21 January 1931
  3. 'Fisher's Alibi' by **E.C. Bentley** - 28 January 1931
  4. 'The Weapon' by **Agatha Christie** – 4 February 1931
  5. 'Tracing Tracey' by **Anthony Berkeley** – 18 February 1931
  6. 'Scotland Yard on the Job' by **Freeman Wills Crofts** – 25 February 1931
  7. 'Beryl in Broad Street' by **Clemence Dane** – 4 March 1931
  8. 'The Sad Truth About Potts' by **E.C. Bentley** – 11 March 1931
  9. 'Bond Street or Broad Street?' by **Anthony Berkeley** – 18 March 1931
  10. 'Beryl Takes the Consequences' by **Clemence Dane** – 25 March 1931
  11. 'Inspector Smart's Nasty Jar' by **Freeman Wills Crofts** – 1 April 1931
  12. 'The Final Scoop' by **Dorothy L. Sayers** – 8 April 1931.

**Publication:** *The Scoop* and *Behind the Screen* were published together in volume form in the UK by Victor Gollancz in January 1983 and in the US by Harper and Row on 2 November 1984.

**Length:** UK 182pp. / US 182pp.

**Price:** UK £ 6.95 / US $13.95 pp

## Post-Publication Appearance

- In the US, 'Behind the Screen' was published in its entirety in *Alfred Hitchcock's Mystery Magazine* in February 1996

# 1931 (UK) / 1932 (US) *The Floating Admiral*

The discovery of Admiral Penistone's body floating in a boat on the Whyn River casts a pall of suspicion and fear over local residents when it is revealed he was stabbed to death. The resourceful Inspector Rudge investigates a case complicated by a second murder before the extraordinary truth is revealed.

## List of contributors

Introduction by **Dorothy L. Sayers**
Prologue: The Three Pipe Dream by **G.K. Chesterton**
Chapter I: Corpse Ahoy! by **Canon Victor L. Whitechurch**
Chapter II: Breaking the News by **G.D.H. and M. Cole**
Chapter III: Bright Thoughts on Tides by **Henry Wade**

———————— Secrets from the Agatha Christie Archives ————————

Chapter IV: Mainly Conversation by **Agatha Christie**
Chapter V: Inspector Rudge Begins to Form a Theory by **John Rhode**
Chapter VI: Inspector Rudge Thinks Better of It by **Milward Kennedy**
Chapter VII: Shocks for the Inspector by **Dorothy L. Sayers**
Chapter VIII: Thirty-Nine Articles of Doubt by **Ronald A. Knox**
Chapter IX: The Visitor in the Night by **Freeman Wills Crofts**
Chapter X: The Bathroom Basin by **Edgar Jepson**
Chapter XI: At the Vicarage by **Clemence Dane**
Chapter XII: Clearing up the Mess by **Anthony Berkeley**
Appendix I: Solutions
Appendix II: NOTES ON MOORING OF BOAT

COUNSEL'S OPINION ON FITZGERALD'S WILL

Although the official solution to the crime is provided by Anthony Berkeley in Chapter XII of the novel, the other contributors – with the exception of G.K Chesterton, Canon Victor L. Whitechurch, and G.D.H. and M. Cole – all propounded their own theories in Appendix I as to who they thought killed Admiral Penistone. Agatha Christie's solution, in addition to being the most ingenious, was also the most admirably succinct.

**Publication:** *The Floating Admiral* was published in hardback in the UK by Hodder and Stoughton on 2 December 1931 and in the US by The Crime Club Inc., an imprint of Doubleday, Doran and Company, on 11 February 1932.

**Length:** UK 351pp. / US 309pp.

**Price:** UK 7s.6d. / US £2.00

**Trivia:** The publication of *The Floating Admiral* inspired a group of Australian writers to try their hand at a similar venture. *Murder Pie* was published by Angus and Robertson in 1936 and involves the mysterious drowning of a secretary on a university campus. Its two editors and co-authors, J.L. Ranken and Jane Clunes Ross, acknowledged *The Floating Admiral* as the source of their inspiration in the book's foreword. The other contributors, all of whom are now largely forgotten, were Walter Murdoch, M. Barnard Eldershaw, S. Elliot Napier, Professor G.V. Portus, Ethel Turner, Professor W.J. Dakin, C.H. Beatie, Ruth Bedford, E. Marie Irvine, Frances Jackson, Noelle Brennan, Allan Clunes Ross, Bruce W. Pratt and Leslie Victor.

# Dodd Mead Omnibus Editions

One of the banes in Agatha Christie's later life was the failure of her British and American publishers to synchronize the publication of each new novel she wrote. Owing to the fickle demands of the serial market, the exigencies of the war and other factors, Dodd Mead sometimes prioritized the publication of an omnibus edition over the latest Christie novel. During the late 1960s, both her UK and US publishers worked much closer together at her request to ensure each new title was released in time for Christmas in the same year. The following is a list of the omnibus editions released by the American publisher throughout her long career.

**30 June 1936** – *Hercule Poirot: Master Detective* featuring *The Murder of Roger Ackroyd, Murder in the Calais Coach* and *Thirteen at Dinner* (US) $1.95 / 928 pp. SPOILER ALERT: The volume contains a foreword in the form of 'A Letter to My Publisher' by Agatha Christie writing as Hercule Poirot, which reveals the name of Roger Ackroyd's killer.

**13 July 1943** – *Triple Threat* featuring *Poirot Investigates, The Mysterious Mr Quin* and *Partners in Crime* (US) $2.50 / 854pp,

**7 September 1954** – *Perilous Journeys of Hercule Poirot* featuring *The Mystery of the Blue Train, Death on the Nile* and *Murder in Mesopotamia* (US) $3.95 / 930pp,

**23 July 1956** – *Surprise Endings by Hercule Poirot* featuring *The ABC Murders, Murder in Three Acts* and *Cards on the Table* (US) $3.50 / 405pp.

**20 May 1957** – *Christie Classics by Agatha Christie* featuring *The Murder of Roger Ackroyd, And Then There Were None*, 'The Witness for the Prosecution', 'Philomel Cottage' and 'Three Blind Mice' (US) $3.50 / 410pp.

**17 October 1960** – *Murder Preferred* featuring *The Patriotic Murders, A Murder is Announced* and *Murder in Retrospect* (US) $4.95 / 410pp.

**9 April 1962** – *Make Mine Murder* featuring *Appointment with Death, Peril at End House* and *Sad Cypress* (US) $4.95 / 473pp.

**30 September 1965** – *Murder International* featuring *So Many Steps to Death, Death Comes as the End, Evil Under the Sun* (US) $4.95 / 478pp.

**17 April 1967** – *Murder in Our Midst* featuring *The Body in the Library, The Murder at the Vicarage* and *The Moving Finger* (US) $5.95 / 444pp.

**2 July 1968** – *Spies Among Us* featuring *They Came to Baghdad, N or M?* and *Murder in Mesopotamia* (US) $6.95 / 543pp.

**21 May 1970** – *The Nursery Rhyme Murders* featuring *A Pocket Full of Rye, Hickory, Dickory, Death* and *Crooked House* (US) $6.95 / 505 pp

**1 May 1972** – *Murder-Go-Round* featuring *Thirteen at Dinner, The ABC Murders* and *Funerals are Fatal* (US) $7.95 / 638pp.

**19 August 1974** – *Murder on Board* featuring *The Mystery of the Blue Train, What Mrs. McGillicuddy Saw!* and *Death in the Air* (US) $7.95 / 601pp.

**1 February 1977** – *Masterpieces of Murder* featuring *The Murder of Roger Ackroyd, And Then There Were None,* 'The Witness for the Prosecution' and *Death on the Nile* (US) $9.95 / 594pp.

**15 February 1977** – *Starring Miss Marple* featuring *A Murder is Announced, The Body in the Library* and *Murder with Mirrors* (US) $10.95 / 630pp.

# The Penguin Millions

From the mid-1930s onwards, Allen Lane, with his brothers John and Richard, revolutionized the British publishing industry by selling high-quality fiction and non-fiction paperbacks to the masses for sixpence apiece under its newly created Penguin imprint.

The first ten Penguin paperbacks were published on 30 July 1935. Agatha Christie holds the distinction of being the only author to have two titles of hers in the original top ten. *The Mysterious Affair at Styles* was the subject of a contractual misunderstanding that led to it being replaced the following year by *The Murder on the Links*. The first ten Penguins were numbered thus: 1) Andre Maurois' *Ariel*, 2) Ernest Hemmingway's *A Farewell to Arms*, 3) Eric Linklater's *Poet's Pub*, 4) Susan Ertz's *Madam Claire*, 5) Dorothy L. Sayer's *The Unpleasantness at the Bellona Club*, **6) Agatha Christie's *The Mysterious Affair at Styles* [replaced in March 1936 with 6A) The Murder on the Links]**, 7) Beverley Nichols' *Twenty-Five*, 8) E. H. Young's *William*, 9) Mary Webb's *Gone to Earth* and 10) Compton Mackenzie's *Carnival*.

In August 1948 Agatha Christie made history when a million copies of her books were published simultaneously by Penguin paperbacks. The ten titles, nos. 682 to 691, each had a print-run of 100,000 copies and the public demand for the ten titles led to further reprints:

No. 682 – *Appointment with Death*
No. 683 – *The ABC Murders*
No. 684 – *The Murder of Roger Ackroyd*
No. 685 – *Lord Edgware Dies*
No. 686 – *The Murder at the Vicarage*
No. 687 – *The Seven Dials Mystery*
No. 688 – *Peril at End House*
No. 689 – *Murder on the Orient Express*
No. 690 – *The Sittaford Mystery*
No. 691 – *The Mystery of the Blue Train*

The venture was deemed so successful – the first set sold around 3.4 million copies – that a second set of ten Christie paperbacks, once again totalling a million copies, was published simultaneously on 22 May 1953. Nos. 924 – 932 featured forewords written especially by the author revealing how she came to write each book or collection of short stories and, not surprisingly, these editions have become highly-sought after by collectors.

    No. 924 – *The Body in the Library*
    No. 925 – *Crooked House*
    No. 926 – *Death Comes as the End*
    No. 927 – *Death on the Nile*
    No. 928 – *The Labours of Hercules* (s/s)
    No. 929 – *Miss Marple and The Thirteen Problems* (s/s)
    No. 930 – *The Moving Finger*
    No. 931 – *The Mysterious Mr Quin* (s/s)
    No. 932 – *Parker Pyne Investigates* (s/s)
    No. 684 – *The Murder of Roger Ackroyd* [Reprinted by popular demand]

# Continuation Cases

Since Agatha Christie's death in 1976, her estate has authorized Hercule Poirot's return to the limelight in a series of books by other authors. More recently, Miss Marple has followed suit in a collection of new stories.

**1992 –** *The D Case, or the Truth About the Mystery of Edward Drood* by Charles Dickens, Carlo Fruttero and Franco Lucentini; originally published in Italy in 1989 and translated into English by Gregory Dowling (San Diego: Harcourt)
Carlo Fruttero and Franco Lucentini bring together the world's great fictional detectives, including Hercule Poirot, Sherlock Holmes and C. Auguste Dupin, at a conference to unravel the mystery of Charles Dickens' unfinished novel *The Mystery of Edwin Drood*.

**1998 –** *Black Coffee* by Charles Osborne (London: HarperCollins)
A novelization of the 1930 play by Agatha Christie in which Hercule Poirot investigates the murder of Claude Amory and the disappearance of a secret formula.

**2014 –** *The Monogram Murders* by Sophie Hannah (London: HarperCollins)
The discovery of three murdered guests at the Bloxom Hotel in London draws Hercule Poirot into one of the most bizarre cases of his career.

**2016 –** *Closed Casket* by Sophie Hannah (London: HarperCollins)
Hercule Poirot solves the murder of an eccentric aristocrat at a country estate in Ireland.

**2018 –** *The Mystery of Three Quarters* by Sophie Hannah (London: HarperCollins)
Hercule Poirot is curious to find out who is sending letters to individuals in his name accusing them of the murder of Barnabus Pandy.

**2020 –** *The Killings at Kingsfisher Hill* by Sophie Hannah (London: HarperCollins)
Hercule Poirot is summoned to the Kingsfisher Hill estate to prove that Richard Devonport's fiancé Helen is innocent of his brother Frank's murder.

**2022 –** *Marple: Twelve New Cases* by Twelve Other Writers (London: HarperCollins)
**Contributors:** 'Evil in Small Places' – Lucy Foley; 'The Second Murder at the Vicarage' – Val McDermid; 'Miss Marple Takes Manhattan' – Alyssa Cole; 'The Unravelling' – Natalia Hayes; 'Miss Marple's Christmas' – Ruth Ware; 'The Open Mind' – Naomi Alderman; 'The Jade Empress' – Jean Kwok; 'A Deadly Wedding Day' – Dreda Say Mitchell; 'Murder at the Villa Rose' – Elly Griffiths; 'The Murdering Sort' – Karen M. McManus; 'The Mystery of the Acid Soil' – Kate Mosse; 'The

Disappearance' – Leigh Bardugo, shortlisted for the Crime Writers' Association's 2023 Short Story Dagger Award.

**2023 –** *Hercule Poirot's Silent Night* by Sophie Hannah (London: HarperCollins)
The Belgian detective stays in a crumbling mansion by the coast while investigating the murder of a man in a Norfolk hospital.

# The World's Thickest Book

Agatha Christie is cited by the Guinness World Records as being the most popular novelist in history as well as author of the world's longest running play, *The Mousetrap*. She entered the Guinness World Records for a third time in 2009 with the publication of the bumper volume *The Complete Miss Marple*; the widest book ever published. It measures 322 mm (12.67 in) and weighs 8.04 kg. According to the Guinness World Records' official website, 'All Agatha Christie's Miss Marple stories – 12 novels and 20 short stories – are collected and published in this volume… There are 68 crimes committed; 11 philandering lovers; 68 secrets and lies; 22 false accusations; 59 red herrings and 21 romances. In all, 43 murders are solved: 12 poisonings; 6 strangulations; 2 drownings; 2 stabbings; a burning; one blow to the head; 1 death by an arrow and 2 people pushed. 143 cups of tea are drunk in the massive volume, there are 66 maids and 47 garments are knitted.'

**Publisher:** *The Complete Miss Marple* was published in the UK by HarperCollins in a limited print edition of 500 copies on 20 May 2009.

**Length:** 4,032pp.

**Price:** £1,000

# The Quotable Christie

**10 September 2015 (UK)** – *Little Grey Cells: The Quotable Poirot* by Agatha Christie, a collection of quotes from the novels and stories, edited by David Brawn, London: HarperCollins.

**Length**: 160pp.

**Price**: £9.99

**5 September 2019 (UK)** – *Murder, She Said: The Quotable Miss Marple* by Agatha Christie, a collection of quotes from the novels and stories, edited by Tony Medawar, London: HarperCollins.

**Length**: 160pp.

**Price**: £9.99

# Part Four
# ADDITIONAL JEWELS IN THE CROWN

# Million-Selling Mary Westmacott

Between 1930 and 1956 Agatha Christie published six novels under the secret nom-de-plume of Mary Westmacott that enabled her to explore various themes close to her own experience such as love, betrayal, abandonment and redemption. In February 1949, she was upset when her pseudonym was exposed in the *Sunday Times* as some of the characters and events in the books were inspired by her family and friends, who had no idea they had been used in this way.

## 1930 – *Giant's Bread*

Vernon Deyre is a brilliant musician whose delightful childhood fails to prepare him for the harsh realities of life. Nor is he aware of the many sacrifices he will have to make to compose his musical masterpiece. Or how his life and all that he holds dear will be jeopardized one night when the ship on which he is sailing across the Atlantic collides with an iceberg.

**Publication:** *Giant's Bread* was published in hardback in the UK by Collins on 14 April 1930 and in the US by Doubleday, Doran and Company, Inc. on 25 July 1930.

**Length:** UK 437pp. / US 358pp.

**Price:** UK 7s.6d / US $1.00

**Word Count:** 102,000

### Post-Publication Serialization

- In Switzerland, *Giant's Bread* appeared in the German language as *Singendes Glas* (*Singing Glass*) in thirty-seven instalments of *Tages-Anzeiger*, the Zurich-based national daily newspaper, from 27 July to 8 September 1973.

## 1934 – *Unfinished Portrait*

An artist befriends a troubled young woman called Celia who is on the brink of suicide. He encourages her to recount her life story to him on a long night's journey into the soul. Her idyllic childhood and success as an adult writer have not prepared her for the shock of losing her husband to another woman. Will she learn to trust and love again, or will she choose death over life?

**Trivia:** The second and most autobiographical of all the Mary Westmacott titles, *Unfinished Portrait* is a fictionalized account of Agatha Christie's childhood, her courting of her first husband Colonel Archie Christie, the birth of their daughter Rosalind and the subsequent breakdown of the couple's marriage.

**Publication:** *Unfinished Portrait* was published in hardback in the UK by William Collins & Sons in March 1934 and in the US by Doubleday, Doran and Company, Inc., on 21 November 1934.

**Length:** UK 316pp. / US 329pp.

**Price:** UK 7s.6d / US $2.00

**Word Count:** 81,000

# 1944 – *Absent in the Spring*

Joan Scudamore has always thought well of herself. On the way home to England after visiting her daughter in Baghdad, she is stranded at a railway resthouse in the desert. The isolation of her harsh surroundings forces her to reflect on her past and go on a journey of the soul in which she is forced to confront the truth about herself and her actions, which have not always been as noble as she claimed.

## Inspiration for the Title

> *From you have I been absent in the spring,*
> *When proud-pied April dress'd in all his trim*
> *Hath put a spirit of youth in everything,*
> *That heavy Saturn laugh'd and leap'd with him.*
> *Yet nor the lays of birds nor the sweet smell*
> *Of different flowers in odour and in hue*
> *Could make me any summer's story tell,*
> *Or from their proud lap pluck them where they grew;*
> *Nor did I wonder at the lily's white,*
> *Nor praise the deep vermilion in the rose;*
> *They were but sweet, but figures of delight,*
> *Drawn after you, you pattern of all those.*
> *Yet seem'd it winter still, and, you away,*
> *As with your shadow I with these did play.*
>
> Sonnet 98, William Shakespeare

## Pre-Publication Serialization

- In the US, *Absent in the Spring* appeared in two instalments of *Good Housekeeping* in July and August 1944.

**Publication:** *Absent in the Spring* was published in hardback in the UK by Collins on 21 August 1944 and in the US by Farrar & Rinehart on 7 September 1944.

**Length:** UK 160pp. / US 250pp.

**Price:** UK 7s.6d. / US $2.00

**Word Count:** 53,000

## 1948 – *The Rose and the Yew Tree*

**Working Title:** *The Soul in the Window Seat* (as cited in Agatha Christie's notebooks)

Hugh Norreys is fascinated by the aristocratic and beautiful Isabella Charteris. Her future seems bright and assured because she is poised to marry her wealthy cousin Rupert following his return from abroad. But she instead falls violently in love with John Gabriel, a selfish and ruthless Second World War hero and runs away with him. Will Isabella's love be enough to redeem him, or will it sow the seeds of her destruction?

### Inspiration for the Title

> *The moment of the rose and the moment of the yew-tree*
> *Are of equal duration. A people without history*
> *Is not redeemed from time, for history is a pattern*
> *Of timeless moments. So, while the light fails*
> *On a winter's afternoon, in a secluded chapel*
> *History is now and England.*
>
> 'Little Gidding' the final poem
> in the *Four Quartets* by T. S. Eliot, 1942

The four poems that comprise the collection (the first three are 'Burnt Cork', 'East Coker', and 'The Dry Salvages') were written by T.S. Eliot in the Second World War during the Blitz and examine perspective, time, humanity and salvation.

### Pre-Publication Serialization

- In the US, *The Rose and the Yew Tree* appeared in two instalments of *Good Housekeeping* in December 1947 and January 1948, illustrated by David Berger.

**Publication:** *The Rose and the Yew Tree* was published in hardback in the UK by William Heinemann Ltd. on 1 November 1948 and in the US by Farrar and Rhinehart on 25 March 1948.

**Length:** UK 221pp. / US 249pp.

**Price:** UK 8s.6d. / US $2.50

**Word Count:** 64,000

## 1952 – *A Daughter's A Daughter*

Ann Prentiss is a widow who has raised her only child Sarah by herself. Now that Sarah is grown up and almost ready to leave the nest, Ann is looking forward to some independence of her own. What Ann is not expecting is to fall in love with a middle-aged widower, who asks her to marry him. Ann's possessive daughter, Sarah, is far from happy at their impending marriage and a bitter and jealous feud erupts between mother and daughter. Are they destined to become enemies for life or will their natural love for each other re-assert itself?

### Inspiration for the Title

The title derives from the well-known proverb 'a son is a son until he takes a wife, but a daughter is a daughter for the rest of your life'.

**Publication:** *A Daughter's a Daughter* was published in hardback in the UK by Heinemann on 24 November 1952 and remained unpublished in the US until it was issued there as a paperback eleven years later by Dell Publishing in September 1963. A hardback edition was eventually released in the US by Arbor Books in March 1972. The novel is based on the play of the same name that Agatha Christie wrote in the late 1930s.

**Length:** UK 200pp. / US Dell 191pp. / US Arbor 191pp.

**Price:** UK 15s. / US Dell .45 cents / US Arbor $5.95

**Word Count:** 57,000

## 1956 – *The Burden* (as Mary Westmacott)

**Working Title**: Angle of Attack (as cited in Agatha Christie's notebooks)

Laura Franklin is a jealous child who lights a candle of intention in the hope her baby sister Shirley will die. But one night, when an unexpected disaster places them both in danger, Laura does not hesitate to save Shirley's life. Her subsequent devotion to Shirley knows no bounds, but as their lives progress into adulthood Laura is to discover that love, like all burdens, comes at a price.

### Inspiration for the Title

> '*For my yoke is easy, and my burden is light*'
> Gospel of St. Matthew, Ch. II, V.30

### Pre-Publication Serialization

- In Canada, *The Burden* appeared as a one-shot serialization in the *Star Weekly Complete Novel*, a Saturday supplement of the *Toronto Star* newspaper, on 10 November 1956.

**Publication:** *The Burden* was published in hardback in the UK by Heinemann on 12 November 1956 and remained unpublished in the US until it was issued as a paperback seven years later by Dell Publishing in September 1963. A hardback edition was eventually released in the US by Arbor Books in June 1973.

**Length:** UK 236pp. / US Dell 233pp. / US Arbor 223pp.

**Price:** UK 12s.6d. / US .45 cents / US Arbor $6.95

**Word Count:** 55,000

## Post-Publication Serialization

- In the UK, *The Burden* appeared in four weekly instalments of *Woman* magazine from 11 August to 1 September 1973, illustrated by John Heseltine.

The first instalment stated that *The Burden* had been 'written some years ago' by Agatha Christie and was 'now serialized for the first time'. Her dual writing identity was highlighted in an article called 'Amazing Agatha, Remarkable Mary'. The remaining three instalments did not cite Agatha Christie's name and merely stated 'Serial by Mary Westmacott'. The first instalment on 11 August 1973 also featured a short story by Agatha Christie called 'Where There's a Will', better known as 'Wireless' from the 1933 UK collection *The Hound of Death* and as 'Where There's a Will' from the 1948 US collection *The Witness for the Prosecution and Other Stories*.

# Autobiographical Writings

## 1946 – *Come, Tell Me How You Live* (as Agatha Christie Mallowan)

*Come, Tell Me How You live* is a travel book that recounts how the bestselling crime writer accompanied her second husband Max Mallowan on his archaeological digs in the Middle East during the 1930s. By her own admission she was the low-brow and he was the high-brow. A light-hearted and frivolous book, with an unerring eye for the humorous side of human foibles, it was written during the Second World War, after Max was posted to Egypt, when Agatha was living alone at Lawn Flats in Hampstead, London, and was feeling nostalgic for their former way of life. The memoir poignantly recaptures the couple's innocent, carefree days in Syria and is full of anecdotes which provide an amusing glimpse of what it is like to excavate ancient cities with a primitive labour force.

### Inspiration for the Title

*Come, Tell Me How You Live* takes its title from verse three of a song the White Knight sings to Alice in chapter eight of *Through the Looking Glass* (1871) by Lewis Carroll. The White Knight refers to the song by several names: *Haddock's Eyes*; *The Aged Man*; *Ways and Means;* and *A-Sitting on a Gate*. The White Knight claims the song is performed to a tune of his invention which Alice recognizes as *My Heart and Lute* by Thomas Moore. The song – sometimes referred to as a poem – is a parody of 'Resolution and Independence', a lyrical poem by William Wandsworth, first composed in 1802 and published in 1807 in *Poems in Two Volumes*. Agatha Christie wrote her own parody of the song called 'A-Sitting on a Tell (With apologies to Lewis Carroll)' for inclusion in *Come, Tell Me How You Live*. The title itself is a wordplay on a 'tell' which is an archaeological term for a mound or site. The first three verses of the White Knight's song are as follows:

>I'll tell thee everything I can:
>   There's little to relate.
>I saw an aged man,
>   A-sitting on a gate.
>"Who are you, aged man?" I said,
>   "And how is it you live?"
>And his answer trickled through my head,
>   Like water through a sieve.

Secrets from the Agatha Christie Archives

> He said, "I look for butterflies
>    That sleep among the wheat:
> I make them into mutton-pies,
>    And sell them in the street.
> I sell them unto men," he said,
>    "Who sail on stormy seas;
> And that's the way I get my bread –
>    A trifle, if you please."
> But I was thinking of a plan
>    To dye one's whiskers green,
> And always use so large a fan
>    That they could not be seen.
> So, having no reply to give
>    To what the old man said,
> I cried, "Come, tell me how you live!"
>    And thumped him on the head.

**Publication:** *Come, Tell Me How You Live* was published in hardback in the UK on 11 November 1946 by William Collins & Sons and in the US by Dodd, Mead and Company on 8 October 1946.

**Length:** UK 192pp. / US 225pp.

**Price:** UK 10s.6d. / US $3.00

**Word Count:** 65,000

**Trivia:** *Come, Tell Me How You Live* was one of two books published as Agatha Christie Mallowan – the other being *Star Over Bethlehem* – so her fans would not be misled into thinking it was a detective story.

# 1977 – *An Autobiography*

Agatha Christie's enthralling murder mysteries are enjoyed by armchair crime solvers around the world. She was an intensely private woman who gave few interviews during her lifetime. It was always her intention that her autobiography should only be published after her death. Rather than adhere to a strict chronology with dates, she has written a fascinating account of her life that is, for the most part, a lucky dip of happy recollections that is sure to delight her legion of fans and add lustre to her reputation as one of the twentieth century's most compelling storytellers.

## Pre-Publication Serialization

- In the UK, *An Autobiography* appeared in four instalments of the *Daily Mail* newspaper (London) from 24 October to 27 October 1977. Since the autobiography makes no reference whatsoever to Agatha Christie's disappearance, the

―――――― Autobiographical Writings ――――――

serialization also included, on 26 October, an article by Harry Weaver detailing the basic facts of what was then an unexplained episode.
- In the US, excerpts from *An Autobiography* appeared in:
  - *Ladies' Home Journal*, October 1977, as 'An Enchanted Childhood'
  - *New York Times* magazine section, 18 September 1977, as 'oirot' First Case'
- In Canada, excerpts from *An Autobiography* appeared in:
  - *The Ottawa Journal*, 29 October 1977, as 'Murderers Are Wicked'
  - *Weekend* magazine, a supplement to the *Whig-Standard* newspaper, 29 October 1977, as 'Murderers Are Wicked'

**Publication:** *An Autobiography* was published in hardback in the UK by Collins on 10 November 1977 and in the US by Dodd, Mead and Company on 14 November 1977.

**Length:** UK 542pp. / US 529pp.

**Price:** UK £7.95 / US $15.00

**Word Count:** 235,000

**Trivia:** In 2009, *An Autobiography* was re-issued in hardback by Harper, an imprint of HarperCollins, with a bonus CD featuring highlights of Agatha Christie's voice dictating portions of her memoir.

## Post-Publication Serialization

- In Australia, New Guinea, New Zealand and Malaysia, *An Autobiography* appeared in five instalments of *The Australian Women's Weekly* from 21 December 1977 to 18 January 1978.
- In the US, excerpts from *An Autobiography*, appeared in:
  - *The Akron Beacon Journal*, 15 – 17 January 1978
  - *The Writer* magazine, volume 9, number 6, June 1978
  - *Andromeda Spaceways Inflight Magazine,* volume ten, number fifty-five, 2012, as 'Ashfield'

# 2012 – *The Grand Tour*

In January 1922, Agatha Christie accompanied her husband Colonel Archibald Christie on a ten-month tour around the world. Archie was employed as the tour's Financial Adviser and it was his job to promote the forthcoming British Empire Exhibition to be held at Wembley on the outskirts of London in 1924. The tour's itinerary included South Africa, Australia, New Zealand, Honolulu, America and Canada. Agatha did her best to take the arduous publicity campaign in her stride, and recorded her recollections in a delightful series of letters, postcards and photographs. The trip was made even more challenging because the tour's leader was the highly irascible and pompous Major Ernest Albert Belcher. Not only did Agatha's adventures during the South African leg of the tour provide her with the background for her 1924 novel *The Man in the Brown Suit*, but the irrepressible Major Belcher himself became the role model for the charming and exasperating character of Sir Eustace Pedlar.

**Publication:** *The Grand Tour: Letters and Photographs from the British Empire Edition* was published in hardback in the UK by HarperCollins on 26 April 2012 and in the US as *The Grand Tour: Around the World with the Queen of Mystery* on 20 November 2012.

**Length:** UK 376pp. / US 384pp.

**Price:** UK £25.00 / $29.99

**Word Count:** 49,000

# The Queen of Crime's Poetry

**1901** – In her autobiography, Agatha Christie reveals that at the age of 11 she wrote a poem to commemorate the first day the trams ran in Ealing, London. She quotes a fragment of the poem *'When the first electric trams did run...'* but if – in accordance with her sometimes erratic recollections – it *was* published, then it has yet to come to light despite the attempts of several researchers.

## 1924 – (UK only) *The Road of Dreams*

### Order of poems in the volume

*A Masque from Italy:*
>'The Prologue: Song by Columbine' / 'Harlequin's Song', / 'Pierrot's Song to the Moon' / 'Pierrette Dancing on the Green' / 'Columbine's Song' / 'Pulcinella' / 'Pierrot's Song by the Hearth' / 'The Last Song of Columbine' / 'Epilogue: Spoken by Punchinello'

*Ballads:*
>'The Ballad of the Flint' / 'Elizabeth of England' / 'The Bells of Brittany' / 'Dark Sheila' / 'Ballad of the Maytime' / 'The Princess Sings'

*Dreams and Fantasies:*
>'The Dream Spinners' / 'Down in the Wood' / 'The Road of Dreams' / 'Beatrice Passes' / 'Heritage' / 'The Wanderer' / 'The Dream City' / 'A Passing'

*Other Poems:*
>'Spring' / 'Young Morning' / 'Hymn to Ra' / 'A Palm Tree in Egypt' (later retitled 'A Palm Tree in the Desert' in the 1973 collection entitled *Poems*) / 'World Hymn, 1914' / 'Easter, 1918' / 'In a Dispensary' / 'To a Beautiful Old Lady' / 'Wild Roses' / 'Love Passes' / 'There Where My Lover Lies' / 'Pierrot Grown Old'

### UK Pre-Publication Appearance

- 'World Hymn' – later retitled 'World Hymn, 1914' – by A.M. Christie appeared in the March / April edition of *Poetry Today* in 1919.

- 'Dark Sheila' by A.M. Christie appeared in the May / June edition of *Poetry Today* in 1919.
- 'A Passing' by A.M. Christie appeared in the November / December edition of *Poetry Today* in 1919.

**Publication:** *The Road of Dreams* was self-published by Agatha Christie and distributed in volume form by Geoffrey Bles in 1924 without the benefit of a copyright date. It is a requirement of law that all publishing houses within the United Kingdom submit a copy of every book they publish to the British Library. Some publishers are tardier than others in sending copies of their books to the library, which has a policy of sending out three reminder letters, after which they do not pursue the matter further. Although the British Library's copy of *The Road of Dreams* has no official publisher's copyright date, the back page bears the stamp of the British Library and the date '17 January 1925', which is when the volume of poetry was recorded in their catalogue system. *The English Catalogue of Books* (volume XI, A – L, January 1921 to December 1925), compiled by the British Library, incorrectly cites 'January 1925' as *The Road of Dreams'* publication date. Consequently, some commenters have mistakenly cited 1925 as the year of publication, but this is factually incorrect. *The English Catalogue of Books* is not an infallible guide to when a book was first published. For instance, *Poirot Lends a Hand* and *Poirot Knows the Murderer* were both published in the UK in March 1946 by Polybooks, an imprint of Todd Publishing, but *Poirot Lends a Hand* has a British Library date stamp of 6 April 1946, while *Poirot Knows the Murderer* has a British Library date stamp of 28 June 1946. Agatha Christie's most famous play *The Mousetrap* (see volume two of this bibliography, entitled *Agatha Christie's Spotlight on Murder*) was published by Samuel French in 1954, but the first edition copy held by the British Library has a date stamp of 14 March 1956. In each instance, the British Library date stamp merely indicates when each title was processed through their vast and complex cataloguing system, which indexes thousands of titles a year. In 1973, Agatha Christie's publisher Collins released a collection of her poetry called *Poems*. The copyright page states unequivocally: 'Volume 1 of this collection was first published by Geoffrey Bles in 1924 under the title *The Road of Dreams*'.

**Length:** 110pp.

**Price:** 5s.

**Word Count:** 5,600

## Post-Publication Appearance

- In the UK, 'Dark Sheila' appeared as an Irish ballad sung by the character of Molly Stanwell in the short story 'Harlequin's Lane', which appeared in issue 241 of *The Story-Teller* magazine in May 1927 prior to inclusion in the 1930 collection *The Mysterious Mr Quin*.
- In Burnie, Australia, the first nine lines of 'The Road of Dreams' appeared in *The Advocate* newspaper on 9 July 1945.
- In Burnie, Australia, the first ten lines of 'Down in the Wood' appeared in *The Advocate* newspaper on 13 July 1945.

- 'Down in the Wood' was also reprinted in Agatha Christie's *An Autobiography* (Collins, 1977) and in *Autumn Chills*, a fresh mix of previously published short stories taken from official Christie collections, HarperCollins, 2023.
- 'In a Dispensary' was reprinted in chapter two of *Agatha Christie: Mistress of Mystery* by Gordon C. Ramsey (published in UK by Collins on 11 November 1968 and in the US by Christie Dodd, Mead and Company on 22 May 1967); as well as in the Agatha Christie based issue of *Lire Magazine Litteraire*, October-Novembre 2020.

**1946 – 'A-Sitting on a Tell (With Apologies to Lewis Carroll)'** from ***Come, Tell Me How You Live*** (an archaeological memoir by Agatha Christie Mallowan), published in the UK by William Collins & Sons and in the US by Dodd, Mead and Company, 1946.

**1965 –** ***Star Over Bethlehem and Other Stories*** **(by Agatha Christie Mallowan) Order of religious poems and stories in the volume:**

*'A Greeting'* (poem)
'STAR OVER BETHLEHEM' (2,200-word short story): Mary and baby Jesus are alone together in a stable when they are confronted by Satan disguised as an angel.

*'A Wreath for Christmas'* (poem)
'THE NAUGHTY DONKEY' (900-word short story): A man and wife, along with their new-born son Jesus, evade their enemies by fleeing into Egypt with the help of a temperamental donkey.

*'Gold, Frankincense and Myrrh'* (poem)
'THE WATER BUS' (3,500-word short story): A woman undergoes a religious transformation on a boat to Greenwich after touching the coat of a passenger.

'IN THE COOL OF THE EVENING' (1,700-word short story): Major and Mrs Grierson return home from a church service to find their desperately ill son has a formed a special friendship.

*'Jenny by the Sky'* (poem)
'PROMOTION TO THE HIGHEST' (3,000-word short story): A group of saints enter the Assembly Chamber in Heaven and petition the Archangel Gabriel so they can return to earth in pity and compassion to help those who need it.

*'The Saints of God'* (poem)
'THE ISLAND' (2,900-word short story): Mary is taken away from the island on which she lives by a man who walks across water.

## UK Pre-Publication Appearance

- The last four lines of the poem 'A Greeting' were quoted in the London *Daily Express* on 16 October 1965.

- 'STAR OVER BETHLEHEM' appeared in *Woman's Journal* in December 1946 and in *Christmas Cheer,* Plymouth Rotary Club's newsletter, December 1954 (UK).
- 'THE NAUGHTY DONKEY' appeared in number 885 of *St. Martin's Review,* the monthly church magazine of St. Martin-in-the-Fields, in December 1964, illustrated by Shephard.

## US Pre-Publication Appearance

- 'THE ISLAND' appeared in the Catholic literary magazine *The Critic* in October 1965, illustrated by Frantz Altschuler

**Publication:** *Star Over Bethlehem* was published in hardback in the UK by Collins on 1 November 1965 and in the US by Dodd, Mead and Company on 15 November 1965.

**Illustrations:** Elsie Wrigley

**Length:** UK 80pp. / US 79pp.

**Price:** UK 13s.6 / US $3.00

**Word Count:** 15,300

**Trivia:** St. Martin-in-the-Fields is an Anglican church at the north-east corner of Trafalgar Square in London. Over the years it has hosted numerous memorial services for famous people and distinguished dignitaries, including Agatha Christie, whose service took place there on 13 May 1976.

## Post-Publication

- 'The Naughty Donkey' was reprinted in *Freunde Marchen, Fabeln und Erzahlung aus all Welt,* (*Friends, Fairytales, Fables and Stories from Around the World*) Reinhard Mohn OHG, Gütersloh 1968 (Germany)
- 'The Water Bus' was reprinted in *A Christmas Treasury of Yuletide Stories and Poems,* edited by James Charlton and Barbara Gilson, Guild America Books 1976 (UK)

# 1973 – *POEMS*

## Order of poems
### VOLUME I

*A Masque from Italy*

'A Masque from Italy' / 'Harlequin's Song' / 'Pierrot's Song to the Moon' / 'Pierrette Dancing on the Green' / 'Columbine's Song' / 'Pulcinella' / 'The Song of Pierrot by the Hearth' / 'The Last Song of Columbine'

'Pierrot Grown Old' / 'Epilogue: 'Spoken by Punchinello'

*Ballads:*
'The Ballard of the Flint' / 'Elizabeth of England' / 'The Bells of Brittany' / 'Isolt of Brittany' / 'Dark Sheila' / 'Ballad of the Maytime' / 'The Princess Sings'

*Dreams and Fantasies:*
'The Dream Spinners' / 'Down in the Wood' / 'The Road of Dreams' / 'Heritage' / 'The Wanderer' / 'The Dream City' / 'A Passing'

*Other Poems:*
'Spring' / 'Young Morning' / 'Hymn to Ra' / 'A Palm Tree in the Desert' (originally published as 'A Palm Tree in Egypt' in the 1924 collection *The Road of Dreams*) / 'World Hymn 1914' / 'Easter 1918' / 'To a Beautiful Old Lady' / 'Wild Roses' / 'Love Passes' / 'Progression' / 'There Where My Lover Lies'

**VOLUME II**

'Beauty' / 'The Water Flows' / 'The Sculptor' / 'A Wandering Time'

*Places:*
'Ctesiphon' / 'In Baghdad' / 'An Island' / 'The Nile' / 'Dartmoor' / 'To a Cedar Tree' / 'Calvary'

*Love Poems and Others:*
'Count Fersen to the Queen' / 'Beatrice Passes' / 'Undine' / 'Hawthorn Trees in Spring: a Lament of Women' / 'The Lament of the Tortured Lover' / 'What is Love?' / 'To M.E.L.M. in Absence' / 'Remembrance' / 'A Choice' / 'My Flower Garden' / 'Enchantment' / 'Jenny by the Sky'

*Verse of Nowadays:*
'From a Grown-Up to a Child' / 'I Wore My New Canary Suit' / 'Racial Musings' / 'Picnic 1960'

**Publication:** *Poems* was published in hardback the UK by Collins on 29 October 1973 and in the US by Dodd, Mead and Company in September 1973. (The *Catalog of Copyright Entries* held by the Library of Congress states 'portion of contents prev. pub. 1924 under the title *The Road of Dreams*' – thus confirming Agatha Christie's self-publishing venture with Geoffrey Bles did not occur in 1925 as mistakenly asserted by some commentators.) The volume was published without a dust jacket.

**Length:** UK 124pp. / US 124pp.

**Price:** UK £1.25 / US $5.95

**Word Count:** 11,900

# Post-Publication Appearance

- The first verse of 'From a Grown-Up to a Child' was quoted in the *Daily Mail* on 1 November 1973

## 1977 – *Mallowan's Memoirs* by Max Mallowan

The autobiography of Agatha Christie's second husband Max Mallowan quotes several odes she wrote about their experiences working on archaeological digs in the Middle East, although he does not always cite each ode's title. She is known to have penned two odes about Max's archaeological assistant Barbara Parker, whom he married after Agatha's death; another about Professor Donald Wiseman, one of Max's dearest friends; one about Peter Hulin, an epigraphist from Oxford University; one about Professor Jorgen Laesso, who fought in the Danish resistance during the Second World War and another about his three Danes; two about Joan and David Oates; one about Nicholas Kindersley; Marjorie Howard; John Reid; Tariq el Madhlum; Max Mallowan himself; and one entitled 'The Saga of the Keeper, the Architect and the Young Epigraphist (Under the auspices of Lewis Carroll)'.

**Publication:** *Mallowan's Memoirs* was published in hardback in the UK by Collins on 15 September 1977 and in the US by Dodd, Mead and Company in February 1978.

**Length:** UK 320pp. / US 320pp.

**Price:** UK £6.95 / US $.10.95

## 2009 (UK only) – *Star Over Bethlehem* and *The Road of Dreams* and *Poems* (as Agatha Christie Mallowan)

A collector's edition featuring *Star Over Bethlehem and Other Stories* (Collins, 1965), together with Agatha Christie's collected poetry from the volumes *The Road of Dream* (Geoffrey Bles, 1924) and *Poems* (Collins, 1973). Surprisingly, her best-known poem 'In a Dispensary' was omitted from this volume until its inclusion in the 50th anniversary collector's edition which was released in the UK on 25 September 2014.

**Length:** 208pp.

**Price:** £12.99

**Word Count:** 39,000

# Unpublished Work

### Poems

- 'The Cowslip' (written April 1901, aged 10); the poem received its first public broadcast when it was read aloud by Poirot actor David Suchet during the television documentary 'Perspectives' *David Suchet: The Mystery of Agatha Christie*, which was broadcast on ITV on 17 March 2013 (UK)
- 'Ode to Christopher Columbus' (c. 1901)
- Untitled, beginning 'Have ye walked in the wood today..?' (aged 13, c. 1903)
- 'Ma Ville Cherie'
- 'The AA Alphabet for 1915'

### Stories

- 'In the Market Place' (under the pseudonym of Sydney West)
- 'The Choice' (under the pseudonym of Sydney West)
- 'Vision'
- 'Being So Very Wilful'
- 'Stronger than Death'
- 'The Green Gate'
- 'The War Bride'
- 'Witch Hazel'

### Novel

- *Snow Upon the Desert*

### First World War Record

- *What We Did in the Great War* (devised by Agatha Christie and Eileen Morris). An illustrated 60-page booklet, featuring an opera *The Young Students*, complete with music, by 'AMC', 'Agony Column', 'Hints on Etiquette' and a parody inspired by Lewis Carroll called 'The Chemist and the Pharmacists' by 'AC'.

### Film Script

- *Bleak House* – based on the 1853 Charles Dickens' novel.

Before her death in 2004, Agatha Christie's daughter Rosalind Hicks expressed the intention of destroying a series of Teddy Bear stories her mother had written for her as a child because she felt they might tarnish the writer's reputation; whether she fulfilled her intention remains unclear.

# Published Stage and Radio Plays

The following list only features plays written directly for the stage by Agatha Christie. The many third-party stage adaptations of her work will be found in the forthcoming *Agatha Christie's Spotlight on Murder.*

**1934 – *Black Coffee*** (an original play by Agatha Christie) (Alfred Ashley and Son) (Samuel French Ltd.1952) The script was updated by Agatha Christie in 1951 when theatre impresario Peter Saunders produced a UK provincial tour of the play starring Kenneth Kent as Hercule Poirot, and this forms the current acting edition licensed by Samuel French Ltd. *Black Coffee* was novelised by Charles Osborne and published by HarperCollins in 1998, despite featuring a copyright date of 1997.

**1944 – *Ten Little Niggers*** (adapted by Agatha Christie) (Samuel French Ltd. 1944)

- (*10 Classic Mystery and Suspense Plays of the Modern Theatre*, edited by Stanley Richards, Dodd, Mead and Company, US 1973; also featuring Joseph Hayes' *The Desperate Hours*, Jack Roffey's *Hostile Witness*, Edward Chodorov's *Kind Lady*, William Archibald's *The Innocents*, Emlyn Williams' *Night Must Fall*, J.B. Priestley's *An Inspector Calls*, Thomas Job's *Uncle Harry*, Edward Percy's and Reginald Denham's *Ladies in Retirement* and George M. Cohan's *Seven Keys to Baldpate*).

**1946 – *Appointment with Death*** (adapted by Agatha Christie from her 1938 novel of the same name) (Samuel French Ltd.)

**1948 – *Murder on the Nile*** (adapted by Agatha Christie from her 1937 novel *Death on the Nile*) (Samuel French Ltd.)

**1952 – *The Hollow*** (adapted by Agatha Christie from her 1946 novel of the same name) (Samuel French Ltd.)

**1954 – *The Mousetrap*** (adapted by Agatha Christie from her 1947 radio play *Three Blind Mice*) (Samuel French Ltd.)

**1954 – *Witness for the Prosecution*** (adapted by Agatha Christie from her 1925 story 'Traitor Hands')

- (*Famous Plays of 1954,* Victor Gollancz, UK 1954; also featuring John Van Druten's *I am a Camera*, N.C. Hunters' *A Day by the Sea*, Clifford Odets' *The Big*

―――――――――――― Published Stage and Radio Plays ――――――――――――

*Knife* and *Carrington V.C.* by husband and wife Campbell and Dorothy Christie – Agatha Christie's former brother-in-law from her first marriage) (Samuel French Ltd. UK 1957 / US 1954)
- (*Best Mystery and Suspense Plays of the Modern Theatre*, edited by Stanley Richards, Dodd, Mead and Company, US 1971; also featuring Hamilton Dean's and John L. Balder's *Dracula*, Anthony Shaffers' *Sleuth*, Frederick Knott's *Dial M for Murder*, Robert Marasco's *Child's Play*, W. Somerset Maugham's *The Letter*, Patrick Hamilton's *Angel Street*, Joseph Kesselring's *Arsenic and Old Lace*, J.B. Priestly's *Dangerous Corner* and Maxwell Anderson's *Bad Seed*).

**1957 – *Spider's Web*** (an original play by Agatha Christie) (Samuel French Ltd.) (Novelized by Charles Osborne and published in the UK in 2000 by HarperCollins and in the US by St. Martin's Press in 1999).

**1958 – *Verdict*** (an original play by Agatha Christie) (Samuel French Ltd.)

**1958 – *The Unexpected Guest*** (an original play by Agatha Christie) (Samuel French Ltd.) (Novelized by Charles Osborne and published in the UK by Harper Collins and in the US by St. Martin's Press in 1999).

**1960 – *Go Back for Murder*** (adapted by Agatha Christie) (Samuel French Ltd.)

**1963 – *Rule of Three*** featuring ***The Rats, Afternoon at the Seaside*** and ***The Patient*** (three original one-act plays by Agatha Christie) (Samuel French Ltd.)

**1973 – *Akhnaton*** (written in 1937 and edited by Agatha Christie in the same year as publication) (Collins UK) (Dodd, Mead and Company US)

**1993 – *The Mousetrap and Other Plays*** (Agatha Christie) comprising *And Then There Were None* (formerly *Ten Little Niggers*), *Appointment with Death, The Hollow, The Mousetrap, Witness for the Prosecution, Towards Zero* (the indoor version by Gerald Verner, edited by Agatha Christie), *Verdict* and *Go Back for Murder*.

- (HarperCollins UK 1993)
- (Dodd, Mead and Company, US 1978, with an introduction by the thriller writer Ira Levin)

**2017** saw several plays by Agatha Christie (with the exception of *The Rats* and *The Patient*) being published for the first time by Samuel French Ltd. in pre-manuscript form prior to their release in traditional acting editions in 2019:

- ***Butter in a Lordly Dish*** (former radio play)
- ***Personal Call*** (former radio play); also reprinted in *Ghosts from the Library: Lost Tales of Terror and the Supernatural* (A *Bodies from the Library* Special) London: Collins Crime Club, 2022
- ***The Wasps' Nest*** (one-act play)
- ***Yellow Iris*** (former radio play)

— Secrets from the Agatha Christie Archives —

- *Murder in the Studio* (aka *Murder on the Air*) comprising **Personal Call, Yellow Iris** and **Butter in a Lordly Dish** (former radio plays)
- *A Daughter's a Daughter* (the original play on which Agatha Christie based her 1952 Mary Westmacott novel)
- *Fiddlers Three* (redrafted version of the 1971 play *Fiddler's Five*)
- *A Poirot Double Bill* comprising **The Wasps' Nest** and **Yellow Iris** (former stage and radio plays)
- *Rule of Thumb* comprising **The Wasps' Nest, The Rats** and **The Patient** (former stage and radio plays)
- *The Secret of Chimneys* (formerly known as *Chimneys,* based on the 1925 novel)
- *The Stranger* (Agatha Christie's 1932 play, which was the basis for Frank Vosper's 1936 play *Love from a Stranger*)
- *Towards Zero* (the outdoor version written by Agatha Christie)

# Unpublished Plays

- *The Conqueror*
- *Teddy Bear*
- *Eugenia and Eugenics*
- *The Last Séance*
  (original working title *The Mother*)
- *Ten Years*
- *Marmalade Moon*
  (original working title *New Moon*)
- *The Clutching Hand*
  (adapted from Arthur B. Reeves' 1915 novel *The Exploits of Elaine*, London: Hodder and Stoughton)
- *The Sister-in-Law*
  (the first draft was entitled *The Lie*)
- *Someone at the Window*
- *Miss Perry*

## A Masque from Italy

'The Prologue: Song by Columbine' / 'Harlequin's Song', / 'Pierrot's Song to the Moon' / 'Pierrette Dancing on the Green' / 'Columbine's Song' / 'Pulcinella' / 'Pierrot's Song by the Hearth' / 'The Last Song of Columbine' / 'Epilogue: Spoken by Punchinello'

Speculation surrounds the nine poems comprising *A Masque from Italy* from Agatha Christie's poetry collection *The Road of Dreams* (Geoffrey Bless, 1924 UK) and whether she actually wrote them to be performed on the stage; it seems highly improbable because in Part IV of her autobiography she says that when she was 17 or 18, she penned 'a series of poems on the Harlequin legend: Harlequin's song, Columbine's, Pierrot, Pierette, etc.' and sent 'one or two of them to *The Poetry Review*' and was very pleased when they were published and she got 'a guinea prize'. She also says she later set some of these poems to music, adding her compositions were not of a 'high order'.

# Forgotten Gems and Articles by Agatha Christie

- Christie, A.M.C., 'One Hour With Thee Valse', a musical composition for waltzing, published by London Weekes and Co., c. late 1900s. The front cover depicts a romantic-looking young woman with auburn curls. Price 2, net. Agatha Christie was especially pleased when her composition was occasionally played the local band in her hometown of Torquay in Devon although in later life, she remarked that an hour is 'a pretty hefty time for a waltz to last'.
- Christie, Agatha, 'Does a Woman's Instinct Make Her a Good Detective?', *The Star,* 14 May 1928 – the article also reproduced the writer's signature; reprinted in *Murder She Wrote: The Quotable Miss Marple*, edited by Tony Medawar, London: HarperCollins (2019)
- Christie, Agatha, 'Agatha Christie Pleads for the Tragic Family of Croydon', *Sunday Chronicle,* 11 August 1929; reprinted in *Six Against the Yard* by members of The Detection Club, Margery Allingham, Anthony Berkeley, Freeman Wills Crofts, Father Ronald Knox, Dorothy L. Sayers, Russell Thorndike, London: HarperCollins, 2013
- Christie, Agatha, 'The Crime Passionnel', *Britannia and Eve*, February 1930
- Christie, Agatha, 'Murder – and Our Sporting Instinct, *Tit-Bits*, 27 September 1930
- Christie, Agatha, 'What I Would Do If I Were Starving', *Britannia and Eve*, July 1931
- Christie, Agatha, 'A Letter to My Publisher' by Hercule Poirot (identifying the killer of *The Murder of Roger Ackroyd*) was published as a foreword to *Hercule Poirot: Master Detective*, New York: Dodd, Mead and Company, 1936, featuring *The Murder of Roger Ackroyd, Murder in the Calais Coach* and *Thirteen at Dinner*; decades later the letter – with the name of Roger Ackroyd's killer removed – was also published in the UK as a pamphlet and released in a special edition box set called *Styles: Hercule Poirot's First and Last Cases* featuring *The Mysterious Affair at Styles* and *Curtain: Poirot's Last Cases*, London: HarperCollins, 2016
- Christie, Agatha, 'Hercule Poirot Fiction's Greatest Detective', *Daily Mail*, 15 January 1938; reprinted in *Agatha Christie Official Centenary Celebration 1890 – 1990*, ed. by Underwood, Lyn, Belgrave Publishing, 1990; also reprinted, in two parts, as 'Living with Poirot' and 'The Last Word' for the introduction and postscript of *Little Grey Cells: The Quotable Poirot* by Agatha Christie, edited by David Brawn, London: HarperCollins, 2015

———————— Forgotten Gems and Articles by Agatha Christie ————————

- Christie, Agatha, 'How I Became a Writer', *Listener*, 11 August 1938
- Christie, Agatha, 'Drugs and Detective Stories', University College Hospital magazine, volume XXVI (6), December 1941–January 1942; reprinted in the two-volume hardback box-set *Styles: Hercule Poirot's First and Last Cases*, featuring *The Mysterious Affair at Styles* and *Curtain: Poirot's Last Case*, London: HarperCollins, 15 September 2016
- Christie, Agatha, 'Detective Writers in England', an article commissioned by the Ministry of Information and published in a Russian magazine – title unknown – in 1945; reprinted in *Ask a Policeman* by members of The Detection Club, Anthony Berkeley, Milward Kennedy, Gladys Mitchell, John Rhode, Dorothy L. Sayers and Helen Simpson, London: HarperCollins 2012
- Christie, Agatha, *A Letter from Agatha Christie*, attributing guilt to Dr Gully in the unsolved murder case of Charles Bravo in 1876, London: *Sunday Times*, 20 October 1968; retitled 'Who I Think Did It' and reprinted in *Cosmopolitan* magazine (New York), May 1969; both publications featured Elizabeth Jenkins' lengthy article 'Poison at the Priory'
- Christie, Agatha, a letter of appeal to Pope Paul VI in defence of the Latin Mass, signed by over fifty leading cultural, academic and political figures, including Robert Graves, Graham Greene, Cecil Day-Lewis, Compton Mackenzie, Max Mallowan and Iris Murdoch, London: *The Times*, 6 July 1971
- Christie, Agatha, introduction to Saunders, Peter, *The Mousetrap Man*, London: Collins, 1972
- Christie, Agatha, 'Cleopatra as the Dark Lady', letter to editor, London: *The Times* newspaper, 3 February 1973; reprinted in *The Second Cuckoo: A New Selection of Letters to The Times*, chosen by Gregory, Kenneth, London: George Allen and Unwin, (1983), as well as *The Times Great Letters: A Century of Notable Correspondence*, edited by James Owen, Glasgow: Times Books, an imprint of HarperCollins, (2007)
- Christie, Agatha, letter citing her dislikes, *My Pet Hate Book*, in aid of the Save the Children Fun, London: Routledge and Kegan Paul Ltd., 1974
- Christie, Agatha, 'Margery Allingham – A Tribute', originally published in the UK in *Penguin Book News*, March 1968; reprinted in *The Return of Mr. Campion: Uncollected Stories*, Allingham, Margery, New York: St Martin's Press, 1989
- Christie, Agatha, 'Enter Allen Lane and the Penguins', *Agatha Christie Official Centenary Celebration 1890 – 1990*, ed. by Underwood, Lyn, Belgrave Publishing, 1990

# Recipes à la Agatha Christie

- Christie, Agatha, 'Omelet Agatha Christie' and 'Mystery Potatoes', *A Kitchen Goes to War: Famous People Contribute 150 Recipes to a Ration-Time Cookery Book*, London: John Miles, 1940
- Christie, Agatha, 'Hot Bean Salad' recipe, ed. Hellman, Renee, *Celebrity Cooking for You: Dishes Chosen by the Famous*, London: Andre Deutsch 1961
- Christie, Agatha, 'Devon Squab Pie' and 'Thunder and Lightning' recipes, Lothian, Elizabeth, *Devonshire Flavour: A Devonshire Treasury of Recipes and Personal Notes*, Exeter: David and Charles Publishers, 1971
- Christie, Agatha, 'Lemon Sole Greenway' recipe, ed. Falk, Betty, *The Shelter Cookery Book: A Collection of Recipes from Famous People*, London: Penguin Books 1971
- Anonymous, *The National Trust Cookbook*, Swindon: National Trust, 2016, featuring Agatha Christie's recipe for Lobster Bisque

# Parodies and Tributes by Other Writers

**1936 – 'The Clue of the Missing Umbrella'** from the February edition of *Punch* Magazine

Hercule Poirot, Lord Peter Wimsey, Dr Thorndyke and Father Brown are travelling with two other passengers on a train. When it emerges from a dark tunnel, one of the men in their compartment has died in mysterious circumstances.

**1936 –** *Case for Three Detectives* by Leo Bruce (London: Geoffrey Bles)

A murder is committed behind closed doors and three amateur detectives take up the challenge to unmask the killer. Agatha Christie's Hercule Poirot is parodied as Amer Picon, Dorothy L. Sayer's Lord Peter Wimsey is reinvented as Lord Simon Plimsoll and G.K Chesterton's Father Brown appears as Monsignor Smith. Each arrives at his own brilliant solution to the case, iron-clad in its logic and startling in its originality. But one and all are upstaged by Sergeant Beef, who sits in the background and declares, 'I know who done it!'

**1937 –** *Gory Knight* by Margaret Rivers Larminie and Jane Langslow (London: Longman's & Co.)

On arriving at an English country house, a quartet of famous detectives find their hostess' cook Dora Knight has disappeared. The discovery of her body precipitates the arrival of the police in the final stages of the novel. The five famous detectives parodied are: Hippolyte Pommeau (Agatha Christie's Hercule Poirot), Lord Robert Money and his manservant Bunyan (Dorothy L. Sayer's Lord Peter Wimsey and Bunter), Dr Vicary (John Rhodes' Dr Priestley), Mr Hazard (H.C. Bailey's Reggie Fortune), and Inspector Quench (Freeman Wills Crofts' Inspector French). The dust jacket quotes the reaction of two of the parodied authors. 'I greatly enjoyed *Gory Night*', says Freeman Wills Crofts. 'Inspector Quench, I am afraid, is a chip off the old block.' John Rhodes writes, 'The author seems to have caught the peculiarities to perfection. I am, of course, principally interested in Dr Vicary, whose conversation and mannerisms move me to an appreciative chuckle.'

**1952 – 'The Murder of Santa Claus'** by Tage La Cour

Translated into English by Paul IV Liebe, this short pastiche was originally published in 1952 in the Danish anthology *Mord til Jul* (*Murder for Christmas*) under the pseudonym of Donald McGuire and pays homage to the thinly disguised 'Hercules Poiro'. It was published as follows:

- *Ellery Queen's Mystery Magazine*, December 1956 (UK)
- *Ellery Queen's Mystery Magazine*, January 1957 (US)
- *Ellery Queen's Mystery Magazine*, March 1957 (AUS)
- *Ellery Queen's Anthology* #10, 1966

**1953 – 'The Unpleasantness at the Stooges' Cub'**, a parody featuring Captain Hastings and other famous fictional sleuths' sidekicks, by W. Heidenfeld, *Ellery Queen's Mystery Magazine*, February 1953 (US).

**1964 –** *Greenmask* by Elizabeth Linington (New York: Harper and Row). A police detective solves a spate of murders after recognizing that the killer has based his plan of action on Agatha Christie's *The ABC Murders*.

**1965 – 'The Teccoomshire Fen Mystery'**, a Hercule Poirot parody, by Cathie Haig Star, *Ellery Queen's Mystery Magazine,* November 1965 (US).

**1966 – 'The Boy Who Read Agatha Christie'** by William Britain, *Ellery Queen's Mystery Magazine*, December 1966 (US).

**1975 – 'Muddle on the Orient Express'** by Lou Silverstone, with artwork by Angelo Torres, is a satire on the 1974 film *Murder on the Orient Express* starring Albert Finney as Hercule Poirot, which appeared in issue 178 of *Mad Magazine* in October 1975. The cover of the US publication features artwork by Jack Davis depicting characters from the films *The Godfather Part II* and *Murder on the Orient Express* congregating in front of the fabled train.

**1977 –** *The Strange Case of the End of Civilization as We Know It* by John Cleese, Jack Hobbs and Joe McGrath (London: W.H. Allen & Co.). This is the published screenplay for the television comedy featuring Sherlock Holmes' grandson's attempts to prevent Moriarty from taking control of the world. Hercule Poirot, Columbo, Sam Spade, Steve Garrett and Sam McCloud add to the ensuing mayhem.

**1974 – 'Murder in the Pantry'**, a Miss Marple parody, by Michele Spirn, *Ellery Queen's Mystery Magazine*, December 1974 (US); the same issue also features a **Crossword Puzzle: 'To Dame Agatha with Love'** by Jack Luzzatto.

**1977 – 'Ode to Agatha on Her Eightieth Birthday: 15 September 1970'** by the crime writer's husband Max Mallowan from *Mallowan's Memoirs*, Collins (UK) / Dodd, Mead (US) September 1977.

**1979 –** *Jeeves: A Gentleman's Gentleman* by C. Northcote Parkinson (London: Macdonald and Jane's, 1979). This continuation novel was written after the death of its creator P.G. Wodehouse. His immortal character Jeeves recounts episodes from his life as a valet, including the brief period he was employed by the ill-fated Montague Todd. After Montague Todd is kidnapped, Hercule Poirot and Lord Peter Wimsey compete to rescue him from his kidnappers, only to be upstaged by Father Brown.

———————— Parodies and Tributes by Other Writers ————————

**1979 –** *The Eleventh Little Nigger*

*The Eleventh Little Nigger* centres around a revival of Agatha Christie's play *Ten Little Niggers*, which is being staged at the Theatre Gerard in Paris. Paul Samsom arrives late at the theatre one night just before the play is due to begin and finds the rest of the cast dead in their dressing-rooms. A further surprise awaits him in his own dressing room, namely the body of an unknown man, his face and hands covered in white greasepaint, whom the media baptize the eleventh little nigger.

Originally published in 1977 as *Le Onzième Petit Negre* by the independent Paris publishing house Regine Deforges, the novel was translated into English by Gordon Latta and published in the UK as *The Eleventh Little Nigger* by Collins and in the US as *The Eleventh Little Indian* by Dodd, Mead and Company in 1979, respectively.

**1989 – 'The Agatha Christie Books by the Window',** a poem from *The Cinnamon Peeler and Selected Poems* by Michael Ondaatje (London: Picador).

**1990 – Agatha Christie Centenary Tribute (1890 – 1990)**

*A Classic English Crime: 13 Stories for the Christie Centenary from the Crime Writers Association*, edited by Tim Heald (London: Headline)

| | |
|---|---|
| 'Means to Murder' | Margaret Yorke |
| 'Smoke Gets in…' | David Williams |
| 'Holocaust at Mayhem Parva' | Julian Symons |
| 'All's Fair in Love' | Susan Moody |
| 'The Lady in the Trunk' | Peter Lovesey |
| 'Jack Fell Down' | H.R.F. Keating |
| 'Experts for the Prosecution' | Tim Heald |
| 'A Fete Worse than Death' | Paula Gosling |
| 'Wednesday Matinee' | Celia Dale |
| 'Spasm' | Liza Cody |
| 'A Little Learning' | Simon Brett |
| 'Good Time Had By All' | Robert Barnard |
| 'Cause and Effects' | Catherine Aird |

**1998 –** *The Affair at Styles***,** a pastiche of Jared Cade's 1998 biography *Agatha Christie and the Eleven Missing Days* (Peter Owen Ltd.) by Humphrey Carpenter, *The Sunday Times Culture Magazine*, 20 December 1998.

**2000 –** *Who Killed Roger Ackroyd?* On 19 October 2000, Fourth Estate published an English language translation by Carol Cosman of French writer Pierre Bayard's *Who Killed Roger Ackroyd?* (*Qui a tué Roger Ackroyd?,* Les Editions de Minuit, Paris 1998). The front cover of the UK edition features the subtitle: *The Murderer who Eluded Hercule Poirot and Deceived Agatha Christie*, while the actual title page inside the book replaces this subtitle with another: *The Mystery Behind the Agatha Christie Mystery*. Pierre Bayard, a psychoanalyst and a professor of literature at the University of Paris, argues an altogether different character was responsible for stabbing Roger Ackroyd to death than the one exposed by Hercule Poirot.

## Secrets from the Agatha Christie Archives

**2000 – 'Who's Afraid of Agatha Christie?'** is the title story in a collection by Ahmed Faqih published by Keegan Paul International; a man sitting in a lobby reading an exciting detective story by Agatha Christie finds himself being distracted by an annoying stranger.

**2006 – 2008 Evadne Mount:**
*The Act of Roger Murgatroyd* is a mystery novel by Gilbert Adair (Faber, 2006) that takes its title from a word-play on Agatha Christie's *The Murder of Roger Ackroyd* and was written in homage to the practitioners of the Golden Age mystery and in particular to the Queen of Crime. It is the first in a trilogy featuring the crime novelist Evadne Mount. *A Mysterious Affair of Style* (Faber 2007) is a wordplay on *The Mysterious Affair at Styles* while the third *And Then There Was No One: The Last of Evadne Mount* (Faber 2008) takes its title from *And Then There Were None*.

**2013 – P.D. James' Homage:** The fictitious village of Wychwood-under-Ashe from Agatha Christie's 1939 novel *Murder is Easy* inspired the poem 'Bleeding-under-Wychwood' by the crime writer PD James in which she remarks Poirot's grey cells are 'ticking' and Miss Marple's needles are 'clicking'. The poem was published in the 14–28 December 2013 edition of *The Spectator* – the oldest continuously published magazine in Britain – and alleges the village of Bleeding-under-Wychwood is such a hotbed of crime it is the perfect place to take a holiday since you can expect to sleep 'without a snore as you've seldom slept before'.

The same issue of *The Spectator* featured an article by PD James called 'A Nice Gentle Murder' in which she argued the pleasures of 'Golden Age' detective fiction can no longer be written. It was an extraordinary point of view for her to adopt as one of the leading living exponents of the classic English murder mystery.

Malice Domestic, established in 1989, is the name given to an annual conference held in Washington, D.C., to salute traditional mystery novels, past and present, as best typified by the works of Agatha Christie. At each conference the board of Malice Domestic presents the Agatha Awards in six different categories: Best Novel; Best First Mystery; Best Historical Novel; Best Short Story; Best Non-Fiction; and Best Children's / Young Adult Mystery. There is also a Poirot Award which is presented from time to time to individuals other than writers who have made an outstanding contribution to the mystery genre.

The author of nineteen crime novels and three non-fiction titles, as well as two posthumous short story collections to date, PD James was born in Oxford in 1920 and died in 2014, leaving behind a personal fortune in excess of £22 million to be divided amongst her heirs, proof positive that crime does pay for those who have a talent for putting pen to paper.

**2017 – 'Hercule Poirot's Birthday'** is a short story by David Gibb from the October edition of *Mystery Weekly*, a US magazine. The Belgian detective is dining at a restaurant when a female guest is poisoned. He is assisted in his investigation by Captain Hastings and Chief Inspector Japp.

# Novels Featuring Agatha Christie as a Character

The following works of fiction are not endorsed, licensed or authorized by the estate of Agatha Christie or Agatha Christie Ltd. because the gulf between the imaginings of their respective authors and the true facts of her life is too wide to be remotely credible:

**1978 –** *Agatha: The Agatha Christie Mystery* by Kathleen Tynan (London: Star Books / New York: Ballantine Books)

A novelization of Kathleen Tynan's original screenplay for the 1979 Warner Bros. film *Agatha* starring Vanessa Redgrave and Dustin Hoffman; the screenplay was subjected to rewrites by Arthur Hopcraft before and during filming.

**1991 –** *Dorothy and Agatha* by Gaylord Nelson (New York: Dutton)

Dorothy L. Sayers is horrified when she finds the body of a dead man slumped over her typewriter – especially when it transpires his apparent suicide is really murder. Unluckily for the killer, Dorothy is determined with the help of her friend, fellow crime writer Agatha Christie, to unravel the mystery.

**1994 –** *The Bette Davis Murder Case* by George Baxter (New York: St. Martin's Press)

American acting legend Bette Davis visits London during the 1930s and hires a house from the archaeologist Virgil Whyn. Following his murder, she turns to her neighbour Mrs Mallowan – otherwise known as mystery writer Agatha Christie – for help in solving the crime.

**2000 –** *The Case of Compartment 7* by Sam McCarver (New York: Signet)

The year is 1914 and John Darnell, a paranormal detective, boards the Orient Express and finds himself travelling with a sultry spy, Marta Hari, a phantom bride and a young Agatha Miller, later to become the crime writing legend Agatha Christie.

**2004 –** *The London Blitz Murders* by Max Allan Collins (New York: Berkeley Prime Crime)

As the Second World War rages, the renowned pathologist Sir Bernard Spilsbury joins forces with Agatha Christie, who is working as a dispenser at University College

## Secrets from the Agatha Christie Archives

Hospital, to expose a Jack-the-Ripper style murderer who kills four women over five nights in central London.

The story is based on a series of four real-life murders committed by Gordon Frederick Cummins during February 1942, for which he was hanged on 25 June 1942. Although Agatha Christie took no part in the real-life investigation, Sir Bernard Spilsbury was, in fact, the pathologist who carried out the post-mortems on the victims.

**2007 – *Christietown* by Susan Kandel (New York: Harper)**

Cece Caruso's latest biographical subject, Agatha Christie, is causing her headaches, not least because her publisher thinks her research into the crime writer's disappearance is extremely weak. She has only a week in which to improve the section while also contending with the opening day festivities of 'Christietown', a retirement community based around the works of the famous mystery writer. To add to the mayhem, an actress playing Miss Marple in a stage play is murdered.

Susan Kandel is represented by the Sandra Dijkstra Literary Agency, who once approached Agatha Christie Ltd. requesting permission for their client to base a series of mysteries around the character of Hercule Poirot's twin brother Achilles. The idea was declined by Agatha Christie Ltd.

**2014 – *Murder Will Out* by Alison Joseph (London: Endeavour Press)**

The peaceful English village of Sunningdale is rocked by a murder at the local vicarage. Was the dead man Cecil Coates the victim of a crime passional – or something far more sinister? The locals are convinced one woman more than any other is capable of finding out the truth; up-and-coming crime writer Agatha Christie.

**2015 – *Hidden Sins* by Alison Joseph (London: Endeavour Press)**

It's June 1925 and Agatha Christie is holidaying at a hotel in Cornwall. One of the guests is found murdered on the tennis court and a revolver belonging to the manager of the hotel is found nearby. As she delves deeper into the lives and secrets of the staff and hotel guests, she begins to suspect the killing may have its roots in the First World War.

**2016 – *The Woman on the Orient Express* by Lindsay Jane Ashford (Seattle: Lake Union Publishing)**

1928 is a difficult year for Agatha Christie, as well as for Katharine Keeling and Nancy Nelson. When all three women find themselves sharing a train journey to the Middle East, each is desperate to overcome their personal demons, but the past is reluctant to let them go and they find their lives intersecting with lasting repercussions.

In real life Agatha Christie travelled alone on the Orient Express to the Middle East and was not accompanied by Katherine Keeling, who was married to the archaeologist Leonard Woolley. The Woolleys were, in fact, busy at that time excavating the archaeological site of Ur, where two years later Agatha Christie met her second husband-to-be, Max Mallowan, who was working for the couple. The fictitious character of Nancy Nelson resembles Nancy Neele, whose affair with Archie Christie led to him divorcing Agatha in 1928 and marrying her immediately afterwards.

―――― Novels Featuring Agatha Christie as a Character ――――

**2016 –** *Death in Disguise* by Alison Joseph (London: Endeavour Press)

Agatha Christie's old friend Patrick Standbridge invites her to the Embassy Theatre in a bid to cheer her up following the misery of her divorce. But events take a sinister turn at the theatre when 26-year-old Romanian dancer Cosmina Balan is found strangled in her dressing-room. A distraught Patrick is convinced she was murdered by her dancing partner Alexei, but Agatha Christie has other ideas.

**2016 –** *On the Blue Train* by Kristell Thornell (Sydney: Allen and Unwin)

Traumatized by the break-down of her marriage, Agatha Christie finds herself unable to trust her loved ones and her old way of life. The solitude and anonymity she seeks is disrupted when a fictitious character called Harry McKenna, bruised from the end of his own marriage, asks her to dance.

**2017 –** *Miss Christie Regrets* by Guy Fraser-Simpson (Chatham: Urbane Publications)

A series of letters written by the late Agatha Christie is linked to the recent murder of the director of an exhibition of Constable paintings. The investigation is complicated by the discovery of the remains of a dead body found in a block of flats where Agatha Christie lived decades earlier during the Second World War.

**2017 –** *A Talent for Murder* by Andrew Wilson (London: Simon and Schuster)

In December 1926, a sinister doctor attempts to blackmail Agatha Christie into murdering his wife. Will she be able to outwit him, or will she be forced to do the unthinkable?

**2018 –** *A Different Kind of Evil* by Andrew Wilson (London: Simon & Schuster)

At the request of the secret service, Agatha Christie sails to Tenerife in the Canary Islands to investigate the murder of an agent whose partly mummified body has been found covered in the sap of a Dragon tree inside a cave.

**2018 –** *Minky Woodcock: The Girl Who Handcuffed Houdini* by Cynthia Von Buhler (London: Titan Comics' Hard Case Crime imprint)

Minky Woodcock, the daughter of a private detective, who met Agatha Christie years earlier at a funeral, writes to the well-known authoress asking for advice on how to become a private detective. Soon afterwards Minky gets a chance to put her skills to the test when the crime writer Sir Arthur Conan Doyle asks her to help him prove that the great Harry Houdini is a fraudulent medium.

**2019 –** *Death in a Desert Land* by Andrew Wilson (London: Simon & Schuster)

Agatha Christie receives a letter from a family believing their late daughter Gertrude Bell has met with foul play. The dead woman was competing with another archaeologist to the right to artefacts found in the Middle East. Could Mrs Leonard Woolley have done the unthinkable by helping Gertrude Bell into the afterlife with an overdose of sleeping medication?

**2020 –** *I Saw Him Die* by Andrew Wilson (London: Simon & Schuster)

On the eve of her marriage to Max Mallowan, Agatha Christie goes undercover for the Secret Intelligence Service at a shooting lodge on the Isle of Sky and finds herself investigating a double murder.

**2020 –** *The Mystery of Mrs Christie* by Marie Benedict (Napperville: Sourcebooks Landmark)

A fictionalized rehashing of the early years of the crime writer's life and disappearance. While it was promoted as an adult novel, the emotional immaturity underscoring the narrative makes it more suitable for young adults.

**2021 –** *Death at Greenway* by Lori Rader-Day (William Morrow: New York)

Set in Agatha Christie's real-life country house in Devon during the Second World War, a disgraced nurse, tasked with looking after ten children evacuated from London, becomes embroiled in a murder after a body washes ashore.

**2021 –** *Murder at Mallowan Hall* by Colleen Cambridge (Kensington Publishing: New York)

Phyllida Bright, a fictitious housekeeper, discovers a dead body during a house party at the equally fictitious home of her employers Agatha Christie and husband Max Mallowan.

**2022 –** *A Trace of Poison* by Colleen Cambridge (Kensington Publishing: New York)

Agatha Christie's fictitious housekeeper Phyllida Bright has a new mystery to solve after a poisoned cocktail is imbued, but was the intended victim really the president of a local writing club or someone else?

**2022 –** *The Christie Affair* by Nina de Gramont (Mantle: London)

The novel rehashes the disappearance from the alleged point of view of the woman who broke up the Christies' marriage. In reality, however, it does no such thing because in this case she goes from being an English woman called Nancy Neele to an Irishwoman called Nan O'Dea, who as an unwed mother is subjected to abuse by catholic nuns.

The most ridiculous and far-fetched of all the entries in this category, it turns on the idea that Archie and Agatha Christie's daughter Rosalind Hicks was supposedly the daughter of Archie Christie and Nan O'Dea, who murders two of her former abusers at Harrogate during the writer's disappearance in December 1926.

**2022 –** *Young Agatha Christie* by William Augel (Los Angeles: Big)

As a young child, Agatha Christie treats each day as one big crime scene. No mystery is too small or large for her curious mind. Possessed of a penchant for puzzles, she imagines

―――――― Novels Featuring Agatha Christie as a Character ――――――

thrilling twists on classic fairytales, turns a tea party into a full-scale investigation and in general drives her family mad with her inquisitiveness.

**2023 –** *Murder by Invitation Only* by Colleen Cambridge (Kensington Publishing: New York)

During a murder game at Beecham House, the host drops dead and Agatha Christie's fictitious housekeeper Phyllida Bright turns sleuth to hunt down the killer.

**2024 –** *Murder Takes the Stage* by Colleen Cambridge (Kensington Publishing: New York)

Agatha Christie's fictitious housekeeper Phyllida Bright turns sleuth once again to track down a killer terrorizing London's theatre-land.

**2025 –** *The Queens of Crime* by Marie Benedict (St. Martin's Press: New York)

London 1930 and the five Queens of Crime – Agatha Christie, Dorothy L. Sayers, Ngaio Marsh, Margery Allingham, and Baroness Emma Orczy – form a secret society and solve the murder of an English nurse in France to prove to their male counterparts in the Detection Club that being female does not make them second class citizens.

In reality, Margery Allingham did not become a member of the Detection Club until 1934 – the same year Ngaio Marsh published her first crime novel *A Man Lay Dead*. Moreover, New Zealand-born Ngaio Marsh did not join the elite ranks of the Detection Club until 1974.

# Select Non-Fiction Articles by Other Writers

Not a day goes by when Agatha Christie is not making news somewhere in the world. The articles written about her are endless. Readers wishing to receive daily notifications about her are advised to go to https://www.google.com/alerts to receive regular notifications.

Aldridge, Mark, 'Love, Crime and Agatha Christie' from *Screening the Dark Side of Love: From Euro Horror to American Cinema,* ed. Ritzenhoff, Karen A. and Randell, Karen, London: Palgrave, Macmillan, 2012

Andrews, Katrina, 'The Great Detectives: Agatha Christie's Tommy and Tuppence', *The Strand Magazine,* no. 11, 2003

Athanason, Arthur Nicholas, 'The Mousetrap Phenomenon', *The Armchair Detective,* Spring 1979

Atticus, 'Men, Women and Memories', *Sunday Times,* 13 and 20 February 1949

Anon, 'Stories That Thrill', *The Herald* (Melbourne), 20 May 1922

Anon, 'Mrs Agatha Christie: Her Own Story of Her Disappearance', *Daily Mail,* 16 February 1928; reprinted in *Agatha Christie and the Eleven Missing Days* by Jared Cade (Peter Owen Ltd. 1998; revised 2011)

Anon, 'From the Golden Era', *Ellery Queen's Mystery Magazine,* March 1955

Anon, 'One Woman's View of a Great English Scandal', *San Francisco Chronicle,* 14 August 1976 Anon, supplementary material from the *New York Times* News Service and the Associated Press, 22 September 1978. (*The New York Times* was not printed at this time because of a newspaper strike, but records were kept, including an article to the effect that a federal judge, Lawrence W. Pierce, had refused to block distribution of a movie and novel based on Agatha Christie's disappearance in 1926. Two lawsuits had been brought by the late writer's estate and by her only child, Rosalind Christie Hicks, and named in the suit as defendants were Ballantine Books, Casablanca Records and Filmworks, First Artist Corporation and Warner Brothers Inc. The film *Agatha,* starring Vanessa Redgrave and Dustin Hoffman, a fictional speculative account of the disappearance, was subsequently released in 1979.

## Select Non-Fiction Articles by Other Writers

Anon, 'Author Hall of Fame: Agatha Christie', *Suspense*, August 2010

Bernstein, Marcelle, 'Hercule Poirot Is 130 – But Then Agatha Christie Is 79', *Observer,* 14 December 1969

Bonner, Hilary, 'David Suchet as Poirot', *Sherlock Holmes: The Detective Magazine*, no. 40, 2000

Booth, Matthew, 'Sherlock Homes-v-Hercule Poirot', *Sherlock Holmes: The Detective Magazine*, no. 40, 2000

Bowen, Michael, 'Great Detectives: Agatha Christie's Hercule Poirot', *The Strand Magazine*, no.7, 2001, and no. 8, 2002

Burgainnier, E.F. 'Agatha Christie's Other Detectives: Parker Pyne and Harley Quin', *The Armchair Detective*, April 1978

Cade, Jared, *Solved: The Mystery of Agatha Christie's Disappearance*, extracts from *Agatha Christie and the Eleven Missing Days* (Peter Owen Ltd. 1998), *The Daily Telegraph*, 24 October 1998

Cade, Jared, *The Agatha Christie Mystery Solved!*, a one-shot publication of *Agatha Christie and the Eleven Missing Days* (Peter Owen Ltd. 1998), *The Australian Women's Weekly*, February 1999 (the magazine went from being a weekly to a monthly publication in 1982)

Cade, Jared, 'Pick of the Poirots: The Mysterious Affair at Styles', *Sherlock Holmes: The Detective Magazine*, no. 40, 2000

Cade, Jared, 'Pick of the Poirots: The Murder of Roger Ackroyd', *Sherlock Holmes: The Detective Magazine*, no. 41, 2001

Cade, Jared, 'Pick of the Poirots: Peril at End House', *Sherlock Holmes: The Detective Magazine*, no. 42, 2001

Cade, Jared, 'Pick of the Poirots: Murder on the Orient Express', *Sherlock Holmes: The Detective Magazine*, no. 43, 2001

Cade, Jared, 'Pick of the Poirots: The ABC Murders', *Sherlock Holmes: The Detective Magazine*, no. 44, 2001

Cade, Jared, 'Pick of the Poirots: Curtain: Poirot's Last Case', *Sherlock Holmes: The Detective Magazine,* no. 45, 2001

Cade, Jared, 'Curtain up on Christie', *Sherlock Holmes: The Detective Magazine*, no.45, 2001; a report on the 2001 Agatha Christie Theatre Festival at Westcliff-on-Sea, England

Cade, Jared, 'Crime, Punishment and Mystery', extract from *Agatha Christie and the Eleven Missing Days* (Peter Owen Ltd. 1998), *The Mammoth Book of Literary Anecdotes*, edited by Philip Gooden (London: Robinson, 2002)

Calder, Ritchie, 'Agatha and I', *New Statesmen,* 30 January 1976

Carr, John Dickson, 'Connoisseurs in Crime', *Woman's Journal*, March 1955

Chapman, Paul M., 'The Other Detectives: Miss Marple', *Sherlock Holmes: The Detective Magazine*, no. 23, 1998

Davies, David Stuart, 'The Miss Marple Files', *Sherlock*, no. 61, 2004

Dueren, Fred, 'Hercule Poirot', *The Armchair Detective*, February 1974

Gray, Judith, 'Agatha Christie Audio by Agatha Christie', *Crime Time*, no. 26, 2002

Hannigan, Shawn Matthew, 'Mystery Sonnet: Agatha Christie', *Ellery Queen's Mystery Magazine*, March/April, 2011

*Herald and Express* (Torquay), 'The Agatha Centenary' (three souvenir supplements issued by the *Herald and Express*), 5, 6 and 8 September 1990

Hicks, Rosalind, 'Agatha Christie, My Mother', *The Times Saturday Review*, 8 September 1990

Hiscock, Eric, 'Personally Speaking', *Bookseller*, 19 April 1980

Johnson, Roger, 'The Other Detectives: Hercule Poirot: Belgian Sleuth Supreme', *The Sherlock Holmes Gazette*, no. 18, 1996

Jordan, Ruth, 'Footprints: Agatha Christie', *Crimespree Magazine*, March-April 2010

Knox, Valerie, 'Agatha Christie at 76 Is Still Plotting Murders', *The Times*, 1 December 1967

Luzzatto, Jack, 'Crossword Puzzle: To Dame Agatha with Love', *Ellery Queen's Mystery Magazine*, December 1974

Nethercott, Michael, 'Introduction to "The Edge"', *Alfred Hitchcock's Mystery Magazine*, September 2010

Murphy, E. A., 'Classics Revisited: *The Murder of Roger Ackroyd*', *Sherlock Holmes: The Detective Magazine*, no. 39, 2000

Pike, B.A. 'Agatha's Stories', *The Armchair Detective*, Winter 1991

Prichard, Mathew, 'Agatha Christie and the Orient', *The Strand Magazine*, no.2, 1999

Ramsey, Gordon C., 'A Teacher Meets Agatha Christie', *Worcester Academy Bulletin*, Spring 1966; reprinted in *The Armchair Detective*, October 1967

Sanderson, Robert, 'The Other Detectives: Harley Quin', *Sherlock*, no. 58 2003

Shibuk, Charles, 'Agatha Christie: Mistress of Mystery, by G.C. Ramsey and Agatha Christie', *The Armchair Detective*, October 1967

Shibuk, Charles, 'Endless Night, by Agatha Christie', *The Armchair Detective*, January 1968

Sova, Dawn, 'The Great Detectives: Agatha Christie's Mr Quin', *The Strand Magazine*, no. 27, 2009

Spirn, Michele, 'Murder in the Pantry', *Ellery Queen's Mystery Magazine*, December 1974

―――――― Select Non-Fiction Articles by Other Writers ――――――

Star, Cathie Haig, 'The Teccomeshire Fen Mystery', *Ellery Queen's Mystery Magazine*, November 1965

Snowdon, Lord, 'The Unsinkable Agatha Christie', *Toronto Star,* 14 December 1974

Symons, Julian, 'Agatha Christie Talks to Julian Symons About the Gentle Art of Murder', *Sunday Times,* 15 October 1961

Thomas, G. W., 'Murder in Mesopotamia: Agatha Christie in the Middle East', *The Armchair Detective*, Summer 1994

Wilson, Edmund, 'Why Do People Read Detective Stories?', *The New Yorker*, 14 October 1944

Wilson, Edmund, 'Who Cares Who Killed Roger Ackroyd?', *The New Yorker*, 20 January 1945

Winn, Godfrey, 'The Real Agatha Christie', *Daily Mail,* 12 September 1970

Wyndham, Francis, 'The Algebra of Agatha Christie', *Sunday Times Weekly Review,* 27 February 1966

# Her Gift is Pure Genius: Non-Fiction Books by Other Writers

Adams, Tom, *Agatha Christie Cover Story,* Limpsfield, Surrey: Paper Tiger, 1981

Adams, Tom, *Tom Adams Uncovered: The Art of Agatha Christie and Beyond*, London: HarperCollins, 2015

Aldridge, Mark, *Agatha Christie on Screen*, London: Palgrave, Macmillan, 2016

Aldridge, Mark, *Agatha Christie's Poirot: The World's Greatest Detective*, London: HarperCollins, 2020

Mark, Aldridge, *Agatha Christie's Marple: Expert on Wickedness*, London: HarperCollins, 2024

Bailey, Frankie Y., *Out of the Woodpile: Black Characters in Crime and Detective Fiction*, Westport, Connecticut: Greenwood Press, 1991

Bargainnier, Earl, *The Gentle Art of Murder: The Detective Fiction of Agatha Christie,* Bowling Green, Ohio: Bowling Green State University Popular Press, 1980

Barnard, Robert, *A Talent to Deceive: An Appreciation of Agatha Christie,* London: Collins, 1980

Barnett, Stuart, *Agatha Christie's And Then There Were None: A Cultural History (Great Authors, Great Works)*, Lanham, Maryland: Rowman and Littlefield, 2019

Baučeková, Silvia, *Dining Room Detectives: Analyzing Food in the Novels of Agatha Christie*, Newcastle-upon-Tyne: Cambridge Scholars Publishing, 2015

Bayard, Pierre, *Who Killed Roger Ackroyd?: The Murderer Who Eluded Hercule Poirot and Deceived Agatha Christie*, London: Fourth Estate, 2000.

Bearne's Auctions & Valuers of Fine Art, *The Greenway Catalogue*, London: ATG Media, 2006

Behre, Frank, *Get, Come, and Go,* Stockholm: Almqvist and Wiksell, 1973

Behre, Frank, *Studies in Agatha Christie's Writings,* Stockholm: Almqvist and Wiksell, 1967

Bennett, Jackie, *The Writer's Garden: How Gardens Inspired our Best-Loved Authors*, London: Francis Lincoln, 2014

—— Her Gift is Pure Genius: Non-Fiction Books by Other Writers ——

Bernthal, J.C., ed., *The Ageless Agatha Christie: Essays on Her Mysteries and Legacy*, Jefferson, Carolina: McFarland and Company Inc., 2016

Black, Jeremy, *The Importance of Being Poirot*, South Bend, Indiana: St. Augustine's Press, 2021

Bloom, Harold, ed., *Modern Critical Views: Agatha Christie*, New York: Chelsea House, 2002

Brown, Antony M., *Poisoned at the Priory: The Death of Charles Bravo,* featuring Agatha Christie's theory, London: Mirror Books, 2020

Bryan, George B., *Black Sheep, Red Herrings and Blue Murder: The Proverbial Agatha Christie,* Bern: Peter Lang, 1993

Cade, Jared, *Agatha Christie and the Eleven Missing Days*, London: Peter Owen Ltd. 1998; revised edition 2011

Campbell, Mark, *The Pocket Essential Agatha Christie*, Harpenden, Hertfordshire: Pocket Essentials, 2001; revised edition, 2005

Cawthorne, Nigel, *A Brief Guide to Agatha Christie, Queen of Crime*, London: Robinson, 2014

Christie Ltd., Agatha, *The Official Agatha Christie Puzzle Book*, London: Laurence King Publishing, 2024

Clanton, Dan W., *God and the Little Grey Cells: Religion in Agatha Christie's Poirot Stories*, T & T Clark: London, 2024

Cook, Cathy, *The Agatha Christie Miscellany*, Stroud, Gloucestershire: The History Press, 2013, aka *Agatha Christie: Inspiring Lives*, 2019

Cook, Michael, *Detective Fiction and the Ghost Story: The Haunted Text*, London: Palgrave Macmillan, 2014

Cotes, Peter, *Thinking Aloud: Fragments of Autobiography,* London: Peter Owen, 1993

Craig, Patricia and Cadogan, Mary, *The Lady Investigates*, New York: St. Martin's Press, 1981

Curran, John, *Agatha Christie's Secret Notebooks: Fifty Years of Mysteries in the Making*, London: HarperCollins, 2009

Curran, John, *Agatha Christie's Murder in the Making: Stories and Secrets from Her Archive*, London: HarperCollins, 2011

Curran, John, *The Hooded Gunman: An Illustrated History of Collins Crime Club*, London: Collins Crime Club, 2019

David, Penny, *More Hidden Gardens*, London: Cassell Illustrated, 2004

Dommermuth-Costa, Carol, *Agatha Christie: Writer of Mystery*, Minneapolis, Minnesota: Lerner Publications, 1997

DuBose, Martha Hailey, *Women of Mystery: The Lives and Works of Notable Women Crime Novelists*, additional essays Thomas, Margaret C., New York: Thomas Dunne Books, 2000

Eames, Andrew, *The 8.55 to Baghdad: From London to Iran on the Trail of Agatha Christie*, New York: Overlook Press, 2005

East, Andy, *The Agatha Christie Quiz Book,* New York: Pocket Books, 1975

Edwards, Martin, *The Golden Age of Murder: The Mystery of the Writers Who Invented the Modern Detective Mystery*, London: HarperCollins, 2015

Edwards, Martin: *The Life of Crime: Detecting the History of Mysteries and Their Creators*, London: Collins Crime Club, 2022

Engsberg Cunningham, Meghan M., *Agatha Christie: Traveler, Archaeologist, and Author* (Fearless Female Soldiers, Explorers and Aviators) New York: Cavendish Square Publishing, 2017

Escott, John, *Agatha Christie: Woman of Mystery,* Oxford: Oxford University Press, 1997

Evans, Mary Anna, and Bernthal, J.C., eds., *The Bloomsbury Handbook to Agatha Christie*, London: Bloomsbury Academia

Everson, William K., *The Detective in Film*, Secaucus, New Jersey: Citadel Press, 1972

Feinman, Jeffrey, *The Mysterious World of Agatha Christie,* New York: Grosset and Dunlap, 1975

Fido, Martin, *The World of Agatha Christie*, London: Carlton Books, 1999

Fitzgibbon, Russell H., *The Agatha Christie Companion,* Bowling Green, Ohio: Bowling Green State University Popular Press, 1980

Grossvogel, David I., *Mystery and Its Fictions: From Oedipus to Agatha Christie*, Baltimore: John Hopkins University Press, 1979

Gerald, Michael C., *The Poisonous World of Agatha Christie,* Austin, Texas: University of Texas, 1993

Gill, Gillian, *Agatha Christie: The Woman and Her Mysteries,* New York: Free Press, 1990

Goddard, John, *Agatha Christie's Golden Age: Volume I An Analysis of Poirot's Golden Age Puzzles*, London: Stylish Eye Press, 2018

Goddard, John, *Agatha Christie's Golden Age: Volume II Miss Marple and Other Golden Age Puzzles*, Wilmslow, Cheshire: Stylish Eye Press, 2021

Hesse, Beatrix, *The English Crime Play in the Twentieth Century* (Crime Files) London: Palgrave Macmillan, 2015

Hoffman, Megan, *Gender and Representation in British 'Golden Age' Crime Fiction* (Crime Files), London: Palgrave Macmillan, 2016

──────── Her Gift is Pure Genius: Non-Fiction Books by Other Writers ────────

Gregg, Hubert, *Agatha and All That Mousetrap,* London: William Kimber, 1980

Green, Julius, *Curtain Up: Agatha Christie A Life in Theatre*, London: HarperCollins 2015; revised and expanded paperback edition (featuring source notes absent from the first edition) retitled *Agatha Christie: A Life in Theatre*, London: HarperCollins, 2018

Green, Raye, *Agatha Christie's Doctors*, Carmarthen: McNidder and Grace, 2024

Gruber, Ursula, *The Spinster Sleuth and the Funny Little Man from Belgium: Domesticity and Traditional Stereotypes as Markers of Femininity in Agatha Christie*, London: Akademiker Verlag, 2013

Gingold, Kate, *Agatha Annotated: Investigating the Books of the 1920s: Obscure Terms and Historical References in the Works of Agatha Christie*, Tucson, Arizona: Gnu Ventures Company, 2023

Grossvogel, David L., *Mystery and its Fictions from Oedipus to Agatha Christie*, Baltimore: The John Hopkins University Press, 1979

Hack, Richard, *Duchess of Death: The Unauthorized Biography of Agatha Christie*, Beverley Hills, California: Phoenix Books, 2009

Hafdahl, Meg and Florence, Kelly, *The Science of Agatha Christie: The Truth Behind Hercule Poirot, Miss Marple and More Iconic Characters from the Queen of Crime*, New York: Skyhorse Publishing, 2023

Haining, Peter, *Agatha Christie's Poirot, A Celebration of the Great Detective,* London: Boxtree, 1995

Haining, Peter, *Murder in Four Acts,* London: Virgin, 1990

Harkup, Kathryn, *A is for Arsenic: The Poisons of Agatha Christie*, London: Bloomsbury Sigma, 2015

Hart, Anne, *The Life and Times of Hercule Poirot,* London: Pavilion Books, 1990

Hart, Anne, *The Life and Times of Miss Jane Marple,* London: Macmillan, 1985

Hawthorne, Bret, *Agatha Christie's Devon*, Wellington, Somerset: Halsgrove, 2009

Haycraft, Howard, *Murder for Pleasure: The Life and Times of the Detective Story*, London: Peter Davies, 1942

Heald, Tim, ed., *A Classic English Crime: 13 Stories for the Christie Centenary from the Crime Writers' Association*, London: Pavilion Books, 1990

Hiscock, Eric, *Last Boat to Folly Bridge,* London: Cassell, 1970

Holgate, Mike, *Stranger Than Fiction: Agatha Christie's True Crime Inspirations*, Stroud, Gloucestershire: History Press, 2010

Hope, Sally and Tony, *Agatha Christie: Plots, Clues and Misdirection*, Market Harborough: The Book Guild, 2023

Hurdle, Judith, *The Getaway Guide to Agatha Christie's England*, Oakland, California: RDR Books, 1999

Jarossi, Robin, and O'Brien, Alison, *Agatha Christie: Shocking Real Murders Behind her Classic Mysteries*, London: Trinity Mirror, 2017

Kabatchnik, Amnon, *Murder in the West End: The Plays of Agatha Christie and Her Disciples Volume 1*, Orlando: BearManor Media, 2024

Kasius, Jennifer, *Agatha Christie's Miss Marple: The Complete Novels in One Sitting*, Philadelphia, USA: Running Press Miniature Editions, 2014

Kasius, Jennifer, *Agatha Christie's Poirot: The Essential Novels in One Sitting*, Philadelphia, USA: Running Press Miniature Editions, 2014

Kaska, Kathleen, *What's Your Agatha Christie IQ?*, Secaucus, New Jersey: Citadel Press, 1996

Keating, H.R.F., ed., *Agatha Christie, First Lady of Crime*, London: Weidenfeld and Nicholson, 1977

Keating, Peter, *Agatha Christie and Shrewd Miss Marple*, Priskus Books, 2017

Keirans, James E., *The John Dickson Carr Companion*, Vancleave, Massachusetts: Ramble Books, 2015

Langton, Jane, *Agatha Christie's Devon*, Bodmin: Bossiney Books, 1990

Lebeau, Guillaume and Martinetti, Anne, *Agatha: The Real Life of Agatha Christie*, London, London: SelfMadeHero Books, 2016

Light, Alison, *Forever England: Femininity, Literature and Conservatism Between the Wars*, London: Routledge, 1991

Lotts, Drew, *Ordeal by Innocence – Behind the Scenes of the 2018 BBC Agatha Christie Adaptation*, Kindle Edition: BTS Books, 2018

Macaskill, Hilary, *Agatha Christie at Home*, London: Frances Lincoln, 2009

MacGrath, Robin, *A Mind of Her Own: The Story of Mystery Writer Agatha Christie*, Beach Lane Books: La Jolla, California: 2024

Maida, Patricia and Spornick, Nicholas, *Murder She Wrote: A Study of Agatha Christie's Detective Fiction*, Bowling Green, Ohio: Bowling Green State University Popular Press, 1982

Makinen, Meria, *Agatha Christie: Investigating Femininity* (Crime Files), London: Palgrave Macmillan, 2006

Mallowan, Max, *Mallowan's Memoirs*, London: Collins, 1977

Martin, Deborah, *The Official Guide to Agatha Christie in Devon*, Paignton, Devon: Creative Media Publishing, 2009

Newbury, Matt, *Agatha Christie's Devon*, Redruth, Cornwall: Orchard Publications, 2019

——— Her Gift is Pure Genius: Non-Fiction Books by Other Writers ———

McCall, Henrietta, *The Life of Max Mallowan: Archaeology and Agatha Christie*, London: The British Museum Press, 2001

Morgan, Janet, *Agatha Christie: A Biography*, London: Collins, 1984

Morselt, Ben, *An A–Z of the Novels and Short Stories of Agatha Christie*, Paradise Valley, Arizona: Phoenix Publishing Associates, 1985

Mullaney, Colleen, *Agatha Whiskey: 50 Cocktails to Celebrate the Bestselling Novelist of All Time*, New York: Skyhorse Publishing, 2023

Murdoch, Derrick, *The Agatha Christie Mystery*, Toronto: Paguarian Press, 1976

Murch, A.D., *The Development of the Detective Story*, London: Peter Owen Ltd., 1957

Norman, Andrew, *Agatha Christie: The Finished Portrait*, Stroud, Gloucestershire:

Tempus Publishing, 2006

Norman, Andrew, *Agatha Christie* (tourism booklet), Stroud, Gloucestershire: Pitkin Publishing, 2009

Norman, Andrew, *Agatha Christie: The Disappearing Novelist*, London: Fonthill Media, 2014

Oats, Jonathan, *Agatha Christie and Ealing: Queen of Crime and Queen of the Suburbs*, Cambridge: Irregular Special Press, 2024

O'Neil, Terence, *Someone to Love Us*, London: HarperCollins, 2010 (the true-life story that inspired events in Agatha Christie's record-breaking play *The Mousetrap*).

Owens, Carole, *The Lost Days of Agatha Christie*, Stockbridge, Massachusetts: Cottage Press Inc., 1995

Osborne, Charles, *The Life and Crimes of Agatha Christie*, London: Collins, 1982

Palmer, Scott, *Agatha Christie's Ten Little Indians on Film and TV*, New York: Cypress Hills Press, 2016

Palmer, Scott, *The Films of Agatha Christie*, London: Batsford, 1993

Palmer, Scott, *The Films of Hercule Poirot*, New York: Cypress Hills Press, 2016

Palmer, Scott, *The Films of Miss Marple*, New York: Cypress Hills Press, 2016

Palmer, Scott, *The Other Films of Agatha Christie*, New York: Cypress Hills Press

Pamboukian, Sylvia A., *Agatha Christie and the Guilty Pleasure of Poison*, London: Palgrave MacMillan, 2022

Peschel, Teresa, *Agatha Christie, She Watched: One Woman's Plot to Watch 21 Agatha Christie Movies Without Murdering the Director, Screenwriter, Cast or Her Husband*, Hershey: Peschel Press, 2023

Pierce, Karen, *Recipes for Murder: 66 Dishes That Celebrate the Mysteries of Agatha Christie*, Taftsville: Countryman Press Inc., 2023

Porter, Tony, *The Great White Palace: Agatha Christie and All That Jazz: The Magical Story of Burgh Island and Its Hotel*, New York: Doubleday, 2002

Poussart, Annick, *Investigating Agatha Christie*, (Souvenir Catalogue), Quebec: Point-a-Calliere, Montreal Archaeology and History Complex, 2015.

Powers, Anne, *True Crime Parallels to the Mysteries of Agatha Christie*, Jefferson: North Carolina, McFarland and Company, 2019

Prideaux, Desirée, *Sleuthing Miss Marple: Gender, Genre and Agency in Agatha Christie's Crime Fiction*, Liverpool: Liverpool University Press, 2024

Pugh, Tison, *Understanding Agatha Christie*, Columbia: University of South Carolina, 2023

Ramsey, Gordon, *Agatha Christie: Mistress of Mystery*, New York: Dodd, Mead and Co., 1967

Rendon, Joni, *Writers Between the Covers: The Scandalous Romantic Lives of Legendary Literary Casanovas, Coquettes, and Cads*, New York: Plume, 2013

Richards, Stuart, *Agatha Christie and Gothic Horror: Adaptations and Televisuality* (Horror and Gothic Media Cultures), Amsterdam: Amsterdam University Press, 2024

Riley, Dick and McAllister, Pam, *The Bedside, Bathtub and Armchair Guide to Agatha Christie,* New York: Frederick Ungar, 1979; revised edition, New York: Frederick Ungar, 1993

Rivière, François, *In the Footsteps of Agatha Christie,* London: Ebury Press, 1997

Roberts, Tom, *Friends and Villains,* London: Hodder and Stoughton, 1987

Robyns, Gwen, *The Mystery of Agatha Christie,* New York: Doubleday, 1978

Rolls, Alistair, *Agatha Christie and New Directions in Reading Detective Fiction: Narratology and Detective Fiction,* (Routledge Studies in Twentieth-Century Literature), Abingdon: Routledge, 2022

Routley, Erik, *The Puritan Pleasures of the Detective Story: From Sherlock Holmes to Van der Valk*, London: Gollancz, 1972

Rowland, Susan, *From Agatha Christie to Ruth Rendell: British Women Fiction Writers in Detective and Crime Fiction*, Basingstoke: Hampshire: Palgrave Macmillan, 2001

Ryan, Richard T., *Agatha Christie Trivia,* Boston: Quinlan Press, 1987

Salem Press, eds., *Detective and Mystery Short Story Writers* (College Support Series), Amenia: Salem Press, 2016

Sanders, Denis and Lovallo, Len, *The Agatha Christie Companion: The Complete Guide to the Life and Works of Agatha Christie,* New York: Delacorte, 1984; revised edition, New York: Berkley Books, 1989

## Her Gift is Pure Genius: Non-Fiction Books by Other Writers

Santangelo, Elena, *Dame Agatha's Shorts*, Rock Hill, South Carolina: Bella Rosa Books, 2009

Saunders, Peter, *The Mousetrap Man*, London: Collins, 1972

Shaw, Marion and Vanacker, Sabine, *Reflecting on Miss Marple*, London: Routledge, 1991

Sherif, Jaber, *Justice in Three Agatha Christie Novels*, London: Lambert Academic Publishing, 2015

Sova, Dawn B., *Agatha Christie A–Z: The Essential Reference to Her Life and Writings*, New York: Facts on File, 1996

Sutherland, John, 'Poirot's Double-Death' from *Where was Rebecca Shot?: Curiosities, Puzzles, and Conundrums in Modern Fiction*, London: Weidenfeld and Nicholson, 1998

Symons, Julian, *Bloody Murder From the Detective Story to the Crime Novel: A History*, Hammondsworth, Middlesex: revised edition, Penguin, 1974

Symons, Julian, *The Great Detectives: Seven Original Investigations*, illustrated by Adams, Tom, London: Orbis, 1981

Thompson, Henry Douglas, *Masters of Mystery: A Study of the Detective Story*, London: William Collins & Sons, 1931

Thompson, Laura, *Agatha Christie: An English Mystery*, London: Headline Review, 2007; retitled *Agatha Christie: A Mysterious Life*, New York: Pegasus, 2018

Toye, Randall, *The Agatha Christie Who's Who*, London: Frederick Muller, 1980

Toye, Randall and Gaffney, Judith Hawkins, *The Agatha Christie Crossword Puzzle Book*, London: Angus and Robertson, 1981

Trethewey, Rachel, *Mothers of the Mind: The Remarkable Women Who Shaped*, Virginia Woolf, Agatha Christie and Sylvia Plath, Cheltenham: History Press, 2023

Trümpler, Charlotte, ed., *Agatha Christie and Archaeology*, London: British Museum Press, 2001

Tynan, Kathleen, *Agatha: The Agatha Christie Mystery*, New York: Ballantine Books, 1978 (a novelisation of an early draft script by Kathleen Tynan of the 1979 Warner Bros. film *Agatha*, starring Vanessa Redgrave and Dustin Hoffman, prior to the film's script being rewritten by Arthur Hopcraft)

Underwood, Lynn, ed., *Agatha Christie Centenary Booklet*, London: Belgrave Publishing (HarperCollins), 1990

Valentine, Carla, *Murder Isn't Easy: The Forensics of Agatha Christie*, London: Sphere, 2021

Vegara, Isabel Sanchez, *Little People, Big Dreams: Agatha Christie*, London: Frances Lincoln, 2017

Wagoner, Mary, *Agatha Christie*, New York: Twayne Publishers, 1986

Wagstaff, Vanessa and Poole, Stephen, *Agatha Christie: A Reader's Companion*, London: Aurum Press, 2004

Wansell, Geoffrey and Suchet, David, *Poirot and Me*, London: Headline, 2014

Wilson, Colin, *Snobbery with Violence: English Crime Stories and Their Audience*, London: Eyrie and Spottiswoode, 1971

Worsley, Lucy, *Agatha Christie: An Elusive Woman*, London: Hodder and Stoughton, 2022

Worsley, Lucy, *The Art of the English Murder: From Jack the Ripper and Sherlock Holmes to Agatha Christie and Alfred Hitchcock*, New York: Pegasus Books, 2014

Wynne, Nancy B., *The Agatha Christie Chronology*, Santa Barbara, California: Ace Books, 1976

York, R.A., *Agatha Christie: Power and Illusion*, New York: Basingstoke, 2007

Zemboy, James, *The Detective Novels of Agatha Christie*, Jefferson, North Carolina: McFarland and Company, 2008

# Index of Titles

## Index of Books and Plays

*4.50 from Paddington* 12, 78-9
*ABC Murders, The* 44-5, 233-35, 266, 275
*Absent in the Spring* (Mary Westmacott) 243-44
*Adventure of the Christmas Pudding, The* 100-1, 124, 128
*After the Funeral* 12, 73
*Agatha Christie Hour, The* 129, 140, 146, 148, 214, 226
*Akhnaton* 259
*And Then There Were None* 10, 52-3, 233-34
*A Poirot Double Bill* (plays) 260
*Appointment with Death* 49, 233, 235, 258, 259
*Appointment with Death* (play) 258
*At Bertram's Hotel* 84
*Autobiography, An* 13, 20, 24, 34, 35, 179, 248-49, 251, 253

*Big Four, The* 28-9, 30-1, 107, 115, 138, 183
*Behind the Screen* 230-31
*Black Coffee* (novelisation) 258
*Black Coffee* (play) 258
*Body in the Library, The* 12, 59, 234, 236
*Burden, The* (Mary Westmacott) 176, 245, 246
*Butter in a Lordly Dish* (radio play) 259-60
*By the Pricking of My Thumbs* 86-7

*Cards on the Table* 12, 46-7, 233
*Caribbean Mystery, A* 83-4
*Cat Among the Pigeons* 79, 80

*Clocks, The* 83
*The Clutching Hand* (play) 261
*Come, Tell Me How You Live* 247-48, 253
*The Conqueror* (play) 161
*Crooked House* 12, 67-8, 234, 236
*Curtain: Poirot's Last Case* 15, 20, 92-3, 210, 262-63, 275

*Daughter's a Daughter, A* (Mary Westmacott) 245, 260
*Dead Man's Folly* 11, 77-8, 134, 218
*Death Comes as the End* 63, 233, 236
*Death in the Clouds* 44
*Death on the Nile* 48, 233-34, 236, 258
*Destination Unknown* 12, 75-6
*Dumb Witness* 12, 47-8, 139

*Elephants Can Remember* 90-1
*Endless Night* 12, 85-6, 276
*Eugenia and Eugenics* (play) 261
*Evil Under the Sun* 11, 12, 56-7, 233

*Fiddlers Five* (play) 260
*Fiddlers Three* (play) 260
*Five Little Pigs* 59, 60, 94
*Floating Admiral, The* 230-32

*Giant's Bread* (Mary Westmacott) 242
*Go Back for Murder* (play) 259
*Grand Tour, The* 249, 250

*Hallowe'en Party* 23, 87-8
*Hercule Poirot and the Greenshore Folly* 134, 218
*Hercule Poirot's Christmas* 50-1
*Hickory Dickory Dock* 12, 76-7
*Hollow, The* 12, 64-6, 258-59

*The Hollow* (play) 258
*Hound of Death, The* 110, 114, 129, 130, 135, 142-43, 153, 160, 164-65, 175, 177, 188-89, 202, 208-9, 219, 222-23, 226, 246

*Labours of Hercules, The* 106-7, 110-11, 119, 125, 127, 131, 135, 144, 155, 166, 197, 200, 222-23, 236
*The Last Séance* (play) 261
*Listerdale Mystery, The* 99, 129, 131, 140, 144, 145, 147, 151, 157, 159, 164, 167, 190-92, 202, 209-10, 222-23, 226
*Little Grey Cells: The Quotable Christie* 92, 104, 149, 179, 194, 197, 210, 240, 262, 279
*Lord Edgware Dies* 38, 235

*Man in the Brown Suit, The* 12, 24-5, 95, 249
*Marmalade Moon* (play) 261
*Mirror Crack'd from Side to Side, The* 82-3, 234, 236
*Miss Marple's Final Cases* 111, 114, 124, 132, 138, 151, 161, 166, 197, 202, 208, 212-14, 222, 226
*Miss Perry* (play) 261
*Mousetrap, The* (play) 169, 177, 202, 239, 252, 258-59, 283
*Moving Finger, The* 12, 60-1
*Mrs McGinty's Dead* 71-2
*Murder at the Vicarage, The* 34-6, 185, 234-5
*Murder in Mesopotamia* 12, 45-6, 220, 233-34, 277
*Murder in the Mews* 12, 120, 139, 149, 152, 166, 171, 194, 201, 204-5, 211-12, 214, 225
*Murder in the Studio* 260
*Murder is Announced, A* 12, 69, 70, 233-34
*Murder is Easy* 51-2
*Murder of Roger Ackroyd, The* 10, 12, 14, 24, 26-8, 164, 220, 233-36, 262, 268, 275-76
*Murder on the Links, The* 20, 23-4, 95, 235

*Murder on the Nile* (play) 258
*Murder on the Orient Express* 39, 40, 235, 266, 275
*Mysterious Affair at Styles, The* 10, 18-9, 20, 95, 235, 262-63, 268, 275
*Mysterious Mr Quin, The* 107, 118, 132, 146, 163, 165, 174, 178, 184-85, 233, 236, 252
*Mystery of the Blue Train, The* 31-2, 157, 204, 211, 225, 233-35

*N or M?* 12, 58, 234
*Nemesis* 89

*One, Two, Buckle My Shoe* 12, 55-6
*Ordeal by Innocence* 12, 79, 80, 282

*Pale Horse, The* 81, 90
*Parker Pyne Investigates* 112-13, 115, 121, 130, 133, 136, 156, 158, 161, 190-92, 194, 222, 226, 236
*Partners in Crime* 103, 105, 108, 117, 119, 126-27, 136, 147, 148, 150, 167, 170, 172, 181, 183, 219, 220, 223, 233
*Passenger to Frankfurt* 89
*Peril at End House* 37, 233, 235, 275
*Personal Call* (radio play) 227, 259, 260
*Pocket Full of Rye, A* 12, 74, 234
*Poems* 141, 244, 251-52, 254-56
*Poirot Investigates* 20, 95, 100, 102-4, 114, 118, 122-23, 138, 141, 145, 150, 154, 162, 166, 170, 173, 176, 179, 225, 233, 237
*Poirot's Early Cases* 99, 102, 105, 115, 118, 123, 137, 142, 144-45, 149, 157, 159, 166, 168, 173-74, 197, 203, 205, 208, 210, 222-23, 225
*Postern of Fate* 91-2
*Problem at Pollensa Bay* 101, 132, 146, 155, 158, 160, 162, 178, 194-97, 202, 204, 210, 214-15, 221, 225-26

*Road of Dreams, The* 251-52, 254-56
*Rose and the Yew Tree, The* (Mary Westmacott) 12, 244
*Rule of Three* (three one-act plays) 259
*Rule of Thumb* (three one-act plays) 260

Index of Titles

*Sad Cypress* 11, 54-5, 233
*Scoop, The* 230-31
*Secret Adversary, The* 20-3, 88, 95
*Secret of Chimneys, The* 25-6, 95, 260
*Seven Dials Mystery, The* 32-33, 235
*The Sister-in-Law* (formerly *The Lie*) (play) 261
*Sittaford Mystery, The* 32-3, 235
*Sleeping Murder* 13, 93-4
*Someone at the Window* (play) 261
*Sparkling Cyanide* 12, 64, 178, 196, 215
*Spider's Web* (play) 259
*Star Over Bethlehem* 248, 253-56
*The Stranger* (play) 260

*Taken at the Flood* 66-7
*Teddy Bear* (play) 261
*Ten Little Niggers / And Then There Were None* 52-3
*Ten Little Niggers / And Then There Were None* (play) 258-59, 267
*Ten Years* (play) 261
*They Came to Baghdad* 70, 234
*They Do It With Mirrors* 12, 72-3
*Third Girl* 85
*Thirteen Problems, The* 12, 104, 108, 109, 117, 118, 121, 128, 134, 137, 140, 152, 170, 171, 186, 223-24, 236
*Three Act Tragedy* 42-3
*Three Blind Mice* 12
*Towards Zero* 12, 62-3
*Towards Zero* (play) 259

*Unexpected Guest, The* (play) 259
*The Unexpected Guest* (novelisation) 259
*Unfinished Portrait* (Mary Westmacott) 242-43

*Verdict* (play) 259

*Wasps' Nest* (radio/stage play) 259, 260
*While the Light Lasts* 99, 101, 125, 136, 145, 149, 153, 175-76, 197, 216
*Why Didn't They Ask Evans?* 40-1
*Witness for the Prosecution* (play) 258-59

## Index of Short Stories

'Accident' 98-99, 190-91, 200-2, 223
'Actress, The' 99, 216-17
'Adventure of the Western Star, The' 104, 179
'Adventure of the Cheap Flat, The' 100, 180
'Adventure of the Christmas Pudding, The' (short version) 203
'Adventure of the Christmas Pudding, The' (novella) 100-1, 124, 128, 132, 154, 172, 197, 203, 205-8, 214, 217, 220-24
'Adventure of the Clapham Cook, The' 102, 205, 210, 225-26
Adventure of the Dartmoor Bungalow, The' 28, 138
'Adventure of the Egyptian Tomb, The' 102, 180
'Adventure of the Italian Nobleman, The' 103, 180
'Adventure of the Sinister Stranger, The' 103-4, 182, 184
'Affair at the Bungalow, The' 104, 188
'Affair at the Victory Ball, The' 104-5, 204, 210, 225-26
'Affair of the Pink Pearl, The' 105, 182-83
'Ambassador's Boots, The' 105-6, 183-4, 219
'Apples of Hesperides, The' 106, 199, 200
'Arcadian Deer, The' 106, 198, 200, 222
'At the Bells and Motley' 107, 185, 222
'Augean Stables, The' 107, 198, 200

'Bird with the Broken Wing, The' 107-8, 186, 223
'Blind Man's Buff' 108, 182, 184
'Bloodstained Pavement, The' 108, 187, 224
'Blue Geranium, The' 109, 186-7, 223-4

'Call of Wings, The' 109-10, 189, 209, 210
'Capture of Cerebus, The' (the 12th labour of Hercules) 110, 199
'Capture of Cerebus, The' (the 13th labour of Hercules) 110, 199, 200

'Case of the Caretaker, The' (short version) 111, 203-4, 213, 224
'Case of the Caretaker's Wife, The' (longer version of 'The Case of the Caretaker') 111, 224
'Case of the City Clerk, The' 111-12, 193
'Case of the Discontented Husband, The' 112, 192
'Case of the Discontented Soldier, The' 112-13, 192, 226
'Case of the Distressed Lady, The' 113, 192, 222
'Case of the Middle-Aged Wife, The' 113, 192, 226
'Case of the Missing Lady, The' 150, 182, 184
'Case of the Missing Will, The' 113-14, 176, 181
'Case of the Perfect Maid, The' 114, 204, 213, 224
'Case of the Rich Woman, The' 115, 193
'Chess Problem, A' 29-9, 30, 115
'Chocolate Box, The' 116, 181, 211, 225
'Christmas Tragedy, A' 116-17, 188
'Clergyman's Daughter, The', and 'Red House, The' 117, 170, 183-4, 219
'Coming of Mr Quin, The' 117-18, 185
'Companion, The' 118, 187, 224
'Cornish Mystery, The' 118-9, 205, 211, 222, 225-26
'Crackler, The' 219, 182, 184

'Dead Harlequin, The' 120, 185
'Dead Man's Mirror' 12, 120, 139, 152, 162, 171, 194, 195, 201, 214, 224, 225
'Death by Drowning' 121, 188
'Death on the Nile, (A)' 121-2, 193
'Disappearance of Mr Davenheim, The' 122, 180
'Double Clue, The' 122-3, 208, 211, 225-6
'Double Sin' 101, 123-4, 132, 143, 161, 174, 189, 207-8, 211, 213, 222-25
'Dream, The' 123-4, 196-7, 206-7
'Dressmaker's Doll, The' 124-5, 208, 213

'Edge, The' 125, 216-7, 276
'Erymanthian Boar, The' 125-6, 198, 200

'Face of Helen, The' 126, 147, 185, 223
'Finessing the King' and 'Gentleman Dressed in Newspaper, The' 127, 182, 183
'Flock of Geryon, The' 127, 199, 200
'Four and Twenty Blackbirds' 12, 73, 127-28, 203, 206
'Four Suspects, The' 128, 187, 223-4
'Fourth Man, The' 129, 189, 201-2, 226
'Fruitful Sunday, A' 129, 191, 209-10

Gate of Baghdad, The 130, 193
'Gipsy, The' 130, 189, 209-10
'Girdle of Hyppolita, The' 130-1, 198, 200, 223
'Girl in the Train, The' 191, 208, 210, 226
'Golden Ball, The' 110, 129, 130-1, 135, 140, 142, 145-47, 155, 159, 165, 167, 189, 191, 209-10, 215, 226
'Greenshaw's Folly' 132, 206-8, 214, 222-224

'Harlequin Tea Set, The' 99, 125, 132, 136, 145, 149, 175-6, 214-7
'Harlequin's Lane' 133, 186, 252
'Have You Got Everything You Want?' 121, 133, 135, 156, 193-4
'Herb of Death, The' 134, 187, 224
'Horses of Diomedes, The' 134-35, 198, 200
'Hound of Death, The' 110, 114, 129, 130, 135, 142-43, 153, 160, 164-5, 175, 177, 188-9, 202, 208-10, 222-3, 225, 246
'House at Shiraz, The' 135-6, 193
'House of Dreams, The' 136, 216-7
'House of Lurking Death, The' 135, 183-4, 219
'How Does Your Garden Grow?' 136-37, 196-7, 212, 225

'Idol House of Astarte, The' 137, 187
'In a Glass Darkly' 138, 196, 213, 226

## Index of Titles

'Incident of the Dog's Ball, The' 47-8, 138-9, 227
'Incredible Theft, The' 139, 166, 194-5, 205, 211, 224
'Ingots of Gold' 140, 186
'In the Cool of the Evening' 253
'Island, The' 253-54

'Jane in Search of a Job' 140, 191, 209-10, 226
'Jewel Robbery at the Grand Metropolitan, The' 140-41, 180

'Kidnapped Prime Minister, The' 140-41, 180
'King of Clubs, The' 142, 205, 211, 225-26

'Lamp, The' 142, 189, 208-10
'Last Séance, The' 143, 175, 189, 208
'Last Séance, The' (radio play) 261
'Lemesurier Inheritance, The' 144, 204-5, 211, 224, 226
'Lernean Hydra, The' 144, 197, 200
'Listerdale Mystery, The' 98, 129, 131, 140, 144, 145, 147, 151, 157, 159, 164, 167, 190, 191-2, 202, 209, 210, 222-23, 226
'Lonely God, The' 145, 217
'Lost Mine, The' 145, 181, 211, 225
'Love Detectives, The' 107, 145-6, 185, 203-4, 214-15

'Magnolia Blossom' 146, 209-10, 214-15, 226
'Man from the Sea, The' 126, 146-7, 185
'Man in the Mist, The' 147, 182, 184, 219
'Man Who Was No. 16, The' 148, 183-84
'Manhood of Edward Robinson, The' 147-48, 190-01, 209-10, 226
'Manx Gold' 148-49, 216-7, 148
'Market Basing Mystery, The' 149, 152, 194, 204-05, 210, 212, 223, 225-26
'Million Dollar Bond Robbery, The' 149, 150, 180
'Motive v Opportunity' 151-52, 187, 224

'Miss Marple Tells a Story' 150-51, 196-97, 213
'Mr Eastwood's Adventure' 151, 191, 201-02, 222, 225
'Murder in the Mews' 12, 120, 139, 149, 152, 166, 171, 194, 201, 204-5, 211-12, 214, 225
'Mystery of Hunter's Lodge, The' 154, 180
'Mystery of the Baghdad Chest, The' 152-54, 196-97, 206-7, 216-17, 221
'Mystery of the Blue Jar, The' 153, 189, 201-2

'Naughty Donkey, The' 253-54
'Nemean Lion, The' 155, 197, 200, 223
'Next to a Dog' 155, 208, 210, 215

'Oracle at Delphi, The' 156, 193

'Philomel Cottage' 156-57, 190-91, 201-2, 233
'Plymouth Express, The' 157-58, 204-5, 211, 222, 225-26
'Pot of Tea, A' 126, 181
'Problem at Pollensa Bay' 101, 132, 146, 155, 158, 161-62, 178, 185, 194, 196-97, 202, 204, 210, 214-15, 221, 225-26
'Problem at Sea' 158-9, 197, 212, 220-21, 225
'Promotion to the Highest' 253

'Rajah's Emerald, The' 159, 191, 209-10
'Red Signal, The' 148-9, 160, 189, 201-2, 226
'Regatta Mystery, The' 124, 137-38, 151, 153, 158-59, 160-1, 178, 194-97, 207, 213-15, 221, 225-26

'S.O.S' 164, 189, 201-2
'Sanctuary' 12, 161, 208, 212-13, 224
'Second Gong, The' 120, 162, 195, 201-2, 214-15
'Shadow on the Glass, The' 162-63, 185
'Sign in the Sky, The' 163, 185

'Sing a Song of Sixpence' 163-64, 190-1, 201-2
'Soul of the Croupier, The' 165, 185
'Star Over Bethlehem' 248, 253-4, 256
'Strange Case of Sir Arthur Carmichael, The' 165, 189, 209-10
'Strange Jest' 165-66, 202, 204, 213, 224
'Stymphalean Birds, The' 166, 198, 200
'Submarine Plans, The' 139, 166-67, 195, 205, 211, 225-26
'Sunningdale Mystery, The' 167, 181, 182-4, 219-20
'Swan Song' 167, 191, 208-10

'Tape-Measure Murder, The' 168, 203, 213, 224
'Third Floor Flat, The' 168-69, 203, 211, 222, 226
'Three Blind Mice' 12, 99, 111, 114, 128, 146, 166, 168-69, 185, 202-3, 215, 222, 224, 226, 233, 258
'Thumb Mark of St Peter, The' 169, 170
'Tragedy at Marsdon Manor, The' 170, 180
Triangle at Rhodes 170, 171, 194, 195
Tuesday Night Club, The 171, 186-87

'Unbreakable Alibi, The' 172, 183-84, 219, 223
'Under Dog, The' 12, 102, 105, 118, 149, 157, 166, 172-73, 204-7, 213, 220, 222-3, 226

'Veiled Lady, The' 173, 181, 212, 221, 225
'Voice in the Dark, The' 174, 185

'Wasps' Nest, The' 174, 207, 212, 225-26
'Water Bus, The' 253-54
'While the Light Lasts' 99, 101, 125, 136, 145, 149, 153, 174-77, 215-17
'Wife of the Kenite, The' 175, 227
'Wireless' 12, 114, 175-76, 189, 201-2, 222-3, 246
'Within a Wall' 176, 217
'Witness for the Prosecution, The' 98, 129, 151, 153-4, 157, 160, 162, 164, 169, 175-77, 188-89, 191, 200-2, 215, 221-23, 225, 233-34, 246, 258

'Yellow Iris' 178, 196-97, 214-15, 259, 260

# Index of Newspapers

*Abeline Morning Reporter-News, The* (Texas) 42
*Aberdeen Evening News* (Scotland) 152
*Advocate-Messenger, The* (Kentucky) 55
*Albany Evening Herald* (Oregon) 22
*Altoona Tribune, The* (Pennsylvania) 42
*American Fork Citizen* (Utah) 21
*Ames Daily Tribune* (Iowa) 33
*Argus, The* (Melbourne, Australia) 64
*Arizona Daily Star, The* (Texas) 78
*Arizona Republic* (Arizona) 37, 161
*Asbury Park Press* (New Jersey) 42
*Atlanta Constitution, The* (Georgia) 34, 106, 125, 165
*Altoona Tribune* (Pennsylvania) 42
*Australian Women's Weekly, The* (Australia) 45, 47, 53, 56-7, 64, 68, 73, 77, 79, 81, 83, 87, 90-1, 93-4, 106-7, 114, 125-7, 131-2, 135, 144, 155, 166, 169, 174, 176, 249, 275

*Bakersfield Californian* (California) 70
*Basellandschaftliche Zeitung* (Liestal, Switzerland) 55
*Beckley Post-Herald* (West Virginia) 30, 32, 55
*Belvidere Daily Republican*, The (Illinois) 55
*Bernardsville News* (New Jersey) 33
*Bicknell Daily News, The* (Indiana) 21
*Big Spring Texas Daily Herald* (Texas) 42
*Birmingham Daily Gazette* (England) 23
*Blockton News, The* (Iowa) 22
*Blue Mound Sun, The* (Kansas) 21
*Bombay Press* (India) 86
*Bonham Daily Favourite, The* (Texas) 63
*Boone News-Republican, The* (Iowa) 62

*Boston Daily Globe, The* (Connecticut) 74
*Bradford Era, The* (Pennsylvania) 30, 55, 62
*Brandon Daily Sun* (Manitoba, Canada) 30, 45, 55
*Brief Stories (Houston, Texas)* 22, 24
*Bradford Era, The* (Pennsylvania) 30, 55, 62
*Brandon Daily Sun* (Manitoba, Canada) 30, 45, 55
*Bristol Courier, The* (Pennsylvania) 30
*Bristol Daily Courier, The* (Pennsylvania) 55
*Brook Report, The* (Indiana) 33
*Brooklyn Daily Eagle, The* (New York) 28
*Brownsburg Record, The* (Indiana) 21
*Buenhogar* (Mexico) 93

*Camden News, The* (Arkansas) 66-7
*Canadian Magazine Star Weekly Novel, The* (Toronto) 87, 90-1
*Carbondale Free Press, The* (Illinois) 63
*Central Queensland Herald, The* 176
*Cherokee Times, The* (Gaffney, South Carolina) 22
*Chicago Daily Tribune, The* 43, 69, 71, 73-5, 78-9
*Chicago Tribune* (Illinois) 12, 93, 178, 196, 215
*Cincinnati Enquirer, The* (Ohio) 159, 171
*Circleville Herald, The* (Ohio) 65, 67
*Citizen, The* (Gloucestershire, England) 34
*Cleveland Sunday News, The* (Ohio) 32
*Clovis Evening News-Journal* (New Mexico) 42
*Colyer Advance, The* (Kansas) 21
*Corsicana Daily Sun, The* (Texas) 41

*Courier, The* (Dundee, Scotland) 20, 26
*Courier-Express, The* (DuBois, Pennsylvania) 65
*Courier-Mail, The* (Brisbane, Australia) 49
*Courier-Post, The* (Camden, New Jersey) 66

*Daily Courier, The* (Connellsville, Pennsylvania) 62, 66
*Daily Boston Globe, The* (Massachusetts) 30, 73, 104-6, 108, 117, 119, 126-7, 136, 147-48, 150, 167, 172, 183
*Daily Clintonian, The* (Clinton, Indiana) 21, 55, 63, 67
*Daily Corvallis Gazette-Times, The* (Oregon) 42
*Daily Courier, The* (Connellsville, Pennsylvania) 55, 62, 66
*Daily Dispatch* (London) 149, 217
*Daily Express* (London) 12, 45, 50-1, 53, 55, 64, 69, 74, 82, 139, 173, 177, 195, 220, 253
*Daily Gazette for Middlesborough* (England) 152
*Daily Herald* (Biloxi, Mississippi) 41
*Daily Herald, The* (Circleville, Ohio) 62
*Daily Herald, The* (Provo, Utah) 22
*Daily Independent, The* (Elizabeth City, North Carolina) 30
*Daily Inter Lake, The* (Kalispell, Montana) 33, 42
*Daily Mail* (East Riding of Yorkshire) 34
*Daily Mail, The* (Hagerstown, Maryland) 41
*Daily Mail* (London) 49, 111, 129, 131-32, 174, 191, 199, 206-9, 212, 248, 255, 162, 274, 277
*Daily Messenger, The* (Canandaigua, New York State) 42
*Daily News, The* (Frederick, Maryland) 41
*Daily News, The* (Huntington, Philadelphia) 65, 69, 73-5, 78-9, 84
*Daily News* (New York City) 34
*Daily News-Journal, The* (Wilmington, Ohio) 41
*Daily Notes, The* (Canonsburg, Pennsylvania) 66-7

*Daily Republican, The* (Monongahela, Pennsylvania) 55, 63, 67
*Daily St. Charles Cosmos-Monitor* (Missouri) 21
*Daily Times* (Davenport, Iowa) 31, 38
*Daily Times, The* (New Philadelphia, Ohio) 33
*Dallas Oil News, The (*Texas) 22
*Daily Press* (Newport, Virginia) 34
*Daily Silver Belt, The* (Miami, Arizona) 21
*Dallas Oil News, The* (Texas) 22
*Daytona Beach Morning Herald* (Florida) 30
*Decatur Evening Herald, The* (Illinois) 19, 27, 31
*Delphos Herald, The* (Ohio) 62
*Delphos Daily Herald* (Ohio) 8, 68
*Denton Record-Chronicle, The* (Texas) 41
*Detroit Free Press* (Michigan) 114, 161, 203, 213
*Detroit Times, The* (Michigan) 45
Des Moines Register, The (Iowa) 27, 110

*East Liverpool Review* (Ohio) 19, 41
*El Paso Times, The* (Texas) 62
*Elwood Call-Leader* (Indiana) 55
*Enquirer and Evening News, The* (Battle Creek, Michigan) 42
*Emporia Daily Gazette, The* (Kansas) 41
*Evening Citizen* (Glasgow) 164
*Evening Citizen, The* (Ottawa, Canada) 66
*Evening Independent, The* (Massillin, Ohio) 62, 65, 124
*Evening Sentinel* (Staffordshire) 34
*Evening Standard* (London) 50-1, 102, 154, 173
*Evening Star* (Washington D.C.) 27
*Evening Telegram, The* (Rocky Mount, North Carolina) 75
*Evening Telegraph and Post* (Dundee, Scotland) 31, 35, 58
*Evening Tribune, The* (Alberta Lea, Minnesota) 41
*Evesham Standard and West Midland Observer, The* (England) 176
*Express, The* (Lock Haven, Pennsylvania) 41

―――――――――――― Index of Newspapers ――――――――――――

*Fairfield Daily Ledger, The* (Iowa) 55
*Fairbanks Daily-News Miner* (Alaska) 70
*Fitchburg Sentinel, The* (Massachusetts) 41
*Florence Morning News* (Eastern South Carolina) 62
*Francesville Tribune, The* (Indiana) 22

*Gaffney Ledger* (South Carolina) 32, 62, 66
*Galveston Daily News, The* (Texas) 42
*Gazette, The* (Montreal, Canada) 74
*Gettysburg Times, The* (Pennsylvania) 41
*Glasgow Evening News* (Scotland) 171
*Great Falls Tribune* (Montana) 36
*Green Bay Press-Gazette, The* (Wisconsin) 42
*Greenville Evening Banner* (Texas) 30

*Hattiesburg American* (Mississippi) 41
*Honolulu Star-Bulletin* (Hawaii) 42
*Hope Star* (Arkansas) 33
*Hudson Herald, The* (Kansas) 21
*Hutchinson News, The* (Kansas) 41

*Index, The* (Hermitage, Missouri) 21
*Index-Journal, The* (South Carolina) 41
*Indianapolis Star, The* (Indiana) 38, 110, 159, 171
*Iron County New* (Hurley, Wisconsin) 22

*Johnson City Pioneer and Journal-News* (Kansas) 21
*Journal-Every Evening* (Wilmington, Delaware) 42
*Journal-News, The* (Nyack, New York State) 62, 66

*Kansas City Times, The* (Missouri) 72
*Kansas City Star, The* (Missouri) 72
*Kena* (Mexico) 86
*Kentucky Advocate* (Danville, Kentucky) 62
*Kingston Daily Freeman, The* (New York) 41
*Kotiliesi* (Finland) 67

*Lafayette Journal and Courier* (Indiana) 32
*Lancashire Daily Post* (England) 160, 176
*Lake Charles American Press, The* (Louisiana) 76
*Lake Park News, The* (Lake Park, Iowa) 22
*L'Anse Sentinel, The* (Michigan) 21
*Lawrence Daily Journal-World* (Kansas) 42
*Leicester Evening Mail* (Leicestershire, England) 35
*Leoti Standard, The* (Kansas) 22
*Lethbridge Herald, The* (Alberta, Canada) 28
*Lincolnshire Echo* (Lincolnshire, England) 34
*Linton Daily Citizen, The* (Indiana) 65, 67
*Liverpool Weekly Post* (England) 24, 27
*Lock Haven Express, The* (Pennsylvania) 55
*Logan Daily News, The* (Ohio) 62, 66
*Logansport Pharos-Tribune, The* (Indiana) 30
*Ludington Daily News, The* (Michigan) 63

*Macon Chronicle-Herald* (Missouri) 62
*Mag-a-Book* (US) 38
*Mail, The* (Adelaide, Australia) 63
*Man* (Australia) 49
*Manitoba Free Press* (Winnipeg, Canada) 27, 33, 35
*Mansfield News, The* (Ohio) 32
*Marion Star, The* (Ohio) 19, 42
*Mason City Globe-Gazette, The* (Iowa) 67
*Maryville Daily Forum*, The (Missouri) 41
*Medford Mail Tribune* (Oregon) 42
*Miami News, The* (Florida) 79
*Minneapolis Tribune, The* (Minnesota) 35
*Monitor-Index and Democrat, The* (Moberly, Missouri) 41
*Monroe Evening Times, The* (Wisconsin) 55, 63

*Monroe Evening Times* (Wisconsin) 55, 63
*Monroe Journal, The* (Carolina) 21
*Monroe Morning Post, The* (Louisiana) 35
*Monroe News-Star, The* (Louisiana) 35
*Montana Standard, The* (Butte, Montana) 63, 65
*Montgomery Advertiser, The* (Alabama) 32
*Morning Bulletin* (Rockhampton / Aus) 177
*Morning Herald, The* (Hagerstown, Maryland) 66-7
*Morning Herald, The* (Uniontown, Pennsylvania) 55
*Morning News, The* (Wilmington, Delaware) 42
*Mon Magazine Policier* (Montreal, Canada) 24-6, 46
*Moorhead Daily News* (Minnesota) 38
*Mount Pleasance News, The* (Iowa) 30
*Muscatine Journal and News-Tribune, The* (Iowa) 31

*Nase Rodino* (Czech Republic) 64
*Nashville Tennessean, The* (Tennessee) 37, 55
*Nanticoke Daily Press* (Pennsylvania) 30
*Newark Advocate, The* (Ohio) 41
*Newcastle Evening Chronicle* (England) 51
*News-Chronicle* (London) 40
*New Zealand Herald, The* (New Zealand) 51-2
*North-Eastern Gazette* (England) 51
*Norwalk Reflector-Herald, The* (Ohio) 66

*Oakland Tribune* (California) 42
*Odessa American, The* (Texas) 55
*Omnibook* (America) 70
*Osawatomie World, The* (Kansas) 22
*Oshkosh Northwestern, The* (Wisconsin) 41
*Otis Reporter* (Kansas) 21
*Ottawa Evening Journal* (Ontario, Canada) 33
*Ottawa Journal, The* (Ontario, Canada) 30, 69, 73, 249

*Owen Leader, The* (Spencer, Indiana) 30
*Oxford Leader, The* (Iowa) 21

*Paducah Sun-Democrat, The* (Kentucky) 74
*Paris News, The* (Texas) 42
*Postville Herald* (Iowa) 21
*Post-Register, The* (Idaho Falls, Idaho) 42
*Philadelphia Inquirer, The* (Pennsylvania) 160
*Philadelphia Sunday Record, The* (Pennsylvania) 26
*Pittsburgh-Post Gazette, The* (Pennsylvania) 34
*Pittsburgh Sun-Telegraph* (Pennsylvania) 69
*Pomeroy Herald, The* (Iowa) 22
*Portsmouth Evening News* (England) 160
*Portsmouth Times, The* (Ohio) 41
*Postville Herald* (Iowa) 21
*Princeton Daily Democrat* (Indiana) 21
*Prostor* (Alma-Ata, Kazakhstan, Russian) 28

*Racine Journal-Times, The* (Wisconsin) 42
*Raleigh Register, The* (Beckley, West Virginia) 67
*Record-Argus, The* (Greenville, Pennsylvania) 67
*Record-Herald, The* (Washington, Ohio) 62
*Republican Tribune* (Union, Missouri) 33
*Reynolds's Illustrated News* (England) 23
*Reveille* (England) 156
*Rochester Democrat and Chronicle* (New York State) 34
*Roseburg News-Review* (Oregon) 30
*Rushville Republican, The* (Indiana) 41
*Ruthven Free Press, The* (Iowa) 21

*Salamanca Republican-Press* (New York State) 41
*Salem News, The* (Ohio) 55
*Salt Lake Tribune, The* (Utah) 69, 101
*San Antonio Light, The* (Texas) 45
*Sandusky Register, The* (Ohio) 32, 42
*San Francisco Examiner* (California) 31

## Index of Newspapers

*San Mateo Times* (California) 30, 55
*Santa Cruz Sentinel* (California) 42
*Satanta Chief, The* (Kansas) 21
*Saturday Evening Post, The* (New York) 12, 39, 40, 43-4, 46-8, 51, 53, 59, 64, 86, 123-4, 196, 206
*Sheboygan Press, The* (Wisconsin) 65, 67
*Sketch, The* (London) 28-9, 31, 99, 100-5, 108, 114-6, 118-9, 122, 126-7, 136, 138-9, 141-2, 145, 147-9, 150, 152, 154, 157, 166-7, 170, 173, 179, 180-3, 194-5, 203-6, 208, 210-12, 216
*Stanberry Headlight* (Missouri) 33
*State Center* Enterprise (Iowa) 22
*State Journal, The* (Lansing, Michigan) 42
*Staunton News Leader, The* (Virginia) 55
*Star, The* (London) 31
*Star Weekly Novel* (Canada) 82, 84, 87, 90-1
*Star Weekly Complete Novel* (Canada) 67, 70, 72, 78-9, 124, 132, 173, 208, 213, 245
*Steubenville Herald-Star* (Ohio) 42
*St. Cloud Daily Times, The* (Minnesota) 41
*St. Louis Star, The* (Missouri) 35
*St. Mary's Star, The* (St. Mary's, Kansas) 22
*Sun, The* (Baltimore, Maryland) 34
*Sunday Advertiser* (Adelaide, Australia) 74
*Sunday Gleaner, The* (Kingston, Jamaica) 55
*Sunday News* (New York) 71, 79, 84, 160, 196, 215
*Sunday News* (Sydney) 129
*Sunday Herald, The* (Provo, Utah) 11
*Sun-Herald, The* (Sydney, Australia) 75
*Sunday Journal and Star* (Nebraska) 36
*Sunday Mail, The* (Brisbane, Australia) 63
*Sunday Mercury* (Birmingham, England)19
*Sunday Milwaukee Journal, The* (Wisconsin) 27
*Sunday Times* (London) *The* 129, 242, 263, 274, 277
*Sun-Herald, The* (Lime Springs, Iowa) 22

*Sunset News, The* (Bluefield, West Virginia) 41
*Svenska Dagbladet* (Sweden) 92
*Swayzee Press, The* (Indiana) 21
*Sydney Morning Herald, The* (Australia) 61, 63, 75, 132
*Sylvia Sun, The* (Kansas) 21
*Syracuse Herald, The* (New York State) 26

*Terre Haute Tribune, The* (Indiana) 67
*Telegraph, The* (Brisbane / AUS) 154
*Thomasville Times-Enterprise* (Georgia) 41
*Tipton Daily Tribune, The* (Indiana) 33
*Times and Daily Leader, The* (San Mateo, California) 55
*Times Recorder, The* (Zanesville, Ohio) 65
*Titusville Herald, The* (Pennsylvania) 63
*Toronto Star, The* (Canada) 12, 27, 37, 67, 70, 72, 79, 82, 84, 124, 132
*Townsville Daily Bulletin, The* (Queensland, Australia) 154
*Traverse City Record-Eagle* (Michigan) 61
*Trybuna Robotnicza* (Poland) 70
*Turon Weekly Press* (Kansas) 21
*Twin Falls News* (Idaho) 21
*Tyrone Daily Herald* (Pennsylvania) 67

*Valley Evening Monitor* (Harlingen, Texas) 55
*Victoria Daily Advocate* (Texas) 30
*Vidette-Messenger, The* (Valparaiso, Indiana) 63, 66

*Warren Times-Mirror, The* (Pennsylvania) 42
*Waukesha Daily Freeman* (Wisconsin) 63, 67
*Warren Times-Mirror, The* (Pennsylvania) 42
*Washington Post, The* (Washington, D.C.) 32
*Waterville Telegraph, The* (Kansas) 21
*Wellsboro Gazette, The* (Pennsylvania) 22

*Wentzville Union, The* (Missouri) 21
*Western Mail, The* (Perth, Australia) 76
*Wilkes-Barre Record, The* (Pennsylvania) 27
*Wilmington News-Journal* (Ohio) 65

*Winnipeg Evening Tribune, The* (Manitoba, Canada) 37, 178
*Yorkshire Evening News* (Yorkshire, England) 177
*Yorkshire Telegraph and Star, The* (Yorkshire, England) 24, 27

# Index of Periodicals

*20-Story Magazine* 99, 127, 131

*Alfred Hitchcock Mystery Magazine* 103, 142, 167
*Alle Kvinner* 111, 169, 172
*Argosy* 98, 110, 114, 119, 125, 126, 128, 146, 155, 157, 161, 177
*Australian Women's Weekly, The* 45, 47, 53, 56-7, 64, 68, 73, 77, 79, 81, 83, 87, 90, 91, 93-4, 106, 107, 114, 125-7, 131-2, 135, 144, 155, 166, 169, 174, 176, 249, 275

*Berlingske Tidende* 171
*Black Mask Detective Magazine* 126
*Blue Book Magazine* 25, 29, 30, 100, 102-5, 114-6, 118, 122, 138-9, 141-2, 144-5, 149, 154, 157, 166, 170, 173, 179, 180-1, 195, 203-4, 205, 208, 210-12
*Britannia and Eve* 146, 185, 262

*Centre View* 117
*Christmas Pie* 164
*Christmas Magpie, The* 144, 204, 211
*Collier's* 12, 49, 50, 54, 56-7, 60-2, 65, 76, 77, 94, 128, 138, 196, 203, 206, 213
*Christmas Story-Teller, The* 109
*Clubman* 108, 118, 120, 126, 147, 163, 165
*Cosmopolitan* 12, 45, 68, 72, 83, 88, 112-13, 115, 121, 130, 133, 135, 156, 169, 192, 193, 194, 202, 263
*Creasey Mystery Magazine* 98, 106-7, 126, 144, 155, 166, 172, 177

*Detective Story Magazine* 108, 123, 137, 140, 151, 168, 170-71, 174, 186-7, 203, 207, 211-12

*Edgar Wallace Mystery Magazine* 120
*Ellery Queen's Mystery Magazine* 12, 13, 98-99, 100, 102-5, 107, 109, 110-11, 113-14, 116-25, 127-29, 130-39, 141-47, 149, 150-58, 160-64, 166-74, 176-78, 197, 199, 217, 266, 274, 276-77
*Everywoman* 130

*Family Magazine* 98
*Flynn's Detective Weekly* 27
*Flynn's Weekly* 107, 126, 133, 146, 165, 172, 176, 178, 184-86, 189, 201, 203, 215
*Flynn's Weekly Detective Fiction* 126, 133, 185, 186

*Ghost Stories* 138, 143, 189, 208
*Grandi Firme* Le 123, 159
*Grand Magazine, The* 23, 39, 106, 117-18, 120, 129, 131, 133, 137, 140, 144, 147, 151, 153, 155, 157, 159, 160-67, 176, 183-85, 189, 190-91, 201, 209-10, 215
*Great American Novel Magazine, The* 28
*Great Detective* 137, 140, 172
*Good Housekeeping* 12, 36, 84, 114, 243-44
*Gothic Stories* 140, 146
*Guide and Ideas Christmas Number* 101

*Holly Leaves* 164, 167, 172, 183, 190, 201
*Holiday Clubman* 147
*Home: An Australian Quarterly, The* 175

299

*Home Journal* 42, 46, 48, 140 150, 167, 196, 213
*Hush* 108, 137, 140, 152, 170
*Hutchinson's Adventure & Mystery Story Magazine* 104, 106, 108, 126, 148, 150, 164, 167, 168, 203, 211

*John Bull* (London) 12, 68, 70, 72, 73, 75-80

*Ladies' Home Journal* 80, 92-3, 137, 162, 196, 201, 212, 214, 217
*Libelle* 176
*Liberty Magazine* 37, 158
*London Magazine, The* 172, 204, 206

*Macfadden Fiction-Lover's Magazine* 151, 191, 201
*MacKill's Mystery Magazine* 108, 113, 120, 131, 133, 144, 147, 152-53, 157, 160, 163, 165, 171, 173, 177
*Magazine of Fantasy and Science Fiction, The* 109, 129, 143
*Mail Magazine, The* (Adelaide, AUS) 130, 177
*Man* 49
*Mata Matters* 174
*Modern Home* 108
*Modern Stories* 170
*Munsey Magazine* 117, 185
*Mystery Magazine, The* 172, 204, 206
*Mysterious Traveler, The* 109, 121

*Nash's Pall Mall Magazine* 121, 130, 133, 135, 156, 187, 193
*Nero Wolfe Magazine* 173
*Novel Magazine, The* 99, 151, 174, 191, 201, 216-17

*Observer, The* (Adelaide / AUS) 145

*Parade: The Middle East Weekly* 106-7, 110, 125, 127, 131, 134, 144, 155, 166, 200
*Pearson's Magazine* 125, 129, 189, 201, 216
*Pictorial Review* 109, 118, 128, 187

*Police Magazine, The* 163, 185
*Reader's Digest Condensed Books* 169
*Red Magazine* 159, 190, 207
*Redbook* 12, 40, 58, 85, 152, 195
*Rex Stout Mystery Quarterly* 128
*Royal Magazine, The* 108, 137, 139, 144, 146, 151, 170-71, 176, 186, 187, 209, 215, 217

*Saint Detective Magazine, The* 100, 108, 118, 126, 158
*Saturday Evening Post, The* 12, 39, 40, 43-4, 46-8, 51, 53, 59, 64, 86, 123-24, 196, 206
*Short Story Magazine* 98, 100, 103-4, 114, 122, 141, 150, 154, 170
*Sketch, The* 28-9, 31, 99, 100-5, 108, 114-16, 118-19, 122, 126-27, 136, 138-39, 141-42, 145, 147, 148-49, 150, 152, 154, 157, 166, 167, 170, 173, 179, 180-3, 194, 195, 203-6, 208, 210-12, 217
*Sovereign Magazine, The* 136, 143, 189, 208, 216
*Star Weekly Complete Novel* 68, 70, 72, 78-9, 124, 132, 173, 208, 213, 245
*Story Digest* 163
*Story-Teller, The* 104, 109, 116, 118, 126, 128, 133-4, 146, 165, 174, 178, 184-8, 203, 215, 252
*Strand Magazine, The* 12, 48, 101, 106, 107, 111, 114, 119, 120, 123, 125, 127-28, 130, 135, 137, 139, 144, 151, 154-5, 158-60, 162, 165-6, 168, 171, 178, 192, 194-8
*Suspense* 98, 102, 114, 124, 169, 170-1, 176, 275
*Summer Pie* 177
*Saturday Journal, The* 140
*Sunday Chronicle Annual 1926* 175, 189, 201
*Sunday Dispatch* 98, 123, 191, 201, 207, 211
*Sunday Times Culture Magazine* 267
*Sunday Sun Magazine, The* 153
*Sydney Mail Christmas Number* 160

## Index of Periodicals

*This Week* 12, 101, 106, 110, 119, 125, 127, 130, 144, 159, 161-2, 165-6, 168, 171, 195-6, 198, 199, 202-3, 206-8, 212-13
*Thriller, The* 98, 112, 157, 259
*Tipperary* 162
*Tit-Bits* 131, 172, 262
*Tit-Bits Summer Special* 131
*Truth* 107-8, 120, 126, 147, 163, 165, 174, 178

*Weldon Ladies' Journal* 163
*Wireless Weekly* 176
*World's News, The* 139, 143, 154
*Woman* (Sydney, Australia) 76-7, 93, 176, 246
*Woman's Day* (Melbourne, later Sydney / AUS) 76
*Woman's Journal* 12, 65, 71-2, 124, 132, 138, 152, 161, 194, 196, 208, 212-13, 254
*Woman's Illustrated Magazine* 101, 154, 206-7
*Woman's Mirror* 81, 173
*Woman's Own* 83-5, 88, 92, 169
*Woman's Realm* 90
*Woman's World* 156
*Women's Magazine* (Perth, Australia) 63, 176
*Writer, The* 89

*Your Car: A Magazine of Romance, Fact and Fiction* 147, 190, 209